Vladimir Putin's Version of *War and Peace*

Vladimir Putin's Version of *War and Peace*

The Battle for the Russian Home Front, 2022–2024

J. L. Black

LEXINGTON BOOKS
Lanham • Boulder • New York • London

Lexington Books
Bloomsbury Publishing Inc, 1385 Broadway, New York, NY 10018, USA
Bloomsbury Publishing Plc, 50 Bedford Square, London, WC1B 3DP, UK
Bloomsbury Publishing Ireland, 29 Earlsfort Terrace, Dublin 2, D02 AY28, Ireland
www.rowman.com

Copyright © 2025 by The Rowman & Littlefield Publishing Group, Inc.

All rights reserved. No part of this publication may be: i) reproduced or transmitted in any form, electronic or mechanical, including photocopying, recording or by means of any information storage or retrieval system without prior permission in writing from the publishers; or ii) used or reproduced in any way for the training, development or operation of artificial intelligence (AI) technologies, including generative AI technologies. The rights holders expressly reserve this publication from the text and data mining exception as per Article 4(3) of the Digital Single Market Directive (EU) 2019/790.

British Library Cataloguing in Publication Information Available

Library of Congress Cataloging-in-Publication Data

Names: Black, J. L. (Joseph Laurence), 1937– author.
Title: Vladimir Putin's version of "War and peace": the battle for the Russian home front, 2022–2024 / J.L. Black.
Other titles: Battle for the Russian home front, 2022–2024
Description: Lanham: Lexington Books, [2025] | Includes bibliographical references and index. | Summary: "For Putin, the home front is a second front. His government's efforts to create and maintain a patriotic, or at least obedient, citizenry is the main subject, along with Moscow's necessary pivot to the East for political and economic succour"— Provided by publisher.
Identifiers: LCCN 2024037203 (print) | LCCN 2024037204 (ebook) | ISBN 9781666958843 (cloth) | ISBN 9781666958850 (epub)
Subjects: LCSH: Russian Invasion of Ukraine, 2022—Public opinion. | Russian Invasion of Ukraine, 2022—Propaganda. | Putin, Vladimir Vladimirovich, 1952– | Russia (Federation)—Politics and government—21st century. | Russia (Federation)—Foreign relations—21st century. | Economic sanctions—Russia (Federation) | State crimes—Russia (Federation) | Propaganda—Russia (Federation) | Public opinion—Russia (Federation)
Classification: LCC DK5467 .B63 2025 (print) | LCC DK5467 (ebook) | DDC 947.706/2—dc23/eng/20241028
LC record available at https://lccn.loc.gov/2024037203
LC ebook record available at https://lccn.loc.gov/2024037204

For product safety related questions contact productsafety@bloomsbury.com.

∞™ The paper used in this publication meets the minimum requirements of American National Standard for Information Sciences—Permanence of Paper for Printed Library Materials, ANSI/NISO Z39.48-1992.

Contents

Preface ... vii
Abbreviations ... ix
Transliteration, Spelling, Punctuation ... xi
Note on Sources ... xiii

Introduction ... 1
1. Opening Salvoes ... 5
2. Explaining Away a Brutal War of Attrition ... 31
3. War into the 'Foreseeable Future' ... 57
4. Putin as *Vozhd* ... 87
5. Net Voine! (No to War!): The Domestic Political Scene ... 121
6. Human and Civil Rights ... 155
7. International Considerations: Are Russians 'Isolated from the Civilized World'? ... 183
8. The Russian Economy Pivots to the East ... 217
9. War of Words: Creating Young Patriots ... 251
10. Ripple Effects: In Lieu of a Conclusion ... 277

Appendix: Further Reading	305
Bibliography	307
Name Index	309
Subject Index	315
About the Author	323

Preface

Like its predecessor *Eternal Putin?: Confronting Navalny, the Pandemic, Sanctions and War with Ukraine* (2023), this book is a chronological and encyclopaedic account of all facets of Russia during a very short period of time. Together with earlier books, *Russia After 2020: Looking Ahead after Two Decades of Putin* (2022), *Putin's Third Term as Russia's President, 2012–18* (2019) and *The Russian Presidency of Dmitry Medvedev, 2008–12* (2015), the sequential volumes provide the most thorough chronicle of the Putin era in Russia, now available anywhere.

These books are histories, albeit of short spurts of modern times. They are purposely descriptive and avoid complex analyses. They all include chapters on Vladimir Putin's presidency, domestic affairs, the economy, international relations and now the consequences of war for the domestic scene.

Even though Putin is everywhere in them, these books are not about Putin per se; rather, they place emphasis upon the domestic scene and Russia in toto. In addition to the Russian political arena, its economy and its media, social issues, such as its citizenry's quality of life, healthcare, human rights, the LGBT and climate change, are dealt with here.

This volume and its predecessors show how Russians see themselves and the outside world, and how the outside world sees Russia. For that reason, they rely heavily on Russian-language sources, many of them representing voices now repressed or muted (see 'Note on Sources').

Chronologically, the current volume begins with the announcement of war ('special military operation') and ends with Putin's all-too-easy victory in the 2024 presidential election, his fifth term.

Abbreviations

ASEAN	Association of Southeast Asian Nations
ATACMS	Army Tactical Missile System (USA)
BRI	Belt and Road Initiative (China)
CB	Central Bank (Bank Rossii)
CICA	Conference on Interaction and Confidence Building in Asia
CIS	Commonwealth of Independent States
DPR	Donetsk People's Republic
FAR	Feminist Anti-War Resistance
FBK	Anti-Corruption Foundation (Navalny)
FOM	Public Opinion Foundation
FSB	Federal Security Service (Federal'naya sluzhba bezopasnosti)
G-7	Group of Seven
G-20	Group of Twenty
GUR	Ukrainian Military Intelligence (Golovne upravlinnia rozvidki)
HIMARS	High Mobility Artillery Rocket Systems (USA)
ICC	International Criminal Court
IOC	International Olympic Committee
ISS	International Space Station
ISW	Institute for the Study of War
LDPR	Liberal Democratic Party of Russia
LPR	Luhansk People's Republic (Lugansk-Russian)
LSR	Freedom of Russia Legion (Legion 'Svoboda Rossii')
MAP	Membership Action Plan (NATO)
MID	Ministry of Foreign Affairs

MoD	Ministry of Defence
MVD	Ministry of the Interior
NASAMS	Norwegian Advanced Surface-to-Air Missile System
NRC	National Resistance Centre (Ukraine)
OCU	Orthodox Church of Ukraine (Ukrainian)
OHCHR	Office of the High Commission of Human Rights (UN)
ONF	All-Russia People's Front
OSCE	Organization for Security and Cooperation in Europe
PACE	Parliamentary Assembly of the Council of Europe
PGO	Procurator (Prosecutor) General's Office
PMC	Private Military Company
RDK	Russian Volunteer Corps (Russkiy dobrovol'cheskiy korpus)
RFE/RL	Radio Free Europe/Radio Liberty
Roscosmos	Russian State Space Corporation
Rosimushchestvo	Agency for state property management
Roskomnadzor	Federal Agency for Supervision of Communications and Mass Media
Rosstat	Federal State Statistics Service
Rostourism	Federal Tourism Agency, abolished 2022
SBU	Security Services of Ukraine (Sluzhba bezpeki Ukrayni)
SCO	Shanghai Cooperation Organizations
siloviki	Russians in positions of power, 'strongmen'
SPIEF	St. Petersburg International Forum
SVO	Special Military Operation (in Ukraine)
SVR	Foreign Intelligence Service (Russia) (Sluzhba vneshnei razvedki)
SWIFT	Society for Worldwide Interbank Financial Telecommunications
TANAP	Trans-Anatolia Pipeline
TAP	Trans-Adriatic Pipeline
UK	United Kingdom
UNGA	United Nations General Assembly
UNSC	United Nations Security Council
UOC	Ukrainian Orthodox Church (Russian)
UR	United Russia Party
US	United States
VEO	Violent Extremist Organization
VOA	Voice of America
VTsIOM	All-Russia Centre for Research on Public Opinion
WTO	World Trade Organization
WWF	World Wildlife Fund

Transliteration, Spelling, Punctuation

Russian transliteration here is based on a modified Library of Congress system, with common-use applications for names and places. Most diacritical marks have been deleted in the main text. Although they both use the Cyrillic alphabet, the Russian and Ukrainian languages have different transliterations for the same names and places, such as Kyiv (Ukrainian) and Kiev (Russian). Some of the conversions have political implications, such as Donbas (Ukrainian) and Donbass (Russian). Except where Russians are quoted, Ukrainian spelling will be used for all place names in Ukraine. Common Western usage is used for popular Russian and Ukrainian names in transliteration, for example, Zelensky.

For reasons of convenience, Crimea is treated here as a separate entity, not as legally part of Ukraine or illegally part of Russia.

British spelling and punctuation are adopted throughout except for personal and textual titles where other spelling systems are appropriate; for example, an American Secretary of Defense and Russian Minister of Defence, or in quotes where the original is maintained.

Note on Sources

In an introductory essay to an issue of *Russian Analytical Digest* devoted to the question, 'How to Study Russia', Marlene Laruelle outlines several structural difficulties with present-day Russian studies, particularly in social science fields.[1] One of these is a habit among Anglophone scholars of limiting their research to English-language studies. They tend also to ignore research completed in disciplines other than their own and focus too much on Putin and Moscow as if those are all there is to the Russian Federation. As an old-time Sovietologist, I start with Russian-language sources, including both official and opposition items, read both the lines and between the lines and try to keep my many personal biases under control.

Russian-language sources provide an insight to what Russians and their leaders believe, or claim to believe, and help one avoid looking at Russia through the singularly 'Western-centric prism' that Laruelle writes about. Independent and government newspapers, Russian-language blogs, party platforms, public opinion surveys, Russian and foreign government documentation and private posts are drawn from here.

Although distribution of information in Russia is once again a monopoly of the government, as it was in Soviet days, there are important exceptions that could never have existed during those earlier times. Russia-based sources from dissident movements and independent accounts of street demonstrations and other opposition behaviours, and police reactions to them, are relatively easy to access via the Internet. These sources include OVD-Info (en.ovdinfo.org), the leading independent Russian website for information on political arrests, criminal proceedings and human rights violations, and the Russian Agency for Legal and Court Information (rapsinews.ru), a source of court proceedings. Many political persons and movements both for and against the war have websites. Activists also enjoy access to all forms of foreign and

Russian social media – such as Facebook, YouTube, Twitter, Instagram, *VK* (*VKontakte*), OK.ru., Yandex, Rutube and, above all, Telegram.

Multiple English-language books, articles and media are cited here as well. Although all major references are documented in the usual way and Russian-language sources dominate, the endnotes include a large number of general, often journalistic essays in English. These are for quick first-start guides for readers who do not have Russian and want to pursue a particular subject. Government and private wire service notations (e.g. AP, AFP, Reuters, Interfax, TASS, RIA Novosti, RBC.ru, Sputnik, UNIAN, Ukrinform) are not intended as analytical or evidential sources, rather they provide exact dates of information releases, context and sequence for the topic at hand. Government press releases present us with what officialdom says, and what it wants readers to believe.

Economic and social data are found in Russian Ministry, Central Bank and Rosstat (Russian statistics) releases. IMF and World Bank reports help confirm or confound Rosstat figures.

Because daily events are crucial to the narrative, there is a greater than usual reliance on mainstream newspaper and television reporting, especially on pieces compiled from the battle and home fronts. These accounts are not used so much for their authors' opinions as they are for timing, the chronology of events and comparative points of view.

Telegram Messenger is particularly important. Founded by Russian brothers Nikolai and Pavel Durov in 2013, headquartered in the British Virgin Islands and operating out of Dubai in over 50 languages, Telegram's messages can be accessed almost everywhere and in multiple formats. With over 700 million active users around the world, Telegram is more popular than Facebook, and in Russia's case, has channels used regularly by both state authorities in Moscow (e.g. by spokesman for the Kremlin, Peskov, and spokeswoman for the Ministry of Foreign Affairs, Sakharova, and even by the Ministry of Defence) and anti-war activists (e.g. Navalny). Regional governors regularly post messages on their Telegram channels.

Readers will also find data from surveys conducted by Russian pollsters such as the independent Levada Centre and the state-funded All-Russia Public Opinion Research Centre (VTsIOM) and the Public Opinion Foundation (FOM). These polls almost always engage a sampling of 1,600 respondents or more above the age of 18, spread over most of the components of the Russian Federation, rural and urban sites, and across generations. Doubtless such polls should not be taken as absolute, especially during wartime when open dissent is dangerous. Since a majority of Russians still obtain their news from state-controlled television, 'public opinion' often mirrors the narrative provided by that venue. Still, a very large percentage of Russians use the Internet regularly. The polls provide a reasonable measure of popular thinking, societal trends and, indeed, often reveal a distrust of government and reflect serious concerns on specific domestic issues.[2]

Some readers may think that various description and accounts recorded here are over-documented in the endnotes, and they may be right. However, many of the descriptions are of events in real time, so the documentation often includes items that reflect typical Russian, Western or Ukrainian versions of the same events so that readers may judge for themselves.

NOTES

1. Marlene Laruelle, 'Russian studies' moment of self-reflection', *Russian Analytical Digest*, No. 293, 3 March 2023, pp. 1–3.

2. See 'The value of public opinion polls' [in Russia], special issue of *Russian Analytical Digest*, No. 292, 22 February 2023.

Introduction

In his fifth century BC treatise *The Art of War*, Sun Tzu is alleged to have written, 'If you know the enemy and know yourself, you need not fear the result of a hundred battles'.

The advertisement for the second edition of Andrew Monaghan's *The New Politics of Russia* offered the same advice, somewhat differently. If we are ever to have constructive relations with Russia, to truly understand it, we must move 'beyond the simplistic, Putin-centric narratives often found in Western accounts'. In short, a broader perspective is necessary if we are to 'know' Russia, even if only as a defensive measure. One such perspective can be found in Richard Sakwa's *The Lost Peace* (2023).[1]

Leaving the war fighting on the ground and air for others to record, this book places the Russian home front under a microscope. It is an immediate continuation of *Eternal Putin?*, where events and developments in Russia from the historic series of amendments to the Russian Constitution ('January Revolution') during the winter of 2020 to the launching of Putin's 'special military operation' in Ukraine on 24 February 2022 were chronicled.

Much has been written about Putin's motives in unleashing an invasion of Ukraine.[2] US president Biden regularly describes the resultant war as one between tyranny and democracy. Others in the West see it as a by-product of the slow but inexorable deterioration of the liberal democratic world order.[3] Western commentators on the war in Ukraine tend to focus on real and alleged Russian infamies and Ukrainian heroics. Russia's advocates tend to focus on the real and alleged villainies of Kyiv and Washington and describe Moscow's action as a defence of the *Russkiy mir* (Russian World). These contradictory visions are not symmetrical ones, as the weight of evidence falls heavily against the Kremlin. But not all of it.

The fact is, we have too little evidence to confirm, without doubt, any of the many theories on why Putin decided to launch his 'special military operation' in Ukraine. As Emeritus Professor Geoffrey Roberts put it, 'The best guidance we have as to what Putin was thinking when he made his decision for war is twofold: what he said and what he did'.[4]

Chronologically, the current book covers what Putin said and what Russia did from the launching of the war in February 2022 to the outcomes of the presidential election in Russia in 2024. The abject failure of Russia's initial blitzkrieg and a sequence of unexpected events in September 2022, such as Ukraine's successful counter-attacks, Russia's 'partial' mobilization, the formal annexation of four regions of Ukraine occupied by Russian forces, and the flood of conscription-age men fleeing Russia, turned the world order upside down and raised fears that a faltering campaign would tempt Putin to deploy nuclear weapons. Western pundits began predicting, yet again, that Putin would be ousted from office by some sort of palace coup.[5] Others repeated the decades-old mantra that Russia was a failed state, fascist and unsustainable,[6] or a 'Mafia state', and was about to self-destruct, finally.[7] Some sought a continuum in Putin's quarter century in high office that made its current position inevitable.[8]

The war was explained as Moscow's 'last stand' by authors who claimed to have foreseen it as a consequence of the West's refusal to recognize Russia's national security interests after 1991. Writing during the war, other scholars believed it an attempt by Putin to guarantee his legacy as the restorer of Russia's status as a Great Power and the West as a conglomerate of paper tigers.[9]

Whatever the case may be, the Russian Federation is still there, though the two-headed eagle on its presidential standard is peering much more eastward now than when Putin first came to office. Highlights of the war other than actual battles include the Western arming of Ukraine, the Prigozhin mutiny and the realm of mis- and disinformation. The implications of these phenomena are featured in the first chapters here.

While checking the course of the war as it impacts the Russian home front, this book looks inside the Russian Federation, delineating messages from the top and responses from below, whether intuitive or coerced, to see how its people are faring.[10]

The course of the war on the battlefield is covered extensively elsewhere and, except for events that have particular consequence for the home front, will be of secondary interest here.[11]

NOTES

1. Richard Sakwa, *The Lost Peace: How the West Failed to Prevent a Second Cold War*. New Haven, CT: Yale UP, 2023. See blurb advertising Andrew Monaghan's, *The New Politics of Russia: Second Edition*. Manchester, UK: Manchester UP, 2024.
2. David R. Marples, 'Russia's war goals in Ukraine', *Canadian Slavonic Papers*, Vol. 64, 2/3 (2022), pp. 207–219.
3. See, e.g. Timothy Snyder, 'Ukraine holds the future: The war between democracy and nihilism', *Foreign Affairs*, September/October, 2022; Sergei Karaganov, 'Ot ne-Zapada k Mirovomu bol'shinstvu', *Rossii v global'noi politike*, No. 5, September/October 2022; Fritze Bartel, *The Triumph of Broken Promises: The End of the Cold War and the Rise of Neoliberalism*. Cambridge, MA: Harvard UP, 2022; Luke Harding, *Invasion: The Inside Story of Russia's Bloody War and Ukraine's Fight for Survival*. London: Vintage, 2022.
4. Geoffrey Roberts, '"Now or never": Putin's decision for war with Ukraine', *Journal of Military and Strategic Studies*, Vol. 22, No. 2 (2022), a special issue on the war in Ukraine.
5. For typical speculations, much of it wishful thinking, Vladimir Zubok, 'Can Putin survive? The lessons of the soviet collapse', *Foreign Affairs*, July/August 2022; Anne Applebaum, 'It's time to prepare for a Ukrainian victory: The liberation of Russian-occupied territory might bring down Vladimir Putin', *The Atlantic*, 11 September 2022; Paul D. Shinkman, 'Kremlin quietly warns against assumptions of Putin's ouster', *US News & World Report,* 13 September 2022; Sergey Radchenko, 'Coups in the Kremlin: What the history of Russia's power struggles says about Putin's future', *Foreign Affairs*, 22 September 2022; Editorial Board, 'Putin's debacle is breaking his country – and he might pay the price', *The Washington Post*, 26 September 2022; Michael Kimmage, Maria Lipman, 'What mobilization means for Russia: The end of Putin's bargain with the people', *Foreign Affairs*, 27 September 2022; Harold Maas, 'Will Ukraine be Putin's downfall?' *The Week*, 29 September 2022; Amy Knight, 'With Russia in crisis, could Vladimir Putin be forced out?' *Globe and Mail*, 1 October 2022.
6. See, e.g. Alexander Motyl, 'Russia is a failed state', *The Hill*, 27 September 2022; Dennis Murphy, 'It's time to brace for Putin's greatest meltdown yet', *The Daily Beast*, 4 October 2022; Tatiana Stanovaya, 'Putin's apocalyptic end game in Ukraine', *Foreign Affairs*, 6 October 2022.
7. See, e.g. volume by Mikhail Khodorkovsky, whom Putin jailed in 2003 for fraud and tax evasion, *The Russia Conundrum: How the West Fell for Putin's Power Gambit – and How To Fix It*. New York: St. Martin's, 2022. Written with Martin Sixsmith.
8. See especially Anna Arutunyan, *Hybrid Warriors: Proxies, Freelancers and Moscow's Struggle for Ukraine*. London: Hurst, 2022; J. L. Black, *Russia After 2020: Looking Ahead After Two Decades of Putin*. Abingdon, UK: Routledge, 2022; Sergei Medvedev, *A War Made in Russia*. Cambridge, UK: Polity, 2023, translated from the Russian by Stephen Dalziel.

9. See, e.g. Liana Fix, Michael Kimmage, 'Putin's last stand: The promise and peril of Russian defeat', *Foreign Affairs*, January/February 2022; Andrei Tsygankov, 'Vladimir Putin's last stand: The sources of Russia's Ukraine policy', *Post-Soviet Affairs*, Vol. 31, No. 4 (2015), pp. 279–303. See also Thomas Graham, *Getting Russia Right*. Cambridge: Polity, 2023, who, while condemning Putin's actions vs. Ukraine, suggests that we got there by refusing to respect Russia as a major power.

10. For a start, see Roger Cohen, 'Life under Putin's forever war', *New York Times International Weekly*, 12–13 August 2023, pp. 1, 6.

11. See especially, daily and weekly reports by the Institute for the Study of War (Washington), 'Ukraine conflict updates', understandingwar.org/backgrounder/ukraine-conflict-updates.

Chapter 1

Opening Salvoes

WHO, WHAT, WHERE, WHEN AND HOW

President Vladimir Putin's early morning televised announcement on 24 February 2022, 'On Conducting a Special Military Operation' (O provedenii spetsial'noi voennoi operatsii – SVO) against Ukraine, took foreign governments and most of Russia's population by surprise. What followed the announcement was a war, though it had to be called something else in Russia. It had been nearly eight years in the making – always in plain sight.[1] Moscow provided the most alarming and uncalled-for drama during those ever-tenser years capped by an invasion of a sovereign country, yet it would be wrong to assume that Kyiv, Washington and Brussels were innocent bystanders in the course of events that led to Putin's serious miscalculation in February 2022.

Details on those events can be found in a vast array of primary and secondary sources, representing a wide cross-section of fact, fiction and opinion.[2] Suffice to list here certain key circumstances: a decision by the president of Ukraine, Viktor Yanukovych, in November 2013 to suspend negotiations on an Association Agreement with the EU; protesters gathered on Independence Square (Maidan Nezalezhnosti) in Kyiv and, as their number grew to several hundreds of thousands (Euromaidans), occupied government buildings until mid-February 2014. The occupation was met with violence on several occasions, the worst of these coming on 18–20 February, when about 100 protesters and 13 police officers were killed.

Appalled by the violence, leaders of all major political parties in Ukraine's parliament (Rada) agreed to a truce on 21 February that would keep Yanukovych in office until an early election could be held, protesters would go home and the special police (Berkut) would step back. The truce was announced on TV and witnessed by foreign ministers from Germany, France and Poland, and a special envoy from Russia. Aroused by right-wing activists such as Dmytro Yarosh of the neo-Nazi *Praviy sektor* (Right Sector), the Euromaidans refused the arrangement. Fearing for his life, the democratically elected Yanukovych fled Kyiv and an interim government was formed on 22 February. Called the Revolution of Dignity by its proponents and a US-brokered coup d'état by its detractors, the formation of a new government saw all the key positions taken by members of the nationalist *Batkivshchyna* (Fatherland) party, whose leader Arseniy Yatsenyuk was named prime minister, and the openly neo-Nazi *Svoboda* (Freedom) party. *Batkivshchyna* held 101 seats in the Rada as a result of the 2012 election, and Svoboda had 37. Neither Ukraine's largest party, the Party of Regions (185 seats), nor its fifth largest, the Communist Party (32 seats), were represented in what was supposed to be 'a coalition of national unity'.

Western parliaments recognized this government even though in 2012 the European Parliament had urged all Ukrainian parties never to form a coalition with *Svoboda*, which it labelled racist, anti-Semitic and xenophobic.[3] The leader of Ukraine's only truly liberal-democratic party, UDAR (40 seats), refused a cabinet post.

Washington's substantial involvement in this outcome, above all the role of the State Department's Victoria Nuland, is well-documented elsewhere.[4]

The interim government's very first action was an attempt to annul Ukraine's language law that, when passed in 2012 after years of divisive argument, granted regional status to Russian and other minority languages in areas where the national minorities exceeded 10 per cent of the population. Ukrainian was still the only official national language. Although the country's acting president vetoed the interim government's first effort to eliminate the language law, the psychological damage was done.

For the next eight years, a programme of promoting the Ukrainian language and culture was accompanied by efforts to diminish the Russian language and culture in Ukraine. Afraid that they were about to lose whatever cultural and political gains they had made since Ukrainian independence in 1991, ethnic Russians in the north, east and south of Ukraine rose up against local administrations and the newly installed interim government they had not voted for and in which they were not represented. In so doing, although they followed the example set by Euromaidans, they were labelled 'terrorists' and the interim government launched an 'anti-terrorist campaign' against them.

Whereas Ukrainians were confirming and strengthening their nationhood, Russians in Russia watched the tribulations face by millions of their long-time friends, relatives and associates in Ukraine with growing concern. The two solitudes, embryonic for decades, had emerged fully grown.

In Crimea, where a referendum (94.3 per cent) in January 1991 and subsequent local elections in 1992 and 1994 all showed a clear preference for independence from Ukraine and accession to Russia, protesters against the new regime occupied government spaces and ousted the Kyiv-appointed governor. On 27 February 2014, one day after NATO announced that its door was open to an application from Ukraine, Russian forces began surreptitiously occupying the peninsula. On 6 March, a stacked Crimean Parliament and the Sevastopol City Council passed resolutions declaring their intention to join Russia. Shortly thereafter, they held referenda to that effect and declared independence from Ukraine. Russia officially proclaimed Crimea part of its Federation on 18 March 2014. This act was considered an illegal annexation by most members of the United Nations, then and now.

The Ukrainian army shelled the separatist parts of the Donbas indiscriminately over the spring and summer of that year. No objections were forthcoming from the West, presumably because they perceived the initial uprising as a Moscow-inspired initiative and refused to consider that the rebels may have had just cause. After about a year, the civil war that saw Ukrainian citizens killing Ukrainian citizens was portrayed in Kyiv as a war against Russia, which was offering limited clandestine help to the rebels. That label and the earlier 'terrorist' tag found resonance in the West, where blaming Russia had long been a national sport.

Ceasefires signed by representatives of Ukraine, Russia, the self-proclaimed separatist republics, and the OSCE, and witnessed by Germany and France, brought periodically broken peace to the region. Signed in 2014 and 2015 and known as the Minsk Protocols, these agreements remained in effect until 2 February 2022, when articles in them guaranteeing special status and language rights for separatist parts of Luhansk and Donetsk, which would remain part of Ukraine, were disavowed by President Volodymyr Zelensky's government in Kyiv.[5] These articles had been agreed by every signatory of the agreements but not acted upon. Twenty days later, Russia recognized the secessionist areas as independent, and eight years of scattered confrontation slid quickly into real war.

Looking back, one can only wonder why the invasion caught almost everyone, including Russians and even the Russian military, unprepared. Those eight years featured accelerated military drills and deployments by the Russian Ministry of Defence (MoD) on its western and southern borders, by NATO in eastern Europe, and by both on the Black Sea. During that time, Western countries re-armed and trained Ukraine's Armed Forces while levelling economic sanctions against Russia. Moscow further Russianized Crimea, brandished new weapons development and waved energy supply red flags at both Europe and Ukraine. Frequent warnings of a coming war from pundits and politicians fell on deaf ears. No one wanted to believe that war was possible.

As US Civil War General William Tecumseh Sherman is credited with saying in 1879, 'war is hell'. Nearly 150 years later, it still means unending death, destruction, fear, anxiety and general mayhem, to date much more for Ukrainians than for Russians. In this volume, however, it will be the Russian home front under the microscope.

There can be no doubt as to who started this tragic war. Putin did. Yet, blaming the Kremlin does not exonerate the West. The inexorable expansion of NATO eastward from the early 1990s, in spite of objections from a much-weakened Russia, humiliated and frightened Russian strategists. Dean of the post-Soviet foreign policy *apparat*, Yevgeny Primakov, predicted as early as 1994 that NATO expansion to the east would have a deep and injurious psychological impact on Russia.[6] Regular pronouncements from Brussels since 2014 that Ukraine would eventually be a member greatly exacerbated the NATO question for Moscow.

Russian politicians and senior military personnel believed, or claimed to believe, that the promise of Ukraine's accession to NATO was the most striking violation yet of earlier OSCE agreements that no state, or group of states, may strengthen their security at the expense of the security of other states. The West's large-scale military and financial aid to Ukraine, while castigating Russia for its much more limited support for separatists, confirmed the Kremlin's suppositions about Western double standards. Both sides may well have been jumping to wrong conclusions, but their policymakers were fenced in by lingering Cold War assumptions about the Other, with Ukraine caught in the middle.

FACETS OF WAR

In announcing the SVO, Putin explained to his startled Russian viewers that he was honouring obligations to 'protect the Russians and our people' in the Donbas, to demilitarize and de-Nazify Ukraine and, above all, to prevent any further expansion of NATO towards Russia's borders. He added that he would not occupy any Ukrainian territory or impose anything by force.[7] These statements might have represented his original expectation for intervention in Ukraine, and he undoubtedly assumed that the MoD's five-pronged blitzkrieg would cause the immediate collapse of the government in Kyiv and a Ukrainian surrender. Whatever his anticipations, the 'special military operation' was initially an utter failure, and a real war ensued.

Putin and his military advisers foresaw a rapid advance to Kyiv, where either his or internal forces would replace the Ukrainian leadership. They expected to be welcomed, especially in eastern Ukraine, and appeared to believe that the Ukrainian army would stand down, or its officers might side with the Russian army as many had in Crimea. None of that happened. Putin's goals were ill-defined, his military neglected to deploy enough troops and protect supply lines and, more importantly in the long run, he failed to prepare the Russian public for war. For that reason, the home front quickly became a second battlefront, of a different sort.

The war was not even to be named a war in Russia. As early as 4 March 2022, the Russian State Duma adopted a law against 'discrediting' Russia's armed forces, or spreading 'fake' news about military operations. In practice, this meant that the truth must not be told or shown. Calling the SVO an 'invasion' and the conflict a 'war' were offences that could result in fines or anywhere from 15 days to 15 years in prison. In July, a law allowed the closure of any foreign media outlet in Russia without recourse if its home base was deemed 'hostile', and also enabled the state to revoke broadcasting licenses of any Russian media outlet that spread 'dangerous information' or 'disrespect' for Russian society and its institutions.

The term 'Russophobia' had long been used by Putin and state officials to frame their notion of Russia as a besieged fortress among the concert of nations. It was now termed 'a misanthropic ideology' by legislation that set fines or prison sentences for perceived acts or statements deemed 'Russophobic', even in absentia.[8]

Patterns of military action and reaction were set in the very first week of conflict. Ukrainian forces fought back successfully around Kharkiv and Kyiv, while the West imposed further sanctions against the Russian economy and cut off airspace to Russian flights. Investors and foreign companies began exiting the country in droves, and the Russian government prepared a list of over 40 'unfriendly' nations with which it would not do business. The United Nations General Assembly (UNGA) voted 154–5 to condemn the Russian attack, and Zelensky embarked on an international video-conference campaign seeking help for Ukraine and censure of Russia. Putin had opened a Pandora's Box and quickly lost control of its content.

In its first ten days, Russian forces were successful in the south. They took Kherson on the Black Sea and Berdyansk on the Sea of Azov, occupied the nuclear power plant (NPP) at Zaporizhzhia and began a bloody siege of Mariupol. And then things started to go wrong. A huge military convoy heading to Kyiv was stopped both by Ukrainian resistance and Russia's own inefficient equipment and fuel supply chain. The West transferred funding and weapons to Ukraine and resistance tightened up. Worry that Russia might resort to nuclear weapons or that NATO might be drawn directly into the conflict dominated the pundit scene. Vague attempts at negotiations never materialized, as Ukrainian forces grew stronger and began to drive Russian troops out of areas they had occupied in the north.

The siege of Mariupol, an important port city on the Sea of Azov, was a sign of things to come. It started on 24 February, the first day of the invasion, and lasted until 20 May, leaving the city in rubble and almost devoid of population. Thousands were killed and the remnants of its last-ditch defenders, troops of the Azov Battalion, were taken prisoner. Mariupol was the first of several Ukrainian cities to suffer a similar fate.

Revenge Taking

As Ukrainian forces liberated areas taken earlier by Russian forces, tales of atrocities committed by Russian troops emerged, the most horrific being a site of mass civilian murders at Bucha, a town of 38,000 in the Kyiv Oblast from which Russian forces withdrew at the end of March.

After a series of minor setbacks, all shrugged off by the Kremlin and its obsequious media, a sudden counter-offensive launched by Ukrainian forces in the Kharkiv region, beginning on 6 September, forced the RF Ministry of Defence (MoD) to rethink its position and the Russian media to begin cautious questioning of the country's military management. NATO voiced more concerns that Russia might resort to tactical nuclear strikes.[9]

Reports of Russian soldiers fleeing the action, abandoning weapons, even tanks, caused Western diplomats and 'experts' gleefully to predict Russia's slide into dysfunction and chaos. Russian official commentators called the hasty retreat a re-grouping of Russian forces to the Donbas and blamed Ukrainian successes on Western mercenaries.[10]

In light of Ukraine's military achievements, the Biden administration announced on 15 September that it would send $600 million in weaponry to feed the counter-offensive with more firepower. Given that just one week prior to that the United States had provided $2.9 billion in financial support on top of another $3 billion in late August, the total amount of US aid to Ukraine since Biden took office reached nearly $16 billion before the first eight months were up.[11]

Further signs of Russian brutalities in areas they had occupied tainted the country's armed forces still more, though those images may not have reached a large portion of the Russian population. For example, the Ukrainian military claimed to have found up to 450 graves near Izyum in the Kharkiv region. RFE/RL's Russian-language TV channel *Nastoiashchee Vremia* (Current Time) displayed photos of graves in an area re-taken by Ukrainian forces, where some of the dead had hands tied and showed signs of torture.[12] Official spokesperson for the Kremlin, Dmitry Peskov, called the reports Ukrainian propaganda. Russian state-controlled media equated the stories with 'lies, like Goebbels', as they had with accounts of the atrocities discovered at Bucha. Russia's still semi-independent print media and Internet channels reported Peskov's responses but were careful not to provide much detail on what he was denying or provide photos of the graves and bodies.[13] Not for the first time, the Russian public was faced with a 'who to believe' conundrum.

The harshness went both ways. As if the long months of control by Russian forces were not enough hardship for citizens of Kharkiv and surrounding areas, officials and police with Ukrainian forces immediately began rounding up hundreds of Ukrainian citizens whom they suspected of collaborating with occupying forces; others fled to Russia. According to the head of Ukraine's national police force, Ihor Klimenko, over 1,300 residents of the area were already under investigation for treason. This number was limited to individuals who had taken official positions in areas occupied by Russian forces, though, as more areas were liberated by Ukrainian forces, the search for 'collaborators' expanded to take in teachers and anyone else deemed to have cooperated with the occupiers.[14] Some were tracked down and shot by Ukrainian partisans without any due process. One Ukrainian official was quoted in the British press saying: 'Our intelligence services are eliminating them, shooting them like pigs'.[15] Neighbours snitching on neighbours in once-occupied areas of Ukraine caught the innocent along with the many guilty with no objections from Western governments.

Negotiations, Casualties, Re-Grouping

By October 2022, Putin may have been regretting that he did not take up peace plans discussed seriously by both sides in March (Minsk) and April (Istanbul), and signed on to by Russia's representative. Negotiations arranged by Turkey's president Recep Tayyip Erdogan and Israeli's prime minister Naftali Bennett and reported to Moscow by Russia's envoy to Kyiv, Dmitry Kozak, included an agreement that Ukraine would stay out of NATO, revert to its original constitutional status as a neutral country and ease its legislation against the Russian language. Russia would withdraw its troops and the Donbas would stay in Ukraine. The status of Crimea would be left for later discussions. Although Western pundits continued to blame him for the breakdown of the talks, Putin later claimed that Russia had initialled the agreement.[16] The settlement that both sides seemed to want broke down in part because the UK's Boris Johnson flew to Kyiv and was presumed to be speaking for the West when he urged Zelensky to fight on. If subsequent accounts by key participants in these talks, for example, German chancellor Gerhard Schröder and Bennett, are accurate, then it would seem that the war might have been halted in the early spring of 2022 if not for Johnson's intervention.[17]

Pressure on the Russian population to participate intensified quickly. As early as May, Russia's evident dearth of manpower and ineffective recruitment programme resulted in a law that abolished the upper age limits for contract soldiers, especially for veterans and specialists. But that wasn't enough. By the fall, Putin had either to declare a potentially very unpopular mass mobilization, or acknowledge that the SVO was lost. Both choices posed serious domestic political risks. A nuclear option proposed by extreme Russian nationalists risked war with NATO. Tightening up what the MoD had already gained in Ukraine – stay the course – was the Kremlin's answer at the time.[18]

Russia still held dominant positions in the Donbas and in the south, around Kherson. The MoD's response to the Kharkiv humiliation was to direct missile strikes against Ukraine's infrastructure, including its power plants and water systems. These caused structural damage and civilian deaths in over 30 towns and villages across Ukraine. In Russia, hardliners in the State Duma began calling for full mobilization. Deputy chair of the Russian Security Council, Dmitry Medvedev, warned that if Western 'half-wits' continue to feed weapons to Ukraine, the 'military campaign will move to another level'. Western countries will be forced out of their comfort zone, he continued: 'Everything around them will be on fire. Their people will experience trouble in full. The earth will be on fire and concrete will melt in the truest sense of the word. We will get to experience big problems as well. Everyone will be in big, big trouble'. He was commenting on a security treaty proposed by Kyiv, in which the United States, the United Kingdom, Canada and a dozen European countries would guarantee Ukraine's security.[19]

Russia Mobilizes

The urge to mobilize materialised again after the United Russia (UR) party swept local and municipal elections in mid-September. Referred to colloquially as 'Putin's Party', the UR took its victory as an indication of a high level of support for the war. Putin's lofty polling ratings and the State Duma's adoption, unanimously, of amendments to laws allowing mass mobilization and making refusal to sign up a criminal offence, bolstered his declaration of a 'partial' military mobilization on 21 September. The call-up of 300,000 referred only to reservists, especially to those who had already served.

To justify the decision, Putin claimed again that he was trying to protect the people of the Donbas against a Nazi government in Kyiv and blamed Washington, London and Brussels for 'pushing Kiev [Kyiv] to shift military action to our territory' and 'plundering all of our country'. He accused NATO countries of encouraging the possibility 'of using weapons of mass destruction against Russia, nuclear weapons'.[20] In short, Putin explained mobilization by insisting that Russia was fighting a de facto war against the West.

Coinciding with the mobilization proclamation, Minister of Defence Sergei Shoigu revealed that Russia's 'losses' since the first days of the SVO were 5,937 dead. That was only the third time the MoD released information on fatalities (2 March – 498; 15 March – 1,351), and as before, they were far below the number of military deaths broadcast by Western and Ukrainian observers who claimed that Russia had suffered about 65,000 military deaths to that date. Neither side could, or would, verify their tallies.[21]

The first stages of the mobilization programme were so muddled that in some regions more than half of the recruited personnel had to be sent home because they did not meet selection criteria. Enlistment officers were dismissed in several recruitment zones and bureaucratic chaos generated higher costs and further communication breakdowns, not unlike the conduct of the war itself.[22] The project was confused as well because the regular fall conscription was scheduled to start on 1 October. Given the time it would take to train recruits for actual battle, even reservists, the possibility of a major infusion of reinforcements remained for some time in the future – or so it was assumed. On 14 October, Putin acknowledged that 16,000 recruits had already been deployed to combat units, some with less than a week of training.[23]

The mobilization decree carried clauses that called for ten-year sentences for voluntary surrender to the enemy, a litany of punishments for no-shows, and up to ten years for refusing to engage in combat.

Anecdotal accounts suggest that recruits lacked proper weapons, gear and food. Tales circulated of officers leaving troops to face their opponents on the battlefield without leadership. Although such tales might be apocryphal, they sounded true, and they were heard throughout Russia.[24] It may be that decades of corruption in the MoD, especially in the procurement division (Oboronservis), were coming home to roost.[25]

To beef up the recruiting effort, on 2 November, Putin signed a law enabling recruiters to enlist individuals with outstanding criminal convictions, though they could not conscript men who had sexually abused children, or were serving sentences for terrorism, hostage-taking or treason. At about the same time, he authorized a law setting out conditions for the creation of volunteer corps. These units have the status of military personnel under contract and are monitored by the MoD, which will set their size, areas of operation, tasks and system of payment. According to the General Staff, more than 15,000 people had signed up for volunteer units by the end of October.[26]

At least one of the mercenary units, the infamous Wagner Group overseen by Yevgeny Prigozhin, admitted that it was recruiting foreign nationals from Russian prisons after a Zambian student serving a nine-year sentence for drug possession was killed while fighting for Russia in Ukraine. The Wagner PMC (private military company) was also accused of freeing rebels from prisons in the Central African Republic (CAR) and sending them to fight in Ukraine, some of them alleged to have raped and killed civilians.[27] This tale was widely circulated but to date remains unproven. At any rate, the role of mercenaries could not be taken lightly. They act in coordination with the MoD, the Federal Security Service (Federal'naia sluzhba bezopasnosti – FSB), and the presidential administration. According to one analyst, they practice 'exterminatory warfare' and specialize in taking urban centres. The Wagner Group already had seen action in Libya, Syria, Sudan and the CAR, and in 2022 was declared a 'terrorist' organization by the United States and the EU. By that time, the number of troops in the Wagner Group fighting in Ukraine may have been as high as 50,000.[28]

The mostly Russian Wagner Group sometimes found itself fighting volunteer units in Ukraine made up of non-Ukrainians and some Russians. For instance, the ethnic-based Freedom for Russia Legion (Russians), the Siberian Legion (Russians), the Georgian Legion (Georgians), the Kastus Kalinouski Battalion (Belarusans), Turan (Turkic-speakers from the Caucasus and Central Asia), and both the Dudaev and Sheikh Mansur Battalions (Chechens), all fought under rather loose monitoring by the Ukrainian Ministry of Defence, though often with post-war agendas of their own. An International Legion of Territorial Defence that absorbed other nationalities was integrated into the Ukrainian army. Many of these volunteers are fluent Russian speakers and are able to infiltrate and undertake sabotaging missions.[29]

'War with the West'

Putin had already settled on the West as the enemy during his explanatory address on the SVO. Citing NATO's military operations against Belgrade, Libya and Syria, and America's invasion of Iraq, he accused the West of 'arrogance' and a sense of 'absolute superiority' that featured the unrelenting advancement of NATO towards Russia and a renewed 'containment policy, all of which posed a real threat . . . to the very existence of our state. Its sovereignty'. The West crossed a red line, he said, with their support for 'extreme nationalism' in Ukraine.[30] Thus, the SVO was deemed an indirect war with the West almost from the beginning, though that was not stated unequivocally until 2024.

Shoigu made the new approach clear as the announcement of mobilization sent a chill through much of the country. He insisted in a televised address that Russia needed to increase its troop strength because the 'US-led collective West continues its military-political course to contain Russia'.[31] Russian Security Council Secretary, Nikolai Patrushev, confirmed the new public posture, saying during a January 2023 interview that the events in Ukraine 'are not a clash between Moscow and Kyiv, this is a military confrontation between NATO, above all the United States and England, and Russia'.[32]

Meanwhile, the MoD conducted daily briefings in which the conflict was presented as a continuum of successful Russian artillery attacks, air strikes, shoot-downs of Ukrainian drones and aircraft, and interceptions of missiles, as if there were no problems that Russian Armed Forces could not handle easily.³³ Referenda conducted in the occupied zones in September and their subsequent annexation to Russia changed the nature of the conflict and contradicted Putin's declaration in February 2022 that he would not make claims on Ukrainian territory.

DRUM BEAT GOES ON

Ukraine's response to the incorporation of Ukrainian territories into the Russian Federation was to apply for immediate accession to NATO, while its counter-offensive racked up another victory by forcing Russian troops to withdraw from the nearly surrounded town of Lyman in the Donetsk region. The site had been an important logistics and transport hub for Russian forces.³⁴ Coming just one day after the annexation announcement, the Ukrainian triumph was humiliating for Putin and prompted Chechnya's head, Ramzan Kadyrov, to demand that Russia use tactical nuclear weapons and that the responsible general be dismissed. Zelensky proclaimed that he would 'never' negotiate with Putin, and Ukrainian representatives began talking of an ultimate Ukrainian victory if only the West would 'increase its supply of sophisticated weaponry' and give NATO a 'rare chance to test its equipment in a real-time, high-intensity operational environment'.³⁵

As it happened, the commander of Russia's Western military district, Col. Gen. Aleksandr Zhuravlev, was fired and replaced by Lt. Gen. Roman Berdnikov. The deputy minister of defence in charge of logistics also was let go and, shortly thereafter, the MoD named a new commander of the invading army on the ground: Army General Sergei Surovikin, former head of the Russian Aerospace Forces. He came to the post hours after an explosion on the Kerch Strait bridge (see 'Attack on the Kerch Strait Bridge'). There was no immediate change on the battlefield. Ukraine's momentum continued with a breakthrough in the Kherson region.

The recently promised permanency of Kherson as part of Russia was in doubt by late October, as Ukrainian forces retook villages in the region and Russia-appointed authorities there urged civilians in the north of the province (oblast) to leave immediately and cross over to the left side of the Dnipro (Dnieper) River. Early in November, Putin added his support to civilian evacuation from parts of the Kherson area, and Russian troops began a 'controlled' withdrawal from the region's northwest. Stories spread that Russian soldiers emptied Kherson's Regional Art Museum of priceless art and antiquities, trucking items to museums in Russia.³⁶

The losses caused splits among Putin's inner circles to widen. The MoD under Shoigu, the Wagner Group and Chechnya's Kadyrov all seemed to be moving in different directions. Prigozhin and Kadyrov were openly critical of the MoD.

Attack on the Kerch Strait Bridge

Russia's troubles grew when, on 8 October, a truck exploded on the automobile side of the 19-kilometre (12-mile) Kerch Strait bridge that connects mainland Russia with Crimea. Three civilians were killed, and a fire broke out in nearby oil tanker cars moving by rail to Crimea. The bridge, an important component of the supply route for Russian forces in Ukraine, was damaged and closed for a short time. Although Kyiv did not claim responsibility at that time, Ukrainian officials and media exulted about it. The Ukrainian post office printed postage stamps celebrating the explosion on the bridge.[37] At a meeting the next day with the head of Russia's Investigative Committee, Aleksandr Bastrykin, Putin was told that the bombing was arranged by 'Ukrainian special services and citizens of Russia and foreign countries'.[38]

Speaking about this incident and others, Zelensky now made it plain that recovering Crimea along with the four annexed territories on mainland Ukraine was one of the conditions that could bring the nine-month war to an end. At that stage, Putin appeared to be left with few options. After proclaiming that the annexed regions were now Russia's 'forever!', he could not give them up without losing face. The call-up project was not working well either, and Ukrainian armed forces were chipping away at Russia's earlier gains. Losses were now admitted, if obliquely, on Russian TV. As the head of the State Duma Defence Committee put it, 'We have to stop lying . . . our people are not stupid'. Not stupid, to be sure, but they were misinformed and cowed. No one dared blame Putin directly, so critics impugned the military leadership instead.[39]

Six weeks after the partial call-up and a few days after the MoD said that the mobilization campaign was completed, Russian recruits were still being sent off to fight without proper training, military equipment or weapons. Stories of strikes by soldiers from Chuvashia who had not received promised wages and bonuses, and other forms of protest, began spreading through social media and dissident information outlets – but not on state-controlled media.[40]

Dmitry Medvedev jumped into this fray by calling on the government to reinstate the death penalty for perpetrators of wartime sabotage. Citing the assassination of Darya Dugina, daughter of the philosopher of Eurasianism, Aleksandr Dugin, attacks on recruiting offices and threats to railways and power lines, and calling the saboteurs 'freaks' with 'thoroughly broken brains', he insisted that the moratorium on capital punishment since 1996 should be lifted. He wrote this as an op-ed piece for *Aktual'nye kommentarii*, a Putinist outlet, and signed it off as the head of the UR.[41] Critics of this potential change believed that the death penalty, suspended by Yeltsin so Russia could join the Council of Europe, would also be used against political opponents of the regime. The Kremlin denied that it was considering restoring capital punishment.

The nuclear option was still there, but that would signal that Russia was losing to Ukraine. None of the obvious Plan B's were good ones for the Kremlin as the first weeks of October unfolded.

Russia Responds

After labelling the damage done to the Kerch bridge a 'terrorist act' perpetrated by the 'failed state of Ukraine', Russian forces intensified attacks on Ukrainian infrastructure. Although the Russian MoD announced that its mass retaliation 'successfully' hit military targets, communication centres, energy and water facilities in about a dozen Ukrainian cities, they were much more random than that and driven by lust for revenge. Dozens of people, many of them children, were killed or injured. Videos of damage were posted around the world to belie Moscow's assertions.[42]

In a speech to the Russian Security Council on 10 October, Putin made it plain that the missiles were directed at Ukrainian cities in retaliation for the Kerch bridge event, and also claimed that Ukraine had conducted 'terrorist' attacks on the Kursk NPP and the TurkStream. He promised further retribution if more strikes against 'Russian territories' occurred.[43] On the other hand, Lavrov told a TV interviewer that Russia was open for talks with the West on the issue of Ukraine, but had not yet received any 'serious' proposals to negotiate, and that Moscow would consider a Putin-Biden meet during the G-20 summit in November.[44] The Kremlin had not yet offered any serious proposals itself and was not likely to do so.

The message to Russians was that Putin wanted peace; Zelensky and the West did not. Since most public protests against the war had been curtailed harshly by that time, the degree to which the Kremlin was believed at home remained a mystery.

ARMING UKRAINE

Armaments and training programmes from NATO countries had been flowing into Ukraine since 2014.[45] The re-provisioning campaign began slowly with small arms, personal gear (helmets, body armour), former Soviet weapons stored in Eastern European countries, drones from Turkey and, of course, money. NATO countries had long hesitated to supply lethal weapons from their own arsenals until, in 2021, the United States sent javelin anti-tank systems to Ukraine. Since then, weapons produced in NATO countries and Australia have poured into the country: armoured vehicles (British Saxons,

Australian Bushmasters), more anti-tank systems (shoulder-fired NLAWs, Javelins), Carl Gustaf anti-tank recoilless rifles (Canada), artillery mounts (French Caesars, American High Mobility Artillery Rocket Systems – HIMARS), plus hundreds of thousands of rounds of ammunition and artillery shells. These were delivered within the first six months of the war. Much, much more was to come.

In November 2022, the White House asked Congress for $38 billion in aid, a sum that would bring the total appropriations for Ukraine up to $100 billion since February. Of the new supplement, $21.7 billion were designated for military and security assistance, the remainder for humanitarian, health care and other support services. A separate sum of $7 billion was requested so that weapons could be transferred to Ukraine from US stocks.[46]

Citing US State Department data in November 2022, and State Department press releases, the Russian MoD and Western journalists calculated that Washington had supplied Ukraine with more than 88,000 tonnes of weaponry since the end of February that year. These supplies comprised 236 artillery systems, among them 36 HIMARS, that is, long-range mobile rocket systems. Over a million artillery shells, 100,000 man-portable anti-tank missile systems, about 1,400 man-portable air defence systems, 15 helicopters, 46 radars, 10,200 assault rifles and pistols, more than 70 million rounds of ammunition for small arms, and 26 patrol boats. The Russian media also reported that, in November, the US Department of Defense provided another $400 million that would allow for the purchase of 45 Czech T-72 tanks. The Russian mainstream media spread detailed inventories of foreign weaponry going to Ukraine, leaving Russians with the clear impression that they were fighting a Washington and NATO proxy.[47] This later became the official message.

The United States also began delivering National Advanced Surface-to-Air Missile Systems (NASAMS) to Ukraine. Two were supplied in November 2022, along with Avenger air defence systems, and additional NASAMS were scheduled after they were built. They have a longer range than any missile launcher used by Ukrainian armed forces up to that time.[48]

The second year, from February 2023, was to bring an even greater amount of lethal and mobile firepower from the West to Ukraine.

Drums of War Continue Apace

Neither Russia nor Ukraine eased the intensity of their war effort in the fall of 2022.

In the south, advancing Ukrainian troops forced over 60,000 civilians to evacuate Kherson, at least to the other side of the Dnipro. At the same time, Russian forces made some gains in the northern Kharkiv region and, during a meeting with his Security Council, Putin declared martial law in the four recently occupied areas of Ukraine. He also granted extra powers to heads of regions in the Russian Federation close to the border with Ukraine, mainly to ensure that decrees related to mobilization and support for the war would be carried out.[49] The decree defined 'response levels' for all of Russia, the strictest covering the six regions bordering Ukraine. In those areas, authorities have the right to forcibly evacuate residents, seize properties and limit transport and other vehicular movement.[50]

In the midst of heightened tension, NATO and Russia conducted long-planned nuclear exercises at about the same time in October, both asserting that they were normal annual undertakings and warning the other not to escalate. Mutual threats piled up anyway, as NATO pledged to provide Ukraine with drone jammers, doubled its naval presence in the Baltic and North Seas, and warned Russia that any use of nuclear weapons against Ukraine would have 'severe consequences'. In turn, Putin cautioned that any clash between Russian and NATO forces would lead to a 'global catastrophe'.[51] Stating the obvious did nothing to slow the intensification of war-fighting.

Before that, Ukrainian missiles hit a power station and a munitions depot in Russia's Belgorod region, killing several civilians.[52] On that same day in October, shelling destroyed the offices of the Russia-appointed government in the city of Donetsk. Both Russia's mainland and territories it occupied in Ukraine were now under attack. Ducking the issue, the Russian media and MoD mostly ignored the strikes on Belgorod and shifted focus from the latter events by claiming victories in other parts of Ukraine. These 'victories' included kamikaze drone attacks on Kyiv.

Though civilian centres were hit and civilians were killed, Russia's primary targets were energy sites, in an attempt to freeze Ukrainian resistance when winter set in. Statements from NATO and Washington to the effect that Russia was 'weaponizing winter' became a steady refrain. Attacks were reported also in Dnipro (Dnipropetrovsk until 2016), Kharkiv, Mykolaiv and Khryvyi Rih. Escalation was in the air. Ukraine's energy operator, Ukrenergo, reported outages in several areas as missile attacks continued in western and central Ukraine, especially in the Volyn, Rivne and Kirovohrad regions. The city of Khmelnytskyi and parts of Odesa suffered extended power outages.

An interview with Russia's General Surovikin on 18 October left no doubt as to the MoD's official version of events: the SVO, he said, was aimed against a 'criminal regime that pushes citizens of Ukraine to their death'. Russians and Ukrainians are one people, he added, and both want to be independent of the West and NATO. Surovikin boasted of the 'enemy's' huge daily losses of life and, disingenuously, of the Russian practice of 'protecting' each of its soldiers and civilians. 'NATO leadership of the armed forces of Ukraine' was a repeated theme of the interview. If Surovikin actually believed his rambling propaganda, then the chances of the war expanding beyond Ukraine's borders grew greater.[53]

It was at this point that Shoigu and his US counterpart, Lloyd Austin, spoke by telephone. They discussed Ukraine and issues of international security for only the second time since Putin launched the invasion. Their presidents had both said recently that they saw no need for a personal meeting at the up-coming G-20 talks in Indonesia. Shoigu and Austin spoke again just three days later, and Shoigu talked on the same day with defence ministers in France (Sebastien Lecornu), Turkey (Hulusi Akar) and the UK (Ben Wallace). Concern about going from bad to worse dominated the conversations, several of the ministers said. In his talk with Akar, Shoigu raised the possibility that Ukraine was creating a 'dirty bomb' to deploy as a false flag on which to blame Russia, and the MoD followed up with a claim that 'the Kiev regime is preparing a bloody provocation with the death of its own civilians'.[54] Foreign ministers of the United States, the United Kingdom and France immediately issued a joint statement ridiculing the 'dirty bomb' allegation as 'transparently false' and a pretext for further action.[55]

While politicians and pundits in Kyiv and Washington continued to warn that Russia might resort to nuclear weapons and Russia continued to deny it, the MID issued a statement saying that nuclear war would be one 'in which there can be no winners and must never be unleashed'. The statement went on to proclaim,

> Russian doctrinal guidelines in this area are very clearly outlined, they are purely defensive in nature and do not allow for broad interpretation. The reaction with the use of nuclear weapons is hypothetically allowed by Russia only in response to aggression carried out with the use of WMD, or aggression with the use of conventional weapons, when the very existence of the state is threatened.[56]

It is not likely that anyone outside Russia was comforted by this clarification. Still, officials in Washington admitted that they saw no evidence that Russia was preparing a nuclear weapon for deployment.[57]

By that time, Lavrov had confirmed that Putin was ready for talks with the West on Ukraine, but only if they are based on 'realistic proposals' related to Russia's security interests. Zelensky said that no negotiations were possible before Russia's full withdrawal from Ukrainian territory. Russia claimed that Zelensky's refusal to negotiate was a result of 'direct instructions' from 'Western sponsors'. French president Emmanuel Macron told participants at a Cry for Peace summit in Rome that the conflict in Ukraine could be settled only on terms set by the government in Kyiv, where more Russian strikes at the end of October left much of the city temporarily without water and electricity. The MoD claimed at the same time that it had successfully targeted military and energy sites across the country with 'high precision long-range and sea-based weapons'.

More civilians died and the possibility of actual negotiations grew dimmer.[58]

Russians Retreat from Kherson

On 9 November, Shoigu announced that Russian forces would draw back from the city of Kherson and re-establish their defences on the left bank of the Dnipro. The announcement came during a televised meeting with Russia's top military personnel, so it was witnessed by Russia's TV news watchers.[59]

The state-owned media called the withdrawal part of an 'approved plan' introduced by Surovikin to 'save the lives of servicemen', free soldiers up for combat elsewhere in Ukraine, and keep Russian weapons and gear out of the hands of the enemy.[60] A leading propagandist for State-owned *Russia Today (RT)*, Margarita Simonyan, compared it to Kutuzov's retreat from Moscow in 1812; that is, saving troops so as to fight another day. Even Kadyrov agreed with Shoigu's decision.[61] Stretching the party line's credibility further, Surovikin told Shoigu that Ukrainian forces had suffered nearly 10,000 fatalities, plus hundreds of tanks, armoured vehicles and artillery pieces, all of these some 7–8 times more than Russian losses. Peskov insisted that Kherson was still a 'subject of the Russian Federation – legally fixed'.[62] All this sugar-coating notwithstanding, the retreat was a major defeat for Russia and Putin. Both sides again hinted at negotiations, though neither offered any concessions.

The Russian mainstream media parroted statements from the MoD and the Kremlin to the effect that 'there were no losses of personnel, weapons, military equipment and materiel of the Russian group', and that the region would still 'definitely be part of Russia'. That first was a lie and the second was wishful thinking.[63]

Shortly thereafter, the Biden administration announced a new package of military aid to Ukraine that contained Avenger air defence systems but still kept back sophisticated drones capable of hitting targets in Russia. As Ukraine strengthened and Western support grew firmer, Zelensky became even less interested in negotiations. Speaking on 14 November via video to the G-20 meeting in Bali, he presented a 10-point plan for negotiations that could start only after Russian forces withdrew from all Ukrainian territory. Other conditions were a ban on using nuclear weapons, a guarantee on energy security, an all-for-all prisoner exchange and a release of deportees. Zelensky also wanted the UN to establish a committee to investigate Russian war crimes, provide a guaranteed end to the war, and re-open the grain export corridor.[64] Knowing full well that Russia would not consider most of his terms, Zelensky's plan was aimed primarily at an international audience.

A day prior to Zelensky's statement to the G-20, the UNGA adopted another non-binding resolution (94-14-73) to hold Russia responsible for human and material damage done in Ukraine, meaning reparations.[65]

Russia's response was a barrage of up to 90 missiles battering civilian and strategic targets in Ukraine. Residences in Kyiv, power stations in Lviv and Kharkiv, city centres in Odesa, Kryvyi Rih, Mykolaiv, Zhytomyr and others were hit. Power outages proliferated in Kyiv and elsewhere. The fractured infrastructure in Ukraine prompted the World Health Organization (WHO) to warn that many Ukrainian lives were at risk because they lacked electricity and ready access to health care.[66]

Less than a month later, the United States decided to deliver a Patriot missile system to Ukraine.

PEACE TALKS?

The flurry of peace proposals in October having come to naught, Russian forces continued to pound Ukrainian electrical, heating and water systems. About 60 per cent of the Kyivan population lost power temporarily. Three entire regions of Ukraine were left without electricity, and all nuclear power plants were disabled. Parts of Moldova that import electricity from Ukraine also suffered power shortages. Talk spread again about a possible truce or even general peace negotiations. According to some sources, the United States put forward a plan that would have Russia withdrawing from all territory it occupied in Ukraine except Crimea and NATO promising not to allow Ukraine accession for at least seven years. After that same seven years, Crimea would hold a referendum on its future. Russia and Ukraine both rejected the proposal outright. Officials in Moscow said Russia would never give up Crimea; officials in Kyiv said Ukraine would never negotiate while a single Russian soldier remained anywhere in their country.[67]

There were mixed messages from the West. Washington lobbied quietly for peace talks while authorizing another $400 million in military aid; the UK's Ben Wallace urged Ukraine to keep fighting and announced that he was sending three British Sea King helicopters plus 10,000 artillery rounds to Ukraine. In a less direct challenge, NATO tested the French MAMBA Surface-Based Air and Missile Defence system in Romania, specifically 'in response to Russia's war against Ukraine'. Testing the system were F-16s from Turkey, Spanish Eurofighters already deployed in Bulgaria on a NATO mission, American Growler electronic warfare aircraft and French Navy Dassault Rafale fighters flying from an aircraft carrier.[68]

At the same time, the 705-member European Parliament adopted a nonbinding resolution, 494 in favour, 58 against and 44 abstentions, to recognize Russia as a 'state sponsor of terrorism', and placed the Wagner Group on the EU's terrorist list.[69] NATO delegations and the US Senate passed resolutions asking their governments to join the EU action. Biden said no, and the Canadian government hesitated in spite of heavy pressure from the Canadian Ukrainian Congress. Zakharova responded that the European Parliament should be recognized as a 'sponsor of idiocy'.[70]

Although leaders in Moscow and Kyiv began insinuating that they were ready for peace talks, on their own terms, there were no signs of flexibility on the battlefield, and NATO grew more adamant in its support for Ukraine. The Alliance promised further financial and military aid and, during a foreign ministers' meeting in Bucharest, 29–30 November, again guaranteed Ukraine's ultimate accession. Two days after the NATO session, Biden said he was willing to sit down for talks with Putin – only after Russian forces withdrew from Ukraine. The Kremlin replied that it too was open to talks but rejected Biden's conditions. German Chancellor Olaf Scholz telephoned Putin and urged him to seek a diplomatic solution to end the catastrophe and stop the airstrikes against civilian infrastructure, only to be told that the strikes were necessary because the West was 'pumping the Kyiv regime with weapons'.[71] While these very limited hints at negotiations were going on, Russian forces withdrew a little further in the Kherson region and advanced a little further in the Donetsk Peoples Republic (DPR).

At the three-quarter mark of the first annus horribilis, Russia's war in Ukraine settled into a war of attrition, with Ukrainian forces slowly advancing and Russian forces digging in on occupied Ukrainian territory. Russian military decisions improved. Its front lines were bolstered by fresh conscripts and, by targeting energy infrastructure and withdrawing from Kherson, Russia had both troops and equipment to deploy elsewhere. The Russian command now had time to re-group.[72]

The opening weeks of 2023 saw more of the same. Foreign diplomats urged truces, talks, or serious negotiations; Ukrainian and Russian leaders set out conditions that neither could accept; hints at nuclear weapon deployments proliferated; the West approved more sanctions against Russia; Russian authorities adopted further repressive measures at home; and both combatants predicted ultimate victory.

NOTES

1. For quick background on this, see Natalia Savelyeva, 'The Donbas dilemma: Examining Russia's path to full-scale intervention', *Russian Analytical Digest*, No. 306 (14 December 2023), pp. 2–7.
2. For three overarching sources on the crisis of 2014 and its context, Richard Sakwa, *Frontline Ukraine: Crisis in the Borderlands*. London: I.B. Taurus, 2015; J. L. Black, *Russia After 2020: Looking Ahead After Two Decades of Putin*. London and New York: Routledge, 2022; Dominique Arel, Jesse Driscoll, *Ukraine's Unnamed War: Before the Russian Invasion of 2022*. Cambridge: Cambridge UP, 2023.
3. European Parliament/Legislative Observatory. Resolution adopted by Parliament, single reading, No. 2889, 13 December 2012. See also European Parliament, 'Motion for a resolution', No. B7-0221/2014, 25 February 2014.
4. Richard Sakwa, *Frontline Ukraine: Crisis in the Borderlands*. London: I.B. Taurus, 2015, pp. 86–87.
5. On this, see J. L. Black, *Eternal Putin?: Confronting Navalny, the Pandemic, Sanctions and War with Ukraine*. Lanham, MD: Lexington Books, 2023, pp. 153–154.
6. On the early impact of NATO expansion, see, J. L. Black, *Russia Faces NATO Expansion*. Lanham, MD: Roman & Littlefield, 2000.
7. 'Obrashenie Prezidenta Rossiiskoi Federatsii', *Kremlin.ru*, 24 February 2022, kremlin.ru/events/president/news/67843.
8. Vërstka, 'Za "rusofobiiu" planiruetsia sazhat' na srok do piati let, vyiasnila "Vërstka"', *Telegram*, 18 May 2023, t.me/svobodnieslova/1968; 'V Dume predlozhili ustanovit' za rusofobiiu ugolovnuiu otvetstvennost', *RIA Novosti*, 12 May 2023; 'Russia eyes 5-year jail terms for "Russophobia"', *The Moscow Times*, 20 May 2023.
9. '"We fight how we can": Russian views on Ukraine's counteroffensive – How it happened and what comes next', *Russia Matters*, 16 September 2022.
10. For updates on the actual fighting, follow the Institute for the Study of War's (ISW) 'Russian offensive campaign assessment', 15 September 2022, and subsequent reports, understandingwar.org/backgrounder/russian-offensive-campaign-assessment-september-15; Alexander J. Motyl, 'Russia is a failed state', *The Hill*, 27 September 2022; 'State-owned Russian media shrugs off Russia's Kharkiv defeat', *The Bell*, 20 September 2022.
11. US Department of State, '$600 million in additional military assistance for Ukraine', Press Statement. Antony J. Blinken, secretary of state, 15 September 2022.
12. 'In Izyum, where the Russian army left, they found a mass grave', *Meduza*, 15 September 2022.
13. See, e.g. Agenstvo Novosti, 'Massovoe zakhoronenie v Iziume na federal'nykh kanalakh nazvali lozh'iu "po Gebbel'su"', *Telegram*, 19 September 2022, t.me/agentstvonews/1333; 'Peskov nazval vran'em zaiavleniia Kieva o "voennykh prestupleniiakh" v Khar'kovskoi oblasti', *Vedomosti*, 19 September 2022.
14. 'Politseys'ki vidkrili 1358 kriminal'nykh provadzhen' za faktami spivpratsi z vorogom – Igor Klimenko', *Uriadoviy portal*, 16 September 2022, kmu.gov.ua/news

/politseiski-vidkryly-1358-kryminalnykh-provadzhen-za-faktamy-spivpratsi-z-voroh om-ihor-klymenko; Mia Jankowicz, 'Ukrainian collaborators who sided with Russia occupation were given top jobs and fancy titles: Now they're being hunted down', *Business Insider*, 23 September 2022; Andrew E. Kramer, Maria Varenikova, 'Who collaborated with the enemy?' *New York Times International*, 1–2 October 2022.

15. For one account, see Ian Birrell, '"We're hunting them down and shooting them like pigs": How the Ukrainians are taking brutal revenge on the collaborators who've betrayed their neighbours – and country – to the Russians', *The Daily Mail*, 5 October 2022.

16. 'Exclusive: As war began, Putin rejected a Ukraine peace deal', *Reuters*, 14 September 2022; 'Putin rejected early Ukraine peace deal to pursue "expanded" annexation goals reuters', *The Moscow Times*, 14 September 2022; Ben Aris, 'Top Ukrainian politician David Arakhamia gives seventh confirmation of Russia-Ukraine peace deal agreed in March 2022', *bne IntelliNews*, 26 November 2023.

17. 'Russia offered to end war in 2022 if Ukraine scrapped NATO ambitions – Zelensky party chief', *Kyiv Post*, 26 November 2023; Bill Bostock, 'Ukraine official negotiating with Russia said the peace talks turned darker after evidence emerged of a massacre in Bucha', *Business Insider*, 8 April 2022; 'Prime Minister Boris Johnson met with President Zelensky in Kyiv and promised him armoured vehicles and anti-ship missile systems', *Business Insider*, 9 April 2022; Rebecca Rommen, 'Russia offered to end its invasion of Ukraine if it dumped plans to join NATO, but Kyiv feared a double-cross, says negotiator', *Business Insider*, 26 November 2023; for the Schröder explanation, see interview in the *Berliner Zeitung*, 23 October 2023, berli ner-zeitung.de/politik-gesellschaft/gerhard-schroeder-im-exklusiv-interview-was-merkel-2015-gemacht-hat-war-politisch-falsch-li.2151196; and 'NATO allies want longer Ukraine war to weaken Moscow, Turkiye says', *MEMO. Middle East Monitor*, 21 April 2022. See also Putin's remarks in 'Meeting with war correspondents', *Kremlin.ru*, 13 June 2023, en.kremlin.ru/events/president/transcripts/71391; Nicolai N. Petro, Ted Snider, 'What's next for Ukraine: The outlines of a peaceful settlement', *Anti-war.com*, 17 November 2023.

For a more detailed discussion, Samuel Charap, Sergey Radchenko, 'The talks that could have ended the war in Ukraine', *Foreign Affairs*, 16 April 2024.

18. See quotes from myriad specialists in David Rothkopf, 'What happens to Russia after it loses?' *The Daily Beast*, 13 September 2022; Brian Wang, 'What happens after Russia loses in Ukraine?' *Next Big Future*, 11 September 2022, nextbigfuture .com/2022/09/what-happens-after-russia-loses-in-ukraine.html; for an earlier assessment, Liana Fix, Michael Kimmage, 'What if Russia loses? A defeat for Moscow won't be a clear victory for the West', *Foreign Affairs*, 4 March 2022.

19. Dmitrii Medvedev in Telegram, 13 September 2022, t.me/medvedev_telegram/177; 'Dmitry Medvedev on NATO-Russia war: Earth will burn and concrete will melt', *Pravda.ru*, 14 September 2022, english.pravda.ru/news/world/153977 -Medvedev_NATO-Russia_war/; 'Garantii bezopasnosti Ukrainy: reaktsii rossiiskikh vlastei', *Aktual'nye kommentarii*, 14 September 2022.

20. Putin, 'Obrashchenie Prezidenta Rossiiskoi Federatsii', *Kremlin.ru*, 21 September 2022, kremlin.ru/events/president/news/69390; 'Ukaz "Ob ob'iavlenii

chastichnoi mobilizatsii v Rossiiskoi Federatsii'", *Kremlin.ru*, 21 September 2022, kremlin.ru/events/president/news/69391. For a discussion, Pavel Luzin, 'The impossible mobilization', *Eurasia Daily Monitor*, 22 September 2022.

21. 'Shoigu rasskazal o poteriakh rossiiskoi armii s nachala SVO', *Vedomosti*, 21 September 2022.

22. Pavel Luzin, 'Mobilization as a triumph of political eschatology', *Eurasia Daily Monitor*, 29 September 2022.

23. For a review, Neil MacFarquhar, 'Toll of Russia's chaotic draft', *New York Times International*, 22–23 October 2022; 'Russian regions walk back ad hoc mobilization after Putin scolding', *The Moscow Times*, 30 September 2022.

24. See, e.g. Anastasia Tenisheva, Yanina Sorokina, '"I don't trust what they say": Russian draft dodgers stay in hiding even as Putin announces mobilization's end', *The Moscow Times*, 2 November 2022; Allison Quinn, '"The command fled": Putin's own troops keep humiliating him', *The Daily Beast*, 6 November 2022.

25. On this, see J. L. Black, *Putin's Third Term as Russia's President, 2012–18*, London & New York: Routledge, 2019, pp. 211–112, 252–253; 'Oboronservis case defendant causes $90 million damage', *TASS*, 14 July 2014.

26. 'Genshtab: V dobrovol'cheskie otriady zapisalis' bolee 15 000 rossiian', *Vedomosti*, 1 November 2022; 'O vnesenii izmenenii v Federal'nyi zakon O mobilizatsionnoi podgotovke i mobilizatsii v Rossiiskoi Federatsii', 2 November 2022, publication.pravo.gov.ru/Document/View/0001202211040008?index=0&rangeSize=1.

27. 'Zambia student killed in Ukraine was Wagner recruit, Prigozhin says', *The Moscow Times*, 29 November 2022; Philip Obaji, 'Putin's prison recruiting scheme takes a big, desperate turn', *The Daily Beast*, 29 November 2022; 'The president of the Russian Federation signed the law on the creation of volunteer units', *Interfax*, 4 November 2022; 'Putin podpisal zakon o sozdanii dobrovol'cheskikh formirovanii', *Vedomosti*, 4 November 2022.

28. Andreas Heinemann-Grüder, 'Russia's state-sponsored killers: The Wagner Group', *Russian Analytical Digest*, No. 290, 22 December 2022. This is a special issue devoted to the Wagner Group.

29. On this, see Carlotta Gall, 'Fighting for Ukraine to take revenge on Russia', *New York Times International*, 21–22 January 2023; Jean-François Ratelle, 'The North caucasus, the future of Russia, and foreign fighters in Ukraine', *Russian Analytical Digest*, No. 295 (2 June 2023), pp. 6–9.

30. The speech was carried in full also in *Rossiiskaia Gazeta*, 24 February 2022.

31. 'Mobilization tasks set – what Shoigu said at defense ministry board', *TASS*, 21 September 2022; 'Inter'viu Ministra oborony Rossiiskoi Federatsii generala armii S.K. Shoigu', *Telegra*, 21 September 2022, telegra.ph/Intervyu-Ministra-oborony-Rossijskoj-Federacii-generala-armii-SKSHojgu-09-21. See also 'Mobilization fallout', *The Bell*, 26 September 2022.

32. '"Rossiiu khotiat prevratit' v Moskoviiu": Nikolai Patrushev – o Zapade i Ukraine', *Argumenty i fakty*, 10 January 2023. Interview conducted by Vitaly Tseplyaev; 'Senior security official says Russia isn't at war with Ukraine', *TASS*, 9 January 2023.

33. See, e.g. 'Daily briefing of the Ministry of Defence of the Russian Federation', *TASS*, 24 September 2022.

34. 'Ukraine recaptures key eastern town of Lyman', *The Moscow Times*, 1 October 2022; see maps provided by the Institute for the Study of War, 'Russian offensive campaign assessment, October 3', storymaps.arcgis.com/stories/36a7f6a6f5a94484 96de641cf64bd375.

35. See, e.g. Andriy Zagorodnyuk, 'Ukraine's path to victory', *Foreign Affairs*, 12 October 2022.

36. Jeffrey Gettleman, Oleksandra Mykolyshyn, 'As Russians steal Ukraine's art, they attack its identity too', *New York Times*, 14 January 2023.

37. 'Reaction to attack on Crimea-Russia bridge and general roundup', *Kyiv Post*, 8 October 2022; 'Na Krymskom mostu podorvan avtomobil' i zagorelis' tsisterny s topilivom. Spiker parlamenta respubliki obvinil v etom Ukrainu', *Vedomosti*, 8 October 2022.

38. 'Vstrecha s Aleksandrom Bastrykinym', *Kremlin.ru*, 9 October 2022, kremlin.ru/events/president/news/69565.

39. 'The blame game', *The Bell*, 4 October 2022. See also Natalie Musumecci, 'Kremlin allows Russian state TV to report on military setbacks in Ukraine as Putin searches for a scapegoat: "We have to stop lying"', *Business Insider*, 6 October 2022.

40. 7x7 – Gorizontal'naia Rossiia, 'Bolee 100 mobilizovannykh iz Chuvashii . . .', *Telegram*, 2 November 2022, t.me/horizontal_russia/16555; see also a Gulagu.net video, SOTA. 'Mobilizovannye, sobrannye v Ul'ianovskogo oblasti . . .', 2 November 2022, t.me/sotaproject/49035; 'Mobilized Russians launch strike to protest lack of payment', *The Moscow Times*, 2 November 2022.

41. Dmitry Medvedev, 'Smertnaia kazn' dlia predatelei', *Aktual'nye kommentarii*, 2 November 2022; 'Ex-President Medvedev backs death penalty for wartime sabotage', *The Moscow Times*, 3 November 2022.

42. Yevgenii Mezdrikov, Dar'ia Mosolkina, 'Udary po Ukraine: voennaia operatsiia vstupaet v novuiu fazu', *Vedomosti*, 10 October 2022; 'Missile strikes on "many cities" of Ukraine', *The Moscow Times*, 10 October 2022; Dan Ladden-Hall, Anna Nemtsova, 'Kids in firing line as rattled Putin revenge-bombs Kyiv', *The Daily Beast*, 10 October 2022.

43. Putin, 'Soveshchanie s postoiannymi chlenami Soveta Bezopasnosti', *Kremlin.ru*, 10 October 2022, kremlin.ru/events/president/news/69568.

44. 'Lavrov answered the question about the possibility of a meeting between Putin and Biden', *RBC.ru*, 11 October 2022.

45. On the politics of this trend, see Alexander Lanoszka, 'The art of partial commitment: The politics of military assistance to Ukraine', *Post-Soviet Affairs*, 1 January 2023 (online).

46. Bryant Harris, 'White House requests $38 billion more in Ukraine aid', *Defense News*, 15 November 2022.

47. 'Pentagon soobshchil o voennoi pomoshchi Ukraine na $400 mln', *Vedomosti*, 4 November 2022; 'SShA postavili Ukraine bolee 88,000 tonna vooruzhenii', *Vedomosti*, 20 November 2022; 'The United States has delivered more than 230 artillery systems to Ukraine', *Interfax*, 20 November 2022; US Department of State, '$400

million in additional military assistance for Ukraine', *Press Statement*, Antony J. Blinken, 10 November 2022.

48. US Department of Defense, Jim Garamone, 'U.S., allies work to supply Ukraine air defense needs', *DOD News*, 29 November 2022.

49. Putin, 'Zasedanie Soveta Bezopasnosti', *Kremlin.ru*, 19 October 2022, kremlin.ru/events/president/news/69636; Emmanuel Peuchot, 'Kremlin proxies flee Kherson as Ukraine advances', *The Moscow Times*, 19 October 2022; 'Ukraine latest: Russian occupation authorities leaving Kherson', *Bloomberg News*, 19 October 2022.

50. 'Explainer: What does Russia's imposition of martial law mean?' *The Moscow Times*, 20 October 2022.

51. 'NATO's annual nuclear exercise gets underway', *NATO Update,* 14 October 2022; Natalia Drozdiak, 'Russia and NATO are both holding nuclear drills despite rising tensions', *Bloomberg*, 13 October 2022; Kira Latukhina, 'Putin predupredil o global'noi katastrofe pri stolknovenii NATO s rossiiskimi voiskami', *Rossiiskaia gazeta*, 14 October 2022.

52. '11 chelovek pogibli v resul'tate terakta na poligone v Belgorodskoi oblasti', *Vedomosti*, 16 October 2022; 'Russia says 11 killed in "terrorist" attack at military site', *The Moscow Time*s, 16 October 2022.

53. 'Ukraine attempts to attack, Russia grinds down enemy forces – commander', *TASS*, 18 October 2022; 'New Russian commander admits situation is "tense" for his forces in Ukraine', *Euractiv*, 19 October 2022.

54. See, e.g. UK Ministry of Defence, 'Statement on Defence Secretary's call with Russian Defence Minister', *GOV.UK*, 23 October 2022; 'U.S., Russian Defense Ministers discuss Ukraine invasion in rare phone call', *RFE/RL*, 21 October 2022; 'Russian Defense Minister, U.S. counterpart discuss Ukraine in rare call', *The Moscow Times*, 21 October 2022; 'Shoigu rasskazal ministru oborony Turtsii o vozmozhnykh provokatsiiakh Ukrainu', *Vedomosti*, 23 October 2022; 'Shoigu obsudil s frantsuzskim kollegoi situatsiiu na Ukraine', *Vedomosti*, 23 October 2022.

55. U.S. Department of State, 'Joint statement on Ukraine', 23 October 2022, state.gov/joint-statement-on-ukraine-2/, and for the UK, gov.uk/government/news/russian-war-in-ukraine-p3-statement.

56. Ministry of Foreign Affairs of the Russian Federation, 'Statement of the Russian Federation on the prevention of nuclear war', *MID.ru*, 2 November 2022, mid.ru/ru/foreign_policy/news/1836575/.

57. Felicia Schwartz, Henry Foy, 'Military briefing: West steps up tracking of possible Russian nuclear intent', *Financial Times*, 26 October 2022.

58. 'The foreign ministry called the conditions for a dialogue with the West to reduce tensions', *RIA Novosti*, 30 October 2022; '"Massive attack" by Russia on Ukrainian energy facilities', *Kyiv Post*, 31 October 2022; 'Ukraine war: Russian strikes hit infrastructure as Moscow exits grain deal', *The Moscow Times*, 31 October 2022.

59. Anastasia Maier, 'Shoigu prikazal pristupit' k otvodu rossiiskikh voisk za Dnepr', *Vedomosti*, 9 November 2022; Mark Santora, Andrew E. Kramer, Dan Bilefsky, Ivan Nechepurenko, Anton Troianovski, 'Russia orders retreat from Kherson, a serious reversal in the Ukraine war', *New York Times*, 9 November 2022.

60. Yurii Gavrilov, 'Minoborony RF: Rossiiskie podrazdeleniia osushchestvliaiut manevr na podgotovlennye pozitsii na levom beregu Dnepra', *Rossiiskaia gazeta*, 10 November 2022.

61. Kadyrov_95. 'Polnost'iu soglasen s mneniem . . . Surovikina . . .', *Telegram*, 9 November 2022, t.me/RKadyrov_95/3080; Margarita Simon'ian@M_Simonyan. '. . . Zamenite slovo "Moskva" na slovo "Kherson". 'Vozmozhno, stanet poniatnee', *Telegram*, 9 November 2022, twitter.com/M_Simonyan/status/1590384186765950976; 'Kremlin loyalists rally behind military as withdrawal set to begin', *The Moscow Times*, 10 November 2022.

62. Chris York, 'How Russia is reacting to the retreat from Kherson', *Kyiv Post*, 12 November 2022; 'Surovikin: na Khersonskom napravlenii rossiiskie poteri v 7–8 razmen'she, chem u VSU', *RT*, 9 November 2022.

63. See, e.g. Anastasia Morozova, 'Minoborony soobshchilo o zavershenii vyvoda voisk iz Khersoina', *Vedomosti*, 11 November 2022.

64. Zelensky, 'Ukraine has always been a leader in peacemaking efforts: If Russia wants to end this war, let it prove it with actions – speech by the president of Ukraine at the G20 summit', 15 November 2022, president.gov.ua/en/news/ukrayina-zavzhdi-bula-liderom-mirotvorchih-zusil-yaksho-rosi-79141.

65. 'UN general assembly calls for Russian reparations to Ukraine', *RFE/RL*, 14 November 2022.

66. 'Ukraine latest: WHO warns of deadly winter health dangers', *Bloomberg*, 22 November 2022; 'Ukraine grid operator: Damage from Russian attacks "colossal"', *Reuters*, 22 November 2022.

67. 'V Kremli vidkrito shantazhuiut' Ukraynu: Vikonaite nashi vimogi i obstrili zypiniat'sia', *Ukrainska Pravda*, 24 November 2022, pravda.com.ua/news/2022/11/24/7377787/; Mark MacKinnon, 'Top Ukraine official says peace deal with Russia not an option', *Globe and Mail*, 23 November 2022; 'Zelens'kiy vimagae sklikati terminove zasidannia Radbezu OON cherez raketni udari RF', *Ukrainska Pravda*, 23 November 2022, pravda.com.ua/news/2022/11/23/7377687/.

68. 'NATO allies test air and missile defences in Romania', *NATO Update*, 23 November 2022.

69. News. European Parliament, Press Release, 'European Parliament declares Russia to be a state sponsor of terrorism', 23 November 2022.

70. 'EU parliament "a sponsor of idiocy" – Moscow', *RT*, 23 November 2022.

71. 'Telefonnyi razgovor s Federal'nym kantslerom Germanii Olafom Shol'tsem', *Kremlin.ru*, 2 December 2022, kremlin.ru/events/president/news/69971; 'Statement by NATO foreign ministers', *NATO Update*, 29 November 2022.

72. On this, see Barry R. Posen, 'Russia's rebound: How Moscow has partly recovered from its military setbacks', *Foreign Affairs*, 4 January 2023.

Chapter 2

Explaining Away a Brutal War of Attrition

As the fighting in Ukraine moved beyond its origins as a 'special military operation' to a multi-pronged invasion of Ukraine, it became clear to Putin and the Russian people that it would not be over within a few weeks, perhaps even days, as they had been promised.

After several months of bloody military advances, Russia had come to occupy some 20 per cent of Ukrainian territory, almost entirely those areas in which the great majority of Ukraine's ethnic Russians and Russian-speaking population lived. Moscow organized referendums and formal annexations of most of these areas and began integrating them into the Russian Federation. In their turn, increasingly heavily armed Ukrainian armed forces pushed back and the conflict settled into a brutal war of attrition.

The invasion had immediate consequences for Russia's bilateral and multilateral international relationships and prompted neighbouring states to upgrade their defences. The ensuing war cast a dark shadow over the politics and economies of all European countries, where fear of a coming general war was such that Finland and Sweden set procedures for accession to NATO in motion. Even states that remained neutral, such as Switzerland, Austria and Ireland, raised their defence budgets.

WAR OF ATTRITION

By the first week of December 2022, Ukrainian armed forces had retaken their northern, Kharkiv region and in the south, forced Russian troops out of the city of Kherson and areas west of the Dnipro River. While Russian forces retrenched some 20 kilometres from the east bank of that river, replenished its troops and armaments, and launched missile and drone strikes against Ukrainian infrastructure, the West supplied Ukraine with more lethal weapons and military training. Both line-ups became deadlier. Russia bolstered its defences in Crimea close to the Ukrainian border and around the captured, heavily damaged but strategically important city of Mariupol.

The theatres of war shifted and, according to US intelligence, the war itself was running at a 'reduced tempo' early in December.[1] In fact, Ukrainian armed forces were on the offensive along most of the 1,000-kilometre front line, while Russian troops dug in in the south and northeast. By December 2022, Ukraine had reclaimed about a third of the territories seized by Russia since February. Worried about how Ukrainian attacks on Russian soil would be perceived in Moscow, the Pentagon insisted that it sent only defensive weapons to Ukraine.

Unwavering in its rosy pictures, on 5 December, the Russian media headlined Putin driving a Mercedes across the Kerch Strait bridge, two months after the truck bomb damaged it. There followed a prisoner exchange of 64 soldiers each. These swaps had become monthly events. The December exchange followed one of 214 each in November; 52 in October and 55 in September. On the last day of the year, 82 each were traded. After every exchange, former Ukrainian POWs were interviewed and provided the Western media with headlines on how badly they were treated. Former Russian prisoners were mostly inaccessible, so it was left to the MoD to complain about its personnel having suffered in 'Kyiv dungeons'. Doubtless, tales from Ukrainian POWs of ill-treatment at the hands of Russian guards and interrogators were mostly true. The Office of the United Nations High Commissioner for Human Rights (OHCHR) pointed out, however, that brutal treatment of prisoners of war was characteristic of both sides.[2]

In the second week of December, Russian forces upgraded their attacks on Odesa, using drones to knock out energy facilities and leaving much of the city temporarily without electricity. Among other things, these renewed strikes on Odesa meant that the port was closed for grain exporting. Two other Ukrainian ports were partially closed. Ukrainian forces countered with strikes against Russian-occupied Melitopol in the Zaporizhzhia region, a city that was central to logistics linking the Russian-held parts of the Kherson region in the south to Mariupol in the northeast. Ukraine's valuable grain exports had fallen victim to the war.

Also targeted by Russia were gas and oil centres in eastern Ukraine. After Naftohaz facilities in Kharkiv were hit by missiles on 19–20 December 2022, the company's CEO said that about 350 natural gas facilities had been attacked over the previous several weeks.[3]

Arms Control

International arms control treaties fell victim next. Just days before it was to gather, Russia unilaterally postponed a meeting of the bilateral commission on the Strategic Arms Reduction and Limitation Treaty (START) scheduled to begin on 29 November in Cairo.[4] No new date was set. After START-3 completed its 10-year term in 2020, incoming president Biden had agreed to extend it for another five years. Of the many arms control treaties signed between Russia and the United States, most of them in the 1980s, New START was the last one standing. It allowed the deployment of 700 strategic weapons (800 in total) and 1,550 deployed warheads.

Because no specific reasons for the cancellation were offered to the public, rumours buzzed about, again, that Russia might bring nuclear weaponry into play against Ukraine. Putin and Lavrov repeatedly said that they would not commit nuclear weapons other than as a last, defensive option. During a televised meeting in December 2022, with the presidential Council for the Development of Civil Society and Human Rights, Putin answered a questioner who was worried about the threat of nuclear war: 'We have not gone crazy, we are aware of what nuclear weapons are . . . we are not going to brandish them'. He complained that it was the Americans who were placing nuclear weapons in Europe, far from their own borders, and training military personnel in their use, and that it was the UK that was most vocal about using them. They are a 'natural deterrent', he said, not a means to expand conflicts.[5] In the long run, the proof will be in this particular pudding.

Conventional Weaponry Escalation

Rumours of nuclear conflagration failed to slow NATO's ever-increasing arms feed to Kyiv. Meeting in Bucharest for two days at the end of November, the Alliance's foreign ministers promised to sustain Ukraine against a Russia that was 'using winter as a weapon of war'. On the side-lines of that meeting, Ukrainian foreign minister Dmytro Kuleba told reporters that his country needed a wide range of weaponry, especially the Patriot surface-to-air missile systems (SAMS). Medvedev responded by warning NATO against providing such systems to Ukraine, while Shoigu told his MoD collegium that Russia should deploy next-generation arms to its forces in Ukraine, among them advanced high-precision long-range weapons, drones and counter-battery warfare systems.[6]

Shoigu also noted that allocations to the MoD's procurement budget for 2023 increased by 'almost one and a half', making it possible, he asserted, to keep Russia military units equipped at a nearly 100 per cent level. According to a *Vedomosti* report, Russian spending on national defence in 2023 would be 1.2 trillion roubles ($20 billion) more than in 2021.[7]

There was an armaments upsurge everywhere, and the aggressive bombast grew more strident on all sides. In January 2023, Germany agreed to send some 40 Marder combat vehicles and a Patriot air defence system to Ukraine by the end of March. The announcement in Berlin was part of a joint statement with the United States. These contributions raised Germany's total aid to Ukraine to that point to 12 billion euros ($12.7Bln) and drew protests from the Russian embassy in Berlin that Germany was merely aggravating the situation. The United States promised to send Bradley Fighting Vehicles, France offered light tanks (AMX-10RCs), and, a few days later, Poland said it would hand over a company of German-made Leopard tanks if Berlin allowed it. Morocco committed 20 Soviet-built T-72B tanks.

On 15 January, British prime minister Rishi Sunak pledged heavy tanks, the Challenger 2, and about 30 armoured artillery vehicles (AS-90s). These up-scale battle tanks complemented what were left of the some 300 re-fitted Soviet tanks that European countries had already passed on to Ukraine. On 18 January, Canada committed to donating 200 armoured personnel carriers. Zelensky said that the armoured vehicles and heavy tanks were what Ukraine needed to win the war, though it would take months for Ukrainian troops to be trained in their use.[8]

THE OCCUPIED ZONES

As early reports that referenda would be held in parts of Ukraine occupied by Russian forces faded in late summer 2022, newly established administrators found their positions increasingly dangerous. Six Russia-installed officials were killed on one day, 16 September, making over 20 such assassinations since Russia began seizing territory. Though these executions were not mentioned at first by Moscow, they were confirmed by local authorities in Telegram and Twitter messages, and described even in some of the mainstream Russian media.[9]

Renewed calls for referendums surfaced after victories by the United Russia in September 2022's local and municipal elections. After Ukraine's counter-offensive drove occupiers out of the Kharkiv area, authorities in the Luhansk People's Republic (LPR) and the DPR quickly announced that they would hold votes on joining the Russian Federation. Administrators appointed in captured territories of the Zaporizhzhia and Kherson regions followed suit.[10] Large billboards extolling the unity of Russians and Ukrainians popped up in cities under Russian control in the Donbas and elsewhere. The dove-turned-hawk, Dmitry Medvedev, explained that a successful referendum, no matter how illegal other states considered it, would allow the Russian MoD to consider any attack by Ukrainian forces on the area in question an attack on Russian soil. In his words, 'Encroachment on the territory of Russia is a crime, the commission of which allows the use of all the forces of self-defence'.[11] Convoluted as that logic was, experience tells us that Moscow would feel no embarrassment about acting on it.

Referendum ballots in the DPR and LPR asked simply, in Russian only, if the voter supported his or her region's 'accession to Russia as a federal subject'. In Kherson and Zaporizhzhia voters were asked in both the Russian and Ukrainian languages: 'Are you in favour of secession from Ukraine, formation of an independent state by the region, and its joining the Russian Federation as a subject of the Russian Federation?' Voting was entirely by paper ballot, with authorized personnel going door-to-door to collect ballots for the first four days, often accompanied by armed soldiers, leaving only the final day for polling station voting. The Ukrainian government and most Western countries objected strongly to the referendums, describing them a farce tainted by voter coercion and called the subsequent annexations illegal (see table 2.1).[12]

Presumably to add an aura of legitimacy to the process, DPR authorities claimed, and the Russian mainstream media reported, that there were nearly 1,000 foreign observers to monitor their referendums and the head of the electoral commission in the Kherson region said that observers from France and the United States were present at the voting there. Others came from Germany, Italy, the Netherlands, Brazil, Serbia, Egypt and several other countries in Africa.[13] No further information on who these were and how they were invited were available.

Foreign observers notwithstanding, the radical depletion of population in the occupied areas over the previous months and the overwhelming presence of armed Russian and separatist monitors ensured that there would be no surprises in the actual voting. Kyiv and Western governments had good reasons to label the process a sham. State-controlled Russian media celebrated the so-called election 'results', and Russian nationalists revelled in them. Echoes of Soviet-style electoral returns were themselves signals that the voting was rigged.

Schemes to Russianize the occupied zones began almost immediately. In addition to the televised pomp and ceremony at the Kremlin marking

Table 2.1. Alleged Results of Referendums in Occupied Ukraine, in Favour of Joining Russia

Luhansk People's Republic	98.2%
Donetsk People's Republic	99.23%
Kherson region	87.05%
Zaporizhzhia region	93.1%

Source: Compiled by author from official sources cited by Anastasia Tenisheva, 'Pro-Russia "victory" in staged Ukraine referendums clears path to annexation', The Moscow Times, 28 September 2022.

the official act of annexation, or 'return' as Putin called it, the Duma began formulating a series of laws to integrate the regions with Russia's economic, financial and legal systems. These were expected to be completed by the end of 2025. The Russian rouble and Russian mobile providers were introduced, and passports issued. Maps of the Russian Federation shown on state TV incorporated the annexed territory.[14]

In his video address to the UN General Assembly on 27 September, Zelensky made it clear that any attempt on Russia's part to recognize the referendums as a legitimate lead-in to annexation would mean that Kyiv could no longer participate in peace negotiations.[15] The very next day, the United States announced a new package of weaponry for Ukraine worth about $1.1 billion. Chief among the weapons were HIMARS, ammunition, anti-drone systems, radar, 150 armoured vehicles and more.[16]

Annexations

The annexation process went ahead. On 29 September 2022, Putin signed decrees recognizing the regions of Kherson and Zaporizhzhia as independent of Ukraine.[17] Without any apparent irony, the documents also referred to the principles of international law, equal rights and self-determination of peoples. In a televised ceremony the next day, Putin boasted that the 'people living in Donetsk, Luhansk, Zaporizhzhia and Kherson are becoming our citizens forever', and cited Article 1 of the UN Charter as justification. He referred again to the dissolution of the USSR in 1991 that cut millions of Russians off from their homeland without any consultations. Denying explicitly that he was trying to resurrect the Soviet Union, he said instead that he was helping to return millions of Russians to their 'historic Fatherland'. After signing the documents, he and Russia-installed leaders of all four districts raised held-hands and chanted 'Rossiia! Rossiia! Rossiia!'. In the accompanying speech, Putin ranted about the 'dictatorship of the Western elite' attempting to 'preserve its neo-colonial system' and turn Russia into a 'crowd of slaves'.[18]

The Russian presidential administration allocated over three billion roubles (approx. US$40 million) to NGOs operating in the four annexed regions for the purpose of assisting residents of the areas and helping refugees. These NGOs were now considered by Moscow to be operating on Russian territory, so they had access to the same presidential grants as organizations in other parts of the Federation. Funds were set aside to help families of soldiers fighting in Ukraine, to be managed by the We Are Together movement, the All-Russia Popular Front and the United Russia Party.[19]

To stiffen Russia's claims to the seized territories for domestic consumption, Moscow's propaganda machine re-cast the war in Ukraine as a struggle against a perfidious West that was trying to weaken, even dismember, Russia.

Medvedev took up this theme up and claimed that Russia was 'fighting NATO and the Western world'. It was recovering 'original Russian lands', he said, and the next world order will be shaped by Russia, 'not by the USA, Great Britain or "dark Kyiv"'.[20]

State-controlled Russian media relished the annexations while less submissive media, such as *Vedomosti*, described the sequence of events accurately, but offered no editorial glorifications. This was a sign that there was some discomfort in Russia, but no one objected in the face of swelling nationalist braggadocio. *Vedomosti* even outlined concessions offered earlier by Zelensky that might well have ended the fighting in March.[21]

Not dissuaded by Western condemnation, in November 2022 Putin told the Xth All-Russian Congress of Judges that Russian federal courts would soon be opened in the annexed territories and that plans for their full integration into the Russian legal system would be completed 'as soon as possible'. These new territories were now part of Russia as 'the results of the referendums, [and] by the will of millions of people', he proclaimed misleadingly.[22]

One consequence of the formal annexations was that the new territorial acquisitions now fall under recent (2020) amendments to the Russian constitution that forbids Russia from ceding any territory once it is integrated into the Federation. That means that Ukrainian attacks on the Donbas or elsewhere in Russian-occupied parts of Ukraine were perceived in Moscow as attacks on the Russian homeland.[23]

THE WEST STEPS UP – OR IN IT

Over 70 states and international agencies were represented at the 'Solidaires du peuple ukrainien' (Standing with the Ukrainian People) conference in Paris. Called by Macron to raise funds to repair Ukraine's damaged infrastructure, it was co-chaired by him, Zelensky (by video), president of the European Commission Ursula Von der Leyen and France's minister for Europe and Foreign Affairs, Catherine Colonna. Zelensky was represented in person by his wife, Olena Zelenska, and Ukraine's prime minister Denys Shmyhal. India and Indonesia sent delegates; China did not. Speaking by video conference, Zelensky said that his country needed emergency assistance of €800 million to fix the energy network destroyed by Russian missile and drone strikes.

He also asked the G-7 countries to provide additional gas supplies to get Ukrainians through the winter, plus more tanks and missiles. Zelensky proposed three steps towards peace: far more military equipment, support for financial and energy stability, and the withdrawal of Russian troops from all of Ukraine. Russia rejected the latter condition out of hand, saying that Kyiv must 'accept the realities' of the Russian annexations. Zelensky delivered a similar address to the Ukrainian World Congress on 9 December, a few days before the gathering in Paris.[24]

The IAEA agreed to deploy permanent teams to Ukraine's five NPP sites, above all at Zaporizhzhia.

The EU raised the ante, agreeing to an unprecedented package for Ukraine of up to €18 billion for 2023, to be paid on a monthly basis over the year. The funds were to be used to sustain essential public services and housing, and were to be accompanied by anti-corruption reform and 'good governance'.[25]

In the meantime, after much hesitation the United States finally prepared to send a Patriot missile battery to Ukraine. The truck-mounted system carries about 90 soldiers in the battery but needs only three to operate it during combat. Several months of training was necessary, but no American troops accompanied it to Ukrainian soil.

A few days later, Putin was in Belarus accompanied by both his foreign and defence ministers. In post-meeting statements, the two presidents claimed to have discussed mostly economic matters.[26] Western pundits, noting separate visits during the week between the two ministries, began predicting greater Belarusan involvement in the war, prompting statements from Putin's and Lukashenka's offices that Belarus would not be drawn into the war – these assertions were not believed in Kyiv.

Not to be outdone, Zelensky flew off to Washington on 21 December, where he met with President Biden, spoke to the US Congress in person and was again promised delivery of a Patriot air defence system. These weapons were part of another $1.85 billion aid package announced at that time. Along with the Patriot battery that includes a command centre, a radar station to detect incoming threats, and missile launchers, the package consisted of tens of thousands of rounds of artillery, rocket and tank ammunition, mortar systems, grenade launchers and body armour.

While Zelensky was in Washington, Medvedev was in Beijing in his capacity as head of the United Russia party, meeting his Communist Party counterpart, Xi Jinping. Although both sides boasted of an unprecedented level of cooperation between their two countries, Xi made it plain that, whereas it would not criticize Russia's military action in Ukraine, China was anxious for peace talks to begin.[27]

MoD Upgrades

Speaking to the Ministry of Defence Board on 21 December, Putin assured members that there were 'no funding restrictions' when it came to equipping Russia's soldiers with gear and weapons. In turn, Shoigu proposed that Russia expand its Armed Forces to 1.5 million troops from its current 1.15

million, and raise the number of its professional soldiers (kontraktniki) to 695,000, thereby easing the need for conscripted fighting men. The Board agreed that the age of conscription should be raised to 21 from 17 years, set the maximum age at 30 and sent this proposal to the State Duma. While Putin spoke of developing the combat readiness of Russia's nuclear forces and new weapons, such as hypersonic Zircon cruise missiles, Shoigu said that Russia would establish naval bases in two occupied port cities, Berdyansk and Mariupol. He acknowledged that the war was not going well, explaining that Russian servicemen were fighting 'the combined forces of the West'.[28] Putin had just said that the SVO was the 'result of the policy of third countries', so Shoigu was merely repeating the mantra that had become a feature of daily domestic propaganda.

Battles around Bakhmut and Soledar in January 2023 exposed an evolving split within Russia's fighting commands. Whereas Prigozhin claimed that Soledar was taken exclusively by his Wagner Group, the MoD announced that it been victorious in Soledar without mentioning the Wagner Group. It was also at this time that mixed reactions to the promotion of Col. Gen. Aleksandr Lapin to Chief of General Staff for Ground Forces were made public. Pro-war bloggers in Russia and Kadyrov criticized the appointment, blaming Lapin for losses at Kharkiv and Lyman.[29]

It turned out that the Lapin appointment was but one of many shifts within Russia's military leadership. On 11 January, Shoigu announced that Chief of the General Staff Valery Gerasimov had been named commander of the entire grouping of Russian forces in Ukraine. He demoted Surovikin to serve as one of three deputy commanders under Gerasimov. Surovikin had held the post as commander for only three months and was favoured by Prigozhin.[30]

Ignoring the confusion around him, at least in public, Putin told an interviewer for Rossiia-1 TV channel that 'the dynamics [of the SVO] are positive. Everything is developing within the framework of the plan of the Ministry of Defence and the General Staff'.[31] As we shall see, pollsters suggest that a majority of Russians still believed him – or wanted to. Still, Putin's optimism seemed to be flying in the face of the heavy weapons from NATO members aiming his way.[32]

WEAPONS CATCH-22

The sudden rise in Western promises of lethal weapons to Ukraine posed a truly Catch-22 dilemma by the end of January 2023. Berlin's hesitation to allow Poland or Finland to re-export its Leopard tanks was caused by worry that such an act would prompt Russia to initiate a nuclear war. Sweden (anti-tank weapons, mine-clearing equipment and tracked vehicles) and Estonia (remote-fire and anti-tank weapons) had joined the chorus of donors, while the US's security aid to Ukraine neared the $30 billion mark. This volume of aid made it easier for Zelensky to fight on without negotiations, and for Russia to fight on because it believed its enemy was now NATO. Patrushev and Lavrov said as much, regularly. Zelensky now supposed Ukraine could win; Putin believed that Russia mustn't lose. All protagonists settled in for the long haul.

When, on 23 January 2023 after much vacillation, Germany finally agreed to allow the re-export of its Leopard tanks, Lavrov's reaction was to say that, 'When we talk about what is happening there, in Ukraine, we are talking about the fact that this is no longer a hybrid war, but almost a real one'. He went on to say that the West was trying to destroy 'everything Russian in Ukraine'.[33] Medvedev had only recently warned, again, that if Russia is defeated in Ukraine it could resort to deploying nuclear weapons.[34]

A few hours after Berlin's promise of Leopards, 62 of them altogether, some coming from other European countries, Washington pledged 31 Abrams tanks. Moscow's reaction was furious, as expected, with its ambassadors in the German and American capitals threatening further escalation.[35] Biden insisted, rather oddly, that the US tanks were not an 'offensive threat to Russia', and noted that they would not be combat ready for months.[36] Training in their use was lengthy, and maintenance (fuel, equipment), was complicated. Together with weaponry already guaranteed: 90 Stryker armoured personnel carriers and 109 Bradley infantry fighting vehicles from the United States, the 40 Marder vehicles from Germany, 14 Challenger 2 heavy tanks from Britain, AMX-10 RC light tanks from France and the 200 armoured vehicles from Canada, all eventually with trained Ukrainian crews, Ukraine was turned into a giant armoured vehicle depot. As one pundit proclaimed, the new 'swarm of tanks' boded ill for Putin. Maybe. State-owned Russian media told its viewers and readers that NATO was 'pumping up' Ukraine with weapons and therefore sustaining the war and causing more deaths.[37]

PEACE TALKS

As foreign diplomats and their governments pressed for peace talks, and both Moscow and Kyiv asserted that they were willing to hold such conversations, the two combatants continued to lay down conditions that they knew the other would not accept. On 26 December 2022, Lavrov reiterated Putin's initial rationale for the SVO, with the added claim on occupied territories: 'Our proposals for the demilitarization and denazification of the territories controlled by the regime, the elimination of threats to Russia's security emanating from there, including our new lands, are well known to the enemy'.

Otherwise, these demands 'will be decided by the Russian army'. Ukraine's Kuleba tweeted on 25 December that 'Ukraine's position is clear: ceasefire, security guarantees, no compromises on territorial integrity. But Russia sticks to ultimatums. To stimulate a more constructive approach we need two things: more sanctions and more military aid for Ukraine'.[38] The next day he said that the door to peace negotiations could be open as early as February, but only if Russia agreed to submit to a war crimes tribunal. In fact, neither side left any room for peace talks, at least in public.

There were no let-ups on the battlefield either. The death toll mounted, along with further devastation of Ukrainian urban centres, with no end to the Russia-led aerial and missile onslaught in sight. Peskov repeated the official mantra at the end of the year. There will be no peace 'that does not take into account current realities regarding Russian territory, with the entry of four regions into Russia', he said.[39] Shoigu confirmed that stance in a New Year's message to military personnel. 'Our victory, like the New Year, is inevitable', he said, because of your 'heroism in the fight against neo-Nazism and terrorism'.[40] The inflexible propaganda message from the top was disseminated across the country by the mainstream media in a flurry of patriotic speech-making while contrary positions faded from sight.

Putin's annual New Year's communication did change, raising the 'special military operation' in Ukraine to the level of a crusade. Surrounded by military personnel as a visual backdrop, and focusing exclusively on Russia's 'heroic' enterprise in Ukraine and the infamy of the West, he delivered the longest New Year's message of his two decades in office: 'Protecting our people on our own historical territories in the new constituent entities of the Russian Federation is what we are fighting for today', was the central theme of Putin's communication. 'Moral, historical correctness is on our side', he declared, claiming that the SVO could determine the very 'fate of Russia'. In its turn, the West 'lied about peace', encouraged the neo-Nazis and 'cynically used Ukraine and its people to weaken and split Russia'. Putin also maintained that the 'sanctions war' declared against Russia by the West was failing.[41] Clearly, Putin now saw success (or failure) in Ukraine as defining his legacy.

THE 'SPECIAL MILITARY OPERATION' AFTER A FULL YEAR

As the first full year of Putin's war in Ukraine came to an end, its repercussions widened. On the battlefront, Ukrainian forces awaited modern tanks offered by Western countries, and Russia raised its level of offense, hoping to force Kyiv to yield before the new weaponry arrived. On the Russian home front, more human rights organizations and anti-war activists were designated 'foreign agents' or 'undesirables'.

Public opinion surveys also revealed that, while a majority still supported the SVO, a surprisingly large part of Russia's population remained disengaged from it. This was true during the entire first year of conflict, with brief exceptions of an initial outburst of shock and dismay in February 2022 and during the later mobilization furore. The numbers held in February 2023, with about 70 per cent supporting Russia's troops (if not necessarily the war itself) and, in response to separate questions, 50 per cent favoured negotiations. Advocacy for peace negotiations was highest among younger respondents (ages 18–39), while a majority of the older generation (55+) wanted the war to continue. Over 60 per cent thought the SVO was going well, nearly 10 per cent higher than in October 2022.[42]

The one-year anniversary was marked by strained celebrations in Russia, rallying commemorations in Ukraine, more commitments of weapons and a new wave of sanctions from the West, and a 12-point peace plan proposed by China.

Preparing for Spring Offensives

As fighting stepped up and both sides readied spring offensives, the Kremlin acted to protect Moscow. Pantsir-S1 surface-to-air defence systems were placed on the roofs of the MoD and other administrative buildings in city centre, and S-400 missile systems set up around the outskirts of the city. Regional and municipal governments, and private individuals, began overhauling public and privately owned Cold War-era bomb shelters of various types as early as the summer of 2022, and these efforts expanded after mobilization. Tenders issued by federal and regional government agencies for improvements in ventilation systems, waterproofing, door replacements, and air filter and lighting installation, heightened fears of nuclear war.[43]

Russians who were paying attention would know that Zelensky was taking his message in person to European and North American capitals, while Putin was going nowhere. The Ukrainian president attended an EU summit in Brussels after making short stops in London and Paris. In London, he met King Charles and the prime minister, and spoke to parliament; in Paris on 8 February, he had dinner with Macron; in Brussels, he addressed the European Parliament. Zelensky was greeted as a hero everywhere he went, but assurances of weapons remained short of what he urged European governments and Washington to donate.

ANNIVERSARY MONTH, FEBRUARY 2023

Munich Security Conference

Meeting from 17 to 19 February 2023, the annual Munich Security Conference heard further appeals from Zelensky for immediate aid because of the presumed forthcoming Russian spring offensive. The conference was preceded by a meeting of NATO's foreign ministers who agreed to work out new contingency plans in light of the war in Ukraine, as well as for a 'persistent threat of terrorism and challenges posed by China'. Priority was granted to replenishing stockpiles of armaments and munitions. Ukraine's defence minister Oleksiy Reznikov joined them to discuss his country's most urgent needs. Stoltenberg brought their conclusions to Munich, where he stressed how important it was that North America and Europe stood together against Russia in Ukraine.[44] The reality was looking more and more like Russia's domestic propaganda claims, that is, the conflict was between Russia and NATO.

These commitments, plus concomitant warnings to China about sending lethal weapons to Russia and Zelensky's rhetoric about winning the war, raised important strategic questions. To actually defeat Russia, Ukraine would probably need to attack munitions and fuel depots deep within Russia, using newly acquired long-range missile launchers. Yet part of the weapons supply agreements was still that they not be used against targets inside Russia.

All of this mostly undiplomatic diplomatic activity was complicated further when Putin announced, during his address to the Federal Assembly on 21 February, that Russia would suspend participation in New START. As we have seen, the Kremlin had put off on-site inspections in 2022. Explaining that it would be 'absurd' to allow US inspectors access to Russia's nuclear facilities under treaty provisions, because they could provide NATO with sufficient intelligence to attack the sites, Putin insisted that Russia would never be the first to use nuclear weapons.[45] Some Western commentators interpreted the postponement as the first step towards Russia actually deploying those very weapons.

On 23 February 2023, the UN General Assembly approved another non-binding motion calling for the immediate withdrawal of Russian troops from Ukraine, 141 in favour, 7 against, 32 abstaining.[46] China and India were among the abstainers.

The next day, NATO commemorated the fact that Ukraine was standing strong after a year of war with Russia and made sure that Russia understood that the Alliance would uphold its expressed obligations to Kyiv. On that day, Stoltenberg attended a celebration of Estonia's Independence Day, and

NATO sent a message to Kyiv restating its 'solidarity with the government and people of Ukraine'.

As Finland moved ahead with its resolution to join NATO and Sweden's accession was slowed by Turkey and Hungary, four Nordic countries (Norway, Sweden, Finland and Denmark) agreed to operate their air forces as a single fleet. Once achieved, the combined force would number about 250 fighter jets, including F-35s and Sweden's own Saab JAS 39 Gripen fighter aircraft.[47] The Western semicircle around Russia tightened.

China's Peace Plan

It was at about this time that China, after its senior diplomats visited several European countries and Russia, released a 12-point plan for peace. The first item of the plan was an appeal to respect 'the sovereignty of all countries' and their 'territorial integrity' in keeping with the United Nations Charter. The second called for an end to Cold War mentalities, that is, forming military blocs; the third requested an immediate 'end to hostilities' and the resumption of peace talks. Other articles provided for resolving the humanitarian crisis; protecting civilians and prisoners of war; protecting nuclear power plants; rejecting the use of nuclear weapons; facilitating grain exports; ending unilateral sanctions; keeping supply chains open; and arranging for post-war reconstruction.[48]

At first reading, the Russian MID welcomed the proposal, thinking it could achieve the goals of the SVO by political means. A few days later, Peskov was more careful, saying that there were conditions that needed to be guaranteed first.[49] Ukraine's foreign ministry was cautiously optimistic about the plan, though making certain that any agreement would have to include Russian troop withdrawals. Zelensky said that he would like to meet with Xi Jinping and discuss the proposals. The US, the EU and NATO challenged its credibility because of Beijing's ties to Moscow. It seemed, almost, that Ukraine's Western allies were less anxious to accept China's suggestions as a starting point than either Kyiv or Moscow.[50]

One day after China unveiled its plan for peace, France's Macron announced that he would visit Beijing in April to try to convince Xi to pressure Putin into ending the war. In this regard, all eyes were on the three-day summit between the Russian president and the Chairman of the CPC in late March 2023. Ukraine was doubtless a priority topic of their conversations and Putin went so far as to embrace Xi's peace plan as a possible blueprint for peace negotiations: 'We believe that many of the provisions of the peace plan put forward by China are consonant with Russian approaches and can be taken as the basis for a peaceful settlement when they are ready for it in the West and in Kiev'.[51]

No wonder. The Chinese plan assumed that Russia would keep territories it had already seized. The fact that neither Ukraine nor its allies would agree to peace terms under those conditions invalidated it from the beginning. In spite of the pomp and ceremony, the Moscow-Beijing summit changed nothing.

RUSSIANS VS. RUSSIANS

On 2 March, a cross-border attack on Russia's Bryansk region by soldiers claiming to be part of the Russian Volunteer Corps (Russkii dobrovol'cheskii korpus – RDK) fighting for Ukraine saw two civilians and a 10-year-old boy killed, and several Russian servicemen injured. Whatever the ethnicity of the perpetrators, Moscow termed the raid a terrorist act of sabotage by neo-Nazi Ukrainian nationalists and appealed to the United Nations, which answered that it could not verify anyone's claims. Kyiv denied any involvement and called it a false-flag provocation by Russia to generate hatred of Ukrainians. From a video posted on Telegram, Russia's most widely used messaging service, one of the participants was recognized as Denis Kapustin (aka Nikitin, White Rex), 'a well-known Russian neo-Nazi who emigrated to Ukraine in 2014'.[52]

The raid became part of narratives used by both sides to augment their versions of the conflict and highlighted the reality of Russians joining Ukrainian battalions or forming their own units in Ukraine. The RDK's manifesto claims that it is fighting to overthrow Putin and create a 'Russia for Russians', which would not incorporate areas of Ukraine where many non-Russians live. Thus, it has quite different ambitions than the ethnic-based foreign volunteer units described in chapter 1. In addition to the Wagner Group, the Russian Armed Forces also has ultra-nationalist volunteer units on its side, the largest of which is the Russian Imperial Legion that is categorized as a terrorist organization in the United States and Canada.[53]

War with the Collective West?

Although the narrative taken up by Putin and Russian propagandists after Ukraine's counterattacks to the effect that the enemy was more the 'collective West' than Ukraine fell flat everywhere other than Russia, the rhetoric from Brussels, Washington and London added a certain substance to Moscow's allegations. Moreover, by the time that the United States announced another military aid package in March 2023, valued at some $400 million, its total contribution in aid and arms transfer passed $75 billion. Along with aid from the EU, NATO and Canada some $165 billion (€150 billion) in weaponry and other funding had reached Ukraine by mid-April 2023. The March bundle included assault bridges to facilitate movement by tanks and armoured vehicles, plus more of the latter vehicles and ammunition, all in expectation of a Russian spring offensive.[54] NATO agreed to send F-16 fighter jets, eventually.

Meeting Zelensky in Kyiv, Stoltenberg said again that NATO would support Ukraine 'for as long as it takes', and that Ukraine's 'rightful place is in the Euro-Atlantic family'.[55] No details or timetable were mentioned. Although there were no regular forces from the West on the ground in Ukraine, Russia's invasion appeared to have unintentionally mutated into a proxy war between Russia and the West, with Ukraine caught in the middle.[56] By that time, NATO member states had shipped 1,550 armoured vehicles and 230 tanks to Ukraine, and had trained at least 30,000 Ukrainian soldiers abroad. Denmark and Germany agreed to transfer 80 Leopards to Ukraine in May.[57] The amount of financial and materiel support from the West seemed huge in volume, but perhaps not yet enough.

Bakhmut as Pivot Point

As Russian forces pushed closer to taking Bakhmut in March 2023, after many months of heavy losses on both sides, mostly Russian, Prigozhin warned that success or failure there by his troops could prove to be the key to Russia's entire effort in Ukraine. He had already complained about a lack of ammunition and modern heavy weaponry, such as new tanks, and hinted that defence ministry officials intentionally were not providing his men with the necessary help. To that time, the Kremlin had omitted the Wagner Group from its press releases about the 'special military operation'.[58]

This battle exacerbated a growing rift within the Russian military command, with Shoigu and Prigozhin on opposite ends. Prigozhin may have gone too far by accusing the defence ministry and the Chief of General Staff of 'high treason', for 'purposely' depriving his troops of ammunition. He made the squabble public via Telegram. Even after Prigozhin finally received more ammunition, he complained that it wasn't enough and alleged that he had been cut off from communication lines with the MoD.[59]

As the Russian army and Wagner Group slowly closed the circle on Bakhmut, Poland's president Andrzej Duda announced that he would donate four MiG-29s, the first fighter jets from a NATO country. The next day, 17 March, Slovakia's Premier Eduard Heger offered 13 more Russian-made MiG-29s, along with a Kub surface-to-air-missile system. Biden's budget requests for 2024, which built in $6 billion for Ukraine, was under discussion in the United States at that time as well. The new allocation provided an extra $753 million to help Ukraine neutralize Russian disinformation projects and provide more cybersecurity.[60] The United States again declined to send the more advanced F-16 fighter bombers, while the United Kingdom announced that it would supply Ukrainian forces with depleted uranium shells capable of penetrating modern tanks and armoured vehicles.

By this time, the city of Bakhmut, once home to 71,000, was almost completely destroyed and nearly devoid of citizens. Kyiv and Moscow continued to reinforce their forces fighting in the city, which had become a symbolic objective for both sides. After seven months, Russian forces surrounded the city on three sides but still had not taken it.

Russians Begin to Pay Attention

Cross-border raids from Ukrainian special forces and the Russian Volunteer Corp were more frequent over March - April, even though they were met with ever-heavier retaliatory strikes against targets in Ukraine.

These strikes did not discourage Ukrainian intrusions into Russia. On 15 March 2023, an explosion and subsequent fire at an FSB building in Rostov-on-Don was reported by TASS as a result of faulty wiring, but it was probably a result of Ukrainian efforts. Whereas Ukrainian officials insisted that their government was not involved, Zelensky's aide Mykhaylo Podolyak said that Ukrainians watched the fire 'with pleasure'.[61]

Later in March, a Ukrainian military drone attacked a Transneft oil pumping station on the Druzhba pipeline in the Bryansk region of Russia, near its border with Ukraine, and an explosion in the city of Dzhanskoi, Crimea, placed power and rail temporarily out of commission.[62] Ukraine said that drones may have destroyed Russian cruise missiles being transported by train, but claimed no responsibility for it. The next day, 22 March, Ukrainian drones attacked the Russian fleet at Sevastopol.

Realizing that its first year of war had not been the resounding success they promised, both the Russian MoD and the Wagner Group began aggressive recruiting campaigns across the country. In March, the Duma finally opened debate on a scheme to shift the age bracket for conscription from 17–27 to 21–30. Although this sounded counter-productive, the fact that many young men avoid conscription by moving from secondary school directly to higher education persuaded proponents of the bill that it would open up the field for more conscripts.[63] Prigozhin's call for more volunteers was abetted by a new law signed by Putin extending punishments for discrediting the Russian army to criticisms of mercenaries.

Existing conscription requirements were tightened up too. A new law adopted on 14 April allowed the MoD to issue online call-up papers, prevented males who are summoned from leaving the country without special permission and created a digital database of everyone eligible for military service. The online notices are valid on being posted, whereas previously a paper summons was valid only on being signed by the recipient. If the draftee fails to report, he could lose his driver's licence and be prevented from leaving the country. In short, the new rules made it easier for the state to call up new soldiers and harder for Russians to dodge conscription.

The MoD's repeated insistence that no new mobilization was planned did not re-assure potential conscripts. The amendments were part of a near-frenzied sign-up drive.[64]

In April and May 2023, as Russians grew more conscious of the war by government and social media reports, sightings of drone attacks and warnings about an upcoming Ukrainian offensive, efforts to attract contract soldiers proliferated in all Russian cities and towns. Mobile sign-up booths and a wide range of posters appealing to patriotism and glorifying the defence of the homeland sprouted up all over the country. Among other things, these pleas referred to soldiering as 'the real job' (nastoiashchaia rabota). The entreaties, bolstered by promises of wages much higher than the average worker's salary, that is a one-time payment of 195,000 roubles ($2,455) and a minimum monthly salary of 204,000 roubles ($2,568), met with success.[65]

International events complicated matters for Moscow. The first of these came when the International Criminal Court (ICC) charged Putin with war crimes, which he defied by announcing trips to Crimea and Mariupol. A second resulted from the state visit to Moscow by China's Xi Jinping that prompted chatter about some sort of peace discussions.

Although neither occasion slowed the course of war in Ukraine, they did squeeze revealing responses out of Moscow. Putin complained to Xi Jinping that the British promise of depleted uranium-tipped shells for Ukraine meant 'that the West [has] decided to fight with Russia to the last Ukrainian – no longer in words, but in deeds. . . . Russia will have to respond accordingly. I mean that the collective West is already beginning to use weapons with a nuclear component'. The ICC warrant for Putin's arrest caused Medvedev also to hint at nuclear war and reveal his belief that: 'Ukraine is generally a part of Russia, to be honest, it is part of Russia . . . and has always been part of Russia in the narrow sense of the word – Great Russia, not little Russia'.[66] On the warrant itself, he tweeted, crudely, 'no need to explain WHERE this paper should be used'.[67]

Putin's strategic response to the UK's decision to provide Ukraine with uranium-tipped armour-piercing rounds was to announce plans to deploy tactical nuclear weapons to Belarus, 'at the request of Minsk'. He pointed out that the United States had been doing the same thing 'for decades', siting similar weapons on the territories of several of its NATO allies (Belgium, Germany, Italy, the Netherlands, Turkey). Programmes to train Belarusan crews to operate the weapons began on 3 April 2023, and the construction of a special storage facility for them was completed later, in the summer.[68]

The plans for Minsk, plus the accelerated inflow of weapons and funds to Ukraine from the West, anticipated a long and ever-escalating war, and rendered a Putin-Xi Joint Statement on Ukraine (22 March) meaningless. That statement featured platitudes about the UN Charter and opposed foreign blocs taking advantage of the war to the 'detriment of the legitimate security interests' of other countries. It called for a peaceful resolution of the conflict, granted mutual support for China's 12-point peace plan, and expressed opposition to sanctions.[69]

On the other hand, when Peskov was asked at the end of March about prospects for the end of the SVO, he redirected that question to the MoD, and continued: 'If you mean war in a broad context – confrontation with hostile states, unfriendly countries, this hybrid war that is unleashed against our country, then this is for a long time. And here we need firmness, loyalty to ourselves, purposefulness, unity around the president'.[70] Thus, he appeared to be echoing the old Bolshevik notion of a world divided between two immutably hostile camps.

While Russian forces were digging in for the much-talked-of Ukrainian counter-offensive, Putin fired Col. Gen. Mikhail Mizintsev, deputy minister of defence in charge of logistics. No reasons were given, though he may have been made a scapegoat for Russia's alleged deficiencies in ammunition supplies and sub-standard kit for mobilized troops. A week later, Mizintsev's place was taken by Col. Gen. Aleksei Kuzmenkov, former head of the Army Logistics Headquarters (2014–2018), Deputy Commander of the Southern Military District for Logistics and, from 2019, deputy director of the National Guard.[71]

Tallies of Russia's war dead and injured were going up, nearing 200,000 according to statements made by American and Norwegian defence officials, and repeated by the *New York Times* in February.[72] Admitting that such numbers are 'notoriously difficult to estimate', the paper went on to accept them anyway and blamed Russian tactics for the heavy losses; that is, deploying poorly trained recruits and former convicts to the front line and sending them directly into enemy fire. Whatever the actual death toll, Russian parents, wives, spouses and children of soldiers knew that their men were in grave danger. The growing list of dead and wounded were not going to be explained away easily.

NOTES

1. 'U.S. intelligence chief says officials seeing "reduced tempo" in Russia-Ukraine war', *The Hill*, 4 December 2022.

2. UN News, 'Ukrainian and Russian POWs tortured and ill-treated: OHCHR', 15 November 2022, news.un.org/en/story/2022/11/1130657.

3. 'Russian missiles hit Naftogaz facility in Kharkiv region at night', *Ukrainian News* (ukranews.com), 20 December 2022; 'Endless cycle of destruction and repair for Ukraine's energy workers', *Kyiv Post*, 20 December 2022.

4. 'Peregovory po DSNB mezhdu Rossiei i SShA perenesli na bolee pozdnii srok', *Vedomosti*, 28 November 2022.

5. 'Zasedanie Soveta po razvitiiu grazhdanskogo obshchestva i pravam cheloveka', *Kremlin.ru*, 7 December 2022, kremlin.ru/events/president/news/70046.

6. 'Theses of the opening speech of the Minister of Defence of the Russian Federation, General of the Army S.K. Shoigu at a meeting of the collegium of the Russian Ministry of Defence', *Telegra*, 30 November 2022, telegra.ph/Tezisy-vstupitelnogo-slova-Ministra-oborony-Rossijskoj-Federacii-generala-armii-SK-SHojgu-na-zasedanii-Kollegii-Minoborony-Rossi-11-30.

7. Inna Sidorkova, Anastasiia Boiko, 'Raskhody na national'nuiu oboronu v etom godu vyrastut na tret'', *Vedomosti*, 23 September 2022; 'Financing of the State Defence Order of the Russian Federation in 2023 will be increased by almost 1.5 times', *Interfax*, 30 November 2022.

8. 'Patriot training for Ukrainian troops about to start', *Kyiv Post*, 7 January 2022; Tweet, Verkhovna Rada of Ukraine – Ukrainian Parliament, @ua_parliament, 'Incredible News !!!', January 2023, twitter.com/ua_parliament/status/1613178266583539712?s=20&t=KqOtkzCVV6IkGKO8IF_qkQ; 'Poland to send German-made Leopard tanks to Ukraine', *Ukrinform*, 11 January 2023; Prime Minister's Office, 10 Downing Street, Press release, 'PM call with President Zelenskyy of Ukraine: 14 January 2023', *GOV.UK*, 14 January 2023.

9. Il'ia Lakstygal, 'Chto izvestno ob atakakh v Donbass, Khersone i Zaporozh'e', *Vedomosti*, 16 September 2022; Vladimir Rogov, 'Terroristy YGIL sovershili dvoinoe ubiistvo v Berdyanske', *Telegram*, 16 September 2022, t.me/vrogov/4909; see also Katerina Gubareva, t.me/k_gubareva/232; 'Bomb kills East Ukraine separatist prosecutor', *The Moscow Times*, 16 September 2022.

10. 'The "party of war" won: The Kremlin decided to immediately annex Ukrainian territories – and is already seriously planning mobilization: Meduza found out how this decision was made', *Meduza*, 20 September 2022.

11. 'Medvedev says referendums for Donbass to join Russia "need to be held"', *TASS*, 20 September 2022; 'Pro-Moscow officials in occupied Ukraine to hold referendums to join Russia', *The Moscow Times*, 20 September 2022; Nikolaus von Twickel, 'Russia's rushed referendums', *The Moscow Times*, 21 September 2022.

12. 'Donbass, Zaporozhye, Kherson regions to vote on accession to Russia', *TASS*, 22 September 2022; Dmytro Gorshkov, 'Russia holds breakaway polls in Ukraine', *The Moscow Times*, 23 September 2022; Timothy Snyder, 'Russia's obscene "referendums": A media exercise in humiliation, and an element of war crimes', *Kyiv Post*, 23 September 2022; Anna Kovaleva, Vladimir Ladnyi, 'Bolee 90% progolosovavshikh na referendumakh podderzhali vkhozhdenie v sostav Rossii', *Rossiiskaia Gazeta*, 27 September 2022; 'Kremlin proxies claiming victory in "sham" annexation votes', *The Moscow Times*, 27 September 2022.

13. 'About 1,000 observers are working at referendum in DPR – local CEC', *TASS*, 23 September 2022; 'At the referendum in the Kherson region there are observers from the United States and France', *RAPSI*, 23 September 2022; 'Russia recruiting foreign "observers" for sham referenda in Ukraine – intelligence source', *Ukrinform*,

22 September 2022; 'Reports of voter coercion as Russia imposes referendums on parts of Ukraine', *RFE/RL*, 23 September 2022.

14. Anastasia Tenisheva, 'Propaganda show: Russia struggles to integrate annexed Ukrainian regions', *The Moscow Times*, 12 November 2022.

15. For details, see Anastasia Tenisheva, 'Pro-Russia "victory" in staged Ukraine referendums clears path to annexation', *The Moscow Times*, 28 September 2022; 'Ukraine "referendums": Full results for annexation polls as Kremlin-backed authorities claim victory', *Euro News*, 28 September 2022.

16. U.S. Department of Defense, Press Release: '$1.1 Billion in additional security assistance for Ukraine', 28 September 2022.

17. For decrees No's 685 and 686, see the Russian Federation's official Internet portal of legal information: publication.pravo.gov.ru/Document/View/0001202209300001; Aisel Gereikhanova, 'Putin podpisal ukazy o priznanii Khersonskom i Zaporozhskoi oblastei nezavisimymi territoriiami', *Rossiiskaia Gazeta*, 30 September 2022.

18. 'Podpisanie dogovorov o priniatii DNR, LNR, Zaporozhskoi i Khersonskogo oblastei v sostav Rossii', *Kremlin.ru*, 30 September 2022, kremlin.ru/events/president/news/69465.

19. 'Rossiia napravit 2,1 mlrd rublei na podderzhku Donbassa, Khersonshchiny i Zaporopzh'ia', *Kommersant*, 29 September 2022.

20. Dmitry Medvedev on Telegram, 12 November 2022, t.me/medvedev_telegram/209; 'Medvedev: Rossiia v odinochku srazhaetsia s NATO i zapadnym mirom', *Vedomosti*, 12 November 2022.

21. Yeketrina Grobman, Yelena Mukhametshina, Anna Naraeva, Gleb Mishutin, 'V Rossii poiavliaiutsia chetyre novykh regiona', *Vedomosti*, 1 October 2022; Yekaterina Kotova, 'Pole bitvy – za bol'shuiu istoricheskuiu Rossiiu', *Rossiiskaia Gazeta*, 2 October 2022, and more.

22. 'Vserossiiskii s'ezd sudei', *Kremlin.ru*, 29 November 2022, kremlin.ru/events/president/news/69949; Yana Surinskaia, 'Putin zaiavil o sozdanii federal'nykh sudov na novykh territoriiakh', *Vedomosti*, 29 November 2022.

23. For comment, see William E. Pomeranz, 'Putin's annexation miscalculation', *Wilson Center, Kennan Institute Blog*, 6 February 2023.

24. Ukrainian World Congress, 'Address by President Volodymyr Zelensky, Dec. 9, 2022', 10 December 2022, ukrainianworldcongress.org/address-by-president-volodymyr-zelensky-dec-9-2022/; Adam Plowright, 'Zelensky urges 800Mln Euros in Ukraine winter help', *The Moscow Times*, 13 December 2022.

25. European Commission, 'Commission proposes stable and predictable support package for Ukraine for 2023 of up to €18 billion', 9 December 2022, ec.europa.eu/commission/presscorner/detail/en/ip_22_6699.

26. 'Rossiisko-belorusskie peregovory', *Kremlin.ru*, 19 December 2022, kremlin.ru/events/president/news/70143.

27. 'Xi tells Russia's Medvedev that China wants talks on Ukraine', *Bloomberg News*, 21 December 2022.

28. 'Zasedanie kollegii Ministerstva oborony', *Kremlin.ru*, 21 December 2022, kremlin.ru/events/president/news/70159; 'Military operation in Ukraine', *Interfax*, 21 December 2022.

29. Press-sluzhba Prigozhina, Telegram, 10 January 2022, t.me/concordgroup_official/254; for the Ukrainian response, 'StratKom ZSU/AFU StratCom', *Telegram*, 11 January 2023, t.me/AFUStratCom/11607; 'Russian pro-war voices lukewarm on sidelined commander's promotion', *The Moscow Times*, 11 January 2023. For MoD position, Anastasiia Selivanova, 'Minoborony RF: Podrazdeleniia VDV blokirovali Soledar s severa i iuga, v goroda idut boi', *Rossiiskaia Gazeta*, 11 January 2023.

30. On Gerasimov's and other appointments, see Minoborony Rossii, in Telegram, 11 January 2023, t.me/mod_russia/23355; Charles R. Davis, 'Russia demoted the "absolutely ruthless" general who has been leading the war in Ukraine less than 3 months after promoting him', *Business Insider*, 11 January 2023; 'The head of the general staff, Valery Gerasimov, will command the Russian invasion of Ukraine', *Meduza*, 11 January 2023.

31. 'Putin polozhitel'no otsenilk dinamiku SVO', *Vesti.ru*, 'Moskva. Kreml'. Putin', 15 January 2023, vesti.ru/article/3147801.

32. On this, see Marcel Plichta, 'The epic arsenal of Western guns coming for Putin this year', *The Daily Beast*, 13 January 2023; 'British decision to send heavy tanks to Ukraine prompts Russian warning', *The Moscow Times*, 15 January 2023.

33. Dmitrii Kulemyakin, 'Lavrov zaiavil, chto voina Zapada s Rossiei uzhe ne gibridnaia, a pochti nastoiashchaia', *Rossiiskaia Gazeta*, 23 January 2023.

34. Sinéad Baker, 'Russia could resort to nuclear weapons if it loses in Ukraine, says former Russian president', *Business Insider*, 20 January 2023.

35. Russian Embassy in Germany, 'Commentary by Russian ambassador to Germany S. Yu. Nechaev on the decision of the German government to supply Ukraine with Leopard 2 tanks', *Embassy News*, 25 January 2023, russische-botschaft.ru/ru/2023/01/25/kommentariy-posla-rossii-v-germanii-s-4/; 'Russia warns of escalation as Germany greenlights Leopard tanks for Ukraine', *The Moscow Times*, 25 January 2023.

36. Laura Kelly, 'Biden says US tanks to Ukraine are not an offensive threat to Russia', *The Hill*, 25 January 2023.

37. Igor Dunaevskii, 'Baiden: SShA peredadut Ukraine 31 tank M1 Abrams dlia kontrnastupleniia', *Rossiiskaia Gazeta*, 25 January 2023, and 'NATO nakachivaet Ukrainu tekhnikoi: SShA peredadut Ukraine tanki M1 Abrams, Germaniia gotovit dva batal'ona Leopard', *Rossiiskaia Gazeta*, 25 January 2023; 'U.S. to provide 31 Abrams tanks to Ukraine amid Russian warnings', *The Moscow Times*, 25 January 2023; Marcel Plichta, 'Swarm of tanks is just the start of Putin's new nightmare', *The Daily Beast*, 25 January 2023.

38. Moscow. Kremlin. Putin. 'The president of the Russian Federation is ready to negotiate with all opponents', 25 December 2022, smotrim.ru/video/2536466?utm_source=internal&utm_medium=main2-news&utm_campaign=main2-news6; 'Russia's proposal on Ukraine's demilitarization should be better accepted – Lavrov', *TASS*, 26 December 2022; Dmytro Kuleba @DmytroKuleba, 'No consensus in negotiations yet . . .', *Tweet*, 25 March 2022.

39. 'Ukraine "peace plan" must factor in Russia's four new regions, Kremlin emphasizes', *TASS*, 28 December 2022.

40. '"Nasha pobeda – neotvratima": Sergei Shoigu pozdravil voennoslyzhashchikh s nastupaiushchim Novym godom', *Rossiiskaia Gazeta*, 31 December 2022.

41. 'Novogodnee obrashchenie k grazhdanam Rossii', *Kremlin.ru*, 31 December 2022, kremlin.ru/events/president/news/70315.

42. On the 'disengaged' Russian population, see Joshua Yaffe, 'The quiescent Russia', *Foreign Affairs*, 23 February 2023; 'Konflikt s Ukrainoi: otsenki fevralia 2023 goda', *Levada-tsentr*, 2 March 2033.

43. See, e.g. 'Vlasti Krasnodara ezhegodno tratiat den'gin a remont bomboubezhishch. Komu dostaiutsia kontrakty i za chto?' *93.ru*, 31 October 2022; Pyotr Kozlov, 'Amid Ukraine war, Kremlin orders nationwide bomb shelter overhaul', *The Moscow Times*, 6 February 2023; 'Kremlin declines to say if Moscow is preparing for air strikes', *The Moscow Times*, 20 January 2023.

44. *NATO Update*, 15 and 17 February 2023.

45. 'Poslanie Prezidenta Federalnomu Sobraniiiu', *Kremlin.ru*, 21 February 2023, kremlin.ru/events/president/news/70565.

46. Ivana Saric, 'UN general assembly demands Russia withdraw from Ukraine', *Axios*, 23 February 2023.

47. Alla Shoab, 'Norway, Sweden, Finland, and Denmark struck a deal to run their 200+ advanced fighter jets as a single fleet, creating a new headache for Russia', *Business Insider*, 25 March 2023.

48. Ministry of Foreign Affairs of the People's Republic of China, 'China's position on the political settlement of the Ukraine crisis, 2023-02-24 09:00', mfa.gov.cn/eng/zxxx_662805/202302/t20230224_11030713.html.

49. 'Kremlin, on China plan, says no conditions for peace "at the moment" in Ukraine', *The Moscow Times*, 27 February 2023.

50. ABC News, 'Biden spells out what's at stake in Ukraine as conflict marks 1 year', *YouTube*, 24 February 2023, youtube.com/watch?v=ohO9aUlvies; George Wright, Jaroslav Lukiv, 'Ukraine war: Zelensky wants Xi Jinping meeting following China's peace plan', *BBC News*, 24 February 2022, bbc.com/news/world-europe-647 62219; Connor Echols, 'Diplomacy watch: China's peace plan draws mixed reactions', *Responsible Statecraft*, 24 February 2024; Alexandra Brzozowski, 'NATO and EU give sceptical reaction to China's peace proposal for Ukraine', *Euractiv*, 24 February 2023.

51. 'Prezident Rossii i Predsedatel' KNR sdelali zaiavleniia dlia pressy', *Kremlin.ru*, 21 March 2023, kremlin.ru/events/president/news/70750.

52. Ekaterina Grobman, Maksim Solovov, 'V Brianskoi oblasti proizoshla odna iz samykh gromkikh diversii za poslednee vremia', *Vedomosti*, 2 March 2023; 'Kremlin says will take "measures" to prevent Ukrainian border incursions', *The Moscow Times*, 3 March 2023; 'Danilov: We will soon hear a lot of Russian volunteers aiming to liberate territories within Russia', *Ukrinform*, 2 March 2023.

53. For the RDK Manifesto, 'Za chto my srazhaetsia?' 24 November 2022, telegra.ph/Za-chto-my-srazhaemsya-11-24. For ultra-nationalist groups on both sides, 'Explainer: Which Russian far-right groups are fighting in Ukraine?' *The Moscow Times*, 18 March 2023. See also J. L. Black, *Eternal Putin?* p. 256.

54. Jim Garamone, 'U.S. sends Ukraine $400 million in military equipment', *U.S. Department of Defense, DoD News*, 3 March 2023.

55. 'Secretary general in Kyiv: NATO stands with Ukraine', *NATO Update*, 20 April 2023.

56. On this, see Richard Haass, Charles Kupchan, 'The West needs a new strategy in Ukraine: A plan for getting from the battlefield to the negotiating table', *Foreign Affairs*, 13 April 2023.

57. Kiel Institute for the World Economy, 'Ukraine support tracker, 2023', accessed 26 April 2023, ifw-kiel.de/topics/war-against-ukraine/ukraine-support-tracker/; 'Daniia sovmestno s Germaniei postavit na Ukrainu 80 tankov Leopard 1', *Vedomosti*, 5 May 2023.

58. For Prigozhin's 4-minute video, see NewsBreak, 4 March 2023, @ABnewsReal, newsbreak.com/news/2946506176164-wagner-boss-appears-to-issue-veiled-threat-to-kremlin-in-ominous-video.

59. 'Wagner head accuses Russia's Defense Ministry of treason', *The Moscow Times*, 21 February 2023; Kepka Prigozhina, 'Publikuem zapros ot redaktsii izdaniia "N'ius Info" i otvet . . .', *Telegram*, 9 March 2023, /t.me/Prigozhin_hat/2817; 'Wagner boss "cut off" from official channels after public ammo plea', *The Moscow Times*, 9 March 2023.

60. 'Russian analytical report, March 6–13, 2023', *Russia Matters*, 13 March 2023.

61. 'Mikhaylo Podolyak @Podolyak_M', *Tweet*, 16 March 2023, twitter.com/Podolyak_M/status/1636340557885612032; Alla Shoaib, 'Ukraine said it was "watching with pleasure" as footage showed a lethal fire at a building of Russia's FSB security service near border', *Business Insider*, 16 March 2023.

62. Aksenyov Z 82. 'V raione Dzhankoia otrabotala PVO . . .', *Telegram*, 20 March 2023, t.me/Aksenov82/2268; 'Crimea drone attack wounds 1, Ukraine claims cruise missiles destroyed', *The Moscow Times*, 21 March 2023; 'Explained: Explosions in Crimea destroys missiles or a school, depending on who you ask', *The Kyiv Post*, 21 March 2023.

63. Matthew Loh, 'Russia wants to replenish its troops by recruiting 400,000 new contract soldiers starting April: Reports', *Business Insider*, 16 March 2023; 'Minoborony nachinaet novyi nabor kontraktnikov, tsel' – 400 tysiach chelovek', *Radio Svoboda* (RFE/RL), 14 March 2023.

64. 'Peskov zaiavil, chto ob elektronnykh povestkakh prizvan ispravit' bardak v voenkomatakh', *TASS*, 12 April 2023; 'Kreml' otvetil na vopros o perspektivakh novoi volny chastichnoi mobilizatsii', *RIA Novosti*, 11 April 2023; 'Confusion and indifference but no panic as Russia tightens draft rules', *The Moscow Times*, 14 April 2023.

65. 'In photos: Russia's military recruitment efforts for home and frontlines', *The Moscow Times*, 15 May 2023.

66. 'Medvedev called Ukraine part of Russia', *RIA Novosti*, 23 March 2023; 'Prezident Rossii i Predsedatel' KNR sdeli zaiavleniia dlia pressy', *Kremlin.ru*, 21 March 2023, kremlin.ru/events/president/news/70750.

67. Dmitry Medvedev @MedvedevRussiaE, Tweet, 17 March 2022, twitter.com/MedvedevRussiaE/status/1636759416807514114?ref_src=twsrc%5Egoogle%7Ctwcamp%5Eserp%7Ctwgr%5Etweet.

68. Vivek Shankar, Anton Troianovski, 'Putin says he could put tactical nuclear weapons in Belarus by summer', *New York Times*, 26 March 2023; 'Russia to deploy

its tactical nuclear weapons in Belarus at request of Minsk, says Putin', *TASS*, 25 March 2023.

69. Ministry of Foreign Affairs of the People's Republic of China, 'President Xi Jinping and Russian President Vladimir Putin sign joint statement of the People's Republic of China and the Russian Federation on deepening the comprehensive strategic partnership of coordination for the new era and stress settling the Ukraine crisis through dialogue', 22 March 2023.

70. 'V Kremle prognoziruiut dolguiu gibridnuiu voinu Zapada protiv RF', *Interfax*, 29 March 2023.

71. Minoborony Rossii, 'Na dolzhnost' zamestitelia Ministra oboronu RF, . . . Kus'menkov', *Telegram*, 30 April 2023, t.me/mod_russia/26067; Polina Khudyakova, 'General-polkovnika Kuz'menkova naznachili zamministra oborony', *Vedomosti*, 30 April 2023.

72. Helene Cooper, Eric Schmitt, Thomas Gibbons-Neff, 'Soaring death toll gives grim insight into Russian tactics', *New York Times*, 2 February 2023.

Chapter 3

War into the 'Foreseeable Future'

The monthly Levada Centre survey on the conflict in Ukraine found that in April 2023, 45 per cent of its 1,600 respondents followed events in Ukraine very or quite closely and another 45 per cent still paid little or no attention to them. The oldest age group (55+) was still more attentive to the war than younger Russians. There was little change in overall backing for the Russian army, which 75 per cent said they support. The percentage of respondents who wanted to see peace negotiations rose from 38 in March to 51 per cent in April. If these polls were reasonably accurate, then Putin's domestic propaganda campaign was holding firm.[1]

CHANGING PERSPECTIVES

According to Russian reports, Ukrainian forces tried to hit Putin's residence in the Kremlin with two drones on 3 May. Kyiv rejected accusations that it was involved, and called the incident staged. Whether this thwarted 'terrorist act' against Putin's person was real or fabricated, the Russian media made much of it, emphasizing that though he may be in danger their president was going about his heavy schedule as usual.[2] State Duma Speaker Vyacheslav Volodin and the Kremlin insisted that the United States was behind the alleged attempt on Putin's life, and Peskov told Russian journalists 'this is all dictated from Washington'.[3] Surveys conducted in late April showed that a clear majority of Russian respondents (61 per cent) did not want to see nuclear weapons deployed against Ukraine.[4]

Having already down-sized the annual Victory Day (9 May) spectacle, the government called off the biennial air show scheduled for July. Thus, Putin lost an opportunity to preen for a domestic and foreign audiences in front of Russia's advanced technology.

It was at this time that Prigozhin threatened to withdraw his troops from Bakhmut and again raged on video against Shoigu and Gerasimov for not supplying his forces with enough ammunition to defend themselves. Spouting obscenities, Prigozhin stood in front of what appeared to be dozens of blood-covered Wagner Group corpses. Within two days he was promised ammunition, but tension between him and the senior MoD command festered.[5]

Whether or not Prigozhin was getting the weapons he needed, Ukraine was. In that same week, the UK sent Ukraine air-launched Storm Shadow cruise missiles that have a strike capacity of up to 300 kilometres (200 miles). At about that time, the Biden administration announced another package valued at about $1.2 billion in ammunition, training programmes and equipment in support of Ukraine's air defence systems. This last included two new anti-drone systems.[6]

Not to be left out, Germany's defence minister announced that Berlin was preparing a €2.7 billion package ($2.95 billion), its largest yet, for Ukraine. The aid bundle listed 30 additional Leopard-1 tanks, Marder armoured vehicles, air defence and surveillance drones.[7]

On 9 May, Prigozhin complained that the Russian army was 'fleeing' ('The 2nd Brigade pissed away three-square kilometres this morning'), a charge that appeared to be confirmed the next day when the Ukrainian military announced that an entire Russian brigade had retreated from its positions around Bakhmut.[8] The MoD in Moscow was not amused.

Even with an obsequious media, the Kremlin was having a difficult time keeping bad news out. Its storyline was wearing a little thin for Russia's armed forces personnel and even the general public. For instance, when train cars filled with grain were derailed by explosives in Crimea on 18 May, near Simferopol, the incident was attributed to the 'intervention of outsiders'. Russians could easily read between the lines – if they wanted to.[9] By the spring of 2023, Ukraine's Armed Forces were much better equipped than they were in 2014, or even in early 2022, much better trained and much better funded, and stood on the moral high ground.[10] Russia's Armed Forces still had the advantage of numbers, but pre-war hype about its sophisticated weaponry had proven hollow. Its conscripted soldiers were under-trained, its mercenaries under-equipped and its collective morale was low.

Then the tide began to change. On 20 May, Prigozhin claimed that the Wagner Group had complete control of Bakhmut, called Artemovsk by Russia. While Putin congratulated him and the MoD for their apparent success, and the Russian media exulted in a 'great victory', soldiers with the Russian

Volunteer Corps infiltrated and shelled the Russian Belgorod region. Using drones, mobile artillery, tanks and armoured vehicles, they destroyed residential houses, administrative buildings and, according to regional governor Vyacheslav Gladkov, a kindergarten. Both the RDK and the Freedom of Russia Legion (Legion 'Svoboda Rossii' – LSR), took credit for the incursion. Peskov claimed that it was an attempt to deflect attention from the 'loss' of Bakhmut, and the Ukrainian MoD still denied any involvement with forays on Russian territory.[11] Clearly, the Russian public now had more to think about.

They couldn't help but hear Prigozhin, whose words were available to Russians via social media. In a remarkably frank interview on RuTube with political strategist Konstantin Dolgov, Prigozhin criticized the SVO for looking for Nazis in Kyiv, finding none and, instead, 'making Ukraine a nation known around the world'. Moreover, instead of 'demilitarization', Russia 'militarized Ukraine', making the Ukrainian army one of the world's strongest. He bitterly chastised the children of Russia's elite for still living a 'fat carefree life' while other mothers cry over their sons, and again asserted that Shoigu and Gerasimov must be replaced by Mizintsev and Surovikin. The expletive-filled interview was undated, but appeared on RuTube during the last week of May 2023 (it was blocked later).[12] Soon afterwards, Wagner Group troops began withdrawing from Bakhmut, leaving the city to Russia's regular army.

Prigozhin's rant coincided with an announcement from Minsk that Russia had begun its promised transfer of tactical nuclear weapons to newly constructed storage facilities in Belarus. Shoigu again explained that this action came because the 'collective West' was conducting an undeclared war against Russia and that Washington had been providing nuclear backup for its NATO allies for decades. The US State Department again warned that the use of such weapons would result in 'severe consequences'.[13] Coupled with further announcements from the Pentagon that Denmark, Norway and the Netherlands would be conducting training sessions for Ukrainian pilots to operate F-16s supplied by the United States, any optimism that the war in Ukraine might be winding down was quickly dispelled.[14]

Asked about the use of tactical nuclear weapons in June, at SPIEF 2023 (St. Petersburg International Economic Forum), Putin noted that the first transfer of parts of these weapons had just then arrived in Belarus and that their use was only a 'theoretical' possibility. They would be deployed only if there was a threat to Russian territorial integrity. 'We have more such weapons than the NATO countries', he added, so if they want to talk of reductions 'fuck them, you know? As our people say. (laughter)'.[15]

Ukraine Pushes for NATO Membership

While Russia appeared to be facing some internal upset at top military and political levels, Zelensky told a large gathering of European leaders in Moldova on 1 June 2023 that NATO and the EU should speed up the process for Ukraine's accession.

The Ukrainian leadership grew more confident of fast-tracked memberships in the EU and NATO while attending June's Ukraine Recovery Conference in London. As well as encouraging Kyiv about accession, the gathering promised huge amounts of aid, both immediate and over time: EU (€50 billion); UK (£3 billion over next 3 years), World Bank (US$1.76 billion); EBRD (€600 million); European Investment Bank (€840 million); USA ($1.3 billion); Germany (€381 million).[16] As the Ukrainian prime minister pointed out and Russian propaganda proclaimed, NATO was in a de facto proxy war with Russia already.

PEACE PLANS?

As these events unfolded, politicians and analysts outside Russia and Ukraine began to treat the war as unwinnable by either side.[17] Pleas for negotiations came from every direction, but no one came up with a plan that could serve as a basis for mediation. Proposals set out already by Kyiv, Moscow, Beijing, the Vatican and Washington failed before their ink dried. Setting aside Donald Trump's bizarre claim that he could end the war in 24 hours, it was not clear to anyone after 16 months how peace could be achieved by anything but violence. Cynics saw the war of attrition going on for years, mostly at the expense of Ukraine.

This did not stop other entities from trying. On 3 June, Indonesia's defence minister urged combatants to establish a demilitarized zone, with troops on both sides pulling back at least 15 kilometres from existing front lines. This zone would be monitored by a UN peacekeeping force that would also organize referenda in the occupied ('disputed') territories. Kyiv dismissed this scheme out of hand, repeating that Russia must withdraw all its troops from Ukrainian territory before any negotiations could take place.[18] Western countries also criticized the plan; China praised it.

Taking their turn, a delegation of African leaders organized a mission they dubbed 'the road to peace', also in June. Led by South African president Cyril Ramaphosa, the group of seven leaders (Uganda, Senegal, Zambia, Republic of Congo, Comoros and Egypt) met with Zelensky and a day later with Putin, hoping to draw them to a joint summit. The African leaders claimed to be non-aligned and concerned over the damage the war was doing to their cost of living and food supply. Analysts correctly foresaw failure.

Are Russians Really Paying Attention?

A series of questions asked by the Levada Centre during the final week of May 2023 suggested that large numbers of Russians were still 'disengaged' (45 per cent of 1,601 respondents) from the 'special military operation'. There was an increase in the percentage who preferred to continue 'hostilities', from 38 per cent in April to 48 per cent in May, with a concomitant drop in the number that preferred peace negotiations (51 per cent to 45 per cent).[19] In early June 2023 it remained to be seen whether shifting Ukrainian tactics to more incursions against Russian territory would lengthen the Russian public's attention span.

A clever Ukrainian destabilizing tactic disrupted some Russian families. The 'I Want to Live' (Khochu zhit') project; that is a hot line operated by Ukrainian intelligence services to help Russian soldiers surrender under the terms of the Geneva Convention. They made the project known by using Russian opponents of the war to distribute leaflets, sticking them on trees, telephone poles, shop windows and so on, with the heading, 'Are they sending you to fight in Ukraine?', followed by contact information on how to avoid having to go by using the project as 'insurance against death'. Leaflets were also distributed by drones. A spokesperson for the Ukrainian MoD claimed that over 6,500 Russian servicemen had surrendered between September 2022, when the hot line was created, and the end of January 2023. Although this tally could not be proven, it was plain that the project met with some success. At least one Russian activist caught posting 'I Want to Live' leaflets died under murky circumstance while in custody in Rostov-on-Don.[20]

A 'War' Is Still a 'War'

Putin worked hard to rally his people around the flag. On Russia Day, 12 June, he handed out 'Hero of Labour' medals and called on all Russians to support the SVO as an act of patriotism and take 'responsibility for the fate of the Fatherland'.[21] At a Kremlin meeting with war correspondents the official narrative was re-played many times; above all, the notions that Russians were fighting the collective West, that annexed territories in Ukraine were historically and rightfully Russian, that the SVO was going well, and that social media photos of destruction in Ukraine were hoaxes.[22] None of the so-called war correspondents present demurred.

Chapter 3

PRIGOZHIN MAKES HIS PLAY

After withdrawing his troops from Bakhmut at the end of May, Prigozhin toured Russia's regions, arranging press conferences in Yekaterinburg, Vladivostok and Novosibirsk, with more to come. Calling for a general mobilization because, he repeated, the 'war' would be a long one. Prigozhin urged the government to stop glossing over the perils of war and toughen up by reintroducing the death penalty and revert to a planned economy. His tour was touted as part of an undefined 'Wagner Second Front'. He also said that had no plans to launch a political career. Maybe not, but Prigozhin's sudden and somewhat unexpected appearances sounded political to many observers.[23]

After he refused to let his mercenary force sign regular contracts with the Russian army, Prigozhin openly accused the country's military leadership of incompetence and deceit.

Complaining that 'there is no management, there are no military successes, the leadership of the Ministry of Defence carefully deceives the president . . . we listen all day about 60 destroyed Leopards, about 3,000 destroyed enemy soldiers . . . complete, total nonsense'.[24] He challenged the official narrative on all counts.

On that same day, 22 June, Prigozhin acted. He called for an armed rebellion against the defence ministry and moved his troops into Russia from occupied territory in eastern Ukraine. Claiming that he was responding to destruction and deaths in his field camps caused by rockets, helicopter gunships and artillery fired by Russia's regular army, Prigozhin's forces moved into the Rostov area, where he met with no resistance. He claimed that his only target was the senior military leadership, not the president or any other government institution. Putin angrily appealed to the 'citizens of Russia' via TV not to support 'those who, by deceit or threats, were dragged into a criminal adventure, pushed onto the path of a serious crime – an armed rebellion'. Without naming Prigozhin, he called the action a betrayal, a 'stab in the back of our country and our people', and promised 'tough' punishments. The Kremlin geared up for civil war.[25]

After seizing the city of Rostov, where they appeared to have been welcomed, the Wagner PMC headed for Moscow, over 1,000 kilometres (689 miles) distant. Calling his cavalcade a 'March of Justice' (Marsha spravedlivosti), Prigozhin targeted the commanders whom he blamed for the failures of the SVO. The Russian media, social and mainstream, filled up with photos of troop convoys on the highways that included battle tanks on flatbed trucks. Caught by surprise, the Ministry of Defence made no attempt to stop them.

In Moscow, heavily armed soldiers patrolled the streets. Armed checkpoints and sandbag-protected machine gun stations set up on the city's outskirts. Russian authorities could not prevent wild speculations and questions about what was going on, among them rumours that Putin had fled to St. Petersburg. Western TV channels revelled in the story. Panels of retired generals, admirals and intelligence officers joined breathless journalists to provide an extraordinary range of possibilities for Russia, Putin and Ukraine – before their pontificating was cut short by a 'deal' reached by the Kremlin and Prigozhin. The rebel leader would move to Belarus. Rebel troops who had reached within 300 kilometres of Moscow turned back towards their bases in Ukraine.[26] Neither they, nor Prigozhin, would be prosecuted. Lavrov confirmed that Lukashenka had brokered the deal and then telephoned Putin to inform him of its results.[27]

Within hours, Wagner PMC forces left Rostov, Voronezh and Lipetsk, highways were re-opened and an uneasy calm set in – at least for the Russian public. Prigozhin said that he did not want to shed Russian blood, all evidence to the contrary, and claimed that he and his troops were patriots, not betrayers. The matter of treason was not yet resolved and, according to *Kommersant*, the criminal case against and FSB investigation of Prigozhin were still underway.[28] Whereas European leaders and Western punditry almost universally saw the unfolding events as a sign that the Putin regime was breaking down, what the bizarre, 24-hour insurrection actually meant for Putin's leadership and the MoD was not immediately obvious.[29] The coup attempt, if that is what it was, was relatively bloodless, though the Wagner PMC shot down several Russian army helicopters and one plane on 24 June, killing their crews.[30] Putin's oft-proclaimed Russian unity and his aura of political invincibility appeared to be on shaky grounds. This time, no one in Russia could pretend it had not happened.

Prigozhin did not stay quiet for long. On 26 June, he released an 11-minute video, from an unknown location, in which he said that the 'march' exposed weaknesses in Russian security. Its purpose, he continued, was 'to avoid the destruction of Wagner and to hold to account the officials who through their unprofessional actions have committed a massive number of errors'. It was not an attack on Putin, he maintained.[31]

Shortly thereafter, Putin was back on TV angrily insisting that Russian unity had saved the day. Visibly unforgiving, he fulminated against 'the organizers of the rebellion, having betrayed their country, their people, and those who were drawn into the crime. They lied to them, pushed them to death, under fire, to shoot their own', and went on to say that a bloody civil war in Russia is what the 'neo-Nazis in Kyiv and their Western patrons' wanted. Without mentioning their leader, Putin guaranteed the freedom of 'patriotic' Wagner soldiers who could go home, go to Belarus or sign up with Russia's regular army.[32] Prigozhin's fate remained murky. Belarus's neighbours, the Baltic states and Poland, made it clear that they did not want the mercenary army close to their borders.

In a much calmer presentation on 27 June, Putin praised Russian soldiers and national guardsmen who 'prevented civil war'. Speaking at a hastily arranged outdoors ceremony at the Kremlin in front of 2,500 servicemen from the MoD, National Guard, Ministry of the Interior and special services, plus Shoigu and the heads of the attending departments, he thanked them for 'saving the Motherland from upheavals'.[33] In fact, they had done very little.

The Kremlin quietly launched a purge of senior military staff. Rumour had it that Gen. Surovikin was arrested amid claims that he supported the mutiny. Other jobs were on the line as Putin looked for scapegoats.[34]

A final chapter in the Prigozhin saga came with his death in a mysterious airplane crash on 23 August 2023.

WAR AGAINST THE WEST?

To make up for numbers lost with the withdrawal of the Wagner forces, the MoD began an aggressive recruiting campaign. Along with men to fill in the depleted ranks, special emphasis was placed this time on attracting women to the front as doctors, surgeon's assistants, nurses and cooks.

Ads encouraging women under the age of 50 to sign up proliferated, and hot lines were set up to make it easy for them to apply. If they agreed to serve for one full year, in the recently annexed areas of Ukraine, they would earn salaries equal to men recruited at the same rank. Shoigu claimed that over 1,000 women were already involved in the SVO.[35]

The Russian MoD still needed more male front-line soldiers. Thus, Putin reneged on his earlier decision to raise the conscription age. A new bill introduced in July retained the minimum age at 18, instead of the 21 promised earlier, and raised the upper limit to 30, from the maximum for eligibility of 27.[36] As we shall see in later chapters, the intense campaigning in the name of patriotism was successful both in the numbers of volunteers it attracted and the support gained by framing the conflict as a defence against a threatening West.

Shoigu made this approach plain in June 2023 when he told senior military officers gathered at the MoD Collegium that, because the 'collective West is waging a proxy war against Russia', he was going to build up forces on Russia's western borders. The statement was triggered by Finland's entry into NATO and Sweden's expected entry, which he called 'serious destabilizing factors'. He added that Poland was the main tool of Washington's anti-Russia policy and so also posed a serious threat, especially since Warsaw was planning to build the 'largest army in Europe' with American weaponry – or so the Collegium was told. These alleged circumstances generated further high-level public conversations in Russia about using nuclear weapons, shunting aside any thought of peace negotiations.[37]

WAR INTO THE 'FORESEEABLE FUTURE'?

Summits purporting to focus on peace talks had no impact whatsoever on the on-going war of attrition, which, by August 2023, featured cruise missiles and drones on land, sky and sea. Notices of hits and misses in Ukraine, occupied Ukraine and Russia became daily fare. Early in that month, Peskov told a *New York Times* journalist that 'there are currently no grounds for an agreement... we will continue the operation for the foreseeable future'.[38] He was responding to a question about the various proposals for peace.

Ukrainian Breakthrough

Both sides escalated their assaults over the summer, Russia dominating the air and Ukraine conducting more and more raids on to Russian territory. The Kerch Strait bridge was regularly under attack, as was Russia's Black Sea Fleet port and ships in Sevastopol. Russia's response tended to be swarms of strikes by drones and cruise missiles, while fighting on the ground bogged down along the front line. Armoured vehicles and tanks became less important because they were too easily targeted and surface-to-air missile defence systems became central to Ukraine's defence. These had to be delivered by the West.

The mainstream press in both combatant countries reported battles and dramatic strikes so differently that one might think they were reporting completely separate phenomena. Peskov's 'unforeseeable' began to look more like 'never-ending'.[39] By August, Russians worried that many of the drone attacks against them originated from within their own country, lending credence to Kyiv's claims that there is an active pro-Ukrainian fifth column operating in Russia. Ukrainian partisans also directed missile strikes, or provided intelligence for acts of sabotage against Russian military and administrative offices and personnel in occupied parts of Ukraine. Orchestrated by Ukraine's special forces by means of a group called the National Resistance Centre (Tsentr natsional'nogo sprotivu), such acts (cutting power sources, sand in gas tanks, displaying Ukrainian symbols and songs) are very hard to prevent and, the NRC says, inflict psychological damage to occupying staff and officials.[40]

Russia-backed politicians in annexed areas were constantly targeted: A deputy in the Luhansk regional parliament and former separatist military commander, Mikhail Filiponenko, was blown up in his car in November

2023, one week after another Russia-supported politician was shot in Crimea. A former deputy in the Luhansk parliament and proponent of the war, Oleg Popov, was killed by a car bomb in December.[41] The SBU also conducted assassinations of Ukrainian 'traitors' within Russia. For example, in December, a former member of Medvedchuk's faction in the Rada was shot to death in a suburb of Moscow. Illia Kyva had been criticizing Ukraine on Russian TV and was under sanction by the UK. His killing was celebrated on Ukrainian media, which circulated gruesome photos of him lying dead in a snowbank.[42] Pro-Russian Ukrainians were no longer safe even in Russia.

Recruiting Campaign Heats Up

The on-going recruiting drive intensified a year after the first mobilization fiasco. According to Dmitry Medvedev in September, 280,000 people had joined the army under contract since the start of 2023.[43] Conducted both online and with large public posters and rallies, the renewed campaign featured mobile recruiting trucks and promises of salaries three times larger than the national average. Colourful brochures highlighting contract military service as the 'choice of a real man', or as the profession of 'defending the Motherland', were effective. The MoD also made it possible for foreigners over the age of 18 and with a secondary school education to sign up.

At year's end, Putin told his annual press conference audience that Russia had recruited 486,000 people to the Armed Forces, and that over 244,000 of them were 'located directly' in the combat zone. 15,000 are joining up daily, he said, so there was no need for a new mobilization.[44]

Patriotism and peer pressure were important to the recruiting effort, but the main lure was still the much higher-than-average wage, plus various bonuses. Yet, the fact that unemployment was at a record low of 2.9 per cent by the end of 2023 and labour shortages were forcing wages up made the recruit target difficult to achieve.

Impasse?

While Medvedev was boasting about Russia's recruiting successes, US Secretary of State Blinken returned to Ukraine for his fourth visit, bringing with him pledges of more than $1 billion in new funding for humanitarian aid and weapons. Some of the money was to be used to remove mines, and some to combat corruption. Over $5 million of the allocation came from assets belonging to Russian oligarchs and seized from US banks. Much of the sum for armaments came in the form of grants, and so would not have to be repaid. Peskov reacted on behalf of the Kremlin by complaining, again, that 'Washington is waging a war to the last Ukrainian'.[45]

By that time, it was unlikely that anyone in Russia who was paying attention believed that the conflict was a mere 'special military operation'.[46]

Ukraine May 'Cease to Exist'

When the first of the promised American M1 Abrams tanks arrived in Ukraine, Volodin told media that unless Ukraine surrenders on Russia's terms it will 'cease to exist'. In this, he echoed earlier threats issued by Dmitry Medvedev, who now claimed that, because the West was supplying more and more weapons to Ukraine, Russia had few options other than 'direct conflict with NATO on the ground'.[47]

Disputing the Volodin-Medvedev assertions, NATO's Stoltenberg paid an unannounced visit to Kyiv on 28 September and, at the first meeting of an International Defence Industry Forum, promised long-term assistance. NATO's 'Support and Procurement Agency is overseeing a number of major initiatives, including framework contracts for €2.4 billion worth of key ammunition, including €1 billion of firm orders', he said. Over 20 countries were represented at the Forum. In a joint press conference, Zelensky told Stoltenberg that Ukraine needed more air defence systems against the almost nightly Russian drone intrusions.[48] Recognizing that it was impossible to keep all this global activity from their public, Russian media manipulators and educators devised entirely new methods to spin the official version of events (see chapter 9).

ARMS UNCONTROLLED

When Russia suspended participation in the New START and the United States followed suit, the international community worried that nuclear weapons would proliferate and eventually be utilized by Russia against Ukraine. Although both sides agreed to abide by the treaty's terms to end of term, 2026, until a new agreement could be worked out, these worries persisted. In the meantime, they blamed each other for a lack of progress in negotiations. In July, Russia's representative to the UN Disarmament Conference, Gennady Gatilov, told an interviewer that there could be no movement on arms control legislation until the United States 'abandoned the destructive course of inflicting a strategic defeat on Russia'.[49] With Americans and Russians preparing for presidential elections in 2024, New START was a dead issue.

So too was the Comprehensive Nuclear Test Ban Treaty (CTBT). On 6 October 2023, Russia's envoy to the CTBT Organization announced on X (Twitter) that Moscow was poised to revoke the Treaty it had ratified in 2000. Washington objected, invoking multiple dangers. Not long afterward, on 17

October, the State Duma voted to de-ratify. American complaints rang a little hollow, for even though 178 other countries had ratified the CTBT by 2023, other signatories, the United States had not. Nor had China. The United States interpreted Russia's action as a means to pressure Western countries against providing weapons to Ukraine. In fact, Simonyan had already said that Russia should test a nuclear bomb in Siberia so as to alert the West to Russia's capabilities. Her glib remark was not received well by Siberiaks.[50]

The fact is, the CTBT had never even come into force because not all of the 44 required signatories had ratified it and Russia claimed that it was now merely getting back on an even footing with the United States. 'We have been waiting 23 years for the United States to ratify this Treaty', Volodin complained. Russia is still a signatory to the treaty and Putin's bill says that the country will continue to abide by its obligations.[51]

The last Cold War Arms Treaty went the way of the Dodo bird in November 2023, when Russia formally withdrew from the 1990 Treaty on Conventional Armed Forces in Europe (CFE). It had withdrawn de facto in June. The original CFE placed limits on the number of conventional weapons that could be deployed by NATO and Warsaw Pact countries. It went through several updates after the Warsaw Pact and the USSR disappeared, and Russia suspended participation in 2015 because, it said, the European signatories failed to confirm several adjustments agreed in 1999. In its turn, NATO shelved its current part in the CFE, while accusing Russia of undermining Euro-Atlantic security.

The War of Attrition Grinds On

With the savage attack on Israeli civilians by Hamas soldiers on 7 October (Putin's birthday) drawing Washington's attention to the sudden Israeli-Hamas war, and Putin in China, the war of attrition in Ukraine took a turn. The Ukrainian General Staff announced that it destroyed multiple helicopters and other materiel in overnight strikes against Russian airfields and equipment in the occupied Luhansk and Berdyansk regions. What was new about this attack was Zelensky's claim that Ukrainian forces used recently acquired ATACMS for the mission. As usual, Russia claimed that it intercepted all the missiles and no real damage was done.[52]

At the time, the United States had not yet admitted to sending the long-range system to Ukraine, though Zelensky expressed his gratitude for them publicly. Putin called their use a mistake, for they would 'simply prolong the agony' in Ukraine. While conceding that the ATACMS posed a threat, he let slip the phrase, 'war is war' (voina est' voina), acknowledging what everyone knew already, but still could not be said in Russia.[53]

According to the Ukrainian defence ministry, the Russian army's renewed offensive in October cost it 1,400 troops and 55 Russian tanks in one 24-hour stretch.[54] Wartime embellishment or not, the conflict was taking far too many lives on both sides.

While Russian missiles besieged Ukraine from afar and ever-increasing numbers of young Russian men lost their lives and limbs in ground actions, Levada Centre surveys suggested that, in October and November, nearly 40 per cent of the general Russian population still claimed to be paying little attention to the war, yet only 37 per cent favoured continuing it. That was a drop of 11 per cent since September. Support for Russia's Armed Forces and Putin remained high.[55] Clearly, although most Russians did not feel directly threatened by the war, they were growing tired of it.

Aggressive harassments from both sides heated up on 11 November, Armistice Day. A day after that, a Ukrainian General Staff 'update' claimed that 1,100 Russian soldiers had been killed in the previous 24 hours and over 310,000 since the war began. These highly embellished totals were widely distributed in Ukrainian propaganda materials, in English-language publications, on Telegram and elsewhere (see table 3.1). These numbers were available to Russian users of social media.

At the same time, Russian media posted accounts of shooting down drones around Belgorod, its Armed Forces winning mythical or exaggerated victories and headlining Ukrainian military desertions and other losses. Generally, however, the Russian print media treated details of the war as a sidebar and concentrated instead on trying to present life going on as usual for Russian citizens.[56]

Table 3.1. Ukrainian General Staff Estimates of Russian Losses as of 11 November 2023

Personnel: 311,750 (+1100)
Tanks: 5,349 (+7)
Armoured Combat Vehicles: 10,073 (+32)
Artillery Systems: 7,559 (+32)
Multiple Launch Rocket Systems: 881 (+2)
Anti-Aircraft Missile Systems: 580 (+1)
Aircrafts: 322 (+0)
Helicopters: 324 (+0)
Tactical Unmanned Aerial Vehicles (UAVs): 5,632 (+12)
Cruise Missiles: 1,560 (+1)
Ships / Boats: 22 (+0)
Submarines: 1 (+0)
Automotive Equipment and Tanks: 9,944 (+19)
Specialized Equipment: 1078 (+9)

Source: General'niy shtab ZSU, 'Orientovni vtrati protivnika sklali', Telegram, 12 November 2023, t.me/GeneralStaffZSU/10888.
Note: The '+' signs refer to additions over the previous 24 hours.

Even as Ukrainian forces were achieving some success in November 2023 prominent Western analysts still recommended that Ukraine shift to a strictly defensive posture and try to negotiate a cease-fire.[57] Winter was coming and a ceasefire, they argued, would save many lives, guarantee Ukrainian security for a time and allow the country to re-set its economy in association with the EU. It did not mean that Kyiv would formally give up the 15 per cent of its territory Russian forces occupied, or stop holding Russia accountable for its aggression. Western 'experts' contended that the West could use the time to help Ukraine modernize even if it was truncated territorially, while it, the West, would then re-adopt a policy of containment against Russia. No matter how appealing these clichéd suggestions might have been to the general populations of the allied governments, and maybe even of the combatants if they knew of them, the likelihood of either Zelensky or Putin accepting them at that time was nil.

Signalling the frailty of hopes for peace talks, in November US Defense Secretary Austin was in Kyiv for the second time, travelling there by train from Poland to announce that the Pentagon would soon send another $100 million in weaponry, including one more HIMARS plus Stinger anti-aircraft missiles and millions of rounds of artillery and small arms ammunition. Cold weather gear was also part of the package. This security assistance was the fifty-first tranche of equipment provided from the US DoD inventory since August 2021.[58] The German foreign minister was also in Kyiv to reveal his country's new parcel of military aid, made up of IRIS-T air defence systems and ammunition.[59] At that same time, the Ukrainian prime minister announced the receipt of a €1.5 billion ($2.2 Bln) tranche from the EU, bringing the bloc's total in aid to Ukraine up to €16.5 billion.

Train Wrecks

Acts of sabotage within Russia accelerated, sometimes with help from Russian anti-war activists. According to a *Mediazona* report in October 2023, a direct action anti-war tactic in Russia came in the form of railway sabotage. Nearly 150 Russians, most them under 25 years in age, had been subjected to prosecution for such acts by that time. Charges ranged from simple hooliganism to acts of terrorism, or treason. At least one defendant was handed a sentence of 13 years. Some were connected to Ukrainian 'curators' or to the Freedom of Russia Legion. In the Ryazan region, at least 15 supply cars were derailed by an explosive device on Armistice Day 2023.[60]

Upgrading its programme of sabotage within Russia, on 1 December, Ukraine's SBU took credit for explosions on a rail line in Siberia, thousands of kilometres away from the front line. A forced derailment of a train passing through Buryatia followed a few days later, as a result of multiple detonations in the Severomuysky Tunnel. These explosions destroyed a fuel train on the Baikal-Amur (BAM) line, temporarily cutting off rail links between Russia and China. Ukrainian sources headlined the deeds' military significance; Russian sources either ignored them or classified the explosion and fire acts as 'terrorism'.[61] Local residents must have known better.

Ukraine Back on Defence

Early in December, Kyiv's presidential adviser posted on Twitter that Ukraine's Armed Forces would adopt a different tactic, 'effective defence in certain areas'. They would remain on the offensive in Crimea and on the Black Sea.[62]

During his annual call-in a few days later, Putin said that Russian troops had regained the initiative and, while proclaiming that southeast Ukraine is 'historically Russian territory', he made it clear that he wanted his forces to take Odesa, 'a Russian city, . . . everyone knows this well'. He also claimed that Western aid was winding down 'little by little' and made it plain that the war would last until Russia achieved its original aims, a 'de-Nazified', 'de-militarized' and neutralized Ukraine.[63] Even if Putin's four-hour 'conversation' was mainly propaganda for his domestic audience, it was obvious from it that the Kremlin planned to wait Ukraine and its allies out.

The second week of December saw mixed news for Russia and Ukraine on the international scene. Moscow was relieved when the US Congress again blocked a budget bill that included the large allocation for Ukraine, and adopted instead a defence policy bill that built in a mere $300 million for Kyiv. Further bad news for Ukraine came when an EU aid package was stalled by objections from Hungary. Russia was irritated, however, when the EU agreed to initiate serious discussions about admitting Ukraine.[64] Even though the US Department of Defense announced another $250 million tranche for Ukraine in late December, a feeling spread that Western support for Ukraine was waning.

The vicious circle of attack, retaliation, blame, denial and more attacks seemed endless to observers. The United Nations called for an immediate end to the devastation of Ukraine; Poland accused Russia of violating its airspace with a missile; and the Committee of Soldiers Mothers of Russia (Komitet soldatskikh Materei Rossii) continued to pester Putin and the MoD for better conditions and leaves for soldiers.[65] All to deaf ears.

During a New Year's Day televised visit to a military hospital in Moscow, Putin railed about Ukrainian attacks on Belgorod, labelling them 'terrorism' and a crime against civilians, raging dishonestly as if Russian forces had not been targeting civilians in Ukraine for nearly two years. Schools in regions close to the Ukrainian border were ordered to extend their Christmas break until 19 January.

Throughout Ukraine, Western-supplied air defence systems, Patriots and NASAMS, were effective against Russia's Kinshal missiles and Shahed drones, but enough got through to cause widespread chaos. The cycle of war continued. So, too, did prisoner-of-war swaps. The UAE mediated an exchange of about 250 each on 3 January 2024, the largest exchange yet.[66]

Russian angst was personified by Dmitry Medvedev. Upset that the French foreign ministry called the attack on Belgorod an act of self-defence by Ukraine, against an aggressor, he threw a tantrum and posted on Telegram that the 'frog-eaters' were 'scum, bastards, freaks'.[67] The Ukrainian media made much of the bizarre outburst; *RT International* tried to defend it.[68]

By the end of 2023, the course of war fighting appeared to be evolving in Russia's favour. On the ground, Ukraine's much-hyped counter-offensive had flopped and Russia's much larger forces had geared up for the long haul. Ukraine's economy was in disarray, large portions of its population were displaced, many of its cities under constant attack and Russia controlled the skies. Russia's economy was recovering. Its armed forces, after initial bungling, was improving and settling in for ground confrontation along a 1,000-kilometre front.[69]

INTO THE UNFORESEEABLE FUTURE?

The fighting continued unabated while Washington debated the question of more aid to Ukraine. On 11 January 2024, White House NSC Coordinator John Kirby told a press conference that American military aid to Ukraine 'had ground to a halt' as of 30 December 2023. The news wasn't all bad for Kyiv, however, for the NATO-Ukraine Council pledged 1,000 Patriot missiles to bolster Ukraine air defences, and the UK guaranteed its support for Ukraine during the next financial year to the increased amount of £2.5 billion ($4.27 Bln).[70] The latter arrangement was part of a new UK-Ukraine Agreement on Security Co-Operation signed on 12 January by Zelensky and the UK's prime minister Rishi Sunak, who was in Kyiv. Sunak also promised a large delivery of drones, most of them built in Britain.

On 16 January, Germany and France agreed to provide more military assistance for Ukraine jointly. Ammunition for Leopard tanks, surveillance drones, armoured personnel carriers, long-range missiles and bombs were part of the multi-billion-dollar aid package. Two days later, France and the United States formed a 23-country coalition to provide Kyiv with artillery and ammunition.[71]

While Zelensky was making a pitch at the World Economic Forum (17–19 January), in Davos, Switzerland, NATO's 31 Chiefs of Defence, plus Sweden as an invitee, gathered in Brussels. They agreed on continued support for Ukraine and finalized arrangements for the Alliance's largest war games since 1988. Steadfast Defender 2024 comprised 90,000 troops from its 31 member states, plus Sweden. Ships, planes and combat vehicles participated in an effort to test how well and how quickly NATO could coordinate and sustain defence against an attack on Europe.[72]

Chair of NATO's Military Committee, Admiral Rob Bauer, left no doubt that they were preparing for a conflict with Russia, though only if Russia attacked a NATO member. Soon afterwards, NATO signed a $1.2 billion contract to manufacture artillery rounds for Ukraine, and the three Baltic states agreed to construct a series of bunkers on their borders with Russia and Belarus in case of any land attack.[73] Lavrov added to the doomsday prognosis by rejecting arms control talks with the United States because, he said, Washington 'has cast us [Russia] as an enemy'. He warned that a 'direct clash of nuclear powers' was possible.[74] This became the most worrisome unknown variable of the year.

This Is a 'War Against the Collective West' – Peskov

Rumours in late January 2024 that Putin was discussing possible settlements with Washington were immediately denied by Moscow and Kyiv.

As Ukrainian forces hit targets in Russia – oil depots, refineries, tank columns, planes on the ground, ships in or near Crimea – and Russian forces advanced slowly on the ground, Peskov told reporters that what began as 'a special military operation against Ukraine over time took the form of a war against the collective West, . . . led by the United States'. The war was now a war and would continue until Russia's objectives were achieved, he declaimed.[75] As if to confirm Peskov's stance, Russian forces kept on making small advances on the front lines in Ukraine and launching missile and artillery strikes against Ukrainian cities.

Hoping to ensure that Kyiv could sustain its war effort while managing its domestic economy, the EU agreed on 1 February to provide a special, long-term aid package valued at €50 billion ($73 Bln) to support Ukraine's economy and help with reconstruction.[76] The package, one-third in grants, two-thirds in loans, was kept separate from EU monies for arms and ammunition.

Perhaps to broadcast feigned indifference to the EU, Russia launched a wave of drones and cruise missiles against Kyiv on 6 February while the head of foreign affairs for the EU, Josep Borrell, was visiting the capital. Residences were hit, at least five killed and dozens wounded. More drone sorties were recorded in Kharkiv and the Lviv region, and Ukrainian troops finally withdrew from Avdiivka on 17 February after eight months of intense fighting. Russia forces crept westward, as Ukrainian forces ran desperately short of ammunition.

Putin continued to fantasize, boasting to defence workers in Tula that Russian weapons were superior to those of NATO: 'They are clearly superior to everyone, this is an obvious fact. I mean missile technology, armoured vehicles, and everything that is used on the battlefield'.[77] Workers in a munitions factory in Tula may have believed him, but Russian troops on the front line might have questioned his enthusiasm.

THE THIRD YEAR

As the second year of war came to an indecisive end, Russia appeared to have the edge. Its much larger pool of soldiers and ammunition stockpiles gained extra advantages by the fact that American support for Ukraine seemed to be flagging, though every Western government spoke grandiosely about their long-term commitment to the Ukrainian cause. Meanwhile, other countries took up the slack.

While Biden waited for the Republican-controlled Congress to agree to his large package of support for Ukraine, France guaranteed up to €3 billion in aid for 2024 and Germany promised €7.1 billion in military provision. At the Munich Security Conference in February, Zelensky, Macron and Scholz signed financial agreements and security guarantees covering a ten-year period. These were similar to a deal signed by Britain's Sunak a month earlier. To mark the anniversary of the first day of war, Canada's Trudeau paid a surprise visit to Kyiv (his third) and promised $2.7 billion in loans to be administered by the IMF, plus over $400 million in military spending and intelligence gathering. A few weeks before that, Ottawa allocated $95 million to manufacture 800 drones for Ukraine.[78] These were to be ready for delivery by the spring.

Standing at a podium in Kyiv with Italy's Meloni, the EU's von der Leyen, Belgium's prime minister Alexander De Croo and Zelensky, Trudeau called Putin a 'coward' and joined the surge of new sanctions imposed against Russia by Western countries in response to Aleksei Navalny's mysterious death. Stoltenberg pronounced that 'Ukraine will join NATO. It is not a question of if, but of when'.[79] What these political and financial promises would lead to remained to be seen.

Changing the course of the war became a hot topic that same week when Macron suggested that NATO should not rule out sending ground troops to Ukraine. Whereas the United States, Germany and others immediately rejected the idea, Putin responded by hinting again at nuclear war: 'We have weapons that can destroy targets on their territory'.[80]

Acting independently of Kyiv, the Freedom of Russia Legion was back, capturing the village of Tyotkino in the Kursk region of Russia, and promised more such raids.⁸¹ Russia claimed to have repelled several incursions, as well as more drone attacks in the Belgorod region, denied the Tyotkino loss (in spite of videos to the contrary) and called Ukrainian attacks in Russia 'terrorist' acts organized by Kyiv. Two other militia groups, the Russian Volunteer Corps and the Siberian Battalion, also conducted swoops into Russian territory, targeting ammunition depots, bridges and communications centres. To counter the bad news, including the crash of a large Russian military transport plane in Ivanovo, the MoD headlined its 'liberation' of several Ukrainian villages in the Donbas.⁸²

In Russia, Levada Centre surveys found little change in the general population's attitudes towards the war. In polls conducted during a week in December 2023 and the final week of January 2024, only 20 per cent of respondents said they were following events in Ukraine 'very closely', and 34 per cent 'fairly closely'. The level of disengagement seemed not to have changed much since the surveys conducted in May. The level of support for Russian troops in Ukraine remained high (77 per cent) and, as in previous months, more respondents preferred peace negotiation (52 per cent) than continuing war (40 per cent). In every category, a split between younger and older age groups was clear, with older groups (55+) showing a greater preference for war and more trust in TV news. Only 22 per cent overall said that the SVO was a mistake. Putin retained an approval rate of over 80 per cent, even though about two-thirds of respondents believed that the cost of war in lives and the economy was too high. These published numbers, accurate or not, could not help but encourage the Kremlin to stay the course.⁸³

More Peace Talks

When Zelensky met Erdogan in Istanbul on 8 March, the Turkish president again offered to broker peace discussions, this time by hosting a summit between Kyiv and Moscow. Zelensky remained adamant that any such talk must be based on the 10-point peace plan he proposed in November 2022. Just two weeks earlier, on the anniversary of the invasion, Switzerland's representative told the UNGA that, acting on Zelensky's request in January, it would invite all nations to a high-level peace conference it was organizing for Ukraine in the coming summer.⁸⁴

The Kremlin watched warily as Zelensky visited dockyards in Turkey where two corvettes were under constructed for Ukraine and urged Erdogan to help keep the grain corridor open. At that time, Kuleba was in Vilnius meeting with the Baltic and French foreign ministers in an attempt to get a more consistent supply of weapons. They were supported indirectly by two events in the United States. Biden harshly condemned Republicans during his state of the nation address for not releasing funds to support Ukraine and, at the Academy Awards night in Hollywood (9 March), *20 Days in Mariupol* won an Oscar for the best documentary. On accepting the statuette, director Mstyslav Chernov wished he hadn't had to make the film and condemned Russia to standing applause.

Election Days in Russia

As Russians began voting for their president on 15 March (see chapter 4), Ukrainian forces stepped up their attacks on Russia's border regions.[85] Strikes against Belgorod and Kursk forced regional Russian authorities again to evacuate schools and shopping malls. At least eight regions were subjected to waves of drones, an oil refinery was set on fire in the Samara region, airports were closed in Moscow and polling stations were hit in occupied areas (e.g. Zaporizhzhia). Many drones were shot down. Putin swore revenge and vowed to hunt down Russian 'traitors' who attacked Russia allied with Ukraine: 'We will punish them without a statute of limitations'. Less than 24 hours after the final election day, 17 March, Russia fired 31 ballistic and cruise missiles at Kyiv, and a day later launched over 100 missiles and drones against Ukraine's energy infrastructure, including the country's largest hydro-electric power plant in Dnipro.[86]

Plus Ça Change, Plus C'est La Mëme Chose – Not

The Russian public was shaken out of its complacency when, in late March, Ukrainian forces struck two more of Russia's landing ships, a military communications centre and Black Sea Fleet infrastructure. Commander of the Ukrainian Air Force, Mykola Oleshchuk, proclaimed on Telegram that 'Crimea is ours!', perhaps a little optimistically.[87] Ukraine's security agency, GUR, then began targeting factories that make Shahed drones and oil refineries as far away as Tatarstan. With US aid to Ukraine still in limbo, the EU decided to allocate European funds to purchase weapons from outside Europe to help Ukraine.

Meanwhile, on the evening of 22 March, Russia was stunned from another, unexpected, direction. With the West and Israel focusing on Hamas and Hezbollah in the Middle East, Islamic State-Khorasan Province (IS-KP) conducted a savage attack against civilians in the Moscow area. Assailants walked almost casually into the Crocus City (Krokus Siti) concert hall in Krasnogorsk and sprayed the audience with assault rifle fire. At least 140 were killed and 150 wounded.[88] They then burned the building with explosives. According to Putin, up to 15 of the assailants were captured over the next several days, several of them caught while fleeing towards Ukraine. Although his first inclination was to blame Ukraine directly, he soon walked that back to concede that 'radical Islam' was behind the attack, but continued to hint that Kyiv and Washington were somehow involved.[89]

The IS-KP attack came just hours after Peskov finally provided Russians with a reality check. He admitted that Russia was 'in a state of war' with Ukraine. It began as a special military operation, Peskov said, but evolved into a war when the 'collective West became a participant on the side of Ukraine'.[90] For many Russians this acknowledgement was ominous in that a de facto war provides the state with rationales for what it was already doing: enlarging its Armed Forces, managing the economy directly and controlling the mind-set of the population. By this time, Levada Centre surveys tell us, up to 60 per cent of Russians were following events in Ukraine 'very closely' (22 per cent) or 'quite closely' (38 per cent).[91] The terrorist attack added an exclamation mark to the wake-up call in Moscow.

A mere two weeks later, Congress finally passed the $61 billion aid for Ukraine bill.[92] The Russian reaction was predictable: Peskov complained that the aid would merely 'enrich America and further ruin Ukraine'; Zakharova, called it an election ploy: 'Ruling elites in the United States . . . are ready to pump up the regime in Kyiv with weapons so it is able to fight to the last Ukrainian'.[93] The ever-more-pithy Dmitry Medvedev called the decision a 'vote of gleeful American bastards'.[94] Surveys conducted by the Levada Centre in July saw the share of Russians who favoured talks to end the war reached 58 per cent, the highest to date.[95] Granted, only 17 per cent believed that Russia should make concessions and about one-third had come to think of the nuclear option as acceptable (52 per cent did not), but the fact that a clear majority wanted the war to end would suggest that the real or feigned rage at the top had not trickled down.

By the late spring of 2024, tens of thousands of soldiers had been killed, wounded or had gone missing on both sides, and there was still no end in sight.

NOTES

1. 'Konflikt s ukrainoi: otsenki aprelia 2023 goda', *Levada-tsentr*, 27 April 2023, levada.ru/2023/04/27/konflikt-s-ukrainoj-otsenki-aprelya-2023-goda/.

2. 'Kievskie bespilotniki noch'iu atakovali Kreml', *TASS*, 3 May 2023; Aysel Gereykhanova, 'Kreml: RF rastsenivaet ataku bespilotnikami na rezidentsiiu prezidenta kak terakt i pokushenie na Putina', *Rossiiskaia Gazeta*, 3 May 2023; 'Zelensky categorically denies Ukrainian involvement in Kremlin drone attack', *The Moscow Times*, 3 May 2023.

3. Sergei Leonov, '"V popytke terakta protiv Putina uchastvovali SShA". V Gosdume gotoviat otvet', *Argumenty i fakty*, 3 May 2023; Yelena Mukhametshina, Dar'ia Mosolkina, 'Peskov obvinil SShA v atake dronov na Kreml', *Vedomosti*, 4

May 2023; Vyascheslav Volodin. 'Terakt v otnoshenii Prezidenta – eto napadenie na Rossiiu', *Telegram*, 3 May 2023, t.me/vv_volodin/640.

4. 'Vozmozhnosti primeniia iadernogo oruzhiia v ukrainskom konflike', *Levada-tsentr*, 12 May 2023.

5. For Prigozhin's tirade against the MoD, 'Press-sluzhbas Prigozhina. #1564 Poteri ChVK "Vagner" za 4 Maia 2023 goda', *Telegram*, 4 May 2023, t.me/concordgroup_official/895, and for his threat, 5 May, t.me/concordgroup_official/896. See also Orkestr Vagnera/Wagner. *Telegram*, 5 May 2023, t.me/orchestra_w/6484; 'Wagner chief says pulling out of Bakhmut after blasting Russian military top brass', *The Moscow Times*, 5 May 2023.

6. US Department of Defense, 'Administration announces additional security assistance for Ukraine', *Immediate Release*, 9 May 2023.

7. 'Germany Unveils 2.7 bn Euro weapon package for Ukraine', *Kyiv Post*, 13 May 2023.

8. 'Ukraine says Russian forces pulling back after Bakhmut attacks', *The Moscow Times*, 10 May 2023; 'Fierce Ukrainian counterattack takes ground in Bakhmut – Prigozhin claims "betrayal"', *Kyiv Post*, 10 May 2023; 'Peskov zaiavil o dostizhenii "opredelennykh tselei" za god spetsoperatsii', *Vedomosti*, 11 May 2023. For Prigozhin's videos, see 'The conflict between Wagner and the Defense Ministry heats up', *The Bell*, 9 May 2023.

9. Anastasia Shvetsova, 'Barony s zernom soshli s rel'sov v Krimu. Chto izvestno', *Vedomosti*, 18 May 2023; 'V Krymu s rel'sov soshli vagony s zernom', *TASS*, 18 May 2023; 'Crimea railway blast derails Russian train – Reports', *The Moscow Times*, 18 May 2023.

10. On this, see Alexandra Chinchilla, Jahara Matisek, 'Ukraine's hidden advantage', *Foreign Affairs*, 11 May 2023.

11. For RDK videos of the incursion, see Russiy Dobrovol'cheskiy Korpus. Telegram, 22 May 2023, t.me/russvolcorps/512, and for Governor Gladkov's descriptions, see Nastoiashchiy Gladkov, 'Na territoriiu Graivoronskogo okruga zashla diversionno-razvedyvatel'naia gruppa VSU.' . . , *Telegram*, 22 May 2023, t.me/vvgladkov/2255; 'Russian border region says Ukrainian "sabotage" unit carried out incursion', *The Moscow Times*, 22 May 2023. See also Legion "Svoboda Rossiy". 'Legion i RDK na sviazi: Derzhim stroi ni dal'she osvobozhdaem nashu Rodinu', *Telegram*, 23 May 2023, t.me/s/legionoffreedom. See also Mykola Vorobiov, 'Anti-Kremlin Russian volunteers launch border incursion into Russia's Belgorod region', *Eurasia Daily Monitor*, 31 May 2023.

12. For a summary of the Prigozhin interview, see, 'I love my Motherland, I obey Putin, I'm sorry for Shoigu, we will continue to fight', *Meduza*, 24 May 2023, and for the original interview in Russian, RUTUBE, rutube.ru/video/cdeb735bc0a754c170e39f45a6cd67b1/?r=a, if it is still available.

13. Aleksei Nikol'skii, Nurlan Gasymov, 'Rossiia i Belorussiia podpisali dokumenty o razmeshchenii iadernogo oruzhiia', *Vedomosti*, 25 May 2023; Lukashenko says Russia has begun moving nuclear weapons to Belarus', *The Moscow Times*, 25 May 2023.

14. US Department of Defense, C. Todd Lopez, 'F-16 training, aircraft, to fill Ukraine's mid-term, long-term defense needs', *DOD News*, 23 May 2023; 'Borrel' zaiavil, chto podgotovka ukrainskikh letchikov na F-16 uzhe nachalas', *TASS*, 23 May 2023; 'Daniia i Niderlandy vozglaviat podgotovku ukrainskikh pilotov k poletam na F-16', *Vedomosti,* 25 May 2023.

15. 'Plenarnoe zasedanie Peterburgskogo mezhdunarodnogo ekonomicheskogo foruma', *Kremlin.ru*, 16 June 2023, kremlin.ru/events/president/news/71445.

16. 'Denys shmyhal: Recovery conference shows unwavering global support for Ukraine', *Ukrainian Government Portal*, 22 June 2023, kmu.gov.ua/en/news/denys-shmyhal-konferentsiia-z-vidnovlennia-demonstruie-nepokhytnu-svitovu-pidtrymku-ukrainy.

17. See, e.g. Samuel Charap, 'An unwinnable war: Washington needs an endgame in Ukraine', *Foreign Affairs*, 5 June 2023.

18. John McBeth, 'No takers for Prabowo's Ukraine peace plan', *Asia Times*, 8 June 2023; Mercedes Ruehl, Kathrin Hille, 'Indonesia floats Ukraine peace plan, triggering sharp western criticism', *Financial Times*, 3 June 2023.

19. 'Konflikt s ukrainoi: otsenki maia 2023 goda', *Levada-tsentr*, 1 June 2023.

20. 'V spetspriemnike Rostova-na-Donu umer aktivist Anatolii Berezikov', *OVD-Info*, 14 June 2023; David Wallace, Shane Reeves, 'Ukraine symposium – The "I Want to Live" project and technologically-enabled surrender', *Lieber Institute, West Point*, 13 January 2023.

21. 'Vruchenie medalei Geroia Truda i Gosudartvennykh premii Rossiiskoi Federatsii', *Kremlin.ru*, 12 June 2023, kremlin.ru/events/president/news/71346.

22. 'Vstrecha s voennymi korrespondentami', *Kremlin.ru*, 13 June 2023, kremlin.ru/events/president/news/71391.

23. See, e.g. 'Osnovatel' ChVK "Vagner" vo Vladivostoke: "Primorskie boitsy samye boesposobnye"', *Vostok Today*, 31 May 2023, vostok.today/46214-osnovatel-chvk-vagner-vo-vladivostoke-primorskie-bojcy-samye-boesposobnye.html; '"Nado ob'iavit' mobilizatsiiu uzhe seichas": Prigozhin vnezapno poiavilsia v Yekaterinburge i ob'iasnil, kak zakonchit' CVO', *E1.Ru*, 31 May 2023, e1.ru/text/politics/2023/05/31/72353093/; 'Esli my voiuem dal'she, nado ob'iavliat' mobilizatiiu uzhe seichas', *Meduza*, 31 May 2023.

24. Press-sluzhba Prigozhina, '#1829 Publikuem pervuiu chast' bol'shogo interv'iuiu Evgeniia Prigozhina', *Telegram*, 23 June 2023, t.me/concordgroup_official/1279; 'Wagner chief accuses Moscow of "misleading Russians" over Ukraine offensive', *The Moscow Times*, 22 June 2023.

25. Putin, 'Obrashchenie k grazhdanam Rossii', *Kremlin.ru*, 24 June 2023, kremlin.ru/events/president/news/71496.

26. Matvei Koporushkin, 'RIA Novosti: Prigozhin zaiavil, chto ChVK "Vagner" razvorachivaet kolonny i ukhodit v obratnom napravlenii', *Rossiiskaia Gazeta*, 24 June 2023; Joshua R. Krocker, 'Progozhin's armed rebellion will have lasting consequences for Russia, Putin and the Ukraine war', *The Moscow Times*, 24 June 2023; 'Putin survives wagner revolt but forced to cut deal', *The Moscow Times*, 25 June 2023.

27. Belta, 'Soobshchenie press-sluzhby Presidenta Respubliki Belarus', *Telegram*, 24 June 2023, t.me/belta_telegramm/204927; 'Segodniia v 9 vechera

Prezidenty Belarusi i Rossii snova pogovorili po telefonu . . .', *Telegram*, 24 June 2023, t.me/belta_telegramm/204935; Inna Greseva, 'Lavrov raskril detali uchastiia Lukashenko v peregovorakh s Prigozhinym Prezident Belorussii sam predlozhil pomoch' razreshit' mirom situatsiiu s popytkoi miatezha', *Vedomosti*, 26 June 2023.

28. 'Yevgenii Prigozhin ostaetsia pod sledstviem po delu o miatezhe', *Kommersant*, 26 June 2023.

29. See, e.g. 'Prigozhin' rebellion, Putin's fate, and Russia's future: A conversation with Stephen Kotkin', *Foreign Affairs*, 24 June 2023.

30. Alexander Khrebet, 'Ukraine's air force: Wagner mercenaries down 6 Russian army helicopters, 1 plane on June 24', *The Kyiv Independent*, 25 June 2023; 'Chef's special – Documenting equipment losses during the 2023 Wagner Group mutiny', *Oryx* (Holland), 24 June 2023, oryxspioenkop.com/2023/06/chefs-special-documenting-equipment.html.

31. 'Wagner leader Prigozhin breaks his silence, issuing first audio statement since mutiny', *Euronews*, 26 June 2023, includes the full video.

32. Putin, 'Obrashchenie k grazhdanam Rossii', *Kremlin.ru*, 26 June 2023, kremlin.ru/events/president/news/71528.

33. 'The criminal case on the fact of the armed rebellion was closed', *TASS*, 27 June 2023; Minoborony Rossii, 'Idet podgotovka k peredache ChVK "Wagner" tiazheloi voennoi tekhniki . . .', *Telegram*, 27 June, t.me/mod_russia/27879; Putin, 'Vystuplenie pered podrazdelenniiami . . .', *Kremlin.ru*, 27 June 2023, kremlin.ru/events/president/news/71533.

34. David Knowles, 'Ukraine: The latest – "General Armageddon" arrested in post-coup purge', *Business Insider*, 29 June 2023; 'Russian sources speculated that Wagner's rebellion is already having widespread impacts on the Russian command structure', *Institute for the Study of War*, 28 June 2023, understandingwar.org/backgrounder/russian-offensive-campaign-assessment-june-28-2023; 'Vladimir Putin freezes out hardliners after Wagner mutiny', *Financial Times*, 29 June 2023.

35. 'Shoigu rasskazal, skol'ko zhenshchin-voennykh uchastvuet v spetsoperatsii', *RIA Novosti*, 3 July 2023; 'Russia military targets women in recruitment ad', *The Moscow Times*, 7 July 2023.

36. 'Nizhnii predel prizyvnogo vozrasta v Rossii reshili ne povyshat' do 21 goda', *Interfaks*, 21 July 2023.

37. Yuri Gavrilov, 'Sergei Shoigu zaiavil, chto Zapad vedet protiv Rossii oposredovannuiu voinu', *Rossiiskaia Gazeta*, 9 August 2023; Andrey Baklitskiy, 'What we learned from recent calls for a Russian nuclear attack', *The Moscow Times*, 24 July 2023; Dmitry V. Trenin, 'Conflict in Ukraine and nuclear weapons', *Russia in Global Affairs*, 22 June 2023.

38. Quoted by Roger Cohen in 'Putin's forever war', *New York Times*, 7 August 2023.

39. Chris York, Maryna Shashkova, 'Ukrainian drones sweep across Russia, military planes destroyed, Kyiv vows to "increase scale"', *Kyiv Post*, 30 August 2023; Anatolii Kazantsev, 'Minoborony: VS Rossii noch'iu nanesli udar po punktam upravleniia i razvedki VSU', *Rossiiskaia Gazeta*, 30 August 2023; 'Kyiv targeted by "most

powerful" aerial attack since spring', *The Moscow Times,* 30 August 2023; 'Regions across Russia targeted in major drone attack', *The Moscow Times,* 30 August 2023.

40. For the National Resistance Center of Ukraine's website in English: sprotyv.mod.gov.ua/en. Kateryna Zakharchenko, Chris York, 'The secretive Ukraine partisan center causing havoc behind enemy lines', *Kyiv Post,* 30 August 2023.

41. 'Ukraine says it was behind car bombing of Russian proxy politician', *The Moscow Times,* 7 November 2023; 'Eks-deputat parlamenta LNR pogib posle podryva avtomobilia', *TASS,* 6 December 2023.

42. 'Ukraine releases footage from assassination site of "top traitor" Illia Kyva', *Kyiv Post,* 11 December 2023; 'NV obtains new photos and videos of the elimination of traitorous ex-MP Ilya Kyva near Moscow', *The New Voice of Ukraine,* 11 December 2023; 'Who was Illya Kyva? Ukrainian "traitor" gunned down near Moscow', *RFE/RL,* 7 December 2023.

43. 'About 280,000 individuals enlisted by contract from January 1 – Medvedev', *TASS,* 3 September 2023.

44. 'Itogi goda s Vladimirom Putinym', *Kremlin.ru,* 14 December 2023, kremlin.ru/events/president/news/72994.

45. 'US pushes Ukraine to war, special military op continues – Kremlin', *TASS,* 6 September 2023.

46. 'Chto izvestno o raketnoi atake VSY na shtab Chernomorskogo flota v Sevatopole', *TASS,* 22 September 2023; Nikolai Grishchenko, 'Mikhail Razvozhaev: VSU nanesli raketnyi udar po shtabu Chernomorskogo flota', *Rossiiskaia Gazeta,* 22 September 2023; Sophia Ankel, '"Difficult to accept": Prominent Russian hardliner admits its navy couldn't defend itself from Ukraine', *Business Insider,* 6 October 2023.

47. 'Medvedev: Rossii ostavliaiut vse men'she vybora, krome priamogo konflikta s NATO', *Vedomosti,* 26 September 2023; 'Ukraine may disappear from world map "as a result of current events" – Medvedev', *TASS,* 21 July 2022. See also Yaroslav Trofimov, *Our Enemies Will Vanish: The Russian Invasion and Ukraine's War of Independence.* Toronto: Random House (Penguin), 2024.

48. 'Zelensky meets with Stoltenberg in Kyiv, discusses key defense issues', *Ukrinform,* 28 September 2023; NATO, 'NATO secretary general addresses first international defence industry forum in Kyiv: There is no defence without industry', 29 September 2023, nato.int/cps/en/natohq/news_218893.htm?selectedLocale=en.

49. Yevgeniia Chukalina, 'The grain deal degenerated from a humanitarian project into a commercial one', *Izvestiia,* 3 July 2023, an interview with Gatilov.

50. NATO, 'North Atlantic Council statement on Russia's withdrawal from the Treaty on Conventional Armed Forces in Europe', 9 June 2023, nato.int/cps/en/natohq/official_texts_215586.htm?selectedLocale=en; 'North Atlantic Council statement on the allied response to Russia's withdrawal from the Treaty on Conventional Armed Forces in Europe', *NATO Update,* 7 November 2023; 'Russia formally quits post-Cold War Arms Treaty with Europe', *The Moscow Times,* 7 November 2023.

51. 'Russia notifies UN of CTBT ratification withdrawal', *Interfax,* 3 November 2023; for the 44 signatures requirement, see *The Comprehensive Nuclear-Test-Ban Treaty,* Annex 2, ctbto.org/our-mission/the-treaty; US Department of State,

'Russia's planned withdrawal of its CTBT ratification', *Press Statement*, Antony J. Blinken, 2 November 2023, state.gov/russias-planned-withdrawal-of-its-ctbt-ratification/.

52. General'niy shtab ZSU/ General Staff of the Armed Forces of Ukraine, 'Operativna informatsiia stanom na 06.00 17 zhovtnia 2023. . . .', *Facebook*, 17 October 2023, facebook.com/GeneralStaff.ua/posts/pfbid02xQdq5uSoxyYfm4G3yS2JiVSYcaoQAZ4DvrDL5D2KLXQnckY8mQUdKiuYnuWXumdVl; 'Ukraine says strikes Russian occupied airfields in East', *The Moscow Times*, 17 October 2023.

53. 'Press-konferentsiia po itogam vizita v Kitai', *Kremlin.ru*, 18 October 2023, kremlin.ru/events/president/news/72532; Natasha Bertrand, Oren Liebermann, 'US has provided Ukraine long-range ATACMS missiles, sources say', *CNN Politics*, 17 October 2023; David E. Sanger, Lara Jakes, Marc Santora, Constant Méheurt, John Ismay, 'Ukraine uses powerful American-supplied missiles for first time', *New York Times*, 17 October 2023.

54. 'Nearly 1400 Russian troops, 55 tanks eliminated over past 24 hours', *The New Voice of Ukraine*, 20 October 2023.

55. 'Konflikt s Ukrainoi: Otsenki oktiabria 2023 goda', *Levada tsentr*, 31 October 2023; 'Konflikt s Ukrainoi: Otsenki noiabria 2023 goda', *Levada tsentr*, 8 December 2023. These surveys were conducted on 19–25 October and 23–29 November among slightly over 1,600 people 18 years of age and older throughout the Federation.

56. General'niy shtab ZSU, 'Orientovni vtrati protivnika sklali', *Telegram*, 12 November 2023, t.me/GeneralStaffZSU/10888; 'Over 1,000 Russian troops eliminated in Ukraine over past 24 hours, says General Staff', *The New Voice of Ukraine*, 12 November 2023. For Russian official, all is well, accounts, read *Rossiiskaia Gazeta* (https://rg.ru).

57. See, e.g. Richard Haass, Charles Kupchan, 'Redefining success in Ukraine', *Foreign Affairs*, 17 November 2023; Eugene Rumer, Andrew S. Weiss, 'It's time to end magical thinking about Russia's defeat', *The Wall Street Journal*, 16 November 2023; Liana Fix, Michael Kimmage, 'A containment strategy for Ukraine', *Foreign Affairs*, 25 November 2023.

58. US Department of Defense, Joseph Clark, 'Austin reaffirms U.S. support during Ukraine visit', *DOD News*, 20 November 2023; 'Biden administration announces new security assistance for Ukraine', *DOD News*, 20 November 2023.

59. 'IRIS-T, chariady i drugoe oruzhe: Pistorius ob'iavil o novom pakete pomoshchi Ukraine', *RBK-Ukrayna*, 21 November 2023, rbc.ua/ukr/news/iris-t-snaryadi-ta-insha-zbroya-pistorius-1700572228.htm.

60. Dima Shvetys, 'Fire tracks: An updated survey of anti-war railway sabotage in Russia', *Mediazona*, 6 October 2023, en.zona.media/article/2023/10/06/sabotage-map; Natalie Musumeci, 'Protesting the Ukraine war is banned in Russia, so young people are sabotaging trains and railroad tracks instead: UK intel', *Business Insider*, 6 November 2023; 'Russia opens "terrorism" inquiry over train derailment', *The Moscow Times*, 11 November 2023.

61. 'In a devastating blow, Ukraine's SBU destroys key railway tunnel connecting Russia and China', *The New Voice of Ukraine*, 30 December 2023; 'Severomuiskiy tonnel': istoriia stroitel'stva, kharakteristiki i krupneishie ChP',

Kommersant, 1 December 2023; Maryna Shashkova, Julia Struck, 'SBU strikes again: Another train blown up on critical Russian rail line', *Kyiv Post*, 1 December 2023.

62. 'Mikhaylo Podoliak @Podolyak_M', X, 4 December 2023, Twitter.com/Podolyak_M/status/1731666848029036585?ref_src=twsrc%5Egoogle%7Ctwcamp%5Eserp%7Ctwgr%5Etweet.

63. 'Itogi goda s vladimirom putinym', *Kremlin.ru*, 14 December 2023, kremlin.ru/events/president/news/72994.

64. For background, see Michael Kimmage, 'Born in the bloodlands: Ukraine and the future of the European project', *Foreign Affairs*, 22 August 2023.

65. Sonam Sheth, 'The angry wives of Russian soldiers are becoming a thorn in Vladimir Putin's sides', *Business Insider*, 29 December 2023; 'Ukraine retaliates against Russian mass missile attack with mass drone attack', *The New Voice of Ukraine*, 30 December 2023; '14 chelovek pogibli v Belgorode v rezul'tate obstrela VSU: chto izvestno k etomu momentu', *Rossiiskaia Gazeta*, 30 December 2023; 'Minoborony soobshchilo ob obstrele Belgoroda kassetnymi boepripasami', *Vedomosti*, 30 December 2023.

66. 'Ukraine, Russia swap hundreds of POWS in U.A.E.-mediated deal', *RFE/RL*, 3 January 2024; 'V Rossiiu iz ukrainskogo plena vozvrashcheny 248 voennykh, Ukraina zaiavila, chto vernula 230 chelovek', *Kommersant*, 3 January 2024.

67. Dmitrii Medvedev, 'My nikogda ne liubili frantsuzov. . . .', *Telegram*, 3 January 2024, t.me/medvedev_telegram/429; for the French statement, see diplomatie.gouv.fr/fr/dossiers-pays/ukraine/evenements/article/ukraine-q-r-extrait-du-point-de-presse-03-01-24.

68. See, e.g., 'Russia's political clown Medvedev calls French "frog eaters" and "f*gs" in unhinged post', *The New Voice of Ukraine*, 4 January 2024; 'Medvedev labels French diplomats "Scum, bastards, freaks"', *RT International*, 3 January 2024.

69. On this, see Katrina Vanden Heuvel, 'Ukraine and the end of magical thinking', *The Nation*, 20 December 2023; Constant Méheut, 'Russia retakes some land hard won by Ukraine during counteroffensive', *New York Times*, 28 December 2023; Sonam Sheth, 'The Russia-Ukraine war appears to be at a stalemate. But soldiers on both sides are losing at the front lines', *Business Insider*, 5 December 2023.

70. 'U.S. suspends military aid to Ukraine – White House', *The New Voice of Ukraine*, 12 January 2024; 'NATO-Ukraine Council meets, Allies pledge further air defence', *NATO Update*, 10 January 2024.

71. Institute for the Study of War (ISW), 'Russian offensive campaign assessment, January17, 2024', understandingwar.org/backgrounder/russian-offensive-campaign-assessment-january-17-2024; Rudy Ruitenberg, 'US, France to lead artillery coalition for Ukraine', *Defense News*, 18 January 2024.

72. 'NATO chiefs discuss deterrence and defence priorities', *NATO Update*, 18 January 2024.

73. Republic of Estonia. Ministry of Defence, 'Baltic countries to build defensive installations on their borders', 19 January 2024, kaitseministeerium.ee/en/news/baltic-countries-build-defensive-installations-their-borders.

74. The Ministry of Foreign Affairs of the Russian Federation, 'Foreign Minister Sergey Lavrov's statement . . . on Russia's foreign policy performance in 2023 . . .', 18 January 2024, mid.ru/en/foreign_policy/news/1926392/.

75. 'Peskov said that the SVO will continue until all its goals are achieved', *TASS*, 14 February 2024, tass.ru/politika/19988073.

76. Lorne Cook, Samuel Petrequin, 'EU seals US$54B aid package for Ukraine despite Hungary's objections', *Global News*, 1 February 2024.

77. 'Strecha s aktivom uchastnikov foruma "Vse dlia pobedy!"', *Kremlin.ru*, 2 February 2024, kremlin.ru/events/president/news/73368.

78. Prime minister of Canada, 'Prime minister visits Kyiv and announces additional support for Ukraine', 24 February 2024.

79. 'NATO secretary general's statement on the second anniversary of Russia's full-scale invasion of Ukraine', *NATO Update*, 24 February 2024; 'Trudeau calls Putin a "coward" and a "weakling" for quashing opposition', *YouTube*, 24 February 2024.

80. 'Poslanie Prezidenta Federal'nomu Sobraniiu', *Kremlin.ru*, 29 February 2024, kremlin.ru/events/president/news/73585.

81. Legion "Svoboda Rossii", 'PGT. Tetkino, Kurskoi oblast polnost'iu pod kontrolem rossiiskikh ozvoboditel'nykh sil', *Telegram*, 12 March 2024, t.me/legionoffreedom/1119; Legion "Svoboda Rossii", 'Sovmestnoe zaiavlenie Legiona "Svoboda Rossii" . . .', *Telegram*, 13 March 2024, t.me/legionoffreedom/1129.

82. 'The Ministry of Defence showed damaged equipment of saboteurs in the Belgorod region', *RBC.ru*, 12 March 2024; 'V Ivanovo poterpel krushenie voenno-transportnyi samolet Il-76', *RIA Novosti*, 12 March 2024; for the denials, RIA Novosti, 'Informatsiia o zakhode v. . .', *Telegram*, 12 March 2024, t.me/rian_ru/234931.

83. 'Konflikt s Ukrainoi: otsenki kontsa 2023 – nachala 2024', *Levada-tsentr*, 6 February 2024, levada.ru/2024/02/06/konflikt-s-ukrainoj-otsenki-kontsa-2023-nachala-2024-goda/.

84. 'Switzerland agrees to Zelenskiy's request to host peace summit', *RFE/RL*, 15 January 2024.

85. 'Russian missile strikes on Odesa kill 20, injure more than 70', *Meduza*, 15 March 2024; Oleksandr Gimanov, 'Russia strikes kill 20, including rescuers, in "vile" Odesa attack', *The Moscow Times*, 15 March 2024.

86. 'Zasedanue kollegii FSB Rossii', *Kremlin.ru*, 19 March 2024, kremlin.ru/events/president/news/73678; 'Russia bombards Kyiv as Zelensky calls for more air defence', *Euronews*, 21 March 2024.

87. Generalnyi shtab ZSU, 'Urasheno . . .', *Telegram*, 24 March 2024, t.me/GeneralStaffZSU/13834; Komanduvach Povitrianikh Sil Mikola Oleshchuk, 'Nebo i more odnogo kol'oru! . . . Krim – NASH!', *Telegram*, 23 March 2024, t.me/ComAFUA/240.

88. 'Chislo postradavshikh pri terakte v "Krokus siti kholle" vozroslo do 360', *TASS*, 27 March 2024.

89. 'Vladimir Putin obratilsia k rossiianam posle terakta v "Krokus Citi". Video i stenogramma', *Rossiiskaia Gazeta*, 23 March 2024; Putin in a video, TASS.

'Rossiiskoe obshchestvo na fone terakta v "Krokus" pokaz . . .', *Telegram*, 25 March 2024, t.me/tass_agency/239950.

90. 'Peskov: Rossiia nakhoditsia v sostoianin voiny, kazhdy dolzhen eto ponimat', *Agumenty i fakty*, 22 March 2024; 'Kremlin says Russia in a "state of war"', *The Moscow Times*, 22 February 2024.

91. 'Konflikt s Ukrainoi: massovye otsenki marta 2024 goda', *Levada Tsentr*, 4 April 2024, levada.ru/2024/04/04/konflikt-s-ukrainoj-massovye-otsenki-marta-2024-goda/.

92. Phillips P. OBrian, 'Analysis: House passes Ukraine aid: How it happened, what it signifies', *Kyiv Post*, 21 April 2024; Victoria Lukovenko, 'Russia claims advances near Chasiv Yar as Ukraine hails new aid', *The Moscow Times*, 21 April 2024.

93. Quoted in Katerina Tishchenko, 'V Rossii isterika iz-za reshenii o pomoshchi SShA Ukraine i konfiskatsii aktivov', *Ukrainskaia pravda*, 20 April 2024; 'Otvet ofitsial'nogo predstavitelia MID Rossii M.V. Zakharovoi na vopros CMI . . . SShA finansovoi pomoshchi Ukraine', *MID*, 21 April 2024, mid.ru/ru/foreign_policy/news/1945280/.

94. Dmitrii Medvedev, 'Eto bylo golosovanie radostnykh shtatovskikh ubliudkov: . . .', *Telegram*, 20 April 2024, t.me/medvedev_telegram/483?ref=en.thebell.io.

95. 'Konflikt s ukrainoi: osnovnye indikatory, otvetstvennost', povody dlia bespokoistva, ugroza stolknoveniia s nato i primeneniia iadernogo oruzhiia', *Levada-tsentr*, 7 July 2024.

Chapter 4

Putin as *Vozhd*

MIRROR, MIRROR ON THE WALL

After two decades of asking the magic mirror on the wall who was the strongest leader of all, a tamed mirror might have answered that Putin had earned an almost invincible image as leader, or *vozhd*, an old term meaning a chieftain who embodies all of Russia.[1] If the mirror could provide reasons for its judgements, there would be notable changes proffered after February 2014, and still more after February 2022. Before those years, Putin had almost single-handedly saved Russia from the soul-destroying crises of the 1990s, re-established his country's status as a major power, assured political stability and restored economic solvency to its people. His decisions related to Crimea in 2014 solidified the reflection of invincibility in the mirror, at least for Russians; his decisions in 2022 saw the first cracks begin to spread in that same mirror.

TURNING VICTORY INTO DEFEAT

The Ukrainian military surge in September 2022 shook Putin's stature as wartime leader. Nationalists who had been cheering Russia's reluctant warriors on, clamouring for annexed territory and urging the total defeat of Ukraine saw their dreams up-ended. They blamed Russia's military leadership, demanded that Putin take immediate action and started even to question his intentions.

A few Russian media personalities dared, very cautiously, to speak up for more transparency. Some public groups and individuals, also cautiously, recommended that peace talks start; others called for mass mobilization. These approaches indirectly challenged the *vozhd*'s decision making and spread doubt about the state-controlled news. The new reality prompted Western voices to speculate, yet again, about Putin's imminent downfall due to competing internal forces.[2]

The Putin team needn't have worried. His popularity had reached astronomical heights before the sudden Ukrainian victories in the Kharkiv region in September. According to the All-Russia Centre for the Study of Public Opinion (VTsIOM), a state-funded polling agency, by 11 September 2022 'trust in Putin' had reached an 81.5 per cent approval rating and his United Russia (UR) supporters won easily in municipal and local elections held across the country a few days later. Two other mainstream polling companies drew similar conclusions.[3] Western and Russian naysayers notwithstanding, Ukraine's counter-offensive caused barely a ripple in the wave of Russian public enthusiasm for their leader.

If Putin had any political problems, they lay within his inner circles, not with the public. Yet, most of the oligarchs and *siloviki*, the systemic opposition and senior military officers appeared to share Putin's view of the West as duplicitous and anti-Russia. Even if, in September 2022, the SVO seemed directionless to moderates among the elite and nationalists alike, they had little choice but to bet on Putin and the newly dominant military caste. But they needed the war to be won.[4]

So did Putin. Although he kept up a busy schedule as 2022 wound down, meeting with senior officials, Russian interest groups and foreign dignitaries, often in televised moments, his personal uncertainty was exposed by the cancellation or postponement of major annual public occasions, such as his address to the Federal Assembly, the Q&A political event (Priamaia liniia s Vladimirom Putinym) and year-end major press conferences. State-controlled media offered facile explanations for these unusual scheduling changes, but subtle questioning grew louder: 'Where is Putin?'

There appeared to be a temporary loss of control. The mass movement of young men out of the country as partial mobilization brought the war closer to millions of Russians who had been disengaged from it, caught officialdom unprepared. So, too, did media acknowledgement of 'minor' defeats, news about the Kerch bridge explosion and spreading photos of missiles hitting Kyiv and other Ukrainian cities.[5] Yet, it was still not clear that the majority of Russians were bothered about the war. At least one knowledgeable scholar suggested that the West's determination to isolate Russia from the world's economic and political world helped the already oppressive state isolate its population from reality. The Kremlin was able to stoke the already intuitive and state-promoted belief in Russia that the West was 'Russophobic and hypocritical' unimpeded, keeping the public on Putin's side as the guardian of their national security against foreign inroads.[6]

His seventieth birthday, 7 October 2022, was greeted with little public fanfare in Russia while he spent much of the day in meetings in St. Petersburg with the CIS heads of state. The one grandiose moment came when Patriarch Kirill proclaimed that 'God put you in power so that you could perform a service of special importance and of great responsibility for the fate of the country and the people entrusted to your care'.[7] The Russian Orthodox Church (Moscow Patriarchate) was a resolute supporter of Putin's war in Ukraine, believing it to be a matter of defending the 'Russian World' (Russkiy mir) against alien Western influences.

Although the term *Russkiy mir* refers to Russia's political and cultural sphere of influence in practice, Orthodoxy takes it to encompass a spiritual realm encompassing Russians everywhere; that is, a cultural-linguistic group at home and abroad (the diaspora) with unique 'Russian' values that warrant protection. Since the Church is usually ranked among the top three most trusted institutions in Russia, along with the presidency and the army, Orthodoxy serves as an important spiritual prop for Putin's brand of conservatism.[8]

Questions of Succession

As mismanagement of the war became increasingly obvious, murmurs about removing Putin grew louder, though still mostly from Russians abroad. Although no-one could foresee a popular uprising, talk of palace coups led either by disgruntled oligarchs or angry generals, or an in-house political upheaval in the name of moderates such as Aleksei Kudrin or Sergei Sobyanin, made the rounds.[9]

The anti-Putin chorus grew louder after Russia's embarrassing retreat from Kherson, though still muted when it came to action. No Russian potential leader dared suggest giving occupied territories back to Ukraine, nor would they propose any change in the course of the war that would endanger their own places of privilege. Above all, none would give up Crimea.[10]

Former president (2008–2012), long-time prime minister and suddenly turned hawk, Dmitry Medvedev, was still available as well. But there is no evidence that he had either a popular base or a supportive clique among the *siloviki*. He was, in fact, the high-level politician most loyal to Putin, with whom he had worked since the early 1990s. Removed from the prime minister's post in January 2020 and named Deputy Head of the Security Council as compensation, and still head of the UR party, Medvedev added the newly created position as first Deputy Chair of the Military Industrial Commission to his portfolio in December 2022. The Commission is chaired by Putin, but the decree announcing the appointment allows the first Deputy to call and conduct meetings, create working groups and set up councils. This is also Medvedev's role in the Security Council, which Putin chairs. Many would say he is little more than Putin's frontman in the UR, commonly known as 'Putin's Party'. If Putin steps down or is forced out, Medvedev will go down with him.[11]

After years of building up nationalist myths that appealed to the Russian population, fulfilling socio-economic promises and stifling political opposition, the very notion of a successor to Putin was anathema to the majority of Russians. Even though his charisma may have been waning and his image as strongman wavering, there were no viable alternatives as 2022 closed out.[12]

The Decision to Invade – Re-Visited

While delivering a speech confirming the annexations, Putin was open about a central, if long disguised, motivation for launching the military assault on Ukraine. The referendums helped redress the 'catastrophic' separation of Russians from their Fatherland in 1991, he said, while rejecting the idea that he was trying to restore the USSR. Instead, he claimed to be restoring the historical unity of Russians, and called on Ukraine to negotiate – meaning Kyiv should give in to the inevitable. As the speech turned into a harangue, Putin raged at the West whose 'dictatorship', he said, had the 'features of Satanism'.[13] The Russian leader thereby portrayed his invasion as a matter of redressing historical grievances and also part of a competition between civilizations.[14]

The State Duma adopted laws on annexation unanimously on 3 October and the Federation Council approved them the next day, also unanimously. When Putin signed the laws only hours later, he made official the appointments of acting heads of the new 'Russian' regions: Denis Pushilin in the DPR, Leonid Pasechnik in the LPR, Vladimir Saldo in the Kherson region, and Yevgeny Balitsky in the Zaporozhye region.

A majority of Russians welcomed the territorial acquisitions. While Western and Ukrainian governments and peoples fulminated about Russia's egregious land grab, the overall Russian sentiment was reflected in the words of Olga Zanko, deputy chair of the Duma's Committee for the Development of Civil Society:

> We are witnesses of history. Novorossia is returning home again. They will tell their grandchildren about it, write about it in textbooks, make films. And we see it with our own eyes. We see how Russia has risen from its knees again and is becoming stronger every day. Becoming stronger thanks to each of us. Thanks to real men who do not stand in lines at the border, but take up arms to defend the country, thanks to women, teachers, scientists, workers, volunteers, who each in their place bring the common victory closer.[15]

Valdai Speech, 27 October 2022

It was at the Valdai International Discussion Club on 27 October that Putin framed the ideological basis for his SVO. The title for the session led the witness: 'The World After Hegemony: Justice and Security for All'. Organizers claimed that 'experts', political leaders, diplomats and economists from 40 countries attended, among them delegations from Afghanistan, Brazil, Egypt, Turkey, China, India, Indonesia, Iran, Kazakhstan, Uzbekistan and South Africa. Although representatives from Germany, France and the United States showed up, to all intents and purposes the West was a no-show.

That may have been just as well, for Putin opened his welcoming address by accusing the West of inciting war in Ukraine and instigating provocations around Taiwan, thereby destabilizing the world's food and energy markets. Most of the remainder of the speech was a tirade against the West for its 'bloody' and 'dirty' attempts to regain hegemony over the world. He condemned Western countries for disregarding any culture not their own and the United States for its 'arrogant desire for world leadership'. Russia, on the other hand, 'being an independent, original civilization, has never considered and does not consider itself an enemy of the West', and he, Putin, has tried from his first year in office to build stable relations with the West and NATO only to receive a consistent 'no' at every turn. 'Russia does not challenge the elites of the West', Putin continued. Instead, 'it simply defends its right to exist and develop freely'.[16]

Whether the long and rambling diatribe was an outburst of frustration over the course of war in Ukraine or a deeply ingrained vision of the world, it certainly set out a dividing line in global affairs.

MANAGING THE FEDERATION IN WARTIME

In addition to a Government Coordination Council set up in October 2022 to manage the economy with Mishustin in the chair, the presidential administration began discussing the abolition of direct election for mayors in the regions. Regional governors, most of them from the UR, would prefer to appoint mayors in cities under their jurisdiction, claiming that this would facilitate coordination with the central government. Several governors suggested that elections were too expensive at a time when funds should be dedicated to the SVO. The political opposition, what there was left of it, objected because it is at the municipal level that they wield their only influence.[17]

Defections were made more difficult as well. Passports for bureaucrats with access to secrets had already been confiscated, and border guards knew who to prevent from leaving. Resignations from government were out of the question because they could be deemed a treasonous act and, in fact, officials hoping to defect might find that they had nowhere to go.

When Putin declared martial law in the occupied areas of Ukraine, he also placed Russia's regions on various levels of alert; that is, 'response regimes'. This official designation gave local officials greater powers when it came to recruiting both for the military and for the economy. Areas close to the occupied parts of Ukraine were designated 'medium level' response. Russia's Central Federal District (Moscow region), was set at 'high-alert regime' and the remainder of the country at the 'basic response' level. At the medium level, authorities can restrict exit and entry, and even movement within their jurisdiction. Governors everywhere set up operational headquarters to manage the military mobilization with the help of security forces. When the first mobilization campaign ended, these agencies were not dissolved.[18]

Maintaining the Image in the Mirror

On 25 November, after some hesitation and much preparation, Putin met with mothers of soldiers fighting in Ukraine, just two days ahead of the celebration of Mother's Day in Russia. These 17 mothers were very carefully chosen. They represented different sections of the country: Dagestan, Krasnodar, Chechnya, Tula, Khakassia, Sakha, St. Petersburg and so on. None of them were there to complain about the war or conscription, though they criticized the red tape involved in applying for assistance and medical support for the wounded. They all spoke of national unity and the heroics of their sons, several of whom had been killed or wounded. One of the mothers represented the All-Russia People's Front (Obshcherossiiskii narodnyi front – ONF), a youth-run organization founded by Putin in 2011. Another hailed from the LPR, whose son fought for the *'Russkiy mir'*, she said, and yet another came from the Kuban Cossack community. There was a Jew and a Muslim. The last one to speak was a UR film-maker who was then encouraged by Putin to make documentaries in support of the 'special military operation'. The word 'invasion' was never uttered and, although the term 'war zone' came up in relation to the SVO, the word 'war' itself was heard only in references to the events of 1941–1945.[19]

In his opening remarks as published by the Kremlin, Putin claimed to share their pain and insisted that images from the internet 'cannot be trusted'. Opposition and other 'mothers' groups complained that Putin's select few were there to serve as propaganda agents in support of the SVO. For example, the Council of Wives and Mothers called the meeting 'shameful', and a member of that Council, Olga Tsukanova, labelled them 'pocket mothers' in a video posted on Telescope.[20] As a result, the Procurator General's Office (PGO) ordered that the Council be excluded from *VKontakte*. Based in St.

Petersburg, *VKontakte* is the largest Russian in-house social media network. Originally private and independent, it is now owned by Gazprombank and one of its subsidiaries. Its CEO is Vladimir Kiriyenko, son of Sergei Kiriyenko, first deputy chief of Putin's presidential administration.

Early in December 2022, during a televised meeting of the presidential Human Rights Council, Putin expounded on the Russian version of human rights, contrasting them with what he believed were Western values:

> The new fashionable Western values have been brought to the point of absurdity, they are simply destructive. It is unlikely that they will be accepted in other parts of the world, but they will bring a lot of harm.
>
> The source of these values is not accidental. The Western concept of rights and freedoms is based on the understanding of man as an autonomous individual. But for many peoples and civilizations, for the majority, individualism is not the main value. National models should take into account religious, historical, cultural specifics.[21]

Under no circumstances would individualism override the rights of the collective in Putin's ideal Russia.

No reason was given for the abrupt cancellation of Putin's annual end-of-year press conference in 2022, for the first time since 2012, though it is reasonable to assume that it was because the administration would not be able to avoid embarrassing questions about Ukraine.[22] The conference usually invited some 500 carefully vetted journalists from Russian and foreign media. When, soon afterwards, Putin postponed his annual address to the Federal Assembly, officials insisted that the president was too busy with the SVO to spend time on these events. Yet his public presence as commander-in-chief seemed to have been fading as well. Military decisions were left for Shoigu to announce. Western media began debating whether Putin's relative absence meant he was shifting blame, losing control or planning something dramatic.[23]

Opponents home and abroad circulated gossip that Putin was ill, insane or otherwise physically and mentally unfit for leadership. For example, the head of Ukraine's military intelligence, Kyrylo Budanov, told ABC News in January 2023 that the Russian president 'has terminal cancer and will die soon'. He said the same thing six months earlier, but at that time granted the Russian president a few more years. Stories that Putin suffered from Parkinson's disease, prostate cancer and disease-driven erratic behaviour regularly made the rounds.[24] In January 2023 Zelensky told an audience at the World Economic Forum at Davos that Putin might not even be alive.[25] Russia watchers began predicting what might happen on Russia's ultimate defeat.[26]

Perhaps aware that he needed to appear as a leader too busy for the big public performances, towards the end of December 2022 Putin chaired multiple televised Cabinet meetings, a session with Lukashenka, and also with the acting heads of the LPR and DPR. He hosted an awards ceremony for individuals described as leaders and 'patriots' in wide-ranging fields, and met with military personnel, 'Mother Heroines', teachers, and so on. At an expanded Ministry of Defence Board session, he claimed that Russia was fighting 'the military potential and capabilities of almost all major NATO countries'.[27]

It was also at this time that the Kremlin issued a video message marking the Day of Security Workers, exhorting them 'to firmly suppress the activities of foreign intelligence services, to quickly identify traitors, spies and saboteurs'.[28] The hunt was on.

The fact that 57 per cent of respondents to a Levada Centre survey conducted from 24 to 30 November 2022 said they preferred a transition to peace talks, may have been a consideration behind Putin's apparent fade into the background. Although over 70 per cent still supported the Russian army, respondents in the age group 18–24 were nearly 70 per cent in favour of ending the war. The Kremlin's narrative held, however. Asked why so many countries condemned Russia's actions in Ukraine, the four most common answers were: they were subservient to the United States (36 per cent); the world was always against Russia (31 per cent); they are afraid that Russia will deal with them as they have with Ukraine (19 per cent) and; disinformation by the Western media (19 per cent). Only a few agreed with what could be deemed 'Western' opinions: they consider that Russia has violated international law and Ukrainian rights (17 per cent); they are angry at the actions of Russia and sympathize with Ukraine (12 per cent). These opinions were expressed in 1,601 face-to-face, confidential interviews in the respondents' homes.[29]

The polls showed that, even if support for the SVO was no longer unequivocal, the traditional tenet that Russia was surrounded by enemies still rang true for most Russians who paid attention to international affairs.

In end-of-year surveys, 2022, state-funded pollsters provided the Kremlin with more comfort: FOM, for example, claimed that 78 per cent of Russians approved the activities of the president and 77 per cent trusted him. VTsIOM found that 74.3 per cent approved Putin's activities and 78.1 per cent trusted him.[30] Accurate or not, Putin could read these results as overwhelming faith in his leadership.

PUTINISM ADJUSTED

The PGO's quickness to move against a mother's group was symptomatic of the evolution of Putinism. The war in Ukraine consolidated various strands that had come to represent Putinism and turn it into a definable ideology that could now be characterized as part of a centuries-old continuum of Slavophiles defending Russia against Westernizers. Putin had made this plain in an essay published in July 2021: 'On the Historical Unity of Russians and Ukrainian', in which he insisted that the West was exploiting Ukraine to undermine and weaken the *Russkiy mir*, by which he meant Russia, Belarus and Ukraine. Aggressive rhetoric against liberal-democracy and a fierce defence of what Putin believes are Russian values: authoritarian political practices and extensive economic paternalism had moved to the top of Putinism's characteristics.[31]

Top down orchestration of the war also revealed the degree to which the regime had become personalized. By claiming that he was holding off Western inroads, he turned the war into a clash between good and evil with him as the white knight. No one in the State Duma, the Federation Council or, with the exception of Yabloko, the mainstream political parties, dared – or perhaps even wanted – to oppose him. His government's blatant use of law enforcement, the courts and legislation to silence any opposition to the war; its vehement denial of the obvious when confronted with information and photos of death and destruction in Ukraine, or stories of rape, torture and looting; and its unabashed eagerness to occupy and annex territories the world knew was not Russia's, erased any respect Putin may once have earned in the West. The rapid descent into a zero-sum regime meant that Putin would have to win in Ukraine, or lose everything.

He made that clear himself during a combative speech delivered at the military parade on Red Square, 9 May 2023, where he again asserted that the West had launched a 'real war' against Russia and that 'the future of our statehood and our people depends on you', meaning Russia's Armed Forces.[32]

By that time, the basic tenets of Putinism had come to represent a re-formulated Russian ideology, the core of which was Russia's assumption of historical uniqueness. Russian 'values' were presented as if they had remained unchanged for centuries. Putin's emphasis upon political sovereignty, populism and anti-Western sentiments were perceived as part of that continuum, encompassing the past, present and future. If Putinism is, in fact, a reflection of the Russian psyche, as Mikhail Suslov suggests, the possibility of Western-style liberal democracy ever gaining a real toe-hold in Russia is slight.[33]

Meetings with State Duma Party Leaders

After meeting separately in February 2023 with leaders of the main parties in the State Duma, the Communist Party of the Russian Federation (CPRF – Gennady Zyuganov), the Liberal Democratic Party of Russia (LDPR – Leonid Slutsky), A Just Russia (Sergei Mironov), New People (Aleksei Nechaev) and the UR (Vladimir Vasiliev) in that order, Putin said that he was looking for feedback on domestic socio-economic policies prior to his already-postponed annual presentation to the Federal Assembly then re-set for 21 February 2023. Needless to say, he did not expect, nor did he get, anything but absolute support for the war in Ukraine. They all echoed in one way or another Zyuganov's depiction of the SVO as defence against a 'crusade declared against our civilization, the entire Russian world'.[34]

Annual Address to the Federal Assembly, 21 February 2023

Delivering the address to the Federal Assembly only days before the one-year anniversary of the invasion, Putin vowed to press on with the 'special operation'. He repeated the official narrative even more aggressively than previously: Western actions forced him to launch the SVO, and the West was fuelling the conflict further in a vain hope to defeat Russia. In its turn, Russians were defending 'historical Russian lands' and those who fled the country to avoid the fighting were 'traitors'.[35]

Coming soon after rousing speeches delivered in Kyiv and Warsaw by Joe Biden, Putin's two-hour lecture to the Federal Assembly could be taken as Russia's battle cry against the West. Several parts of the speech are left to appropriate chapters ahead, but for Putin's leadership it could be called an exercise in cheerleading for Russia's armed forces, a 'rally around the flag' exhortation embellished with a litany of calumnies suffered by Russia at the hands of the West.

Other takeaways from the speech to offer glimpses of Putin's leadership profile were pledges to increase the minimum wage and provide social benefits to citizens in areas annexed from Ukraine. He again boasted that Western sanctions were not impeding the Russian economy, suspended arms control measures (New START), and urged big businesses to cut ties with the West and invest in their homeland.[36]

One day after the big address, Putin gave a short address (4 minutes) to a patriotic rally concert presented under the title, 'Glory to the Defenders of the Fatherland' (Slava zashchitnikam Otechestva), surrounded on stage by be-medalled soldiers and sailors in the Luzhniki stadium in Moscow. A statutory holiday to celebrate veterans of all Russia's wars, the Defender of the Fatherland Day had long been an annual event, but was granted special significance in 2022. The carefully orchestrated occasion featured war-supporting performances, one of them a band of accordion players wearing caps with the letter 'Z' (one of the symbols of the war) on them, presentations by wounded veterans of the Donbas civil war, and people in traditional Russian clothing from around the country. To make certain that the televised show was seen as a sign that the SVO was widely supported by Russians, public sector workers were given a day off to attend. Free tickets went to senior bureaucrats and UR party members, and concert goers were bussed or trained in from distant locations. The stadium was opened up to everyone at the last moment so that it would appear full. Flag wavers abounded.[37]

In that same week, Putin granted an interview for the channel Rossiia-1, in which he repeated accusations that NATO was participating directly by providing Ukraine with weapons and training and that its ambition was to dismember the Russian Federation. Polls suggested that this message was still believed by a majority of the Russian population, who also continued to support him as their *vozhd*.[38]

Out of Touch

According to a defector from the Federal Guard Service, the body responsible for the president's safety, Putin was becoming increasingly isolated from the 'outside world'. Gleb Karakulov told an interviewer that Putin did not use Internet or a mobile phone and got all his information from trusted inner circle personnel and Russian TV. He places 'barriers between himself and the world . . . His perception of reality is distorted'.[39] Although the depiction originated with a hostile witness, there was a ring of reality to it.

Aware that he needed to be seen, Putin flew to Crimea to celebrate the ninth anniversary of what Russians call the 'reunification' of the peninsula with Russia. Coming days after the International Criminal Court (ICC) issued a warrant for his arrest for alleged 'unlawful deportation' of thousands of Ukrainian children, Putin's visit to Crimea and a surprise side trip to Mariupol by helicopter dominated the Russian media. State TV carried a video of Putin driving himself around Mariupol at night in the company of Deputy Prime Minister Marat Khusnullin. The carefully choreographed 'spontaneous' tour exposed no signs of damage to viewers; rather, they saw a relatively busy highway, with cars and buses, bright road signs and a busy city centre. Putin also walked through restored buildings, such as the Mariupol Chamber Philharmonic building, with Khusnullin gushing in the background. Uninformed viewers would have no inkling of the devastation wreaked on the city by Russian shelling.[40] He chatted with small groups of people, presumably all carefully selected for state TV and social media platforms.

The Mariupol visit was the closest Putin had been to the front line and served both as a response to the ICC (he toured a children's centre) and to hawks at home who had hinted that he was increasingly out of touch with the actual war effort. The state-controlled media was effusive about the wondrous recovery of Mariupol, and responded to the ICC's warrant at first by ignoring it and, when the news had clearly leaked out in Russia, by attacking the credibility of the court.[41]

Prior to leaving Moscow for Crimea, Putin chaired a video-conference dedicated to the social-economic development of Crimea and Sevastopol. He and his cabinet-member interlocutors bragged of enormous advances made in almost all sectors (e.g. economic, health, education, infrastructure construction) in the peninsula since 2014, with special emphasis on facilities for children and orphans. He told an interviewer that Russia had not wanted confrontation with Ukraine; rather, Russian authorities were forced to launch the SVO 'precisely because they [Crimeans] were attacked, . . . by the Nazis'.[42] These three days of active participation in domestic and international affairs, and his creative delusions about Crimea, were intended, in part, to offset whatever little Russians might have learned of the ICC decision.

Attempting to legitimize annexing territories for public consumption, Putin also flew into Kherson by military helicopter and then visited the Vostok National Guard HQ in the Luhansk region. Both trips were to military headquarters and were announced after the fact when the Kremlin released videos for public viewing. Their dates were not made public. He heard reports from commanders, wished the troops a happy Easter and distributed icons. Neither Shoigu nor Gerasimov accompanied the president because, Peskov said, it was too great a risk for all of them to travel together. They participated in the meetings by video link, leaving Putin to play at front-line leader.[43]

Outwardly unworried about any problems his people and country might be facing, Putin demonstrated a calm complacency when he told workers at an aviation plant in Ulan-Ude, Buryatia, that 2022 had been a beneficial year for Russia because it left them 'more sovereign and independent in the field of economy and finance'. He called the actions taken by the West against Russia's economy a failure, and went on to describe the 'struggle' in Ukraine as a matter of the 'survival of Russian statehood' and a defence of the *Russkiy mir*.[44] He probably believed his own mythology.

Rumours and denials circulated in April that Putin might forego the 9 May Victory Day parade in Moscow for 'security' reasons. Unwilling to miss an opportunity to nurture patriotism on a grand scale, the traditional Moscow event was maintained. To be safe, the Federal Guard Service closed Red Square to the public a full two weeks before the annual event, the longest closure ever, and some 25 cities called off their Victory Day parades for security reasons. The Immortal Regiment march, in which Russians, among them Putin, carry photos of relatives killed in the Second World War was cancelled.[45]

On the day of the Victory Day parade, seven leaders of former Soviet republics joined Putin on Red Square: Armenian prime minister Nikol Pashinyan, Belarusan president Alyaksandr Lukashenka, Kazakh president Kassym-Jomart Tokaev, Kyrgyzstan's president Sadyr Japarov, Tajik president Emomali Rahmon, Uzbek leader Shavkat Mirziyoyev and Turkmen president Serdar Berdimuhamedow. Except for Japarov, who committed himself well in advance, these appeared to be last-minute decisions. It is not known if other leaders were invited.

PRESIDENTIAL ELECTION LOOMING

Preparations for the presidential election set for March 2024 began as early as January 2023 when Putin was named Russian politician of the previous year by VTsIOM, a rating he has been granted almost every year since 2006. State-controlled pollsters and the Levada Centre gave him high marks in terms of trust and confidence and Putin easily topped VTsIOM's telephone query about who the responders saw as Russia's top three politicians of 2022 (see table 4.1).

Setting the stage for the campaign itself, executives of the UR told members that they should take every opportunity to collate the SVO with Soviet victories in the Second World War. The Party was also instructed to conduct special financial courses for secondary school students to teach them the merits of the UR's 'People's Programme'. Weekly topics for party candidates to puff up began with the celebration of the eightieth anniversary of Soviet victory in the Battle of Stalingrad (17 July 1942–2 February 1943). UR aspirants were encouraged to apply the Stalingrad slogan, a 'line beyond which it is impossible to retreat', to the present. Lessons in courage were other matters for candidates to dwell on. To mark that anniversary more dramatically, a new monument to Stalin was unveiled at the site of the famous victory.

Table 4.1. VTsIOM's Poll on Top Politicians for 2022

Name	Percentage of Respondents
Putin	55
Mishustin	21
Lavrov	13
Shoigu	10
Zhirinovsky	5
None	7
Difficult to answer	25

Source: 'Russians name top three politicians of the year for 2022', TASS, 13 January 2023.

Putin visited the city during the celebrations, and the ruling party unleashed a campaign to portray its leader as a Stalin-like victorious wartime leader.[46]

In January 2023, Russian pundits began pondering the campaigning roles of hawks who wanted to accelerate the war effort and pragmatists who preferred to negotiate peace terms, and offering predictions of potential personnel changes in senior political ranks.[47] Regional gubernatorial elections were set for 20 regions in the fall of 2023, along with 16 elections to legislative assemblies. Polls were set up in the annexed territories of Ukraine. These served as a test for the presidential election the next year.

Western commentators began again to re-visit earlier assumptions that Russia's elite supported the war effort, concluding that some leading members of the political and business classes were losing confidence in Putin and even in the likelihood of a Russian victory in Ukraine. According to Tatiana Stanovaya, a senior fellow at the Carnegie Russia Eurasia Centre, many senior Russian officials and business leaders were tired of the hostilities and hoped for a negotiated settlement. Like Karakulov, they also saw Putin as isolated and poorly informed, though they dared not say so openly.[48] Indeed, the sanctioning regimes left Russia's oligarchs with little choice but to rally around the Kremlin. That is where their bread was buttered.

Ironically, an adamant propagandist for Putin and the SVO, *RT*'s editor-in-chief Margarita Simonyan was one of the first of the in-house image-makers to urge authorities to seek peace because Russia itself was now under attack. She offered this recommendation on TV in a programme hosted on 4 June by the most prominent proponent of the war, Vladimir Solovyov.[49] Simonyan's previous stance was an aggressive pursuit of victory. She was taken to task by other talking heads, but seeds may have been sewn.

Russia Day, 12 June 2023

Putin could not afford to cancel another annual event just as the long-awaited Ukrainian spring offensive began to chip away at Russian-held areas in Ukraine, and Russia's border regions increasingly came under attack. He had to be seen as an active *vozhd*.

On 12 June, at an elaborate celebration of Russia Day held in the Grand Kremlin Palace, Putin handed out gold medals and state prizes to individuals for their accomplishments in science, technology, literature, art, human rights, education and charitable work in 2022. His opening words set the tone, proclaiming that the public holiday was a sign of 'the inseparability of centuries-old history, the greatness and glory of the Fatherland, [and] affirms the unity of our multinational people, our devotion to our country, a warm, sincere attitude towards our beloved Fatherland'. He went on to link the awardees' accomplishments to Russian patriotism and success in the 'special military operation'. The prize winners followed suit; for instance, winner of the State Prize for Human Rights said in all seriousness that 'the SVO was a human rights operation'.[50]

Mutiny

The mutinous events in June were a shock to the Putin regime. As the dust began to settle, Peskov proclaimed that it was Putin who had saved the day by avoiding bloodshed. The president's brief open-air speech to military and security personnel who, he claimed, had safeguarded Moscow, was hailed by the state media as a 'new page in the history of the Kremlin'.[51] It was delivered at the Palace of Facets on Cathedral Square, 27 June. There were no secrets this time, the Russian mainstream media co-opted social media's playing field and spewed out 'explanations' for what happened, and carried myriad opinion pieces about Prigozhin. Only a few suggested that he was a threat to Putin's authority, or even implied that there might be weaknesses in Russia's power vertical.[52] It was left to Western analysts to treat the mutiny as the beginning of the end for Putin, and the US State Department's Blinken to insist that the affair revealed 'cracks' in Putin's hold on power.[53] These opinions also revealed more wishful thinking than thoughtful analysis.

Russian public opinion was mixed. A Levada Centre survey conducted from 22 to 28 June, that is, over the period of the mutiny, saw Shoigu's approval rate drop from 60 to 51 per cent, and Prigozhin's slip from 58 to 30 per cent. Significantly, the percentage of respondents who wanted the war to continue also fell slightly, from 48 per cent in May to 40 per cent at the end of June, and supporters of peace negotiations rose from 45 to 53 per cent. Sixty per cent were concerned that the situation in Ukraine could escalate into a Russian confrontation with NATO, a jump of 12 per cent from the same time in 2022.[54] This latter fear was a result of Putin's re-formulated narrative about the cause and course of the war. Proponents of peace talks were mainly in the younger age categories, women and people who do not get all their news from TV.

Surveys conducted by the Levada Centre a week later revealed that, (a) an unusually high percentage of respondents was 'highly aware' of the mutinous incident (92 per cent), (b) nearly half of them got their information about it from state-controlled TV (44 per cent), 29 per cent by word of mouth and the rest from the Internet, (c) support for Prigozhin fell further, to 22 per cent by July, and, (d) among authorities (e.g. Putin, Mishustin, Lavrov) only Shoigu's reputation suffered, and that only somewhat.[55] It would appear that the Russian population was in a 'wait and see' mode.

Navalny chipped in from prison, writing on Instagram that he at first thought the stories about Prigozhin's insurrection was a prank pulled on him by court officers. When he learned it was real, he wrote that the greater threat to Russia was Putin, for it was he who allowed Prigozhin to recruit convicts and brought Russia close to civil war. He pointed out that when the military columns neared Moscow, 'no one stood up to protect Putin', and that the idea that Russia was unified was a myth.[56]

In this last charge, Navalny was partly right. Russians hearing of, or seeing via social media, the unimpeded progress of the Wagner PMC from Rostov towards Moscow with no one trying to stop them, were perplexed. Several areas reported a run on their banks as individuals withdrew cash. Stores reported that people were stocking up on food supplies. Some senior officials and managers booked flights out of Moscow to safer parts of Russia and a few of the oligarchs with private jets in Moscow flew to St. Petersburg, or even to Turkey. There were no spontaneous public displays of support for Putin, or of rage against Prigozhin. Whether this was because of lack of information, an intuitive fatalism or a certain indifference towards the *vozhd* is unclear.

As the Kremlin began seeking people to blame for the Prigozhin fiasco, Putin undertook a public relations campaign to create the impression that all was well. On 28 June, he travelled to Dagestan, walked among the public shaking hands and allowing selfies, visited a mosque and toured a UNESCO historical site. His session with Sergei Melikov, head of the republic, in which they touted the area for tourism, was televised.[57] The next day, he spoke in Moscow at the opening of the annual forum of the Agency for Strategic Initiatives, titled, 'Strong Ideas for the New Times' (Sil'nye idei dlia novogo vremeni) after visiting several of its many exhibitions. The purpose of the Agency, founded in 2011, is to develop products in Russia to replace items traditionally imported from the West. He took the time also to chair a televised meeting on the development of tourism.[58]

Addressing a video-conferenced summit of Shanghai Cooperation Organization's (SCO) hosted by India, Putin thanked its members for their support during the aborted mutiny and told them that the Russian people were 'united as never before'. The entire Russian society stood as a 'united front against the attempted armed rebellion', he said disingenuously.[59]

A 'united' and loyal citizenry notwithstanding, about a month after the botched mutiny, Putin signed a law providing for 'specialized para-military enterprises' to defend Russia's borders and combat attempts at sabotage. These units will be armed by the MoD, but overseen by regional governors and under the direct control of Putin. Called 'special enterprises' they have a mandate to stop any unmanned vehicles (drones) on air, land and water and can be used for crowd control. They are authorized to fight against 'illegal armed groups'.[60] A few weeks later Putin agreed that the 200,000-person national guard (Rosgvardia) should be equipped with heavy weaponry; that is, artillery and attack helicopters.[61] Although this law was created in the name of national security, the security of the *vozhd*'s regime was more to the point.

Bills submitted to the State Duma in September 2023 permitted the National Guard to include volunteer formations within their composition. Former Wagner Group soldiers were allowed to register. These formations will be based on contracts and the volunteers will be neither military personnel, nor employees of the National Guard. They may be created directly by the president and will be managed under the same rules as volunteer units within the MoD, which has about 40 of them.[62] Members of volunteer formations must all swear an oath of allegiance before the Russian flag.

Prigozhin Killed

The question of what to do about Prigozhin came to a sudden conclusion on 23 August 2023, when he and all aboard a private jet crashed in the Tver region, near Moscow.[63] According to the plane's manifest, other senior Wagner officers among the dead were Dmitry Utkin, former GRU officer and an original member, Valery Chekalov, a logistics specialist, and several field commanders. The pilot, co-pilot and flight attendant were also Wagner employees.[64] Cause of the crash remained unknown, though speculation ran amok. At least one group linked to Wagner claimed that the plane was shot down by the MoD; Western and Ukrainian media assumed Putin ordered it; the Russian media remained vague or called it an accident; and dissidents warned that it was a clear warning to 'anyone who had any subversive thoughts' about the SVO or Russian realities in general.[65]

Navalny posted from prison: 'Here is the subtle work of Putin's killers. Shoot down/blow up a passenger plane over Russia'. Prigozhin supporters promised revenge. Peskov rejected all rumours of a political assassination as 'absolute lies', in a futile attempt to quell rampant conjecture to that effect.[66] Gossip spread that Prigozhin faked his place on the plane and was still alive and plotting somewhere, perhaps in Africa; others predicted that the event could lead to civil war. On 26 August, using genetic analysis, the Investigative Committee confirmed Prigozhin's death, thereby stifling, but not eliminating, theories that he was still alive and planning a comeback.[67]

A spokesman for the US Department of Defence told CNN that they saw no evidence that the plane was shot down by a surface-to-air missile, as Prigozhin-advocate Russian blogger GrayZone proclaimed. Other sites circulated visuals that seemed to show explosions on board the plane. In a televised conversation with the DPR's Pushilin, Putin expressed 'condolences to the families of all the victims' and said that Prigozhin 'made serious mistakes in his life, but he achieved the right results'. A full investigation was underway, he added.[68]

Makeshift memorials with flowers and placards mourning Prigozhin's death appeared spontaneously in Moscow, St. Petersburg, Novosibirsk and other centres. These were observed closely but not removed by police. Levada Centre polls in August showed that 39 per cent of Russians approved Prigozhin's actions and 37 per cent did not; 26 per cent believed that the plane crash was an accident, 20 per cent blamed Russian authorities; 16 per cent believed that Prigozhin was still alive, and 14 per cent held foreign intelligence services responsible for the deed. If these numbers were truly representative, then the Russian population appeared to have little faith in the Kremlin's narrative of events.[69]

Putin Still in Charge

It was at this moment that Peskov posted a theoretical suggestion that the scheduled presidential election might not be held, because it was 'obvious' that the incumbent would win. Putin seemed to have beaten back public opposition from aggressive right-wing nationalists.[70] Nevertheless, despite the fact that Prigozhin was dead, Surovikin dismissed and Igor Girkin, head of the Club of Angry Patriots, was in prison (see chapter 5), their supporters were still there. The Kremlin continued to clamp down on pro-war ultra-nationalist military bloggers who criticized the MoD, accused senior officers of incompetence, revealed tactical mistakes or leaked stories from disenchanted troops.[71]

So as to avoid demonstrations, Prigozhin's funeral was kept secret until after the fact. Police continued to guard the site at the Porokhovskoe cemetery in St. Petersburg for several days after the interment while cars filled with mourners, or curious sightseers, lined up at the entrance for several kilometres.[72]

Meanwhile, Putin turned his attention to securing a fifth term as president. Perhaps worried about the public reaction to the Prigozhin affair, he catered to his base by keeping inflation down and legislating social benefits for poor citizen, for troops on the ground, veterans and their families. With a fourth quarter growth spurt in the economy and the poverty level lower than it had been in decades, at 9.8 per cent, there were no economic reasons for the general population to challenge his leadership.[73]

Putin had another opportunity to vent against the West in September 2023 at the Eastern Economic Forum held in Vladivostok. There, he insisted that Ukraine's counter-offensive had failed and that it was Kyiv that refused to hold peace talks. He used the 'persecution' of Donald Trump to illustrate how 'rotten' the US political system was and complained that, while 'many' Americans wanted better relations with Russia, US officialdom saw Russia as an 'existential enemy'.[74] The growing number of attacks within Russia were conducted by Ukrainian saboteurs trained by the British secret service, he said. It is unknown how these remarks were received by participants from mainly Far Eastern countries, but they revealed a sense of unease in Putin's world view.

That sense was expressed in another way on 30 September and again on 1 October 2023 when Russia marked both the one-year anniversary of the annexation of four Ukrainian regions and the annual Ground Forces Day. For the former event, Putin released a video message in which he congratulated the peoples of the DPR, LPR, Zaporizhzhia and Kherson regions who 'made their choice – to be with their Fatherland'. Moscow celebrated the annexations, which Putin pretended was conducted 'in full compliance with international standards', with a large-scale concert on Red Square. During Ground Forces Day, Putin and Shoigu congratulated Russian troops for 'effectively carrying out their assigned tasks' without admitting to any military-related problems.

The Putin team decided that he should take a more visible international role as well. For instance, his participation in a G-20 summit via video-link on 22 November 2023 was his first direct involvement in the G-20 since 2019, having sent Lavrov in his place previously. The day before that, he participated in a virtual BRICS summit chaired by South Africa's Ramaphosa for the purpose of finding a common response to the Israel-Hamas war and, on the 23rd, he attended a CSTO session in Minsk.

His election team need not have worried. The monthly Levada Centre survey of Russian opinions about the 'conflict in Ukraine' for September again found that less than half of the respondents were paying close attention, and support for Russia's Armed Forces remained high at 72 per cent. As previously, respondents who got their news from TV were much more likely to support the military operation (80 per cent) than those who found news on Telegram channels (65 per cent), although both sets of viewers supported the Army – if not necessarily the war. At about the same time, state-funded VTsIOM and FOM surveys proclaimed that trust in Putin had risen during the first week of October, reaching 78.3 and 74 per cent approval respectively.[75]

Asked by *The Bell*'s co-founder to explain Putin's continued popularity, head of research at the Levada Centre Aleksei Levinson replied that Russians believe the war in Ukraine is an indirect conflict with the West and only Putin was capable of preserving the country's sovereignty in the face of the West's unremitting hostility. He also said that, because it was very difficult for Russians to grasp that they were fighting against fraternal Ukrainians, it was easier for them to accept that their real enemies were located in Washington and Brussels.[76]

Still taking no chances, Putin's electoral team began preparing lists of prominent people for an 'initiative group' to nominate and support him for the presidential campaign. It included a cross-section of academics, scientists, cultural and political figures. On the populist side, he signed laws allowing voting in areas under martial law, and guaranteeing wage and pension increases for military personnel in 2024.[77] After a rare public demonstration in Moscow (7 November) on the part of soldier's wives and mothers who demanded that men who had been deployed for a year be rotated away from the front line, regional officials were ordered to provide wives of soldiers their husbands' salaries as soon as possible. The protest was quickly broken up, but the fact that more were planned by this clearly influential section of the population worried the Kremlin.[78] In December, the families of men conscripted and not allowed leave posted a video on Telegram titled 'The Way Home' (Put' domoi) calling on Putin to send the soldiers home.[79]

All of a sudden, Putin was everywhere on television: opening new medical facilities in the regions via video link (Sochi, 28 November), speaking via video-conference to the World Russian People's Council (Sochi, 28 November), presenting the Volunteer of the Year Award in Moscow (28 November), attending in person the III Congress of Young Scientists (Moscow, 29 November), meeting the head of Rosfinmonitoring (Novo-Ogarevo, 30 November), chairing a session with the permanent members of the Russian Security Council (Novo-Ogarevo, 1 December), signing a decree expanding the size of Russia's Armed Forces (Kremlin, 1 December), accepting credentials from 21 new ambassadors (Kremlin, 4 December), touring the 'Russia' exhibition with a group of children (Moscow, 4 December).

Immediately following this flurry of domestic activity, Putin flew to the UAE and Saudi Arabia to court oil-producing friends and leave the impression that Russia was still a player in the Middle East even as the Israeli-Hamas struggle escalated. He was back in Moscow on 7 December just in time to deliver the opening address to the 14th VTB International Investment Forum, 'Russia Calling!' (Rossiia zovet!), and a few days after that held a combined nearly five-hour large press conference and call-in programme titled 'Results of the Year with Vladimir Putin'. The last two events, usually separate and annual, were the first since he launched the war in Ukraine.

Six days before the call-in, Putin announced his formal candidacy for the presidency.[80] Of the many groups and movements that quickly came out in his support, UR was the most important. At its party forum, Medvedev described the value of the presidency: 'It is the president . . . who consolidates our country'.[81] Indirectly, he and other speakers invoked the image of the president as *vozhd*, a designation confirmed by mainstream Russian polls that placed his approval rates at between 78 and 83 per cent for December.[82]

New Year's Address for 2024

In contrast to the previous New Year's message broadcast with military personnel standing behind him, Putin delivered the 31 December 2023 greeting with the normal Kremlin backdrop. The address was more subdued and stressed a return to normalcy and unity. Russia's successes in 2023, he said, were defence of our 'national interests, our freedom and security, our values'. Other than glowing praise for front line soldiers who, he said, were fighting for 'truth and justice', the conflict in Ukraine went unmentioned.[83]

A month or so later, in his much-hyped interview with Tucker Carlson (see chapter 9), Putin reiterated the tired explanation of why he invaded Ukraine. Starting with a half-hour explanation that Russia has an historical claim on Ukraine, he several times blamed NATO expansion for the current situation.[84]

THE ELECTION, 2024

No matter the vicissitudes of war over the spring and summer of 2023, there was no apparent decline in public support for Putin. His approval rate for April (83 per cent) and May (82 per cent), and the 68 and 67 per cent respectively of respondents who believed that the country was moving in the right direction, were consistent with earlier Levada Centre results. Asked in an open-ended question in May to name politicians whom they most trusted, Putin came out on top again (42 per cent), followed by Mishustin (18 per cent), Lavrov (14 per cent) and Shoigu (11 per cent). For the first time, Prigozhin appeared in the top ten (4 per cent).[85] His botched mutiny in June spelled an end to that brief moment of relative popularity.

After visiting Moscow, an American journalist wrote in August 2023 that sanctions appeared to have little effect on the city: 'The subway is spotless; restaurants . . . overflow; people make contactless payments for most things using their phones; there is a ridiculous concentration of luxury cars; the internet functions impeccably, as it does in all of Russia'. It was not said exactly when he was in Moscow, but his and other first-hand accounts reveal an astonishing public detachment from the war, even as drones sometimes harassed the city.[86]

All this confidence aside, director of the Central Election Commission (CEC), Ella Pamfilova, and other Russian officials launched a campaign in the fall of 2023 to persuade Russians to vote. One feature of this effort was a nationwide lesson broadcast in every school as part of the weekly compulsory viewing called 'Conversations about Important Matters' (see chapter 9). Introducing the lesson herself, Pamfilova outlined the importance of elections and asserted that Russia had the 'most progressive' electoral procedure anywhere. Children in the first two grades were encouraged to hold mock elections with cartoon characters and make posters for polling stations; older students were taught about the country's voting practices and given instructions on Russia's system of democracy.[87]

Candidates

In her announcement on 7 December that made 17 March 2024 the official election date, Chair of the Federation Council Valentina Matviyenko appealed for national unity behind Putin's government and said that the annexed regions of Ukraine would be included in the voting. The election would be held over three days, 15–17 March, and that up to 30 of Russia's regions would be able to use remote electronic systems. Voting abroad would be paper ballot only, and available in fewer countries than in previous years because of opposition from Western governments.

Nominees from the five parties represented in the Duma were eligible to run without collecting supportive signatures; all other party entrants had to submit 100,000 voter signatures to the CEC within 25 days of the official start. Self-nominated aspirants had to provide 300,000 names. There were 25 political parties with the right to offer candidates.[88] As a self-nominee, Putin had first to be supported by 500 or more citizens meeting as an 'initiative group', which was quickly arranged. It was held at the ONF office in Moscow, where he also was endorsed by the UR party. Putin's team set up a website especially for the campaign (putin2024.ru).

One day after the president announced his candidacy, Navalny urged voters to support anyone but Putin. From exile, Leonid Volkov initiated a telephone and on-line project in an attempt to consolidate anti-Putin sentiments, even to setting up large billboards in Russian cities wishing everyone 'Happy New Year' (S Novom godom), with QR codes and an address that led to a website titled 'Russia Without Putin' (neputin.org). Navalny's Anti-Corruption Foundation paid for them. Slow to react, authorities began removing the billboards after two days. Also from exile, the *Novaia Gazeta Evropa* called Putin the 'reigning death candidate' and warned that his campaign would promise economic and social benefits but would actually mean eternal war.[89] This was going to be a battle of words, even if one side was heard only faintly in Russia.

Earlier in December, Grigory Yavlinsky, former deputy prime minister and founder of Yabloko, told an interviewer for RBC that he was collecting signatures for a presidential campaign. Portraying himself as the only leading politician in Russia to advocate a ceasefire in Ukraine, he dropped out before the end of the month for lack of signatures. He wanted 10 million, but got only one million – or so he said.[90]

The flood gates opened. Peace activist Yekaterina Duntsova threw her name into the hat. Endorsed by 500 supporters gathered in one place on 17

December, she then had to find 300,000 unique voter signatures to submit to the CEC for review. Her campaign opened with the comment: 'I believe that together we can win and make Russia a free and peaceful country!'[91] Her name was excluded from the ballot even before she began to collect the larger number, because of typos and errors in her original application, the CEC said.[92]

Boris Nadezhdin announced next. Former municipal councillor in Moscow and Duma deputy, also opposed to the war, he had support from the centre-right Civic Initiative party. Whereas the LPDR nominated its leader, Slutsky, leaders of the CPRF and the New People party declined to contend. The CPRF put Nikolai Kharitonov's (Agrarian Party) name forward in place of Zyuganov, and New People offered Vladislav Davankov instead of its founding leader Aleksei Nechaev. The absence of party leaders weakened the slate. The CEC had received at least 30 applicants before the deadline of 27 December.[93]

Fringe qualifiers began dropping out in January, usually calling on their supporters to back Putin. Most of the remaining applicants failed to fulfil requirements, leaving only four registered candidates by the end of January: Nadezhdin came closest to joining them. He had to collect over 100,000 signatures, with a limit of 2,500 from each of the dozens of the vast country's regions.[94] At first count, the CEC said there were flaws in about 15 per cent of the 105,000 signatures submitted by Nadezhdin.[95] A few days later, after losing appeals to both the CEC and the Supreme Court, he took his family on a 'vacation' outside the country.[96] While it was not surprising that the anti-war candidate was excluded from the ballot, the strength of his campaign and the fact that he raised nearly 100,000 legitimate signatures, many of them from people who lined up in the cold to sign on, was revealing.

The final ballot for the presidential election was therefore left to Putin (self-nomination), Slutsky (LDPR), Kharitonov (CPRF) and Davankov (New People).

Meanwhile, after he spoke out against Putin's election campaign in December, Navalny had a 'serious health-related incident' and was no longer connected by video link to court hearings conducted in his prison. He showed up in a prison colony north of Russia's Arctic Circle some weeks later where, no doubt, the authorities were trying to keep him out of sight and mind as the presidential election campaign got underway.[97]

Navalny's sudden and unexplained death in a remote prison colony a month prior to the election sent a chill through the progressive portion of the electorate.

As February 2024 wound down and the second anniversary of the launch of the SVO passed unmentioned by the Kremlin and Russia's mainstream media, Putin lavished praise on Russia's Armed Forces on Defender of the

Fatherland Day (23 February), more subdued than in the previous year, and on the Special Operations Forces Day (27 February), an annual holiday established in 2015 to mark the anniversary of Russia's take-over of Crimea. He then repeated these messages in his annual address to the Federal Assembly (29 February). In that speech, he again blamed the West for instigating the war in Ukraine and warned of nuclear war if NATO put troops on the ground in Ukraine. That, of course, was the part of the two-hour oration that Western commentators picked up on, mostly ignoring his boasts about the resilience of Russia's economy in spite of Western sanctions and promises that the quality of life for Russians would improve. As he concluded the state of the nation address, however, Putin highlighted the 'main thing'; that is, 'the implementation of all planned plans today directly depends on our soldiers, officers, volunteers – all military personnel'.[98] He had to win in Ukraine!

Putin made a special effort to sway Russia's youth in his favour. Needing a large turnout and their support, the Kremlin instructed regional officials, enterprise bosses and higher education school administrators to get young people out. Putin spoke to youth organizations himself, urging them to be patriotic, vote and ignore opposition members who deserted the country.[99]

THE ELECTION

Voting for the Russian president started very early; that is, on 25 February in 15 hard-to-reach parts of Russia and in the regions of Ukraine annexed by Russia.[100] As the election got underway in the rest of Russia on 15 March, officials offered incentives to draw people to the polls (free lunches, lotteries, amusement park tickets, hair styling, even smart phones). Activists tried to upset the process by pouring green dye into ballot boxes in at least ten regions, ranging from Moscow to Novosibirsk. Several polling stations were targets of Molotov cocktails. While Ukraine stepped up its aerial attacks on border regions so as to disrupt voting, Russian authorities up-graded security throughout and their army launched its massive missile bombardment of Odesa. The CEC was especially concerned about Yulia Navalnaia's call for a 'Noon against Putin' general protest.[101]

In the case of the spoiled ballots, senior officials came up with other classic buck-passing. Pamfilova pronounced that the 'West trained the violators' and paid them 'Judas money' to spread fake news; others blamed the protest actions on 'psychologically damaged' Russians, or Russians with financial grievances, such as debts. Dozens of so-called 'provocateurs' were detained and faced heavy fines or up to five years in prison for 'obstructing the work of the electoral commission'.[102]

'Noon against Putin' demonstrations did take place. Thousands showed up at polling stations across the country, protesting peacefully. At least 80 were detained in more than a dozen cities, while Pamfilova railed that the protesters, 'Zelensky greenshirts', were pathetic and disgusting and caused more people to come out and vote for Putin.[103]

RESULTS

The seriously tainted election, rife with voting infractions and pre-election manipulations, gave Putin free reign to do what he wished with the war in Ukraine.[104] He claimed nearly 88 per cent of the votes cast and a 76.3 per cent turnout, both records. Putin gloated about this in his victory speech ('No one has ever succeeded in anything like this in history'), and blamed the West for all the disruptions. Going on to praise Russia's troops in Ukraine and Moscow's relationship with Beijing as a source of strength, he warned also of a possible the Third World War and even mentioned Navalny by name, calling his death a 'sad occurrence'.[105] While he, Russia's compliant media and, presumably, a large part of the population, basked in their *vozhd's* re-anointment, Ukraine and the West readied for more war.

Putin's first post-election address was to the FSB, whom he encouraged on 19 March to take over management of affairs in the occupied areas of Ukraine so as to combat 'the neo-Nazi Kiev regime – again with support, and often on direct orders [from the West] – that has switched to terrorist methods', and also 'to continue systemic anti-corruption work, paying special attention to the area of defence procurement'.[106] Having been head of the FSB himself, in 1998, Putin had come full circle. The FSB was again in charge, as senior officers in the MoD were soon to find out.

The circumstances were rendered more volatile by the savage, almost casual slaughter of innocents on the outskirts of Moscow by terrorists affiliated with the Islamic State, less than a week after the presidential election. That event and the clearly false impression of unanimity left by the election were signs that 'fortress Russia' may have sprung a leak. Having survived the Prigozhin affair apparently unscathed the first cracks in Putin's strong-man image in the mirror were beginning to show on another front.

NOTES

1. On this, see Fred Weir, 'With Russians feeling besieged, some give Putin a loaded title: Vozhd', *Christian Science Monitor*, 2 April 2018. Weir is a Canadian journalist, long-time resident of Russia, and a regular contributor to the CSM.

2. See Andrey Pertsev, 'Kremlin must placate its supporters amid outrage over Kharkiv retreat', *Carnegie Endowment for International Peace*, 13 September 2022; Shannon Vavra, 'Former Kremlin aide says Putin ouster could be right around the corner', *The Daily Beast*, 15 September 2022. Writers, like Pertsev, who previously were employed by the Carnegie Moscow Center, had to switch to the US-based parent institution because the Russian government closed Carnegie's Moscow branch.

3. 'Doverie politikam', *VTsIOM Novosti*, 15 September 2022, wciom.ru/ratings/doverie-politikam/; 'Vladimir Putin: otsenki raboty, otnoshenie', *FOM*, 16 September 2022, fom.ru/Politika/10946; 'Approval of institutions, ratings of politicians', *Levada-Center*, 14 September 2022, levada.ru/en/2022/09/14/approval-of-institutions-ratings-of-politicians/.

4. For a discussion, Tatiana Stanovaya, 'What Russia's elites think of Putin now', *Foreign Policy*, 19 September 2022.

5. 'At 70, is Putin still the Russian public's irreplaceable man?' *RFE/RL*, 10 October 2022.

6. For an interesting discussion of this, Anna Arutuyan, 'Protests alone won't topple the Kremlin', *Globe and Mail*, 8 October 2022. See also her book, *Hybrid Warriors: Proxies, Freelancers and Moscow's Struggle for Ukraine*. London: Hurst, 2022.

7. '7 oktiabr Prezident primet uchastie v neformal'noi vstreche rukovoditelei gosudarstva – uchastnikov SNG', *Kremlin.ru*, 7 October 2022, kremlin.ru/press/announcements/69526; Anastasia Tenisheva, 'Muted festivities for Putin's 70th birthday amid war, international isolation', *The Moscow Times*, 7 October 2022; '"God put you in power": Russian Orthodox leader tells Putin on 70th birthday', *The Moscow Times*, 7 October 2022.

8. See Regina Elsner, 'Ideological pillow and strange partner: The Russian Orthodox Church and the war', *Russian Analytical Digest*, No. 286 (17 October 2022), pp. 2–5, and Veera Laine, Iiris Saarelainen, 'Spirituality as a political instrument: The Church, the Kremlin, and the creation of the "Russian World"', FIIA (Finnish Institute of International Affairs), *Working Paper 98*, September, 2017.

9. See, e.g. Nicholas James, 'Ukraine war: What, if any, are the chances of toppling Putin and who might take over?' *The Conversation*, 27 October 2022; Lili Bayer, 'Planning for the chaotic post-Putin world', *Politico*, 17 October 2022; Andrei Kolesnikov, 'Is it possible to plan for life after Putin?' *The Moscow Times*, 28 October 2022; Richard D. Hooker Jr., 'The West should not fear the prospect of a post-Putin Russia', *Atlantic Council*, 26 September 2022; Sergey Radchenko, 'Coups in the Kremlin', *Foreign Affairs*, 22 September 2022.

10. On this, see Tatiana Stanovaya, 'Russia's missing peacemakers: Why the country's elites are struggling to break with Putin', *Foreign Affairs*, 18 November 2022.

11. For a long list of Medvedev's commentary on recent events, see 'Dmitry Medvedev in his own words: From modernizing liberal to hateful hawk', *Russia Matters*, 4 January 2023.

12. On this, see Daniel Treisman, 'What could bring Putin down?' *Foreign Affairs*, 2 November 2022, and John Mueller, 'Why Putin may endure', *Foreign*

Affairs, 29 November 2022. For background, see Bo Petersson, *The Putin Predicament: Problems of Legitimacy and Succession in Russia*. Stuttgart: Ibidem-Verlag, 2021.

13. 'Vystuplenie Vladimira Putina v sviazi s priniatiem novykh territorii v sostav RF. Onlain', *Rossiiskaia Gazeta*, 30 September 2022.

14. On this, see Vadim Shtepa, 'Can Muscovy be considered a "state civilization?"', *Foreign Affairs*, 17 April 2023.

15. 'Obshchestvennitsa nazvala istoricheskim obrashchenue Putina', *RAPSI*, 30 September 2022.

16. Putin, 'Zasedanie Mezhdunarodnogo diskussionnogo kluba "Valdai"', *Kremlin.ru*, 27 October 2022, kremlin.ru/events/president/news/69695.

17. Yekaterina Grobman, Yelena Mukhametshina, 'V regionakh nachali obsuzhdat' otmenu priamykh vyborov merov', *Vedomosti*, 3 November 2022.

18. On this, see 'Russia officially moves to a war economy', *The Bell*, 25 October 2022.

19. 'Vstrecha s materiami voennosluzhashchikh – uchastnikov SVO', *Kremlin.ru*, 25 November 2022, kremlin.ru/events.president/news/69935; Yelena Mukhametshina, 'Vladimir Putin pogovoril s materiami rossiiskikh voennykh', *Vedomosti*, 26 November 2022.

20. 'Putin meets with carefully selected group of soldiers' mothers', *The Moscow Times*, 26 November 2022; Isabel van Brugen, 'Mothers of Russian soldiers slam "shameful" Putin meeting', *Newsweek*, 25 November 2022; 'Mozhem ob'iasnit'', *Telegram*, 25 November 2022; for the video from Olga Tsukanova, Telescope @ sovetmateri, telesco.pe/SOVETMATERI/113.

21. 'Zasedanie Soveta po razvitiiu grazhdanskogo obshchestva i pravam cheloveka', *Kremlin.ru*, 7 December 2022, kremlin.ru/events/president/news/70046.

22. 'Bol'shoi press-konferentsii Putina do Novogo goda ne budet', *TASS*, 12 December 2022.

23. See, e.g. Anna Arutunyan, 'Is Putin losing control, or playing his familiar blame game?' *Globe and Mail*, 19 December 2022; Anna Nemtsova, 'Russia can finally see that Putin's "days are numbered"', *The Daily Beast*, 17 December 2022.

24. See, e.g. Brendon Cole, 'Rumors of Putin's ill-health persist amid intelligence updates', *Newsweek*, 5 January 2023; 'Putin sick with "terminal cancer", his DEATH is "coming soon", claims Ukrainian spy chief', *Times Now*, 5 January 2023; Oleg Sukhov, 'Is Vladimir Putin dying of cancer?: Despite rife rumors, evidence runs scarce', *The Kyiv Independent*, 15 August 2022; Olena Roshchina, 'Ukraine's intelligence chief: Putin has a number of illnesses, but he still has a few years left', *Ukrainska pravda*, 24 May 2022, pravda.com.ua/eng/news/2022/05/24/7348167/.

25. Tat'iana Lozovenko, 'Zelenskiy: Ya ne sosem uveren, chto Putin eshche zhiv', *Ukrainskaia pravda*, 19 January 2023; RBK, 'Glavnye zaiavleniia Dmitriia Peskova segodnia', *Telegram*, 19 January 2023, t.me/rbc_news/66868.

26. See, e.g. Liana Fix, Michael Kimmage, 'Putin's last stand: The promise and peril of Russian defeat', *Foreign Affairs*, January/February 2023.

27. 'Zasedanie kollegii Ministerstva oborony', *Kremlin.ru*, 21 December 2022, kremlin.ru/events/president/news/70159.

28. Putin, 'Video address on Security Agency Worker's Day', *Kremlin.ru*, 20 December 2022, en.kremlin.ru/events/president/news/70146.

29. 'Konflikt s Ukrainoi: noiabr' 2022 goda', *Levada-tsentr*, 2 December 2022, levada.ru/2022/12/02/konflikt-s-ukrainoj-noyabr-2022-goda/.

30. 'Deiatel'nost' Putina odobriaet 78% oproshennykh rossiian – FOM', *RAPSI*, 23 December 2022; 'Vladimir Putin: Otsenki raboty, otnoshenie', *FOM*, 16 December 2022, fom.ru/Politika/10946; 'Doverie politikam', *VTsIOM*, 18 December 2022, wciom .ru /ratings /doverie -politi kam/.

31. On this, see Andrei Kolesnikov, 'Scientific Putinism: Shaping official ideology in Russia', *Carnegie Endowment for International Peace*, 21 November 2022; Fiona Hill, Angela Stent, 'The world Putin wants', *Foreign Affairs*, September/October 2022, and Maria Sneglovaya, Michael Kimmage, Jade McGlynn, 'Putin the ideologue', *Foreign Affairs*, 16 November 2023.

32. 'Parad Pobedy na Krasnoi ploshchadi', *Kremlin.ru*, 9 May 2023, kremlin.ru/events/president/news/71104.

33. On this, see Mikhail Suslov, *Putinism: Post-Soviet Russian Regime Ideology*. Abingdon, UK: Routledge, 2024.

34. 'Vstrecha s liderom KPRF Gennadiem Zyuganovym', *Kremlin.ru*, 13 February 2023, kremlin.ru/events/president/news/70505; 'Vstrecha s liderom partii "Spravedlivaia Rossia – Za pravdu" Sergeem Mironovym', *Kremlin.ru*, 14 February 2023, kremlin.ru/events/president/news/70511; 'Vstrecha s liderom LDPR Leonidom Slutskim', *Kremlin.ru*, 13 February 2023, kremlin.ru, evets/president/news/70506.

35. 'Poslanie Prezidenta Federal'nomu Sobraniiu', *Kremlin.ru*, 21 February 2023, kremlin.ru/events/president/news/70565.

36. On this, see 'Five takeaways from Putin's speech on war anniversary', *The Bell*, 28 February 2023; 'Poslanie Prezidenta Federal'nomu Sobranii', *Kremlin.ru*, 21 February 2023, kremlin.ru/events/president/news/70565.

37. For a negative account by a member of the audience, see '"We went to Moscow to warm ourselves in the toilet for three hours" . . .', *Meduza*, 22 February 2023; for a positive view from another member of the audience, 'Thousands of Russians cheer for Putin at patriotic rally', rfi.fr/en/international-news/20230222-thousands -of-russians-cheer-for-putin-at-patriotic-rally, 22 February 2023; for Putin's speech, 'Kontsert "Slava zashchitnikam Otechestva"', *Kremlin.ru*, 22 February 2023, kremlin .ru/events/president/news/70574.

38. This is corroborated by both state-owned and independent pollsters: 'Russians' level of trust in Putin exceeds 78%, poll shows', *TASS*, 20 January 2023; 'Vladimir Putin: Otsenki raboty, otnoshenie', *FOM*, 24 February 2023, fom.ru/Politika/10 946; 'Level of trust in Vladimir Putin in Russia 2019–2023', *Statista*, 21 February 2023; 'Russian support for Putin's war in Ukraine is hardening', *Bloomberg News*, 23 February 2023; Andrei Kolesnikov, 'How Russians learned to stop worrying and love the war', *Foreign Affairs*, 1 February 2023.

39. 'Security officer who fled Russia tells of Putin's growing isolation', *The Bell*, 11 April 2023; '"The Russian president is a war criminal": Interview with the Federal Guard Service officer who worked with Putin and who fled Russia', *Dossier*, 4 April

2023, dossier.center/fso-en/?ref=en.the bell.io. Dossier is funded by the bitterly anti-Putin Mikhail Khodorkovsky.

40. Aisel Gereikhanova, 'Kak Vladimir Putin za rulem ezdil po Mariupoliu. Opublikovany videokradry', *Rossiiskaia Gazeta*, 19 March 2023; 'Putin visits Mariupol in first trip to fallen city', *The Moscow Times*, 19 March 2023; Denis Kurenev, 'Putin nazval prioritetnymi voprosy bezopasnosti Kryma i Sevastopolia', *Vedomosti*, 17 March 2023.

41. For details, see 'How Russia propaganda tried to explain away an arrest warrant for Putin', *The Bell*, 21 March 2023.

42. Viktoriia Il'ina, 'Putin: Rossiia ne stremilas' k konfrontatsii na Ukraine', *Rossiiskaia Gazeta*, 19 March 2023; 'Soveshchanie po voprosam sotsial'no-ekonomicheskogo razvitiia Kryma i Sevastopolia', *Kremlin.ru*, 17 March 2023, kremlin.ru/events/president/news/70702.

43. 'Vladimir Putin posetil shtab gruppirovki voik "Dnepr" i shtab national'noi gvardii "Vostok"', *Kremlin.ru*, 18 April 2023, kremlin.ru/events/president/news/70944; Aisel Gereikhanova, 'Peskov ob'iasnil otsutstvie Shoigu i Gerasimova v poezdke s Putinym v LNR i Khersonskuiu oblast'iu bol'shim riskom sobirat'sia v odnom meste', *Rossiiskaia Gazeta*, 18 April 2023.

44. 'Poseshchenie Ulan-Udenskogo aviatsionnogo zavoda', *Kremlin.ru*, 14 March 2023, kremlin.ru/events/president/news/70674.

45. 'Krasnuiu ploshchad' zakroiut dlia posetitelei s 27 aprelia po 10 maia', *TASS*, 25 April 2023; 'Russia scraps WWII remembrance march on security concerns', *The Moscow Times*, 18 April 2023; Verstka, 'Gde v Rossii otmenili parady 9 maia', *Telegram*, 4 May 2023, t.me/svobodnieslova/1903.

46. 'Edinorossy postoiat za Stalingrad', *Kommersant*, 31 January 2023; 'Stalin monument unveiled to mark 80th anniversary of Stalingrad victory', *The Moscow Times*, 1 February 2023; 'Volgograd dosrochno pereimenovali v Stalingrad', *V1.RU*, 30 January 2023, v1.ru/text/gorod/2023/01/30/72017675/.

47. See, e.g. Andrei Vinokurov, 'Vybory ne za gorami', *Kommersant*, 13 January 2023; 'Kremlin readies for Putin's 2024 re-election under shadow of war – Kommersant', *The Moscow Times*, 13 January 2023. See also Tatiana Stanovaya, 'Russia faces three pivotal moments in 2023', *Carnegie Endowment for International Peace*, 9 January 2023.

48. Joshua Zitser, 'Putin lives in an "information vacuum" and never used a cellphone or the internet, a Russian intelligence officer who defected says', *Business Insider*, 4 April 2023; Isaac Chotiner, 'Why Russia's elites think Putin's war is doomed to fail', *The New Yorker*, 3 May 2023, an interview with Stanovaya; 'Russia's elites are starting to sour on Putin's chances of winning the war in Ukraine', *Bloomberg*, 8 June 2023.

49. See 'Vecher s Vladimirom Solov'evym', 5 June 2023, smotrim.ru/video/2626760; 'Margarita Simon'ian predlozhila prekratit' voinu – potomu chto VSU "poluchat rakety po nam"', *Meduza*, 7 June 2023.

50. 'Vruchenie medalei Geroia Truda i Gosudarstvennykh premii Rossiiskoi Federatsii', *Kremlin.ru*, 12 June 2023, kremlin.ru/events/president/news/71346.

51. 'RIA Novosti: Rech' Putina pered voennymi stanet "novoi stranitsei v istorii Kremlia"', *MKRU* (Moskovsky komsomolets), 27 June 2023.

52. See, e.g. 'Putin na minnom pole: opasnye kapkany dlia vlasti v postprigozhinskii period', *MKRU* (Moskovsky komsomolets), 27 June 2023.

53. See, e.g. Liana Fix, Michael Kimmage, 'The beginning of the end for Putin?', *Foreign Affairs*, 27 June 2023; 'Prigozhin's attempted mutiny exposes cracks in the Russian regime', *The Bell*, 27 June 2023; U.S. State Department, interview: 'Secretary Antony J. Blinken with Dana Bash of CNN state of the union', 25 June 2023; Ana Gaguy, 'Russia's Wagner rebellion "shows real cracks" in Putin's regime, Blinken says', *Forbes*, 25 June 2023; Andrew D'Anieri, 'Putin's weakness has been revealed. Here's how Russia's neighbors are reacting', *Atlantic Council*, 25 June 2023; Joshua R. Krocker, 'Despite the Kremlin's best efforts, Putin's façade has cracked', *The Moscow Times*, 13 July 2023.

54. 'Konflikt s Ukrainoi: otsenki kontsa iiunia 2023 goda'', *Levada-Tsentr*, 30 June, 2023, levada.ru/2023/06/30/konflikt-s-ukrainoj-otsenki-kontsa-iyunya-2023-goda/.

55. Denis Volkov, 'Sotsiologiia miatezha: kakoi otpechatok ostavili sobytiia 24 iunia v obshchestvennom mnenii', *Levada-tsentr*, 7 July 2023, levada.ru/2023/07/05/sotsiologiya-myatezha-kakoj-otpechatok-ostavili-sobytiya-24-iyunya-v-obshhestvennom-mnenii/.

56. Navalny. Podpisat'sia, 'S 1 iunia v moei kamere otkliuchili dazhe radio, drugikh liudei ya pochti ne vizhu . . .', *Instagram*, 27 June 2023, instagram.com/p/CuABw2oNlyD/?hl=ru; '"No one stood up to defend Putin. There was no unity of the nation around him." Alexei Navalny on Yevgeny Prigozhin's rebellion', *Meduza*, 27 June 2023.

57. 'Zachem Vladimir Putin ezdil v Dagestan', *Vedomosti*, 29 June 2023.

58. 'Forum ASI "Sil'nye idei dlia novogo vremeni"', *Kremlin.ru*, 29 June 2023, kremlin.ru/events/president/news/71554; 'Putin to speak at ASI forum strong ideas for a new time', *TASS*, 28 June 2023.

59. 'Zasedanie Soveta glav gosudarstv – chlenov ShOS', *Kremlin.ru*, 4 July 2023, kremlin.ru/event/president/news/71578.

60. 'Glavam rossiiskikh regionov razreshili sozdavat' voenizirovanye kompanii', *Meduza*, 25 July 2023.

61. 'Vladimir Putin podpisal zakon o nadelenii Rosgvardii pravom imet' na vooruzhenii tiazheluiu tekhniku', *Tsentr analiza mirovoi torgovli oruzhiem*, 4 August 2023; Sinéad Baker, 'Russia's 200,000-strong national guard is getting armed with heavy weapons, in a sign of its growing importance to Putin, UK intel says', *Business Insider*, 8 August 2023.

62. Denis Kurenev, 'V Gosdumu vnesli zakonoproekty o formirovanniakh dobrovol'tsev v Rosgvardii', *Vedomosti*, 22 September 2023.

63. 'Yevgeny Prigozhin listed as passenger of plane crashed in Tver region – Agency', *TASS*, 23 August 2023; 'MChS Rossii. V Tverskoi oblasti blizi . . .', *Telegram*, 23 August 2023, t.me/mchs_official/10806.

64. 'RIA Novosti. Rosaviatsiia podtverdila, chto bortu razbivshchegosiia v Tver . . .', *Telegram*, 23 August 2023, t.me/rian_ru/213016.

65. See, e.g. Ksenia Sobchak, 'Krovavaia baryna: Absoliutno chetkii signal vsem elitam, . . .', *Telegram*, 23 August 2023, t.me/bloodysx/30226; 'Plane carrying Yevgeny Prigozhin crashes in Russia', *The Moscow Times*, 23 August 2023; Tatiana Stanovaya, 'Why Putin wanted Prigozhin dead', *Foreign Affairs*, 23 August 2023.

66. 'Kremlin dismisses Prigozhin assassination rumors as "absolute lies"', *The Moscow Times*, 25 August 2023.

67. Marina Krylova, 'SK RF podtverdil gibel' Evgeniia Prigozhina pri krushenii samoleta pod Tver'iu', *Rossiiskaia Gazeta*, 27 August 2023. For rumours that Prigozhin lives, see Aleksandr Eliseev, 'Prigozhin Pravda zhiv? Piat' faktov, kotorye mogut ukazyvat' na eto', *Vedomosti*, 27 August 2023.

68. GREY ZONE . . . 'Napomnim, chto samolet byl sbit v nebe nad Tverskoi oblast'iu silami PVO', *Telegram*, 23 August 2023, t.me/grey_zone/20170l; 'Vstrecha s vrio glavy DNR Denisom Pushilinym', *Kremlin.ru*, 24 August 2023, kremlin.ru/events/president/news/72100.

69. 'Zapomnivshiesa sobytiia avgusta, smert' Prigozhin', *Levada-tsentr*, 1 September 2023. The surveys were conducted in the homes of 16,060 respondents in fifty of the constituent entities of the RF during the last week of August.

70. On this, see Boris Grozovski, 'Russia's party of war seeks to turn the war with Ukraine into a national cause: It will fail', *Wilson Center: The Russia File*, 19 September 2022; Ivan Fomin, 'Prigozhin has lost, but Putin is struggling to win', *The Moscow Times*, 24 August 2023.

71. Michael Peck, 'Recent arrests suggest Putin is quietly trying to rein in some of his most effective promoters of the war in Ukraine', *Business Insider*, 15 December 2023; Donald J. Jenson, Angela Howard, 'How Russia's military bloggers shape the course of Putin's war', *The Kyiv Independent*, 8 August 2023.

72. Press-sluzhba Prigozhina, 'Proshchanie s Evgeniem Viktorovichem sostoialos' v zakrytom formate: Zhelaiushchie prostit'sia mogut posetit' Porokhovskoe kladbishche', *Telegram*, 29 August 2023, t.me/concordgroup_official/1305; 'Mnogokilometrovaia probka skopilas' u kladbishcha, gde zakhoronen Prigozhin', *Fontanka.ru*, 30 August 2023, ontanka.ru/2023/08/30/72652016/.

73. 'Number of Russians living below poverty line falls to under 10% for the first time in 20 years', *bne Intellinews*, 3 May 2023.

74. 'Plenarnoe zasedanie Vos'mogo Vostochnogo ekonomicheskogo foruma', *Kremlin.ru*, 12 September 2023, kremlin.ru/events/president/news/72259.

75. 'Konflikt s Ukrainoi: otsenki sentiabria 2023 goda', *Levada-tsentr*, 3 October 2023; 'Putinu doveriaiut 78.3% oproshennykh rossiian – VTsIOM', *RAPSI*, 13 October 2023; 'Prezidentu Putinu doveriaiut 79% oproshennykh rossiian – VTsIOM', *RAPSI*, 10 November 2023.

76. 'Why Russians trust Putin', *The Bell*, 12 October 2023.

77. Andrei Vinokurov, 'Kak v pervyi raz', *Kommersant*, 13 November 2023; 'The Kremlin gears up to launch Putin's re-election campaign', *The Bell*, 14 November 2023; 'Gozduma utverdila zakonoproekt o povyshenii pensii voennym na 4,5% v 2024 godu', *Vedomosti*, 14 November 2023.

78. Alia Shoaib, 'Putin fears the wrath of soldiers' wives, as the Kremlin tries to buy-off potential protesters, report says', *Business Insider*, 26 November 2023; Defence Intelligence, 'Update on Ukraine', 20 November 2023, twitter.com/DefenceHQ/status/1726521140477038990.

79. 'Put' Domoi', *Telegram*, 7 December 2023, t.me/PYTY_DOMOY/525; 'Families of military conscripts make video appeal to Putin', *Novaia Gazeta Evropa*, 7 December 2023.

80. 'Putin announced plans to run for a new presidential term', *RIA Novosti*, 8 December 2023.

81. '"Budushchee Rossii": "Edinaia Rossiia" provela zakliuchitel'nuiu diskussionnuiu ploshchadku pered S'ezdom', *Edinaia Rossiia*, 13 December 2023, er.ru/activity/news/budushee-rossii-edinaya-rossiya-provela-zaklyuchitelnuyu-diskussionnuyu-ploshadku-pered-sezdom.

82. 'Putinu doveriaiut bolee 79% oproshennykh rossiian – VtSIOM', *RAPSI*, 22 December 2023; 'Odobrenie institutov, dela v strane, doverie politikam: Dekabr' 2023 goda', *Levada-tsentr*, 21 December 2023.

83. 'Novogodnee obrashchenie k grazhdanam Rossii', *Kremlin.ru*, 31 December 2023, kremlin.ru/events/president/news/73200.

84. Charlie Hancock, '5 Claims from Putin's Tucker Carlson interview, fact-checked', *The Moscow Times*, 9 February 2024.

85. 'Odobrenie institutov, reitingi politikov: Mai 2023 goda', *Levada-tsentr*, 31 May 2023.

86. Roger Cohen, 'Life under Putin's forever war', *The New York Times: International Weekly*, 12–13 August 2023, pp. 1, 6.

87. 'Izbiratel'naia Sistema Rossii (30 let TsIK), *Razgovor o vazhnom*, razgovor.edsoo.ru/video/2966/, accessed 1 November 2023; Pyotr Kozlov, 'As Putin's re-election looms, Kremlin pushes to indoctrinate a new generation of voters', *The Moscow Times*, 30 October 2023.

88. Dmitriy Goncharuk, Galina Mislivskaya, 'Vybory prezidenta Rossii sostoiatsia 17 marta 2024 goda', *Rossiiskaia Gazeta*, 7 December 2023.

89. 'Prezidentskie vybory-2024. Agitirovat' i golosovat' protiv Putina', 7 December 2023, navalny.com/p/6672/; Leonid Gozman, 'Reigning death candidate', *Novaia Gazeta Evropa*, 9 December 2023.

90. 'Yavlinsky – RBK: "Dlia menia Rossiia i Ukraina – kak pravaia i levaia ruka"', *RBC.ru*, 5 December 2023, rbc.ru/interview/politics/05/12/2023/; 'Putin's liberal critic opts not to run in presidential campaign', *Bloomberg News*, 23 December 2023.

91. 'Ekaterina Duntsova – kandidat v prezidenty Rossii', *Telegram*, 17 December 2023, t.me/Duntsova/66.

92. 'BBC News/Russkaia sluzhba', *Telegram*, 23 December 2023, t.me/bbcrussian/58330.

93. 'Number of candidates for presidential election exceeds 30 – Central Election Commission', *TASS*, 26 December 2023.

94. Andrey Pertsev, 'Anti-war presidential bid causes headache for Kremlin', *Carnegie Endowment for International Peace*, 29 January 2024.

95. 'Artem'ev Igor: pro kampaniiu Borisa Nadezhdin . . .', *Telegram*, 5 February 2024, t.me/artemevi/272.

96. 'Zasedanie TsIK o registratsii Borisa Nadezhdina, 8 fevralia 11:00', *YouTube*, 8 February 2024, youtube.com/watch?v=WEitluwA0v0; Anastasia Tenisheva, Pyotr Kozlov, Nurbek Savitahunov, 'Russian election authority rejects peace hopeful Nadezhdin's presidential bid', *The Moscow Times*, 8 February 2024.

97. Post. Alexey Navalny, @navalny, X, 26 December 2023, twitter.com/navalny/status/1739557690060210196.

98. 'Poslanie Prezidenta Federal'nomu Sobraniiu', *Kremlin.ru*, 29 February 2024, kremlin.ru/events/president/news/73585.

99. See, e.g. 'Meeting with participants in the World Youth Festival', *Kremlin.ru*, 6 March 2024, kremlin.ru/events/president/news/73616/videos; '"Make the young fall in love with Putin": Young Russians pressured to vote as Kremlin demands record turnout', *The Moscow Times*, 12 March 2024.

100. Valentin Loginov, 'Punkt i znachenie: v Rossii nachalos' dosrochnoe golosovanie', *Izvestiia*, 25 February 2024.

101. 'V TsIK prizvali usilit' okhranu urn iz-za porchi biulletenei chernilami', *RBC.ru*, 15 March 2024, rbc.ru/politics/15/03/2024/65f40f849a7947cb8cd20209; 'Bread rolls and Dyson hair stylers: Russia lures voters with election day freebies', *The Moscow Times*, 14 March 2024.

102. Yuliia Maleeva, Yana Surinskaia, 'Izbiratel'nye urny v regionakh stali zalivat' zelenkoi', *Vedomosti*, 15 March 2024; Tatiana Zamakhina, 'Nabliudateli: Vybory idut v shtatnom rezhime, provokatsii ni na chto ne vliiaiut', *Rossiskaia Gazeta*, 16 March 2024.

103. 'At least 47 people detained across Russia on final election day', *Novaia Gazeta Evropa*, 17 March 2024; 'Live: Russians protest Putin in final day of voting', *The Moscow Times*, 17 March 2024, with photos & videos; Anastasiia Larina, 'Pamfilova: chislo zhelaiushchikh progolosovat' vyroslo posle porchi urn s biulleteniami', *Kommersant*, 17 March 2024.

104. 'New-Europe study: About half of votes for Vladimir Putin in the presidential elections were stuffed', *Novaia Gazeta Evropa*, 18 March 2024; 'Fraud, violations and pressure: Election observers describe Russian 2024 presidential vote', *The Moscow Times*, 21 March 2024.

105. Quoted in 'Putin vows Russia cannot be held back in victory speech', *The Moscow Times*, 18 March 2024; 'Navalny's death is sad, but inmates die in US, too – Putin', *TASS*, 18 March 2024; 'Putin describes Russian-Chinese relations as factor of stability', *TASS*, 18 March 2024.

106. Putin, 'Zasedanie kollegii FSB Rossii', *Kremlin.ru*, 19 March 2024, kremlin.ru/events/president/news/73678.

Chapter 5

Net Voine! (No to War!)
The Domestic Political Scene

With the exception of Yabloko, all mainstream political parties in Russia supported the SVO, as did a majority of the population, consistently. Nevertheless, after the initial flurry of action and reaction, anti-war activists did not give up; rather, they changed tactics, turning to more subtle modes of protest than street demonstrations or single picket stands. They were helped by social media accounts from abroad and by the realities of war on the home front. In the political arena, the state became the only real actor, taking over the airwaves and shutting out opposing opinions in the print media, the TV and on the streets. Body-bags notwithstanding, nationalist and patriotic voices drowned out all others.

IF NOT PUTIN, WHO?

Futile Western speculations on when the Russian people would turn against the war, or maybe even rise up against it, were founded on assumptions about the degree to which sanctions and the psychology of isolation would disrupt Russian daily life. Expectations that exiled Russian activist journalists feeding Russian social media images of devastation in Ukraine would persuade the Russian public to reject the SVO proved futile.

Some analysts believed that anti-war collaboration against Putin by disaffected members of the oligarchic elite whose business enterprises were being ruined, or even among the senior officer corps disappointed with the conduct of the war, was possible.[1] It wasn't. Instead, the oligarch class either left, sullenly acquiesced, or became eager war profiteers. Several of Russia's dual-citizen billionaires gave up their Russian passports, among them Facebook investor Yuri Milner (Israel), Freedom Holding retail brokerage founder Timur Turlov

(Kazakhstan), financier Ruben Vardanyan (Armenia) and CEO of the British digital bank Revolut, Nik Stronsky (UK). Founder of Yandex, Arkady Volozh, spoke out aggressively against the Russian action – from Israel. These men were already living outside the country, and their departure did not spill over into an anti-Putin movement in Russia itself. Still, by February 2024, at least seven billionaires had renounced their Russian citizenships.[2] The military officer caste was kept in such a state of flux that organized opposition was rendered impractical, and the institution's innate sense of loyalty made it improbable.

A few members of the wealthy caste left in protest of the war, such as privatization guru under Yeltsin, head of Rusnano, and Putin's envoy for relations with international agencies, Anatoly Chubais. Some members of the elite who had left the country before the war found it difficult to return even if they wanted to. Speaker of the State Duma Volodin proposed close vetting of all of them to be certain they had not supported Ukraine during their absence. Recommendations for their treatment ranged from seizing assets to prison terms.[3] By the ninth month of hostilities, if there was to be a change at the top of Russian society, it would have to come at the behest of the citizenry at the bottom. That was not going to happen anytime soon, if ever.

Local Elections, September 2022

Helped by restrictions on press freedoms, the accelerated repression of opposition voices, and a general sense of patriotism, government supporters swept regional and local elections in September 2022. United Russia candidates won gubernatorial contests in all 14 regions where the post was on the ballot and also took majorities in the six regional legislatures up for re-election. In Moscow, the UR gained nearly 80 per cent of the 1,400 seats available in its municipal elections.[4]

Navalny's voting strategy, known as 'smart voting' (Ymnoe golosovanie) that urged voters to support anyone who had a chance to defeat a pro-Kremlin contestant played a much smaller role than in previous election campaigns, in part because Roskomnadzor blocked access to websites listing his preferred candidates. Roskomnadzor also ordered YouTube, Apple and Google to remove accounts and apps linked to Navalny's team members.

ANTI-WAR POLITICAL ACTIVITIES

Early Acts of Defiance

An especially brazen journalistic act of defiance showed up in magazine racks on the SVO's very first day. An issue of *Novaia Gazeta*, all in black with the blazing white all-capital headline: 'Russia. Bombs. Ukraine.' drew attention to book stalls. There followed on the same cover: 'The editors of "Novaia Gazeta" recognize war as mindless. The editors of "Novaia" do not recognize the Ukrainian people as an enemy, or the Ukrainian language as the language of an enemy. In this number, we will publish important texts in the Russian and Ukrainian languages'. Signed by editor-in-chief, Dmitry Muratov, Nobel Peace Prize winner for 2021. By March, *Novaia Gazeta* was closed down in Russia and re-established in Latvia as *Novaia Gazeta Evropa*.

The first half year of war in Ukraine saw many more instances of anti-war dissent, a few of the most daring of which are represented here. Given that it was already illegal to call the war a 'war' and the invasion an 'invasion', Marina Ovsyannikova's display on 14 March 2022 was a particularly memorable moment for the 'No to war!' (Net Voine!) community. During a live national TV programme, *Vremia*, for which she had worked for a decade, Ovsyannikova sneaked up behind the broadcaster, who seemed not to notice her, and brandished a large poster on which was written, in mixed English and Russian, 'NO WAR. Stop the War. Don't believe the propaganda. They are lying to you here'. For this extraordinarily brave action, she was arrested, fined heavily, and lost her job. Police apprehended her again in July for displaying an anti-war placard on the bank of the Moskva River across from the Kremlin. This time, her large sign read, all in Russian: 'Putin is a murderer. His soldiers are fascists; 352 children died. How many more should die for you to stop?' She placed three child's dolls on the ground in front of her, daubed with red paint representing blood. Seized and confined to house arrest awaiting trial, Ovsyannikova escaped the country with her 11-year-old daughter in September 2022 and was put on the federal wanted list.[5]

A year later, Moscow's Basmanny Court sentenced her in absentia to eight and a half years for spreading 'fake information' about the Russian army ('feik ob armii').[6] In turn, she accused Russian authorities of attempting to poison her at her dwelling in France.[7]

In another heroic feat of defiance, one day after Ovsyannikova's first act of rebellion, Anna Parshkova stood alone in front of the Christ the Saviour Cathedral in Moscow holding a placard saying, in Russian: '6th Commandment: Thou shalt not kill'. She, too, was arrested.[8]

There were more subtle occasions of protest, often headed often by women, some of them belonging to the Feminist Anti-War Resistance (@femagainstwar_bot), or FAR.[9] Spreading their message via Telegram, they also stuck small flyers with names of soldiers who were killed 'Today' (Segodnia ubivaiut) or gone missing (Propal chelovek) on sign posts, information-stands or shop windows with little danger of getting caught.[10]

Among the more innovative acts of protest, the action of artist and LGBT activist Sasha Skochilenko stands out for its imagination. In April, she replaced a price tag in a Perekrestok supermarket with data on the death toll in Ukraine, and on another that Putin had been lying to Russians on TV for 20 years, making it easier to justify war now. She altered six tags in all. An elderly lady snitched on her. Arrested and charged with disseminating 'knowingly false information', Skochilenko remained in detention before coming to trial in December, a week after the Ilya Yashin sentencing (see ahead). A court in St. Petersburg sentenced her to seven years in prison for spreading 'false information about the Russian military' on the basis of 'political hatred'.[11]

On 26 October 2022 FSB agents raided the home of former television star and presidential aspirant (2018), Ksenia Sobchak. They suspected her of involvement in some kind of subversive activity together with her media director, Kirill Sukhanov, who was arrested on charges of extortion a few days earlier. Daughter of Anatoly Sobchak, a liberal mayor of St. Petersburg for whom Putin served as a deputy in the 1990s, Ksenia Sobchak has 9.4 million followers on Instagram. Although she is criticized by Navalny and other 'liberals' as a leading light among Russia's wealthy social elite, the official allegations against her could be taken as a warning to potentially malcontent oligarchs.[12] She showed up in Lithuania on an Israeli passport a few days later.

As well as FAR, the following anti-war groups are dominated by women in Russia: The Eighth Initiative Group (Vos'maia initsiativnaia gruppa – 8IG), t.me/Femspb; SotsFem Alternative (SotsFem Al'ternativa), instagram.com/socfemalt/; Soft Power (Miagkaia sila), t.me/myagkaya_sila_ru; and Project "Labyrinth" (Labirint), labirint.online/ru/.

Cross-Country Objections to War

According to OVD-Info, as of 17 August 2022, 16,437 Russians had been arrested since 24 February for illegal protests. By far the greater number of these were participants in street demonstrations, but 138 of them were for anti-war posts on social networks; 118 individuals were arrested for flaunting anti-war symbols and 62 arrests were the result of direct anti-war actions.[13] The number of detainees grew to 19,673 by the end of April 2023, more than 2,000 of those related to anti-mobilization arrests. At that time, nearly 400 citizens were on trial for disrespecting and disseminating 'hatred' of Russia's armed forces. Others had already received sentences of between three (61-year-old Vladimir Rumyantsev) and 8.5 years (Ilya Yashin). The number of detainees reached 19,855 after two full years of war in Ukraine.[14]

These data are provided on a regular basis by OVD-Info, the leading independent Russian website for information on arrests, criminal proceedings for activities related to politics, and human rights violations in Russia. Founded in 2013 after the infamous Bolotnaya Square arrests of demonstrators, OVD-Info took its name from its main 'enemy', the Department of Internal Affairs (Otdel Vnutrennykh Del). Although designated a 'foreign agent' on 29 September 2022, the website remains active and runs a 24/7 hotline for reports on abuses and arrests.

Spreading 'knowingly false information' about Russia's armed forces became the catch-all phrase used by the courts against any objection to the war effort. So, too, was the label 'fake news', for which Siberian journalist Maria Ponomarenko was sentenced to six years on the first anniversary of the war.[15] A few weeks later, the PGO handed a sentence of 8.5 years to the head of the Protesting MGU's (Moscow State University) Telegram channel (Protestnyi MGU, t.me/msuprotest), 23-year old Dmitry Ivanov, for 'spreading false information' about the Russian Armed Forces.[16]

In March, Yevgeny Roizman, former mayor of Yekaterinburg, was given 15 days in jail for re-posting Navalny organization material, and later stood trial for 'discrediting' the Russian military.[17] He and prominent opposition leader Vladimir Kara-Murza awaited more serious charges. Already labelled a 'foreign agent', in April, Kara-Murza was handed a 25-year sentence in a 'strict regime colony' for 'high treason and fake news about Russian servicemen' and other 'crimes'.[18]

The inventory of absurd sentences grew longer. In late April, authorities picked up Aleksei Mosin, head of Memorial's branch in Yekaterinburg, and charged him with 'discrediting' the Russian army. Having dissolved Memorial, Russia's most famous human rights group, in December 2021, the government now began to harass its personnel. Authorities put the organization's co-chair, Oleg Orlov, on trial in June 2023, for repeatedly 'discrediting' Russia's military in single pickets. He had been arrested a year before that and fined 50,000 roubles for unfurling a banner on Red Square proclaiming 'USSR 1945 is a country that defeated fascism. Russia 2022 is the country of victorious fascism'.[19]

One of the few prominent anti-war activists to remain in Russia, Orlov delivered a passionate defence of truth in his final words to the court. Offering no apologies for what he had said and written, he predicted that it wouldn't be 'long before Russia emerges from the darkness in which it is currently immersed'. Russian patriotism, he said, is now 'synonymous with imperialism' and went on to proclaim that Russians were now living in Orwell's *1984*, where the slogan of the dystopian Oceania was 'war is peace, freedom is slavery'.[20] Citing his age (70) and testimonies from many supporters, the court limited his new punishment to a heavy fine. A former police officer, Semiel Vedel, was sentenced to seven years in prison after a telephone tap caught him criticizing the SVO and referring to Russia as a 'murderer country'.²¹ Meanwhile, the Orthodox Church weeded out objecting priests.²²

Among the wide array of citizens accused in April was a 22-year-old Moscow baker, Anastasia Chernysheva, who was fined ₽35,000 (US$446) for posting photos of anti-war cakes and cookies for sale on Instagram. Some of the offending cakes and cookies were created in Ukrainian colours, others were decorated with the slogan 'Net voine!' and some carried obscene references as to what Putin could do to himself.²³

A much older woman living in Buryatia paid her dues to the anti-war movement as well. Natalia Filonova, age 61, was detained in November 2022 for rallying against mobilization, and awaited a trial set for May 2023. While she was incarcerated, her 16-year-old son was placed in juvenile detention and subjected to severe prison conditions even though he had family who pleaded to keep him. Filonova had been editor of an independent local newspaper and co-chair of the Trans-Baikal region branch of the liberal-democratic Solidarity (Solidarnost) movement. A group of some 30 journalists, activists, priests, artists and politicians from the Buryatia region signed an open letter in her defence.²⁴ All to no avail. The courts condemned her to three years in prison. Known anti-war leadership figures active within Russia are about to become extinct.

Snitching Encouraged

In a speech delivered on 16 March, Putin encouraged the public to hunt down opponents of the war by accusing the 'collective West' of creating a fifth column in Russia so as to 'provoke civil confrontation'. Such efforts will fail, he said, because 'the Russian people will always be able to distinguish true patriots from scum and traitors and simply spit them out like a midge that accidentally flew into their mouths, spit them out on the sidewalk. I am convinced that such a natural and necessary self-purification of society will only strengthen our country, our solidarity, cohesion and readiness to respond to any challenges'.²⁵ In this way, he inspired neighbours to snitch on neighbours, children to tattle on classmates or teachers and workers to betray co-workers.

The degree to which societal 'self-purification' practices, called 'denunciations' in Soviet times, slowed anti-war agitation is not clear, but they certainly encouraged snitching in neighbourhoods, work places and schools. For example, in one incident an art teacher in the Tula region reported to her principal that 12-year-old Masha Moskaleva had drawn an anti-war picture; the principal reported the incident to local authorities. Subsequent focus on the child's father, Aleksei Moskalev, a single parent, saw him arrested and charged with 'discrediting' Russia's Armed Forces. He had posted items about Bucha and the murder of Ukrainian POWs. After he escaped from house arrest and fled the country, a court handed him a two-year sentence in absentia and his daughter was sent into foster care.[26] She was later placed in the care of her mother, with whom she had had little contact for the previous seven years. Police found Moskalev in Minsk in April, extradited him to Russia and, in July, sentenced him to two years in a penal colony.[27]

In another case, authorities arrested 19-year-old university student Olesya Krivtsova in Arkhangel'sk for re-posting anti-war themes on *VKontakte* and Instagram. She had complained online about government-organized pro-war rallies, was snitched on by her Arctic Federal University classmates in January 2023, and faced up to 10 years in a penal colony.[28] While under house arrest, she fled to Lithuania and was placed on Rosfinmonitoring's list of terrorists and extremists.[29]

Several political parties set up websites to collect information from snitchers. For example, the Social Revolutionaries and A Just Russia (#Sprosim-Bastrykina) used what were called 'denunciation' bots through which people could complain about neighbours whom they suspected of sympathy for Ukraine. Local officials sent out notices asking citizens to report on people who spread 'fake news'. A Telegram bot with one of the main symbols of the war, the letter 'Z' from the roman alphabet presented in St. George ribbon colours, was made available for reports on 'provocateurs and scammers'. It is not known how many names found their way to the authorities by these means, but their existence demonstrated a core of activity echoing the time of Soviet Pioneers and Pavel (Pavlik) Morozov, who was killed by family members in the 1930s for snitching on his parents.[30]

Denunciations submitted to Roskomnadzor and other state agencies numbered 300,000 in 2022 alone, ranging from minor to major violations that could be termed treasonous. Lost jobs, lost friends, ostracism and societal distrust were among the results of snitching.[31] By the end of 2023, police complained that they were overwhelmed by reports filed against noisy neighbours, irritating colleagues, and even strangers. One woman boasted to the BBC that she had already denounced over 1,000 people and planned to keep on doing it.[32]

Partial Mobilization

Arrests related to opposition by Russians to the war in Ukraine rose dramatically after Putin declared a partial mobilization on 21 September 2022. At least one organization, the Youth Democratic Movement *Vesna* (Spring), called for an all-Russia protest against mobilization that very day, before amendments to legislation adopted by the State Duma to make refusal to participate a criminal offense came into force. The appeal urged call-ups either not to report or to surrender once they were dragooned into the armed forces, proclaiming: 'Thousands of Russian men – our fathers, brothers and husbands – will be thrown into the meat grinder of war. What will they die for? Why will mothers and children shed tears? For Putin's Palace?'[33]

The partial mobilization proclamation saw a renewal of large-scale anti-war activities across the country. This time, OVD-Info tallied at least 1,310 detentions in 39 Russian cities, 530 of them in Moscow, 536 in St. Petersburg, 47 in Yekaterinburg, and the rest spread throughout.[34] In the North Caucasus, brawls between protesters and police occurred in Makhachkala, Dagestan and also in Nalchik, Kabardino-Balkaria.[35] Large numbers of young men avoided, or tried to avoid, conscription by leaving the country. Direct flights to visa-free Armenia, Turkey, Azerbaijan and Uzbekistan were sold out quickly. On the ground, traffic at Finland's border with Russia 'intensified' overnight, and Russia's borders with Georgia and Kazakhstan were overwhelmed with traffic.[36]

Applications for asylum in EU countries almost tripled, to 8,820, during the first eight months of fighting, though the success rate was low and the process slowed to a near halt. Entry into Finland, the Czech Republic and the Baltic states was almost impossible. The US reported processing about 23,000 asylum requests during that same period, also slowly and resulting in deferred application letters so that individuals would be sent back to Russia whenever the war ended.[37]

The newly resurrected and independent *Novaia Gazeta Evropa* claimed on 25 September that up to 261,000 young men had fled the country already. Videos of long line-ups and huge crowds at airports and border cross points suggest that this astronomical number may not have been too greatly exaggerated.[38] A Telegram channel titled 'Relocation Guide from the Russian Federation' listed options for emigration, which countries were accessible, how to find work abroad, how to deal with border control, and so on. Visits to the 'Guide' that was created by Istanbul-based Ira Lobanovskaya in February 2022, soared after partial mobilization was announced, achieving 1.5 million visits the day following the call-up.[39]

As plane tickets sold out, their prices skyrocketed. The Duma adopted legislation setting long prison terms for desertion (10 years) and 'voluntary surrender' (15 years), defining draft dodging during a period of mobilization or war as desertion. Conscientious objectors risked a three-year term.[40] Even after Putin signed a separate decree exempting full-and part-time students in post-secondary education and vocational training from the mobilization programme, the outflow did not slow.[41] This was true especially in those areas of Russia where non-Russians believed they were singled out for service disproportionately, and in Chechnya, whose head Ramzan Kadyrov claimed that the conscription decree should not apply because the republic had already sent more than its share of soldiers to the conflict.[42]

The mobilization process itself was so chaotic and inefficient that faith in the military apparatus was shaken again. Officials had to send home thousands of men who did not fit the criteria for selection. The situation worsened when citizens learned from social media that thousands of recruits had been deployed to combat units with very little training and poor equipment. To counter the wave of anger and frustration against the enlistment fiasco, the MoD distributed videos showing happy and well-prepared young men going off to fight for their motherland. It was left for body bags to tell the real story.

Public Anti-War Activity Slowdown

Although public anti-war demonstrations faded into the background because of severe restrictions, not everyone gave up. And no one was safe. For instance, in January 2023, authorities charged a deputy in the St. Petersburg legislative assembly, Boris Vishnevsky, with 'discrediting the Russian army'. He and a former deputy, Maksim Reznik, had published an open letter to the chair of Russia's Investigative Committee, Aleksandr Bastrykin, calling on him to open an investigation of the atrocities at Bucha. Reznik had already left the country, but Vishnevsky remained and faced a large fine.[43] Another member of the St. Petersburg assembly, Aleksandr Shishkov, was fined for similar offences in October 2022. All three targets of the court were members of the Yabloko party, as was Muratov, who was attacked and sprayed with red paint while on a train, presumably for his opposition to the war.[44]

Even in 2024, journalists were still the easiest target. Sergei Sokolov, editor of the truncated version of *Novaia Gazeta* that continued to function in Russia, was fined in February 2024 for 'discrediting' Russia's Armed Forces. Not officially connected to its European forebear, it publishes on its channel on Telegram and on YouTube.[45]

Instances of quiet opposition continued to crop up. For example, after the bombing of civilian residences in Dnipro on 14 January 2023 Russians placed flowers and mementos on statues and memorials honouring Ukraine and Ukrainians in at least 50 cities around the country. In Moscow, the statue of Ukrainian poet Lesya Ukrainka was a popular spot for such favours until police placed it under surveillance and several individuals were arrested. In Yekaterinburg, the famous Memorial to Victims of Political Repression was a site at which Russian citizens arranged flowers to express dismay at the actions of their government. In St. Petersburg and elsewhere, statues of famous Ukrainian poet Taras Shevchenko were showered with improvised signs of sympathy, flowers and children's toys. These discreet acts of disobedience were still going on three weeks later in many cities across the country.[46]

A more artistic mode of protest came in the form of sophisticated street graffiti. Members of the Yav (Reality) art group, openly, anonymously, or with code names (e.g. Zoom, Ffchw) painted murals on the sides of deserted buildings or fences. Many of them were equal to Banksy in quality. If the artist was identified, he or she would be detained and fined for 'petty hooliganism'.[47] Offending street art is white-washed by authorities and posters are taken down, but often reappear. One prominent graffiti artist, Vladimir Ovchinnikov (b. 1938), keeps painting anti-war murals, is fined, and then goes back to paint somewhere else. One example of his work was painted on the side of a dilapidated building in Borovsk, a village close to Moscow where he lives. It was whitewashed, and he was fined 35,000 roubles (circa $350). Undaunted, he later drew doves over the spot.[48]

Subtle resistance continued as the second year of war commenced. Coded language appeared on public display. For example, arrested for posting a sign proclaiming 'Net v***e!', which authorities took to mean 'Net Voine!', an activist claimed that the reference really referred to 'Net Voble!' (No to Vobla), a fish called Wobbly in English. She didn't like fish. She was released and drawings of fish soon appeared on telephone poles and other sites; so, too, did three and five dots or images (e.g. of ballerinas) also taken by observers to mean 'Net Voine!', but for which the source, if found, could not be charged easily.[49]

Telegram Messenger Persists

In the midst of the ongoing but subdued opposition in Russia, Roskomnadzor tried to delete banned content from the Internet, even from Telegram. The popular messaging service had been blocked as early as April 2018 because it refused FSB access to users' encrypted messages. The ban was ignored by almost everyone: Peskov continued to use it; Sberbank told employees how to get around the ban; and the messenger became more popular than it had been previously. By February 2023, Roskomnadzor found it necessary to launch a web crawler (Oculus) to scour the Internet for banned materials; for example, videos of the war, images of protesters, LGBT 'propaganda', 'extremist' themes, anti-Putin memes and so on. Successful bans on western social media resulted in the number of Telegram's users more than double during the first year of the war.

According to a representative of Russia's General Radio Frequency Centre (Glavnyi radiochastotnyi tsentr), Oculus helped to delete or block more than 100,000 websites and about 12,000 news items, posts, and reports on Russia's military losses. Depictions of civilian deaths and destruction in Ukraine were removed from Russia's largest search engine, Yandex, and also Mail.r u, *VKontakte* and YouTube. Even at that, the Oculus system will not be fully operable until 2025.[50]

Before Oculus came on the scene, Roskomnadzor employed another automated system for identifying unwanted materials on the Internet. Called *Vepr* (Boar), the system was tasked with finding materials that touched on the topics of territorial integrity, ethnic strife and migration. Its role was expanded in 2022 to catch:

- negative attitudes towards the first person of the state, state structures and interstate organizations;
- fakes about the first persons of the state, about the state and the country as a whole;
- manipulation of public opinion and polarization of society (e.g. on the topics of non-systemic opposition, sanctions pressure, etc.); and
- substitution and discrediting of traditional values.[51]

Russia appears to have returned to the heyday of the Soviet state and self-censorship system under the aegis of Glavlit.

Media personnel sometimes pushed back. When the FSB arrested Evan Gershkovich, an American journalist for the *Wall Street Journal*, and charged him with espionage, some 220 independent Russian journalists signed an open letter demanding his immediate release. Calling the arrest 'preposterous and unjust', they deemed both charges political and without evidence.[52] Needless to say, the petition carried by the anti-Putin *Mediazona,* which was founded in 2013 by the famous punk rock protest group Pussy Riot and blocked in Russia in 2022, went unheeded by the FSB and probably unnoticed by the Russian public.

The pressure against oppositionists did not ease off. In April 2023, authorities opened three criminal investigations against Roman Ivanov, a RusNews journalist whose Telegram channel had 1,600 subscribers. Amnesty International called for his unconditional release, uselessly.[53] In May, director Yevgeniya (Zhenya) Berkovich and playwright Svetlana Petriychuk were detained in Moscow, suspected of justifying terrorism because their company put on a play titled Finist the Brave Falcon (Finist Yasnyi Sokol) about Russian women who fell in love with Islamist militants, married them, and moved to Syria. The 2022 version was anti-patriarchal and anti-terrorism, and was nominated for several awards. Berkovich may have been targeted because of a solo picket against the invasion of Ukraine on 24 February 2022, for which she served 11 days in detention. Subsequently, she wrote anti-war poems and posted them on Facebook. Her over-arching 'crime' in Russia, however, was most likely her feminist activism.[54]

A year later, a military court extended the pre-trial detention of both Berkovich and Petriychuk for another six months and, in July 2024, they were both sentenced to six years in prison for 'justifying terrorism'.[55]

After a year and a half of conflict, the persecution of opponents to the war intensified even as the number of targets diminished. A court in the Trans-Baikal region fined a student 30,000 roubles (circa $350) for stating in her class that 'Russia started the war, attacked Ukraine. Russia is an aggressor, it kills innocent residents of Ukraine'. The student claimed that she had been led into this statement by the teacher and her words were taken out of context. No matter, she was found guilty of 'discrediting the use of the RF Armed Forces', denounced by her own teacher and university classmates.[56]

Since the invasion of Ukraine, foreign journalists have been required to re-apply for visa and media accreditation every three months, rather than the previous annual applications. In August 2023, Russia's Foreign Ministry expelled Eva Hartog, a Dutch correspondent for *Politico Europe*, and Anna-Lena Laurén, a reporter for the Swedish newspaper, *Dagens Nyheter*. Their visa renewals and accreditation applications were rejected with no reasons offered, and they were given six days to leave the country. They were the first foreign journalists to be so treated since the SVO started.[57] The arrest of Gershkovich had been a sign of things to come.

There were even signs of governments-in-exile forming abroad. For instance, Ilya Ponomarev announced a secret National Republican Army during a YouTube message posted on Telegram in which he credited this body with the assassination of Dugina in August 2022.[58] Ponomarev, the only State Duma deputy to vote against the annexation of Crimea in 2014, and others used a Telegram app, February Morning (Utro fevralya), to counter state propaganda about the war in Ukraine. According to one source, at that time, February Morning had '27 regional outlets each with its own Telegram channel where activists and journalists mingle to gather and share news of anti-Putin actions', with about 70 journalists spread around Russia and Ukraine. They set up another Telegram channel called Russian Partisan (Rospartizan), which provided them with a link to the not-so-secret National Republican Army, and also to the militant Freedom of Russia Legion.[59]

Protesters-in-exile and at home had more to worry about when, in January 2024, the State Duma adopted, unanimously, legislation allowing authorities to confiscate the property of anyone convicted of spreading 'fake news' about Russia's army or inciting 'extremist' action. Speaking in support of the bill, Volodin labelled such individuals as 'traitors'.[60]

PRO-WAR POLITICAL ACTIVITIES

On top of the constant barrage of information, misinformation and disinformation from the state apparatus in support of the SVO, dozens of public organizations formed specifically to promote it. Some of these took shape spontaneously, others grew out of existing movements, while still more were created by federal, republic or municipal agencies. In January 2023, for instance, the Soldiers Widows (Soldatskie vdovy) of Russia urged Putin to call for general mobilization after the slaughter of Russian troops at Makiivka on New Years' eve, and to forbid men of military age from leaving the country. They cited the example of Stalin, who thought only 'in terms of victory'.[61]

Long-existing organizations were called into action as well. In June 2022, the ONF launched a fund-raising project to support the military. Called 'Everything for Victory' (Vse dlia pobedy!), it collected about six billion roubles by April 2023 and used it to buy ammunition, clothing and other equipment for Russian troops. The ONF also instituted a service system for wounded veterans, and maintained a large photographic exhibition of smiling soldiers and military equipment in the Grand Kremlin Palace for the months of May and June in 2023.[62]

At the children's level, private clubs, like For Victory! (Za Pobedy!), coordinated volunteers to help children write letters to soldiers at the front, often giving them the right things to say. At a cruder level, the Committee for the Protection of National Interests listed 'traitors' and 'cowards and runaways' with their photos and job descriptions on its website (inagent.info), plus an 'Encyclopaedia of Foreign Agents'.

A 'White Armbands' flash mob (#whitepovyazka) circulated photos depicting groups of private citizens, teachers and schoolchildren all wearing a white armband in solidarity with the Russian army. And the letters 'Z' and 'V' appeared everywhere as symbols of support for the army, on T-shirts, walls, posters, toques and peaked caps. T-shirts sporting the slogan 'I am not ashamed' (Mne ne stydno) or 'We are not ashamed' (Nam ne stydno), along with a small Russian flag, were marketed aggressively and also displayed on posters, bumper stickers and on Internet memes.[63]

Dozens of pro-war bloggers, with thousands of followers, aggressively glorified the war effort. Prominent among these were GrayZone (thegrayzone.com/category/Russia/); Reverse Side of the Medal (t.me/s/rsotmdivision); and Rybar (t-me/rybar), with hundreds of thousands of followers between them.

The most commonly accessed of these was Rybar (Fisherman), which publishes detailed reports and accurate maps of the front lines. It is sometimes used by Western media (CNN, Bloomberg) and military analysts

(Institute for the Study of War), though it is strongly biased on the side of Russia. Rybar posts 5–6 detailed reports each day in its channel on Telegram. The blog started in 2018 to study Middle East issues, with about 30,000 followers and rose to about 1.1 million after Putin launched the SVO.[64]

The assassinated Tatarsky had co-hosted a programme on the Rybar site. Matviyenko, Zakharova and Patriarch Kirill issued statements claiming that Tatarsky told the 'truth' and, with nearly 600,000 followers on his Telegram channel, implied that his efforts were key instruments in the state's domestic propaganda about the SVO.[65] Putin granted him the Order of Courage posthumously. The accused assassin, Daria Trepova, who admitted that she delivered the bomb disguised in a golden bust of Tatarsky, was later handed down a sentence of 27 years, said to be the harshest to a woman in post-Soviet Russia. She insisted that she didn't know the gift was a bomb; authorities claimed she was acting on behalf of Ukrainian 'terrorists'.[66]

Other celebrity advocates of the war became targets of anti-war activists. In addition to Dugina and Tatarsky, an attempt was made on well-known novelist and Russian nationalist Zakhar Prilepin, whose car was blown up in the Nizhny Novgorod region. He was injured; his driver died. In 2020, Prilepin formed the For Truth (Za pravdu) political party that later merged with A Just Russia. At least two groups took credit for the assassination, the 'Atesh' partisan movement of Crimean Tatars, Ukrainians and Russians fighting against Russia in occupied Ukraine, and Ponomarev's National Republican Army.[67] Not wanting to acknowledge these groups, police made an arrest, the official media posted many photos of the deed and the arrestee who, the GPO claimed, confessed to acting on instructions from the Ukrainian special services.[68]

The more extreme nationalist bloggers were targeted by Putin as well, especially after Prigozhin's aborted mutiny. A cross section of hard-line pro-war hawks, such as those mentioned above, were now perceived as threats to the Kremlin's leadership. The clampdown began with the arrest of Igor Girkin, former commander of separatist units in the Donbas with some 800,000 subscribers to his blog. Under sanction by Western countries for his alleged role in shooting down the Malaysian Airline Flight 17 in 2014 and founder of a social movement called the Club of Angry Patriots (Klub rasserzhennykh patriotov) in April 2023, he crossed a line by calling for Putin's resignation. The charge against him was 'public incitement of extremist activity'. Girkin and others had helped Putin instil nationalist fervour in grassroots patriotic movements from the onset of war, but their growing criticism of the MoD and even of Putin went too far.[69]

In January 2024, a Moscow court sentenced Girkin to four years in prison for extremism related to his denigration of the MoD's war strategy. Police arrested several of his supporters who were part of a demonstration on his behalf outside the courtroom.[70]

These arrests did not stop Russia hardliners from expressing their opinions. Mourners at the cemetery where Prigozhin was buried called him a true Russian 'warrior', and nationalist bloggers continued to disparage the way in which the war was conducted – demanding more, not less. For instance, after the strike on a military airfield in Pskov, Rybar and other bloggers complained that Russian air defences had not adjusted to drone attacks and that Russia should report such attacks immediately so as to prepare the public.[71] They wanted the war to be fought more aggressively and, to achieve that, regularly reported problems within the military that the MoD tried to keep secret.[72]

POLITICAL PARTIES IN LIMBO

With the war in Ukraine dominating all political activity and opposition movements muffled either by irrelevance or by oppressive laws, the traditional between-election carping among political parties was noticeably absent in 2022. The radical liberal opposition party, the Party of People's Freedom (PARNAS), was closed down by the Russian Supreme Court in May 2023, leaving only Yabloko to object to the war. Founded first in 1990, dissolved in 2004, and resurrected three years later, Yabloko was one of the oldest progressive parties in post-Soviet Russia. Now led by Nikolai Rybakov, its prior leadership had included Mikhail Kasyanov (fled the country in 2022), Boris Nemtsov (assassinated in 2012), Vladimir Kara-Murza and Ilya Yashin (both in prison).[73] To survive, other mainstream parties ramped up their patriotic credentials.

Perennial third-place party, the LDPR, was rudderless since the death of its founder Vladimir Zhirinovsky in April. It was embarrassed when Prigozhin turned down an offer of membership with a rather scathing reference to the current party leader, Slutsky.

The communists took advantage of the government's evocation of the victory over the Nazis in 1945 to resurrect the image of Stalin as a wartime leader. More than a 1,000 people took part in a ceremony conducted by the CPRF in Red Square to commemorate the seventieth anniversary of the dictator's death. They hoped that the gradual restoration of Stalin's image would help them in national elections.[74] Hoping as well to co-opt the surge of patriotism related to the SVO, the CPRF conducted its 2023 induction ceremony of Young Pioneers on Red Square on 19 May. Nearly 5,000 children between the ages of 9–14 from 45 cities and their parents gathered wearing red caps and neckerchiefs to hear Zyuganov praise their loyalty to Soviet traditions and urge them to spread patriotism among their peers.[75]

To seize the mantle of the most patriotic of parties, the UR began solidifying its dominant hold on the electorate in late 2022 by purging its ranks of anyone deemed an opponent of the war in Ukraine. To do this, the UR scanned the social networks *VKontakte* and *Odnoklassniki* for party members who opposed the SVO directly or indirectly. This process cut the signed-up membership base by about half but opened up its ranks for a larger war-supporting base.[76]

Party leader Vasiliev met again with Putin in March 2023 in a televised one-on-one session and outlined what amounted to a political campaign agenda. After proclaiming that the UR 'takes an absolutely patriotic position', he went on take credit for some 20 new laws. These were a mixed bag of legislation on integrating the annexed regions of Ukraine and their remaining populations into the Russian Federation, protecting the social welfare of all Russians, the environment, entrepreneurial activities and labour relations, health and education. Above all, Vasiliev stressed work done to ameliorate hardships faced by participants in the SVO, veterans and their families. Very few details came with the list of accomplishment presented by him and acknowledged by Putin.[77]

At any rate, if the results of Levada Centre polls conducted in February 2023 may be taken as accurate, there was little need for the UR to worry. Approval rates for Putin, Mishustin, the government and even the State Duma had risen consistently since the autumn of 2022 (see table 5.1).

Table 5.1. Approval Rates: National Direction, Putin, Mishustin, Government and State Duma

1. Is the country moving in the right direction or wrong direction?				
	Sept 2022	Dec 2022	Jan 2023	Feb 2023
Right direction	60	62	66	68
Wrong direction	27	24	24	21
Difficult to answer	12	13	10	11
2. Do you approve or disapprove of Vladimir Putin's activities as president?				
Approve	77	81	82	83
Don't approve	21	17	16	14
No answer	2	2	2	2
3. Do you approve or disapprove of the activity of Prime Minister Mishustin?				
Approve	66	71	70	70
Don't approve	28	23	23	20
No answer	6	6	7	10
4. Do you approve or disapprove of the activities of the Russian government?				
Approve	63	68	67	69
Don't approve	34	28	29	29
No answer	3	4	4	6

Table 5.1.

5. Do you approve or disapprove of the activities of the State Duma?				
Approve	54	57	55	59
Don't approve	41	37	40	34
No answer	5	6	5	7

Source: Compiled by the author from 'Odobrenie institutov v reitinge politikov: Fevral' 2023 goda', Levada-tsentr, 1 March 2023, levada.ru/2023/03/01/odobrenie-institutov-i-rejtingi-politikov-fevral-2023-goda/.

Approval rating for political parties and leaders was one thing, getting the general population on-side with any of them was another matter, particularly since the war in Ukraine soaked up all the political oxygen. Nevertheless, street demonstrations to express social and economic grievances were not curbed, as long as Ukraine was not mentioned. For instance, in April, a crowd gathered in Ulyanovsk to demand the return of direct elections for the city mayor. In Novosibirsk and Perm, gatherings protested high utility prices. These rallies required permission from the authorities and were often organized by political parties, most often the CPRF.[78]

Preparing for the September 2023 Elections

Draft amendments to the federal election law promised to streamline the electoral process. They abolished absentee ballots, allowed public chambers to appoint observers, and enabled individuals who are lodged in pre-trial detention centres and have not lost their voting rights to vote locally.[79] At the same time, however, the number of polling booths were reduced, by about 40 per cent in Moscow and elsewhere by 10 per cent or less. The CEC claimed that this would reduce costs and make it easier for parties to arrange for observers. It said also that fewer booths were possible because of the greatly increased use of electronic voting. This last explanation, critics said, made voting much more vulnerable to corruption and rigging by state authorities.[80]

When CEC director, Pamfilova, unveiled its official logo for September's regional elections, it featured a huge 'V' presented in the colours of the Russian flag, making certain that the SVO was a central consideration for voters.

As all political parties prepped for September's electoral cycle, in-house fighting seemed not to have changed much. For example, the communist movement fragmented yet again. Already divided between the dominant CPRF and the Communists of Russia, the latter group split further as a struggle for leadership emerged between former leader Maksim Suraykin and current leader Sergei Malinkovich. A Party Congress held in Moscow on 14 May returned Suraykin to the leadership post, unanimously, and nominated him to run in September for the position of Mayor of Moscow.[81]

When it came to actual campaigning, all major parties positioned the war in Ukraine on top of their platforms and blamed the West for nurturing it. They competed with each other for the 'most patriotic' label and shoved pressing domestic issues into the background. Leaders of the CPRF and the LDPR even suggested that opposition parties merge into some sort of single patriotic party. While this did not happen, the lack of political opposition among the systemic parties and the state-directed stifling of opposition among extra-systemic parties made it clear that there was but one acceptable current of thought in the political arena – Putin's.[82]

While the State Duma was taken up with the Prigozhin insurrection, the LDPR took a moment to propose an economic innovation. Slutsky submitted a draft law on abolishing all personal income taxes for individuals earning less than 30,000 roubles per month, an amount nearly double the cost of living at the time. The personal income tax rate in Russia was still 15 per cent for those whose annual income exceeded five million roubles, and 13 per cent for everyone else.[83]

At first, the UR made certain of its unique dedication to the SVO by picking 100 of its candidates in primaries from among direct participants in the conflict. Over half of them were combat veterans, others worked in humanitarian capacities in occupied territories, and 28 of the aspirants were still on the battlefield. It was assumed that most of these would win in their primary contests and be on September's ballot. The UR primaries began on 22 May.[84]

After the Prigozhin disaster, UR nominees tended to downplay the SVO and discussed day-to-day issues instead. A month prior to the elections, VTsIOM reported that the UR held 37.7 per cent of popular support, the CPRF 10.2 and the LDPR 9 per cent.[85]

Local Elections, September 2023

The September 2023 elections were held in 49 of the Federation's regions, as well as in Crimea and the four areas annexed from Ukraine the previous year. Independent observers and journalists were not invited to the polling stations.[86] They began during the first week of the month in the Russian-occupied parts of Ukraine, with soldiers standing by, and then took place in Russia on the weekend of 8–9 September. As the first day wound down, the independent election monitoring agency *Golos* (Voice) recorded up to 600 voting irregularities. According to *Golos*, intimidation, vote buying and people prevented from casting their ballots were the most common complaints. There were also tales of ballot box stuffing and so-called 'carousel voting', where a voter casts multiple ballots by traveling between different polling stations.[87]

The first notable victory came in quickly, with Sergei Sobyanin easily winning his third term as Mayor of Moscow. Campaigning as a member of the UR, he far surpassed contenders from other parties, none of whom earned two-digit returns. Turnout in Moscow was more than 40 per cent of eligible voters, the highest in two decades.[88] Although Sobyanin would likely have won anyway, *Golos* listed reports of voter intimidation and procedural violations in Moscow and criticized the online voting system's lack of transparency.

As expected, UR candidates held their seats almost everywhere by wide margins, aided by a new electronic voting system that increased turnout, a rally around the flag atmosphere that made 'Putin's party' a logical choice, and Putin's own campaign tactic that focused on large development projects. All three by-elections to the State Duma were taken by UR contestants; incumbents won in all 21 gubernatorial campaigns, and the UR dominated voting in local legislatures in all but two of the 16 contests. The two failures (Oryol, Khakasia) were taken by the CPRF. Elections in the occupied parts of Ukraine returned over 70 per cent UR in each electoral district.

THE NAVALNY FACTOR

Always looming, first at the forefront and after October 2022 in the background, was the Navalny network. Disbanded officially in 2021 on being designated an 'extremist' organization, it reconstituted itself precisely to oppose the war in Ukraine and mobilization. Former director of Navalny's Anti-Corruption Foundation (Fond bor'by s korruptsiei – FBK), Ivan Zhdanov, and Leonid Volkov announced from exile that the new body would operate as a 'partisan underground', distributing information, providing legal assistance, and even sabotaging recruiting offices.[89]

In response, according to Navalny, the state opened up another criminal case against him, this time for promoting terrorism and extremism. Navalny's status in prison was unclear by January 2023, when during yet another court hearing he said he was ill and that he had been refused proper medical treatment. The hearing was postponed. His wife, Yulia Navalnaia, charged on Telegram that 'Putin is still trying to kill Navalny but in a quieter and slower manner compared to the Novichok poisoning', and the international media began expressing concern about his fate, again.[90] Illness did not stop Navalny from speaking out from inside. Remarking on the second anniversary of his return to Russia and arrest, he posted on Twitter that, 'Our miserable, exhausted Motherland needs to be saved. It has been pillaged, wounded, dragged into an aggressive war, and turned into a prison run by the most unscrupulous and deceitful scoundrels'.[91]

On 20 February, four days prior to the anniversary of Putin's SVO, Navalny tweeted, one at a time, '15 theses of a Russian citizen who desires the best for his country'. The list opened with 'the combination of aggressive warfare, corruption, inept generals, weak economy and heroism and high motivation of the defending forces can only result in defeat'. He argued for the dissolution of the 'Putin regime and its dictatorship', using Russia's energy revenues as reparations for Ukraine, and making Russia part of Europe – otherwise Russia would remain weak, isolated and under-developed. The theses were not mentioned by Russia's mainstream media, but were circulated via Twitter thread, and also by the exiled *Meduza* and *The Moscow Times*.[92]

According to Russia's Human Rights Commissioner, Tatiana Moskalkova, Navalny had appealed to her office 50 times during the first year of his incarceration and each of these had been investigated by the Prosecutor General's Office and the Federal Penitentiary Service. As far as they were concerned, his rights to a lawyer, reasonable living conditions and opportunity to work were adhered to just as they would have been for any prisoner – for whatever that was worth. She was objecting to the EU's inclusion of her name on its 24 February 2023 black list.[93]

The Russian prisoner won the foreign public relations battle, however, when the Canadian-made film, *Navalny*, earned an Oscar for the best documentary in 2022 at the Academy Awards ceremony in Hollywood. Navalnaia and their children, Daria and Zakhar, stood on the stage with director, Daniel Roher, and told the audience that her husband was jailed for protesting against 'Putin's unjust war of aggression in Ukraine' and that she dreamed of the day when her husband and her country would both be free.[94] Although the Russian opposition press in exile exulted in the film's success, wherever the Hollywood ceremonies were mentioned in the Russian mainstream media the documentary was ignored. Interfax reported it in two sentences, with no commentary. Questioned about it, Peskov said he had not seen the film but assumed it was politicized.[95] *RT* published a longer piece on the film, including photos of Navalny's family on stage, and used it to cast doubt on whether he had been poisoned and to justify his imprisonment on returning to Russia ('He had broken his parole. . . . The violation activated his suspended sentence').[96]

Navalny's standing in prison grew murkier. On 19 April 2023, he was returned to solitary confinement for 'another 15 days'. According to reports from his team, Navalny still was suffering from ill health. He complained that, 'I was limited in buying food (we have new rules now), my daily walk is now at 7 am (it's important, because if your walk is in the afternoon, you can get lucky enough to stand in a sunny spot for a while), I now get barely any time to read letters'.[97] Within a day of his release from solitary in May, he was returned there for 15 more days, this time for failing to 'submit to correctional work'.[98]

Coping with a military court by video in April, bringing the number of criminal cases launched against him since his earlier sentence of nine years to ten, he faced life imprisonment on new charges of terrorism. His team shared Navalny's opinion of the charges as 'absurd' on Twitter, noting that he could hardly invoke a terrorist uprising while in prison.[99] He was given 10 days to study the hundreds of pages of documentation against him. At the same time, prosecutors asked for a 12-year sentence for the former head of the Navalny foundation's office in Ufa, Lilia Chanysheva. Arrested first in November 2021 she was charged in 2023 with creating an 'extremist community'.[100] In June, a court sentenced Chanysheva to 7.5 years in prison. Just a few weeks later, another Navalny ally, Vadim Ostanin, was sent to prison for nine years, also on 'extremist' charges. He had been the coordinator of Navalny's political team in Barnaul, Siberia.[101]

Shortly before the new trial, the Navalny team orchestrated an international series of demonstrations in his support. The actual occasion was his third birthday while serving the prison sentence. Russians and their supporters in over 100 cities world-wide rallied for the release of Navalny and all political prisoners in Russia. Brave individuals came out in Russia as well, mostly as single pickets holding simple signs, often in English 'Free Navalny'. Over 100 citizens were arrested across the country, about half of them in Moscow. Slogans, such as 'Freedom to Navalny' (Svobodu Naval'nomu) were spray painted on buildings.[102]

Facing still more charges later in June 2023, Navalny renewed his campaign against Putin and the war in Ukraine from the court room prisoner's box in Melekhovo. In a separate filing, Navalny lost an appeal to the Russian Supreme Court against a regulation that allows prison officials to deprive him of pen and paper. Appearing in court via video link, he argued that, without writing materials, he could not write complaints or correspond with family.[103] Back in court in July, where the prosecution was seeking a 20-year sentence for 'extremism', a wan and thin Navalny again commented bitterly: Russia 'is floundering in a pool of either mud or blood, with broken bones, with a poor and robbed population, and around it lie tens of thousands of people killed in the most stupid and senseless war of the 21st century'. Although the trial was closed, his team circulated Navalny's words on its Telegram site.[104]

Finally, he was sentenced to 19 more years in a special regime colony, which differed from the strict regime colony where he was imprisoned in that he can receive fewer visitors, parcels and letters. The court found him guilty of 'organizing an extremist community, rehabilitating Nazism, creating an NGO that infringes on the personality and rights of citizens, financing extremism, inciting extremism and involving minors in dangerous acts'. His co-defendant, Daniel Kholodny, former technical director of Navalny LIVE, received eight years in a general regime colony.[105] They both lost appeals of this additional sentence in late September.

Navalny released a blistering 2000-word essay titled 'My Fear and Hatred'. He hated Yeltsin and 'those who sold, drank, squandered the historical chance that our country had in the early nineties'. Currently, he 'hates' the present-day oligarchs who benefit from 'the rules of the game' set by their predecessors for Putin to use: 'You can steal, falsify, censor, and all the courts are under your control'. He advised viewers to 'stay true to yourselves and tirelessly explain . . . that democratic principles – pragmatism, and independent court, fair elections and equality before the law – are the best mechanism for a harsh real life on the path to prosperity'. Their time would come, he promised, though not very optimistically.[106]

For this outburst, and others, he was returned to solitary confinement and deprived of writing materials. This was his twenty-first stay in solitary amounting to nearly a year in total days.[107] Not satisfied, the authorities pressed new criminal charges against Navalny. This time, the charge was vandalism, the fourteenth criminal case brought against him. Here is how he described the news on X (Twitter):

1/5 I have no idea which word to use to describe my latest news. Whether it's sad, funny or absurd.
   They bring me letters:
- Any letters from my wife?
- Censored.
- Any papers from the lawyer?
- Censored.
- And what do you have?
- There's one from the investigator.[108]

The letter from the 'investigator' outlined the new charges. Most independent observers go with 'absurd'.

On 16 February 2024, Russian prison officials announced Navalny's death in prison. Claiming that the 47-year old 'felt unwell after a walk and almost immediately lost consciousness', they said he received medical attention right away and that the unexplained death would be investigated thoroughly.[109] Joe Biden, Zelensky, most Western leaders and pundits and Russian oppositionists in exile, instantly blamed Putin, many of them calling it murder. Sakharova and Peskov ridiculed them for not waiting the results of an investigation.[110] Volodin carried the Russian blame attribution habit to new heights, or depths, by charging 'Washington and Brussels' with responsibility for Navalny's death and went on to point fingers at Stoltenberg, Biden, Scholz, Sunak and Zelensky.[111] The nightmarish fictional world of Kafka appeared to have become a reality in Russia.

It wasn't clear how the Russian people would react, though small crowds gathered spontaneously in many of Russia's major cities and laid flowers at makeshift memorials to Navalny and existing monuments dedicated to Soviet victims of political repression. Nearly 300 mourners were detained across the country on the first day, 100 of them in St. Petersburg where a priest who planned to lead a service for Navalny also was arrested. These numbers kept growing at home, while Russians abroad laid flowers or picketed at the gates of Russian embassies.[112] The government's relative silence was countered by messages and accusations that flooded into Russia via domestic social media (e.g. Telegram) and exiled news outlets (e.g. *Dozhd, The Moscow Times*).

As Navalny's mother tried to retrieve her son's body, Navalnaia vowed to carry on his cause and launched a social media platform on X (Twitter) that drew 82,001 followers the first day (twitter.com/yulia_Navalnaia). The site was suspended for a day, but soon re-appeared. Her YouTube statement that she would continue her husband's work had over 5 million views.[113] Navalny's mother finally got to see her son's body, but was told to hold a funeral in secret. She refused. Her message to this effect, on Aleksei Navalny's YouTube site, had over two million viewers and 25,000 comments as of 23 February.[114] As the United States, the United Kingdom and the EU launched hundreds of new sanctions against Russia, she threatened a lawsuit and was allowed to take possession of the body a few days later.[115]

Although Western media immediately began lionizing Navalnaia as the new leader among Russian dissidents abroad, highlighting a hug from Joe Biden and her speech at the Munich Security Conference, it wasn't clear how, or if, she might succeed.[116] There is no guarantee either that the cause espoused by Navalny and his followers will ever gain much traction in Russia, not only because of the repressive nature of the state, but also because of widespread distrust of notions that are perceived to be by-products of Western 'liberalism'.

On the other hand, thousands of people began gathering for Navalny's memorial service and funeral in Moscow, filing past police lines chanting Navalny's name and raising cut flowers over their heads. Some also shouted 'No to war!', 'Russia without Putin!', or 'Free political prisoners!'. The service was conducted at an Orthodox Church in Maryino and Navalny was buried at the Borisovsk cemetery. Navalny's parents, politicians Nadezhdin and Duntsova, and several Western ambassadors (e.g. from the United States, Canada, Czech Republic, France, Germany), attended and tens of thousands watched on YouTube provided by *Dozhd* and Navalny's organization. In other cities, mourners brought flowers to memorials for victims of political oppression. Russia's official press mentioned the event only in passing, making much of the fact that his wife and children were not there without noting that they were in political exile, and repeating that Navalny was a 'terrorist and extremist'.[117] Around more 400 mourners were detained in 39 cities across the country.[118]

On 6 March, Navalnaia tested the reins of leadership and used YouTube to urge Russians to hold protests at polling stations, spoil their ballots or vote against Putin when the election process started. Hoping to cut such activity off at the pass, a week later police raided the homes of known anti-war artists and activist in Moscow and St. Petersburg, including the home of Pussy Riot members still in Russia. In what was probably a Russian special services action, Leonid Volkov was attacked and badly beaten in Vilnius, just a few days before the Russian presidential election.[119]

At about the same time, a court in Moscow sentenced two university students to 3.5 years in prison for being part of Navalny's 'extremist community' and police raided the homes of people in the Stavropol region who worked on Nadezhdin's campaign.[120]

It was left to that election to define the political scene in Russia as it moved into the third year of Putin's war in Ukraine. During the build-up towards that election senior officials worked hard to persuade Russians that their country's democracy was unique. In addition to Pamfilovas's lecture to schoolchildren about the merits of Russia's electoral system, Peskov insisted at the World Youth Festival in the Krasnodar region that 'our democracy is the best'. Speaking at the same affair, Medvedev contributed more aggressive rhetoric, twisting history to justify the war on Ukraine, calling the current Ukrainian state a slave of a 'decrepit' Europe and insisting that 'Ukraine is, of course, Russia'.[121]

After Putin's resounding victory in the presidential election, *Golos* listed hundreds of violations and complained that 'never before have we seen a presidential campaign that fell so far short of constitutional standards'.[122] No matter, the *vozhd*'s message now reigned supreme.

NOTES

1. On this, see Lisa McIntosh Sundstrom, 'The improbable path to peace through domestic political change in Russia', *Canadian Slavonic Papers*, 14 September 2022 (on-line).

2. Mariia Abakumova, 'Vasilii Anisimov stal sed'mym milliarderon, vyshedshim iz rossiiskogo grazhdanstva', *Forbes Russia*, 8 February 2024.

3. 'Volodin: podderzhavshim kievskii rezhim relokantam po vozvrashchenii v RF "obespechen Magadan"', *TASS*, 10 October 2023; 'Fridman heads home, as pro-war lobby push for punishments against emigrants', *The Bell*, 18 October 2023.

4. 'More than 1.1 thousand seats in the municipal elections in Moscow receive the candidates of United Russia', *TASS*, 12 September 2022; Ivan Nechepurenko, 'Amid wartime repression, pro-Putin candidates sweep to victory in regional and local elections', *New York Times*, 12 September 2022.

5. 'Eks-redaktora "Pervogo kanala" Marinu Ovsyannikovy ob'iavili v rozysk', *OVD-Info*, 3 September 2022, ovd.news/express-news/2022/10/03/eks-redaktora-per vogo-kanala-marinu-ovsyannikovu-obyavili-v-rozysk.

6. SOTA, 'Basmannyi sud Moskvy zaochno progovoril . . . Ovsyannikovu k 8,5 godam . . .', *Telegram*, 4 October 2023, t.me/sotaproject/67427.

7. 'French investigators looking into alleged poisoning of ex-Russian TV journalist', *TASS*, 12 October 2023; this item could not be found in TASS's Russian-language press releases; 'France probes suspected poisoning of Russian journalist who staged TV protest', *The Moscow Times*, 13 October 2023.

8. Avtozak LIVE, Telegram, 15 March 2022, t.me/avtozaklive/13077, include photo.

9. On this, see Riley Farrell, 'Russian women run Ukraine anti-war protests despite danger', *ABC News*, 12 October 2022, abcnews.go.com/International/russian-women-run-ukraine-anti-war-protests-danger/story?id=91378202.

10. To access via Telegram, t.me/femagainstwar_bot.

11. 'Trial of Russian artist for anti-war supermarket protest begins', *The Moscow Times*, 16 December 2022; Mediazona, 'Sashu Skochilenko prigovorili k 7 godam kolonii po delu o "feikakh" iz-za antivoennykh tsennikov', *Telegram*, 16 November 2023, t.me/mediazzzona/13608; '"I just wanted to stop the war": Russian artist sentenced to 7 years for price tag protest', *The Moscow Times*, 16 November 2023; 'Seven years in jail for supermarket sticker protestor', *The Bell*, 22 November 2023.

12. 'Sud arestoval kommercheskogo direktora Sobchak po delu o vymogatel'stve', *RAPSI*, 26 October 2022; 'Investigators raid home of Russian Celeb Ksenia Sobchak', *The Moscow Times*, 26 October 2022.

13. OVD-Info, '16,437 zaderzhanii za antivoennuiu pozitsiiu, nachinaia s 24 fevralia 2022', 17 August 2022, data.ovdinfo.org/svodka-antivoennyh-repressiy-polg oda-voyny#1. For photos of protests as they took place on 24 February 2022, see Alan Taylor, 'Anti-war protests in Russia', *The Atlantic*, 24 February 2022.

14. OVD-Info (en.ovdinfo.org/), accessed 26 February 2024.

15. Pavel Chikov, 'Kolichestvo ugolovnykh del o voennykh feikakh', *Telegram*, 22 December 2022, t.me/pchikov/5336.

16. OVD-Info, 23 December 2022 and 7 January 2023, accessed 4 November. See also 'Russia Jails man for 3 years over Ukraine remarks', *The Moscow Times*, 23 December 2022; 'Russian journalist Maria Ponomarenko sentenced to 6 years in jail over post on Mariupol strike', *Politico*, 15 February 2023; 'Russia jails anti-war journalist 6 years for "fake" news', *The Moscow Times*, 15 February 2023, see t.me/free_dmivanov/8; 'Avtora "Protestnogo MGU" Dmitriia Ivanova prigovorili k 8,5 godam kolonii iz-za postov v telegrame', *OVD-Info*, 7 March 2023.

17. 'Former opposition mayor Roizman on trial for "discrediting" Russian army', *The Moscow Times*, 26 April 2023; 'Russian court orders release of former mayor charged with "discrediting armed forces"', *RFE/RL*, 25 August 2023.

18. 'Journalist Kara-Murza to stay in jail over fake news allegations', *RAPSI*, 9 June 2022; 'Kremlin critic Kara-Murza goes on trial for treason', *Euractiv and the Moscow Times*, 14 March 2023.

19. '"Sud otkazalsia priostanovit" ugolovnoe delo sopredsedatelia TsEPCh "Memorial" Olega Orlova', *OVD-Info*, 8 June 2023; 'Russia's Memorial rights group co-chair on trial over Ukraine criticism', *The Moscow Times*, 8 June 2023; Tsentr Memorial, 'Sud priznal Orlova vinovnym . . .', *Telegram*, 11 October 2023, t.me/polniypc/5523.

20. Memorial Tsentr Zashchitu Prav Cheloveka, 'Poslednee Slovo Olega Orlova', 12 October 2023, memorialcenter.org/news/poslednee-slovo-olega-orlova. For an English-language translation, '"Russia will emerge from the darkness": Memorial co-chair Orlov's final words in court', *The Moscow Time*, 11 October 2023.

21. Obshchestvo Memorial, Telegram 27 April 2023, t.me/toposmemoru/2981; 'Memorial's yekaterinburg head accused of double army "discreditation"', *The Moscow Times*, 27 April 2023; 'Former law enforcement officer sentenced to seven years . . .', *Meduza*, 24 April 2023.

22. See, e.g. 'Patriarch Kirill defrocked protodeaccon Andrei Kuraev, who criticizes the Russian Orthodox Church and the Russian authorities', *OVD-Info*, 28 April 2023.

23. For Chernysheva, Thread. @Sota)_Vision, 'V Moskve prishli s obyskom i zaderzhali devushku-konditera iz-za torta s nadpisiami "Net voine": – OVD-Info', *Twitter*, 27 April 2023, and 'Moscow baker faces fine for anti-war cakes', *The Moscow Times*, 28 April 2023; Will Stewart, Rachel Hagan, 'Woman, 22, who baked "f*** Vladimir Putin" cakes detained by Russian police', *The Daily Mirror*, 28 April 2023.

24. 'Open Letter. Svobodu Filonovoi!. Sait podderzhki Natal'i Ivanovny Filonovoi; filonova.online/?p=208; 'Russian anti-war activist's son held in "prison conditions" in juvenile detention', *The Moscow Times*, 2 May 2023; Liudi Baikala, *Telegram*, 31 August 2023, t.me/Baikal_People/3303.

25. 'Soveshchnie o merakh sotsial'no-ekonomicheskoi podderzhki regionov', *Kremlin.ru*, 16 March 2022, kremlin.ru/events/president/news/67996.

26. 'The father of the girl who drew the anti-war drawing was detained in the case of repeated discrediting of the army', *OVD-Info*, 1 March 2023, ovd.news/express-news/2023/03/01/otca-devochki-narisovavshey-antivoennyy-risunok-zaderzhali-po-delu-o; 'Russian man arrested for daughter's anti-war drawing', *The Moscow Times*, 1 March 2022, with photos of the girl, her father and the drawing; 'Mediazona – Sud prigovoril k dvum godam kolonii Tul'skogo ottsa-odnochku Alekseia Moskaleva. . . .', *Telegram*, 28 March 2023, t.me/mediazzzona/11082; 'Delo Alekseia i Mashi Moskalevykh: khronologiia', *OVD-Info*, 28 March 2023.

27. 'Delo Alekseia i Masha Moskalevykh: khronika', *OVD-Info*, 3 April 2023; 'Alekseiu Moskalevu uzhestochili prigovor posle apelliatsii', *OVD-Info*, 3 July 2023.

28. Georgii Chentemirov, Elizaveta Vereykina, '"Let the whole world know that there are people like my daughter." Snitches and a sledgehammer: The case of Olesya Krivtsova', *The Barents Observer*, 23 February 2023.

29. 'Rosfinmonitoring added to the list of terrorists 19-year old student Olesya Krivtsova, suspected of "discrediting" the RF armed forces', *Novaia Gazeta Evropa*,

10 January 2023; 'Russian student who fled "army discrediting" charges added to wanted list', *The Moscow Times*, 20 March 2023.

30. 'Naiti vragov gosudarstva: Kak v Rossiiu vozvrashchaetsia institute donosov', *OVD-Info*, 25 March 2022; 'Socialist-revolutionaries launched a website for questions from the UK [investigative committee] about "poests" in government', *RIA Novosti*, 21 March 2022.

31. Anastaia Kalugina, 'As Ukraine conflict drags on, Russians continue to snitch on each other for anti-war views', *The Moscow Times*, 11 October 2023; '"Moi donos" – prilozhenie shutochnoe donoschiki nastoiashchie', *Shkola 'Poligon Media'*, 8 October 2023.

32. Amalia Zatari, 'Ukraine war: The Russians snitching on colleagues and strangers', *BBC Russkaia sluzhba*, 18 November 2023, bbc.com/news/world-europe-67427422; Tom Porter, 'Russian police are overwhelmed by the number of people snitching on neighbors and colleagues: Report', *Business Insider*, 20 November 2023.

33. Dvizhenie 'Vesna', 'Net mogilizatsii! Vserossiiskaia aktsiia protesta: Segodnia, 21 sentiabria, v 19:00. Tsentry vsekh gorodov', 21 September 2022, t.me/vesna_democrat/3630. Misspelling was in original purposely.

34. 'Harsh detentions and summonses to the military enlistment office: Results of actions against mobilization on September 21', *OVD-Info*, 22 September 2022, ovd.news/news/2022/09/22/zhestkie-zaderzhaniya-i-povestki-v-voenkomat-itogi-akciy-protiv-mobilizacii-21.

35. 'New spontaneous rallies against mobilization begin in Dagestan', *Kavkaz.Realii* (RFE/RL), 26 September 2022, with lots of videos; 'Actions against mobilization resumed in Dagestan', *Meduza*, 26 September 2022.

36. 'There are no tickets left on the airline websites for the next flights', *RBC.ru*, 21 September 2022; Mathew Roscoe, 'WATCH: More than 600 arrests made as anti-mobilization protests continue in Russia', *Euroweekly*, 21 September 2022, includes videos and photos; 'Queues on the border of Russia and Georgia', *Kavkaz.Realii* (RFE/RL), 22 September 2022, with videos, kavkazr.com/a/32045785.html. See details and videos, see 'Russian border traffic surges after "partial" draft announcement', *The Moscow Times*, 22 September 2022.

37. 'File: F4 share of citizenship in first-time asylum applicants in the EU, October 2021-October 2022 (%) v3.png', *Eurostat: Statistics Explained*, ec.europa.eu/eurostat/statistics-explained/index.php?title=File:F4_Share_of_citizenship_in_first-time_asylum_applicants_in_the_EU,_October_2021_-_October_2022_(%25)_v3.png, accessed 8 February 2023; '"I will not go back": Anti-war Russians stuck in EU asylum limbo', *The Moscow Times*, 8 February 2023; Miriam Jordan, 'Antiwar activists who flee Russia find detention, not freedom, in the U.S.', *New York Times*, 28 November 2022.

38. 'Istochniki: v FSB naschitali bolee 260 tysiach pokinuvshikh Rossiiu muzhchin. Siloviki khotiat zakryt' granitsu, no Putyin ne naznachaet obsuzhdenii', *Novaia Gazeta Evropa*, 25 September 2022; Anastasia Tenisheva, '"Total chaos": Russian mobilization exodus accelerates amid border closure rumors', *The Moscow Times*, 26 September 2022.

39. 'Gaid v svobodnyi mir. Kak uyekhat' iz Rossii', Telegram Relocation. Guide (Gaid po relokatsiia iz RF) '"Emigration from Russia to the free world" – a chat for 100,000 people', truerussia.org/en/projects/guide-of-relocation/, accessed 18 July 2023.

40. 'Russia introduces harsh punishments for wartime desertion, refusal to serve', *The Moscow Times*, 24 September 2022.

41. 'Putin podpisal ukaz ob otsrochke ot chastichnoi mobilizatsii studentov i poluchaiushchikh srednee profobrazovanie', *Rossiiskaia Gazeta*, 24 September 2022.

42. For Kadyrov's claim of exemption, see Kadyrov_95, Telegram, t.me/RKadyrov_95/2864.

43. 'Na Vishnevskogo i Reznika sostavili protokoly o diskreditatsii armii', *ZAKS.RU* (St. Petersburg), 9 January 2023, zaks.ru/new/archive/view/234829; 'St. Petersburg politician charged over bucha massacre claims', *The Moscow Times*, 9 January 2023.

44. 'Neizvestnyi napal na glavreda "Novoi gazety" . . . Dmitriia Muratova', *Instagram*, 7 April 2022, instagram.com/p/CcDu49pJXUM/, with photo.

45. Novaia Gazeta, 'Glavred "Novoi gazety" Sergei Sokolov priznan vinovnym . . .', *Telegram*, 29 February 2024, t.me/novaya_pishet/43990.

46. Daria Dergacheva, '"We are asking forgiveness that we know we will never receive": In Russia, people are bringing flowers to monuments of Ukrainians', *Global Voices Post*, 24 January 2023; Valerie Hopkins, Nanna Heitmann, 'In Moscow, a quiet anti-war protest with flowers and plush toys', *New York Times*, 23 January 2023; 'Makeshift Russian memorials to dnipro victims enter third week', *The Moscow Times*, 30 January 2023; Anastasia Tenisheva, '"I couldn't stay silent": Anti-war "flower protests" spread to 60 cities across Russia', *The Moscow Times*, 10 February 2023.

47. 'Yav art group: To protest, it helps to know the law', *The Moscow Times*, 14 December 2022, with reproductions.

48. Jane Aaron, 'Anti-war street artists still working inside Russia', *The Moscow Times*, 2 January 2023; Valerie Hopkins, 'Paintbrush in hand, a Russian muralist wages his own war', *New York Times*, 19 December 2022.

49. On these protests see, Vera Dubina, '"No wobble": Silent protest in contemporary Russia', *Russian Analytical Digest*, No. 291 (27 January 2023), pp. 8–11.

50. Marina Tiuniaeva (Bochkareva), 'Roskomnadzor zapustil sistemu abtomaticheskogo poiska zapreshchennogo kontenta "Okulus"', *Vedomosti*, 12 February 2023; 'Russia launches web crawler for anti-putin memes, banned content', *The Moscow Times*, 13 February 2023; Andrei Pertsev, 'The Telegram ban is forcing ordinary Russians to break the law (Op-ed)', *The Moscow Times*, 24 April 2018; Mike Eckel, Daniil Belovodyev, Anton Bayev, 'Inside the obscure Russian agency that censors the internet: An RFE/RL investigation', *RFE./RL*, 8 February 2023.

51. Alesa Marokhovskaia, Irina Dolinina, Sonya Savina, Polina Bonch-Osmolovskaya, Editorial Staff, 'Vnutri mashiny tsenzury', *iVazhnye istorii*, 8 February 2023, storage.googleapis.com/istories/stories/2023/02/08/vnutri-mashini-tsenzuri/index.html. English-language version, 'Inside the censorship machine', ibid.

52. 'We demand the immediate release of our colleague Evan Gershkovich! A letter from Russian independent journalists', *Mediazona*, 4 April 2023, en.zona.media/article/2023/04/04/evan; for a list of the original names, only available in Russian, see 'Otpustite Evana! Pis'mo zhurnalistov v podderzhku arestovannogo FSB korrespondenta wall street journal', *Mediazona*, 4 April 2023, zona.media/article/2023/04/04/free-evan; 'Russian journalists sign letter demanding U.S. reporter's release', *The Moscow Times*, 5 March 2023.

53. 'Zhurnalista RuNews iz Koroleva otpravili v SIZO iz-za postov o voine v Ukraine', *OVD-Info*, 12 April 2023; Amnesty International, 'Russian Federation: Journalist Roman Ivanov must be released immediately and without conditions', 14 November 2023, amnesty.org/en/documents/eur46/7412/2023/en/.

54. 'Director Zhenya Berkovich and playwright Svetlana Petriychuk are suspected of "justifying terrorism"', *Meduza*, 4 May 2023; 'Rezhisserku i stsenaristku spektaklia "Finist Yasnyi Sokol" zaderzhali po delu ob opravdanii terrorizma', *OVD-Info*, 4 May 2023.

55. 'Delo "Finista" v voennom sude. Onlain', *Mediazona*, 3 May 2024; RIA Novosti, 'Sud prigovoril k 6 godam Berkovich i Petriychuk po delu ob opravdanii terrorisma...', *Telegram*, 8 July 2024, t.me/rian_ru/252513.

56. 'Sud oshtrafoval studentku kolledzha za diskreditatsiiu armii RF na lektsii', *RAPSI*, 30 June 2023.

57. Claudia Chiappa, 'Russia expels POLITICO reporter', *Politico*, 16 August 2023.

58. YouTube, 'V Rossii sozdana natsional'naia respublikanskaia armiia, osushchestvivshaia pokushenie na Dugina', #dugina #ponomarev, 21 August 2022, youtube.com/watch?v=pofT8V8vytc&t=127s.

59. Guillaume Ptak, 'The Telegram-powered news outlet waging guerrilla war on Russia', *Wired*, 29 August 2022, wired.com/story/february-morning-russia-ukraine-war/.

60. Viacheslav Volodin, 'Zakon o negodiaiakh priniat', *Telegram*, 31 January 2024, t.me/vv_volodin/750; 'The State Duma adopts a law on confiscation of property for crimes against the interests of the Russian Federation', *RAPSI*, 31 January 2024, rapsinews.ru/legislation_news/20240131/309582689.html.

61. Guy Faulconbridge, 'Soldiers' widows group calls on Putin to order major mobilization for Ukraine war', *Reuters*, 3 January 2023.

62. 'Narodnyi front prezidentoval vystavku "Vse dlia pobedy!" v Bol'shom Kremlevskom dvortse', *RAPSI*, 4 May 2023.

63. See 'Pro-war new year's decorations appear in Russian cities', *The Moscow Times*, 20 December 2022. See also, 'What is the letter Z: "New swastika" or Kremlin flash mob?' *BBC News: Russkaia sluzhba*, 9 March 2022; Anonymous, 'Russia's new motto: "We are not ashamed": A letter from St. Petersburg', *Mother Jones*, 14 April 2022; Andrei Kolesnikov, 'How "I am not ashamed" T-shirts have become a symbol for Russia's new normal', *Carnegie Endowment for International Peace*, 27 April 2022. See also #NamNeStydno.

64. See 'Unmasking Russia's influential pro-war "Rybar" Telegram channel', *The Bell*, 21 November 2022.

65. Daria Mosolkina, '"Gibel" voenkora Tatarkogo: Chto sluchilos, *Vedomosti*, 3 April 2023.

66. 'Delo ob ubiistve Tatarskogo: Prigovor', *Mediazona*, 25 January 2024.

67. 'He wanted to unwind and go to the presidency: Then it turned out that this swamp is stronger', *Meduza*, 6 May 2023.

68. Natal'ia Kozlova, 'SK RF obnarodoval video doprosa podozrevaemogo v pokushenii na Zakhara Prilepina', *Rossiiskaia Gazeta*, 6 May 2023; Maria Krylova, 'Sud arestoval na dva mesiatsa obviniaemogo v pokushenii na Zakhara Prilepina', *Rossiiskaya hazeta*, 8 May 2023.

69. 'Siloviki zaderzhali Igora Strelkova', *RBC.ru*, 21 July 2023, rbc.ru/politics/21/07/2023/64ba599b9a79475c690f3df2?from=newsfeed; 'Kremlin brings "party of war" to heel ahead of key regional, presidential elections', *The Moscow Times*, 1 August 2023.

70. 'The court sentenced Strelkov to 4 years in prison for calls for extremism', *RAPSI*, 25 January 2024.

71. Rybar, 'Otkyda imenno bylo naneseny udary po Pskovu – neizvestno. . . .', *Telegram*, 30 August 2023, t.me/rybar/51327.

72. See Sinéad Baker, 'Russian hardliners are fuming that the Kremlin wasn't able to stop a string of embarrassing attacks on home soil', *Business Insider*, 31 August 2023.

73. 'Verkhovnyi sud likvidiroval partiiu PARNAS', *Mediazona*, 25 May 2023.

74. 'Russian communists mark 70-year anniversary of Stalin's death', *The Moscow Times*, 6 February 2023.

75. Communist Party of the Russian Federation, 'Pioneers', 20 May 2023, cprf.ru/?s=Young+Pioneers; for photos, see 'Photos: Russian communists organize red square induction for young pioneers', *The Moscow Times*, 23 May 2023.

76. Yelena Mukhametshina, Maksim Ivanov, '"Edinaia Rossiia" iskliuchit protivnikov spetsoperatsii iz chisla svoikh storonnikov', *Vedomosti*, 9 January 2023.

77. 'Vstrecha s glavoi fraktsii "Edinaia Rossiia" v Gosdume Vladimirom Vasil'evym', *Kremlin.ru*, 22 March 2023, kremlin.ru/events/president/news/70753.

78. See, e.g. KPRF, 'KPRF vo glave narodnogo protesta', kprf.ru/actions/kprf/, accessed 20 April 2023. For photos, see Leyla Latypova, 'Russia's local activists find room for protest – Just don't mention the war', *The Moscow Times*, 19 April 2023.

79. 'Eksperty NOM privetstvuiut izmenenniia v FZ o vyborakh', *RAPSI*, 28 March 2023.

80. 'Virtually unlimited possibilities for fraud', *Meduza*, 5 April 2023; 'V Moskve chislo izbiratel'nykh uchastkov sokratiat s 3428 do 2058', *Interfaks*, 16 March 2023.

81. Yekaterina Grobman, '"Kommunisty Rossii" raskalyvaiutsia pered vyborami', *Vedomosti*, 14 May 2023; Aleksandr Tikhonov, 'Soratniki Maksima Suraykina vernuli emu post lidera "Kommunistov Rossii" i resheli vydvinut' v meru Moskvy', *Vedomosti*, 15 May 2023.

82. On this, see Jan Matti Dollbaum, 'Party politics in Russia: Two and a half scenarios', *Russian Analytical Digest*, No. 294 (19 May 2023), pp. 12–13.

83. Laura Keffer, 'Deputaty ot LDPR predlozhili otmenit' NDFL pri dokhodakh nizhe 30 tys. rublei', *Kommersant*, 27 June 2023.

84. 'S fronta na praimeriz. "Edinaya Rossiia" proveriaet politicheskiy potentsial uchastnikov spetsoperatsii', *Kommersant*, 23 May 2023.

85. 'Reitingi doveriia politikam, otsenki raboty prezidenta i pravitel'stva, podderzhka politicheskikh partii', *VTsIOM*, 18 August 2023.

86. 'Putin podpisal zakon, pozvoliaiushchii provodit' vybory pri voennom polozhenii', *TASS*, 29 May 2023.

87. Golos, 'Karta narushenii na vyborakh', 10 September 2023, kartanarusheniy.org.

88. RIA Novosti, 'Sobyanin pobezhdaet . . .', *Telegram*, 11 September 2023, t.me/rian_ru/214793.

89. See Tweet from Leonid Volkov @leonidvolkov, 'Snova otkryvaem shtaby Naval'nogo. Protiv Putina, voiny i mobilizatsii', 4 October 2022, twitter.com/leonidvolkov/status/1577255547963072514; for background on Navalny, see David Herszenhorn, *The Dissident: Alexey Navalny: Profile of a Political Prisoner*. New York: Twelve, 2023.

90. 'Russian critic Navalny says prison denying hospital care', *The Moscow Times*, 12 January 2023.

91. Alexey Navalny @navalny, Twitter, 17 January 2023, twitter.com/navalny/status/1615258155063156737.

92. Twitter thread. 'Alexey Navalny @navalny, 20 February 2023, twitter.com/navalny/status/1627632111220817921?s=61&t=VHziTUIJcWyZNsvUQ_4efQ; 'Alexei Navalny published 15 principles of his political platform – about the war and the post-war structure of Russia', *Meduza*, 20 February 2023; 'Navalny sets out 15-point plan for Russia's postwar development', *The Moscow Times*, 20 February 2020.

93. TASS, 'Moskalkova soobshchila, chto poluchila ot otbyvaiushchego nakazanie Alekseia Naval'nogo bolee 50 obrashchenii', *Telegram*, 27 February 2023, t.me/tass_agency/182381.

94. Judy Kurtz, 'Russian opposition leader's wife gives emotional speech after "Navalny" wins Oscar', *The Hill*, 12 March 2023; 'I dream of the day when you will be free and when our whole country will be free', *Meduza*, 13 March 2023; '"Navalny" wins oscar for best documentary film', *The Moscow Times*, 13 March 2023.

95. See, e.g. 'Kto poluchil "Oskar" – 2023', *Vedomosti*, 13 March 2023; '"Naval'nyi" zavoeval "Oskar" kak luchshii dokumental'nyi fil'm', *Interfaks*, 13 March 2023.

96. 'Navalny documentary wins Oscar', *RT*, 13 March 2023.

97. Twitter thread, Alexey Navalny@navalny – 2/11, 3/11, 19 April 2023, twitter.com/navalny/status/1645829621370290176; 'Navalny in solitary confinement for 13th time despite health issues', *The Moscow Times*, 11 April 2023.

98. Twitter. Alexey Navalny @navalny, 'Yesterday at 8 in the evening I was released from solitary confinement: Today at 9:30 in the morning, I was again in solitary confinement . . .', 11 May 2023, twitter.com/navalny/status/1656592446497718272.

99. Twitter. Komanda Naval'nogo @teamnavalny, 'Naval'nyi: Oni vydvinuli absurdnye obvineniia, po kotorym mne grozit 30 let kolonii. . . .', 26 April 2023, twitter.com/teamnavalny/status/1651128778058285058.

100. Zhdanov, 'Chanyshevoi zaprosili 12 let lisheniia svobody: Suki', *Telegram*, 26 April 2023, t.me/ioannZH/1597; Ivan Zhdanov, 'The state prosecution requested 12 years in prison for Navalny's associate Lilia Chanysheva', *Medusa*, 26 April 2023.

101. 'Eks-koordinatora shtaba Naval'nogo v Barnaule prigovorili k 9 godam kolonii', *OVD-Info*, 24 July 2023.

102. 'Zaderzhaniia iz-za aktsii 4 iiunia v podderzhku Alekseia Naval'nogo', *OVD-Info*, 2 June 2023.

103. 'VS RF otkazal Naval'nomu v iske o poriadke vydachi osuzhdennym ruchki i bumagi', *RAPSI*, 22 June 2023.

104. Komanda Naval'nogo. Forwarded from Navaln'nyi, 'Sud nad Alekseem Naval'nym i . . .', *Telegram*, 20 July 2023, t.me/teamnavalny/20274; 'Alekseiu Naval'nomu zaprosili 20 let kolonii osobogo rezhima po delu ob ekstremistskom soobshchestve', *OVD-Info*, 20 July 2023; Zhdanov, 'Naval'nomu zaprosili 20 let lisheniia svobody . . .', *Telegram*, 20 July 2023, t.me/ioannZH/1902.

105. Yana Surinskaya, 'Mosgorsud prigovoril Naval'nogo k 19 godam kolonii osobogo rezhima', *Vedomosti*, 4 August 2023; 'Moscow city court sentenced Alexei Navalny to 19 years in a special regime colony', *OVD-Info*, 4 August 2023.

106. Navalny, 'Moi strakh i nenavist', 11 August 2023, navalny.com/p/6651/.

107. Tatyana Makeyeva, 'Navalny back in solitary confinement after writing materials taken away', *The Moscow Times*, 24 October 2023; 'Navalny back in solitary after team releases investigation into prison system's cabbage purchases', *RFE/RL*, 11 April 2023.

108. Post. Alexey Navalny @navalny, X, 1 December 2023, twitter.com/navalny/status/1730497810401788262.

109. Daria Snegova, Yekaterina Grobman, 'FSIN soobshchila o smerti Alekseia Naval'nogo', *Vedomosti*, 16 February 2024; SU SK Rossii po Yamala-Nenetskomu avtonomnomu . . .. 'Organizovana protsessual'naia proverka po faktu smerti Alekseia Naval'nogo', *Telegram*, 16 February 2024, t.me/su_skr89/1578; 'Alexei Navalny dies in Jail – prison service', *The Moscow Times*, 16 February 2024.

110. Maria Zakharova, 'Momental'naia reaktsiia liderov stran NATO na smert' Naval'nogo . . .', *Telegram*, 16 February 2024, t.me/MariaVladimirovnaZakharova/7100; Zarubin, 'Peskov pro soobshcheniia o smerti Naval'nogo', *Telegram*, 16 Februatry2024, t.me/zarubinreporter/2069; 'President Biden delivers remarks on the reported death of Aleksey Navalny', *YouTube*, 16 February 2024, youtube.com/watch?v=cvqMXRooFCo.

111. Viacheslav Volodin, 'V smerti Navalnogo vinovaty Vashington i Briussel', *Telegram*, 16 February 2024, t.me/vv_volodin/759.

112. Pyotr Kozlov, '"A great loss": Russian lay flowers at monuments, embassies after Navalny's death', *The Moscow Times*, 16 February 2024; 'In St. Petersburg, Priest Grigory Mikhnov-Vatenko was detained leaving his house', *OVD-Info*, 17 February 2024; 'Navalny was murdered: OVD-Info statement', 16 February 2024, en.ovdinfo.org/navalny-murdered.

113. 'I will continue Alexei Navalny's work', *YouTube,* youtube.com/watch?v=RIrYWhjdK_o, accessed 20 February 2024.

114. Aleksei Naval'nyi, 'They want to secretly bury Navalny: They threaten his mother', *YouTube,* youtube.com/watch?v=w2iysafhiXM, accessed 23 February 2024.

115. James Gregory, James Landale, 'Alexei Navalny: UK sanctions Russian prison chiefs after activist's death', *BBC News,* 21 February 2024; 'US targets Russia with more than 500 new sanctions', *BBC News,* 23 February 2024.

116. See, e.g. Shannon Vavra, 'The hero rising from Navalny's Shadow – and gunning for Putin', *The Daily Beast,* 25 February 2024; Clare Sebastian, 'Yulia Navalnaia is raising hopes for a renewed Russian opposition: She will face huge challenges', *CNN News,* 20 February 2024.

117. For videos, see 'Live: Navalny supporters bid farewell at late activist's funeral', *The Moscow Times,* 1 March 2024. 'Navalny was buried at the Borisov cemetery in Moscow', *TASS,* 1 March 2024; Vasilii Kohkin, 'Alekseya Naval'nogo pokhoronili v Moskve', *Rossiiskaia Gazeta,* 1 March 2024.

118. 'Navalny vigils crackdown', *OVD-Info,* en.ovdinfo.org/, accessed 1 March 2024.

119. Setevye Svobodu, 'Massovye obyski u khudozhnikov i aktivistov. . .', *Telegram,* 12 March 2024, t.me/NetFreedomsProject/993; 'Police search the homes of artists and activists across Russia', *Meduza,* 12 March 2024; 'Attack on Navalny ally Volkov likely "organized by Russia" – Lithuania', *The Moscow Times,* 13 March 2024.

120. 'Siloviki prishli s obyskami k storonnikam Nedezhdina na Stavropol'e', *Kavkazskii Uzel,* 14 March 2024; Mediazona. Ekskliuziv, 'Studentke i vypuskniky NIU VShE, kotorykh . . . Naval'nogo, naznachili po 3,5 goda kolonii', *Telegram,* 14 March 2024, t.me/mediazona_exclusive/1166.

121. Na video vidno (Smotri), '. . . nasha demokratiia samaia luchshaia – Peskov', *Telegram,* 6 March 2024, t.me/navideovidno/72102; Anastasia Mayer, 'Medvedev rasskazal molodezhi o strategicheskoi pozitsii Rossii', *Vedomosti,* 4 March 2024.

122. 'Express view of public observation on the third day and final of voting March 17, 2024', *Golos,* 18 March 2024, golosinfo.org/en/articles/146795; Lucy Papachristou, 'Independent Russian vote monitor says election was a mockery', *Reuters,* 18 March 2024.

Chapter 6

Human and Civil Rights

When the presidential Human Rights Council met on 7 December 2022 with Putin in the chair, human rights topics related to the conduct of the war were not on the agenda. Purged of its anti-war members in November, the 47-member Council was now filled with known supporters of the war. New additions included a right-wing war correspondent who once claimed that the atrocities at Bucha were staged by Kyiv, an official from the All-Russian People's Front and a member of the Free Donbas party.[1]

The future of human rights agencies in Russia quickly grew hopeless after February 2022. They had already been isolated from international forums in April, when the UN General Assembly voted (93-24-58) to suspend Russian from its Human Rights Council. Bidding the next year to re-gain that seat, Russia (83 votes) lost out to Albanian (130) and Bulgaria (160). Council's 47 member-states are chosen by region.[2] Reasons for the UNGA's approbation were clear.

CLEANING HOUSE

Just as the Russian Human Rights Council convened, the NGO *Vesna* was designated an extremist organization by a closed St. Petersburg court, the prosecutor's office having accused it of 'undermining public security and constitutional order'. Although anyone who cooperates with a body deemed extremist faces legal consequences in Russia, and such organizations are forbidden to operate in the country, *Vesna* vowed to continue its work both abroad and at home.[3]

Late in January 2023 a court in Moscow ordered the closure of Russia's oldest human rights organization, the Moscow Helsinki Group. With

Memorial also closed down, Russia's two prominent long-standing civil rights organizations, both with roots in Soviet times and commanding international respect, were gone.[4] A final blow to Russia's traditional human rights groups came on 16 April 2023, when the Sakharov Centre held its final public event prior to shutting its building in central Moscow. Evicted from the site where an exhibition dedicated to Yelena Bonner, Sakharov's wife, had been housed, the Centre marked the event with speeches and poetry readings from human rights activists. The Sakharov Centre said in a press release that its eviction was a result of its status as a 'foreign agent' that meant it could receive no support from the state. The premises had been leased free of charge since 1993. The government's decision, the Centre had said shortly after its 'foreign agent' label came into effect, was further evidence that,

> Uncontrolled power that corrupts society with myths based on fear, hatred and a false sense of superiority, power that manipulates real and imaginary national traumas, cynically exploiting even the most exalted people's feelings, inevitably follows the path of repression, arbitrariness, destruction and bloodshed. Sakharov warned about this, we see it with our own eyes today.[5]

According to Vyacheslav Bakhmin, chairman of its board, the work of the human rights group would continue on-line.[6]

Russia's independent human and civil rights agencies were following the same road to extinction walked by the country's individual activist leaders. In April, a court ordered the termination of SOVA, a research centre in Moscow that monitors nationalist and racist movements in Russia.[7] In June, the Ministry of Justice (Minjust) opened an investigation into the Yeltsin Centre in Yekaterinburg after several Duma deputies accused it of serving as a 'foreign agent'. Opened in 2015, the Centre housed a museum of the 1990s, an art gallery, conference rooms and children's centres. It had issued a statement calling for an 'immediate end to the military operation in Ukraine' just one day after the SVO launch, but had long since taken the declaration down.[8]

INTERNATIONAL ACCLAIM DOOMS RUSSIAN DISSIDENTS

Underscoring Putin and Russia's increasing disassociation from mainstream Europe, the Nobel Peace Prize for 2022 went to three co-winners, Russia's Memorial, the Belarusian human rights activist Ales Byalyatski and Ukraine's Centre for Civil Liberties. According to the Nobel selection committee, the winners 'represent civil society in their countries. For many years they have defended the right to criticize the authorities and defend the basic rights of citizens. They have made outstanding efforts to document war crimes, human rights violations and abuses of power'.[9] Although the committee made a point of stressing that their choices were not directed against Putin, the fact that the announcement came on the day of his 70th birthday rendered that qualification suspect.

A week or so later, the Parliamentary Assembly of the Council of Europe (PACE) awarded the Vlacav Havel Human Rights prize to Vladimir Kara-Murza, who, as we have seen, was later sentenced to 25 years in a Russian prison. The prize, accepted by his wife in Strasbourg in October 2022, came with €60,000 ($58,300). She dedicated the award to Russians who spoke out against the war.[10]

The actual charge against Kara-Murza is worth printing here, as reported in RAPSI, because it was typical of the most serious Putinist condemnations:

> The journalist was found guilty of committing a crime under Article 275 of the Criminal Code of the Russian Federation (high treason), paragraph 'e' of Part 2 of Article 207.3 of the Criminal Code of the Russian Federation (public dissemination of knowingly false information about the use of the Armed Forces of the Russian Federation) and Part 1 of Article 284.1 of the Criminal Code of the Russian Federation (collaboration with unwanted organizations).[11]

Memorial refused to go quietly. Many of its members continued to present reminders of Russia's Stalinist past in public art and exhibitions and provide legal assistance for individuals whose rights needed defending at home and from abroad. Its executive director, Yelena Zhemkova, who had to flee the country, continued to arrange Memorial's 'Returning the Names' annual ceremonies where the names of Stalin's victims are read aloud. No longer allowed in Russia, these events were held abroad in over 70 cities.[12] State persecution of Memorial associate in Russia did not fade either. On 21 March 2023, police conducted massive raids on the homes of prominent members and the organization's offices. These raids were connected to on-going criminal cases under the rubric of 'rehabilitation of Nazism' and allegations that Memorial's vast data base of more than three million victims of Stalinism included a few names of Russian collaborators with Nazis.[13]

The EU's Prize for Freedom of Thought named after Sakharov also irritated Russia, for it went to Navalny in 2021 and to Zelensky in 2022.

Artists, actors and opposition politicians who stayed in Russia were all aware of the risks they were taking and, presumably, so was the acquiescent population. In a final statement before his sentencing, Ilya Yashin said, 'I must stay in Russia, I must speak the truth loudly'. Addressing Putin, 'the man responsible for this bloodbath' who is forcing hundreds of thousands to flee the country, he warned, 'People are running from you, Mr. President.

Can't you see'.[14] Like Navalny, Yashin refused to keep quiet even while incarcerated. *Time* magazine published his 'Message to the World from Inside a Russian Prison' on 10 February 2023. In it, he said that Putin had 'become a true symbol of evil, cursed around the world', and went on to urge the people of Russia to resist the war and the international community to assist them.[15] Other arrestees left similar messages as they were carted off to serve long sentences. Attention from the West had sealed their fate; and not many Russian heard them.

After a year of war and repression, there was not much anti-war individuals could do inside Russia other than talk quietly in their kitchens with like-minded people.[16] Or they could engage in subtle subversions such as the acts described in the previous chapter.

'FOREIGN AGENTS' FRENZY

In July 2022, Putin signed a law to expand the foreign agent appellation to cover anyone and any organization that appeared to fall under 'foreign influence', rather than merely those who collected foreign funding. Anyone who worked with a 'foreign agent' also became vulnerable and could be deemed a traitor by the state. As of 1 December, when the law came into effect, the government began publishing personal data on individuals and groups labelled 'foreign agent'. Roskomnadzor could now block a 'foreign agent's' website without a court order, and individuals so labelled are barred from teaching at any level, producing information for children, organizing public events or even having their bank deposits insured.[17]

When famous Russian pop singer, 73-year-old Alla Pugacheva posted her opposition to the war after her husband, comedian and singer Maksim Galkin, was declared a 'foreign agent', she was barred from the air waves. Lashing out via Instagram, she called war advocates lackeys and slaves ('kholopami, stali rabami), and asked Minjust to include her on its record of foreign agents 'in solidarity' with her husband. Pugacheva and her family left the country.[18] She wasn't alone. Pop singer Monetochka (Liza Gyrdymova) was declared a 'foreign agent' and moved to Lithuania; film producer Aleksandr Rodnyansky and journalists Aleksandr Plyushchev, Mikhail Zygar and Tatyana Felgenhauer were added to the list. So, too, were the head of the Russian branch of Transparency International, Ilya Shumanov, the former head of Navalny's Chuvash headquarters Semyon Kochkin, the widow of the late businessman Dmitry Bosov, Katerina Bosova and Bashkir activist Ruslan Gabbasov.[19] Authorities declared cartoonists Oleg Kuyayev and Pavel Muntyan foreign agents in 2023 and because they both had left the country, the MVD issued warrants for their arrest.[20]

Putin enacted a law that could lead to a five-year prison sentence for any 'foreign agent' who violated assigned protocols twice in the same year.[21]

Also in that month, Minjust added *The Bell,* a weekly publication by Russians-in-exile in the United States, to its blacklist.[22] The year-end saw a flurry of new names. Three more journalists and a human rights activist were labelled 'foreign agents', along with the Feminist Anti-War Resistance movement, the human rights project Roskomsvoboda, the Anti-Corruption Foundation Inc. (foreign structure of FBK), and the autonomous non-profit organization of social and sports programs, Sports LGBT Community.[23]

Additions to the Foreign Agent list, announced almost every Friday, reached 740 by the end of 2023 and did not stop there.[24] No profession or person was immune to the appellation. On Friday, 26 May 2023, for instance, the following assortment of names was added to the file:

- Irina Alleman – host of the Popular Politics YouTube channel;
- Alexandra Arkhipova – anthropologist;
- Levi Bi-2 (Yegor Bortnik, soloist);
- Vladislav Inozemtsev – economist;
- Magomed Gadzhiev – former State Duma deputy;
- Alexander Gabuev, sinologist, director of the Carnegie Centre for Russian and Eurasian Studies in Berlin;
- Olga Tsukanova – head of the 'Council of Mothers and Wives';
- Sergey Chernyshov – former director of the Novosibirsk City Open College;
- Anna Pshenichnaya – journalist;
- National Union for the Revival of Russia; and
- Social movement 'Council of Mothers and Wives'.[25]

A few weeks later, Minjust entered the names of senior officers of the Bookmate book service, and the company itself, into the 'foreign agents' registry of media outlets.[26] A month after that, Minjust added the host of *Dozhd* (Rain), Anna Mongait, and several other of its broadcasters, along with Yevgeny Roizman, a former mayor of Yekaterinburg and opponent of the war in Ukraine. The new roster named a lawyer for FBK, a coordinator for *Golos,* a journalist in Sakhalin and the head of the Free Buryatia Foundation. In July 2023, *Dozhd* joined the more stringent 'undesirable' category.

The flood of 'foreign agent' designations seemed to have no bounds. Journalists, bloggers, politicians and writers swelled the list. Prominent politician Gennady Gudkov and economist Sergei Guriev were among them. New entities so labelled included the World Wildlife Foundation (WWF), charged in March with distributing 'false information' around the world about Russia's environmental policies.[27] Minjust declared the independent environmental news outlet, *Kedr* (Cedar), a 'foreign agent' in November. It closed down in January 2024 because of threats to staff members that they too might be branded.[28]

Complementing the 'foreign agents' catch-all was a rapidly expanding registry of persons whom the Ministry of Justice said were 'affiliated with foreign agents'. As of 31 December 2022, this record stored information on 861 individuals, made up in part by heads and employees of organizations so-designated.[29]

The 'undesirable' category expanded as well. Labelled 'undesirable' in March, Transparency International was forced to dissolve as a legal entity in Russia. Anyone who cooperates with it was now vulnerable to felony charges.[30] The international organization's Corruption Perceptions Index consistently had placed Russia low to very low in its rankings. Its Russia branch re-launched abroad in October.

In August, powers that be declared the co-chair of *Golos,* Grigoriy Melkonyants, an 'undesirable' and raided the homes of 14 of his colleagues in Moscow, St. Petersburg and six other regions in Russia. *Golos* itself was not named an 'undesirable' organization, though a number of its legal entities were registered as 'foreign agents'.[31]

This flurry of additions came just a week or so after the government decided to change the compulsory template for every publication and posting so-designated.[32] As of 1 December 2022, the template must be worded as follows:

> This message (material) was created and (or) distributed by a foreign media performing the function of a foreign agent and (or) a Russian legal entity performing the functions of a foreign agent.

In May, the PGO identified Greenpeace International as an 'undesirable' organization, and in June the well-known legal and human rights Russian group Agora was added to that directory, because, the PGO claimed, its activities 'pose a threat to the foundations of the constitutional order and the security of the Russian Federation'. Agora is an association of some 50 lawyers who have represented Pussy Riot and other dissenters. Based originally in Kazan, it moved its head office out of the country when its founder, Pavel Chikov, was named a foreign agent in March 2023.[33]

The beat went on in 2023. At a meeting following the Crocus City terrorist act in March 2024, head of the MVD, Vladimir Kolokoltsev, told Putin that 44 organizations were designated 'undesirable' in 2023, which meant that they were not able to operate within Russia and any engagement with them could be deemed criminal. By then, 129 individuals and 37 legal entities were included on the register of 'foreign agents'.[34]

Meduza earned the title of 'undesirable' in January 2023, making it illegal for anyone or any entity to distribute articles written by a *Meduza* journalist or, indeed, have any contact with the publication. Already declared a 'foreign agent' in 2021, *Meduza* retained an audience in Russia though its size is unknown. On announcing this development to its readership, the editorship appealed: 'Read Medusa. Overcome fear. Russia will be free. Those who are supposed to go to hell have been there for a long time'.[35]

After boasting of the dozens of international NGOs that had been declared undesirable in Russia by mid-March, General Procurator Ivan Krasnov told a meeting of the Collegium of Procurator Generals that 'more than 125,000 Internet pages related to the spread of fakes about SVO and mobilization' were blocked.[36] Putin was on the stage. In June, the PGO raised the WWF from its 'foreign agent' status to 'undesirable', accusing it of enabling 'large foreign enterprises' to gather information on Russia's environmental situation. The *Novaia Gazeta Evropa* graduated to that level as well.[37]

That infamous list continued to grow in 2024 when, in January, the independent youth news outlet DOXA was affixed to it on the urging of the GPO.[38] Authorities accused DOXA of pretending to be a student publication while actually serving as a subversive agency. No hard evidence of that was revealed. The Duma expanded existing legislation on 'undesirable' organizations in February to include state-sponsored entities along with NGOs. By mid-February that year, the database of Russia's Ministry of Justice listed 137 'undesirable' organizations, aiming at Russian branches of RFE/RL, the BBC and Deutsche Welle.[39]

The frenetic search for 'foreign agents' had taken on a life of its own. The number of designees grew exponentially and without any particular guidelines. In March 2023, authorities stripped the entire family of climate activist Arshak Makichyan of their Russian citizenships.[40] In the first two weeks of April, Minjust appended artist Semyon Slepakov, publicist Igor Yakovenko, journalist Pavel Kanygin, as well as the Rainbow Association, the Carnegie Endowment for International Peace and the Polygon Shop and Bookstore to the roster. Journalist Arkady Babchenko and the limited liability company Khroniker were added to the Ministry of Justice's register of foreign agents.[41] Minjust catalogued two more journalists, a Moscow politician, another human rights organization (Shkola prizyvnika) and a legal advocacy group (Advokatskaya ulitsa) as foreign agents the next week, all of them accused of spreading a 'negative image' of Russia.[42]

On 1 September, Muratov was placed on the list of foreign agents, charged with using 'foreign platforms to disseminate opinions aimed at forming a negative attitude towards the foreign and domestic policy of the Russian Federation'. Eight journalists, scholars, politicians, writers and a comedian joined the swelling roster during August. Among these were Ruslan Bely, a well-known comedian and TV star; Yulia Goralik, an LGBT activist; and Sargylana Kondakova, an advocate for the 'Free Yakutia Foundation'.[43]

More ominously, the FSB and snitchers found 'traitors' in all corners of Russian society. For instance, in July 2023, a court sentenced the founder of one of the country's leading cybersecurity firms, Ilya Sachkov, to 14 years in prison for treason. One anti-war Russian publication, *Kholod* (Cold) proclaimed that the Sachkov case was but one of 82 indictments for treason brought to Russian courts during the first eight months of 2023, a fourfold increase over 2022. *Kholod* is an independent Russian publication founded by journalist Taisiya Bekbulatova. *Perviy Otdel* (First Section), an anti-government Russian human rights project, alleged that there were more such cases under investigation but not made public and that many of the prisoners tried for treason were tortured. Most of the defendants were accused of working for Ukraine, but some were charged with acting on behalf of China, the United States, the United Kingdom or Germany.[44]

The potential for long prison sentences also increased significantly in the spring of 2023 when Putin signed an amendment to the Criminal Code raising sentences to a maximum of five years for assisting international associations in which Russia does not participate, 20 years for sabotage and life imprisonment for treason.[45] Another law, adopted by the State Duma on 19 July, allowed for unscheduled inspections and fines for anyone interacting with 'foreign agents'.[46]

At the end of May, the FSB began rounding up anyone whom they thought were connected to Ilya Ponomarev. Police raided the home and Moscow State University office of professor and CPRF member Mikhail Lobanov, Yabloko member Nodari Khananashvili, editor of a magazine in St. Petersburg Aleksandr Kalinin, musician Boris Grebenshchikov and others. They were all accused of spreading 'fake news' or 'discrediting' the Russian army.[47] Before the year was out, the Ministry of Education began requiring universities to provide information on all professors and students who participated in international scholarly events that year and in the future. In short, authorities were compiling personal data on all academics who were in contact with foreigners, just as the state did during the Soviet era.[48]

One victim of this file was Ivan Kurilla, an historian who studies Russian-American relations. Dismissed in March 2024 from his post with the European University at St. Petersburg for 'absenteeism' even though he was on sabbatical leave, his name stayed on a list of hundreds of 'potential' foreign agents compiled by Roskomnadzor in 2023.[49]

Still up-dating its 'foreign agents' list on Fridays, Minjust added widely read exiled writer Boris Akunin (Grigory Chkhartishvili) in January 2024 for opposing the SVO. Already labelled an extremist by Rosfinmonitoring, Akunin was co-founder of a campaign platform called 'True Russia'

(Nastoiashchaia Rossiia) that gathers Russian cultural figures to help Ukrainian refugees and Russians who fled their country.[50] Another high-profile figure fled Russia towards the end of January after a Duma deputy called her a 'traitor' on his Telegram channel and disclosed her home address. Asya Kazantseva, a prominent science journalist whose public lectures had been cancelled by several Moscow and Tver bookstores, escaped to Tbilisi. Posting on Facebook that she had been subjected to 'waves of hate' from pro-war bloggers and government officials, she said that she would return when 'better times' come.[51]

The frenzy didn't slow as the third year of war opened. On 1 March, another Friday, Minjust named celebrated novelist, playwright and candidate for a Nobel Prize in literature, 81-year old Lyudmila Ulitskaya, a 'foreign agent' for opposing the war and carrying out 'LGBT propaganda'. Now living in Germany, she was attacked angrily by state media for sending her royalties to help Ukraine.[52] At the end of February 2024, the number of 'foreign agents' had reached 406, 86 of whom were under criminal investigation.[53] Not done yet, Putin signed a law in March forbidding individual Russian citizens and businesses from advertising their products or services with any individual or entity designated as a 'foreign agent'. This law makes it very difficult for independent media outlets or journalists to earn income.[54]

Russians could not be blamed if they were to believe that the cultural elements of Soviet society had re-surfaced with a vengeance

Entry and Exit Restrictions

Elements of Soviet era exit and entry restrictions re-appeared too, when amendments to procedures for leaving and entering Russia were adopted in May 2023. In addition to existing grounds for invalidating passports – misplaced, change of full name, gender or other personal information, death of the owner, termination of Russian citizenship – they can now be taken from a person who concludes an employment contract with a Russian company that has access to secrets, and from individuals who have not reported to a registry office within five days of receiving a conscription summons. Current and former FSB officers, diplomats abroad, persons involved in bankruptcies or have criminal records, must now obtain special permission to travel abroad. These rules apply even to movement within the Commonwealth of Independent States (CIS), which is comprised of nine former Soviet republics.[55]

LGBT Woes Worsen

Keeping up with the 'foreign agent' roster expansion, the already stringent law against distributing 'non-traditional relations propaganda' among children was amended to make it apply to all age groups. The amendment included off-line statements and publications in the print media, the Internet, social networks, as well as products in on-line cinemas.[56] The Duma held public hearings on the subject in October, and heard speakers claim that 'unconventional values are imposed by [Russia's] enemies in order to enslave us'. Linking the discussion to the war in Ukraine, *Meduza* reported that one theme was, 'sodomy is a mortal sin, it is the core of Satanism. Against this Satanism, our brothers and sons are dying on Ukrainian soil. This law will be equal to a major military victory'.[57]

The Duma voted unanimously to broaden the law. The new version expanded the type of information prohibited for distribution to children, and increased the fines that individuals or legal entities could be charged for any such offence.[58] The long struggle by the LGBT community for equal rights in Russia reached a nadir when, on 5 December 2022, Putin signed the law into force. Almost immediately, book sellers began removing LGBT-themed books from their shelves and catalogues. Chitai-Gorod, the largest bookstore chain in Russia with over 700 outlets, pulled hundreds of titles.[59]

In effect, the law banned any mention of LGBT in books. Since books written by 'foreign agents' also now pose problems for book sellers, they too are disappearing from Russian libraries and book dealerships. Authors whose books were removed from stores by LitRes service, a group of book brokers, were asked to re-write so as to avoid the law.[60]

The first investigation prompted by the extended law against 'LGBT propaganda' came against Popcorn Books, a publishing house that sponsors LGBT literature. The case was pushed by a UR deputy who raged against a bestseller called *Leto v pionerskom galstuke* (Summer in a Pioneer Necktie) about a relationship between a camper and a counsellor in a summer camp for Pioneers.[61]

The anti-gay law presumed to ban displays such as flying a rainbow flag during pride month, as the US and UK embassies had done in June. For Putin, the Orthodox Church and many Russians, legislation against the LGBT community was appropriate protection against decadent Western influences. For some, the law served as a defensive weapon in what they saw as a clash between civilizations, that is *Russkiy mir* vs. Western liberalism. Russian nationalists viewed the war in Ukraine as a piece of the same struggle.

The Orthodox Church actively supported anti-gay legislation as a means to 'protect our children from being defiled'.[62] By 2023, anti-LGBT rhetoric had become part of Putin's ideological narrative, especially when he was defending what he deemed to be Russia's 'traditional values' against Western liberalism.[63]

Even when faced by enormous obstacles to its freedom of expression, the LGBT community refused to fade from public sight. At least one human rights organizations that defended LGBT, for which it was banned by the regime as a 'foreign agent' in April 2022, sprang back into life in 2023. The Sphere Foundation (spherequeer.org) began operating again in January, purposely to fight against the above-mentioned law. Its leader, Dilya Gafurova, said the agency would function unlicensed and prepare letters and petitions against the state's definition of 'LGBT propaganda'. She ridiculed the state for its ignorance and portrayed legislation against gay and lesbian activism as a by-product of Putin's desperate and futile ideological confrontation with the West.[64] The enormous pressures placed on LGBT individuals in Russia have been described thoroughly by openly queer LGBTQ Russian activist, Elena Kostyuchenko, in *I Love Russia*, a book recently published abroad.[65] The book won the 2024 Pushkin House Book Prize.

While venting against the West in his address to the Federal Assembly in 2023, Putin took another swipe at the LGBT community. He accused the 'elites of the West', where 'the destruction of the family, cultural and national identity, perversion, abuse of children, up to paedophilia, are declared the norm, the norm of their life, and clergy, priests are forced to bless same-sex marriages', of trying to defeat Russia on both the battlefield and in the cultural domain. The family, he said 'is a union of a man and a woman', and we have to 'protect our children from degradation and degeneration'. He went on to suggest that people who abetted Western cultural inroads in Russia were 'traitors' selling 'poisons' to weaken Russians.[66]

As a result of new laws, best-selling foreign books that included references to gays (e.g. Truman Capote, Virginia Woolf), movies from commercial streaming services (e.g. *Brokeback Mountain*), and artworks from LGBT displays disappeared from Russian book store shelves. Plays were cancelled or re-scripted. A lot of the changes were the result of self-censorship by editors, publishers, book dealers, or curators who wanted to avoid fines. One librarian leaked a list of over 50 books that, he said, libraries were forced to remove.[67]

Films with content deemed to be 'LGBT propaganda' to minors were targeted as well; for example, Kinopoisk, a movie portal owned by Yandex, faced an administrative court case brought by Roskomnadzor. The site has more than 150 million visitors monthly. A similar case was brought against TV-3, an entertainment channel owned by Gazprom. They both faced heavy fines. According to *Vedomosti* in June 2023, Roskomnadzor had launched 33 such cases since the 'LGBT propaganda' law came into effect.[68]

Slamming more doors shut, the State Duma voted in July to outlaw all legalistic and surgical gender changes. At first reading in June, all 365 deputies present voted in favour of a 'barrier' against 'Western anti-family ideology'. Some proponents of the bill went so far as to claim that men were changing their gender so as to avoid conscription. Speaker Volodin proclaimed that gender re-assignment was a form of 'molestation of children' and that it would lead to 'degeneration of the nation'.⁶⁹ Human rights proponents in Russia warned that the policy would lead to a dangerous underground surgical market, increased secret hormone therapy, raise anxieties in the transgender community and perhaps lead to suicides. No matter – the UR-dominated Duma overwhelmingly accepted the Putinist view that all such notions were products of wicked Western values.⁷⁰

In this connection, the Ministry of Justice filed motions in November to label international LGBT movements extremist, even though there is no such thing as an organized international LGBT administrative community with a desire to 'incite social discord'. The Russian Supreme Court designated all such vaguely defined movements 'extremist' anyway. The decision, handed down on 28 November 2023 in effect criminalizes any type of LGBT advocacy in Russia.⁷¹ Rosfinmonitoring added the still un-defined 'international LGBT public movement' to its list of terrorists and extremists in March 2024, making the bank accounts of groups and individuals subjected to freezing.⁷²

One day later, police raided gay-friendly nightclubs, bars and saunas in Moscow, claiming that they were looking for drugs. In St. Petersburg, a gay club was evicted from space it had rented for years. Obviously, the Supreme Court ruling made the LGBT community in Russia fair game for persecution by authorities and public alike.⁷³

The Russian Supreme Court also declared the gay pride rainbow flag an 'extremist symbol'. Shortly thereafter police arrested a photographer for posting a rainbow flag on-line and a woman who wore earrings with a rainbow design. In the latter case, she was snitched on by members of the public who spotted them on her while she was sitting with a friend at a table in a café.⁷⁴

Female LGBT artist activists were especially targeted by the tightened-up anti-LGBT legislation. Among these was Yulia Tsvetkova, who was prosecuted on pornography charges related to her presentation of pictures in the 'Vagina Monologues', but acquitted by a court in Khabarovsk. In June 2022, she was added to the list of media 'foreign agents'. Although she was acquitted, again, her exhibition was banned in November 2022. She left the country to join the growing Russian artistic diaspora.⁷⁵ Tsvetkova was the founder of the 'Woman – Not Doll' project and organizer of the Saffron Flower art festival. The vicissitudes of Russia's judicial system struck again in March 2023, when a court in Vladivostok overturned her earlier acquittals and set the pornography charge up for another round of trials.⁷⁶

Putin's electoral victory in March 2024 ensured that that the LGBT community would come under ever increasing pressure.

Women

On the last day of 2022, the Russian government approved a new National Strategy for Action in the Interests of Russian Women for 2023–2030, the purpose of which, its general provisions proclaimed, was 'to ensure the principle of equal rights and freedoms for men and women and create equal opportunities for their implementation'. If no one noticed a ripple of excitement in Russia's female circles, that was because the National Strategy was not much different from its predecessor signed into law in 2017, which accomplished nothing.

The document featured ways and means for women to combine full employment and career development with 'family responsibilities and raising children', and to narrow the large wage gap between men and women doing the same job. Offering vague promises to prevent 'women's troubles', it said nothing specific about domestic abuse.[77]

Women's rights came under attack in July when Minister of Health Mikhail Murashko began pushing for legislative restrictions against abortions, while he in turn was lobbied by the Orthodox Church to ban abortion altogether so as to defend 'traditional Christian values'.[78] Putin doubled down on this message in a video address delivered on International Women's Day (8 March 2024). While many other countries, and women's organizations, used that day to extol gender equality and highlight women's rights issue, Putin again told Russian women that their greatest gift was 'childbirth', and their most important task was 'tireless care of children'.[79] Insisting that women grant priority to having children and signing legislation to restrict reproduction rights had become central features of Putinism. He had already declared 2024 the Year of the Family.

Feminist Activism

The Feminist Anti-War Resistance movement had its formal beginning one day after Putin's forces invaded Ukraine. On that day, FAR posted a Manifesto on Telegram that concluded with the statement: 'We are the opposition to the war, to patriarchy, to authoritarianism and militarism. We – are the future and we will win'.[80]

FAR's activities spread to dozens of Russian cities, where it continues to disseminate anti-war and anti-conscription messaging. It works closely with *Vesna*, even as many of the leaders of both movements had to flee the country because of surveillance and harassment from authorities. On International Women's Day, 8 March 2022, FAR members asked that they not be given flowers, as was the tradition; rather, flowers bound with blue and yellow ribbons (Ukrainian colours) should be laid at war memorials throughout Russia. This act of defiance occurred in at least 94 Russian cities and towns.[81]

While Putin gushed about the 'enduring importance of motherhood and the traditional values of our country' and presented Mother Heroine awards to mothers of 11 and 13 children on Women's Day, FAR, *Vesna, Uznik.Online* (Prisoner.Online), the SotsFem Alternative, the Eighth Initiative Group, and other activist bodies spoke out against the official portrayal of women. They all pointed out that Russia did not protect women from domestic abuse and objected to the state's propaganda exploiting Women's Day.[82]

The Eight Initiative Group, a united feminist movement based in St. Petersburg, posted on Telegram that 'despite many years of work by the feminist community, the state is still deaf to the problem of violence against women'.[83] The SotsFem Alternative and FAR took Putin and the Orthodox Church to task for trying to solve Russia's demographic problems by limiting access to abortions: 'instead of stopping the costly, senseless military operations that are killing Russians, or instead of fighting poverty and developing effective programs to support childhood, motherhood and responsible parenthood'. Soft Power, a women's social-political movement, complained of militarism permeating all levels of schooling, from kindergarten to universities, and protested the growing number of female political prisoners.[84]

FAR also distributes a newspaper titled *Female Truth* (Zhenskaia Pravda), an 'anti-war newspaper that it is not ashamed to show to mothers and grandmothers!'[85]

Another form of female activism emerged first in November 2023 and then gathered momentum in 2024. Every weekend in January until arrests started in February 2024 women relatives of mobilized soldiers wearing white scarves placed red carnations at the Tomb of the Unknown Soldier close to the Kremlin walls, and called on the government to bring their male relatives home. While some of them were members of the *Put' domoi* (The Way Home) movement, many were there as mothers, wives or daughters of men conscripted and sent to fight in Ukraine. Some carried signs saying, 'Return my husband' (Vernite muzha). Although police arrested journalists covering the protests and detained a few demonstrators for questioning, authorities had to be very careful about arresting wives and mothers of fighting men. State media was careful not to give them publicity.[86]

To counter public embarrassment for the Kremlin, the Russian government organized counter-groups of more openly loyal wives and mothers, and labelled information posted on the *Put' domoi* Telegram channel (40,000 followers) as fake. Nationalist media calls them foreign agents, though as of March 2024 they had not yet been so named by the government. They were one of the first dissident movements to call for nation-wide protests after Navalny's sudden death in February 2024.

Another such movement, supported by mothers and directed towards men who did not want to be conscripted fell under the general rubric Kovcheg

(Noah's Ark), and was called 'Go by the Forest' (Idite lesom). Complementing Ukraine's 'I Want to Live' project, it used Telegram and Instagram to provide legal and other information, accommodations in foreign countries and other support for anyone who wished to avoid mobilization.[87]

Meanwhile, the state-directed campaign against feminists continued unabated. In April 2024, a Russian court opened criminal cases against two prominent Russian feminist activists – Daria Serenko, one of the founders of FAR, and Zalina Marshenkulova, who openly opposed the invasion of Ukraine – in absentia. They had both moved abroad.[88]

Religion

The Russian Orthodox Church plays a key role in maintaining public support for Putin's war. Along with blessing military units before the MoD sends them off to fight, the Orthodox hierarchy proselytizes for the conflict from pulpits. In April, Patriarch Kirill proclaimed that dying in Ukraine would 'wash away all sins' from Russian soldiers and, as the war passed its ninth month, Russia's goals in Ukraine were termed 'sacred' by Medvedev and others. In fact, Medvedev went so far as to declare on Telegram that: 'We are listening to the words of the Creator in our hearts and obeying them. . . . the goal is to stop the supreme ruler of Hell, whatever name he uses – Satan, Lucifer or Iblis', from governing in Ukraine.[89]

Depicting the SVO in terms of a Christian crusade became more common as the war went on. Dozens of priests were sent to the front to provide religious and moral guidance to soldiers. This was not always considered a desirable assignment.[90] There were scattered examples of priests objecting to the war, but they were quickly silenced by church and lay authorities, ostracized by their communities or, in a few cases, forced to leave the country. Although anti-war sermons inevitably resulted in fines or lost positions, nearly 300 Orthodox priests signed an open letter in March calling for an end to the 'fratricidal war in Ukraine'.[91]

The Buddhist leader in Russia fled the country, the Dalai Lama's representative was designated a 'foreign agent' and the Chief Rabbi of Moscow moved to Israel after condemning the war. He, too, was tagged a 'foreign agent'. Islamic leaders, with much larger constituencies than other non-Orthodox adherents, kept silent.[92]

Also in the sphere of religion, the state acted against Jehovah's Witnesses in December 2022 sentenced nine members to six years in prison in trials held in Birobidzhan and Blagoveshchensk. In some cases, they were charged with extremism and in others with undermining Russian state security. These sentences raised the number of Witnesses sent to prison in 2022 to 40. Designated an 'extremist' organization since 2017, members of the sect have been subjected to raids at their homes, a process that accelerated after February 2022, because they are pacifist and have their headquarters in the United States.

Russian Orthodoxy suffered a setback in Ukraine when the Ukrainian Ministry of Culture ordered all Ukrainian Orthodox Church (UOC) monks off the eleventh-century Kyiv-Pechersk Lavra (Monastery of the Caves) property by the end of March 2023. This order fell in line with Zelensky's decree of December 2022 imposing sanctions against all representatives of any religious organization associated with Russia. Although the UN's Human Rights Commission (OHCHR) called these actions against the UOC discriminatory, complaints from Moscow went unheeded and, in contrast to its usual response to incidents of religious persecution, the US State Department issued no comment.[93]

On 1 April, the SBU arrested Metropolitan Pavel, abbot of the Kyiv-Pechersk Lavra, accusing him of justifying Russian aggression, and inciting national and religious hatred. He was placed under house arrest for two months and forced to wear a monitoring bracelet around his ankle. Earlier, the monk had threatened Zelensky with damnation.[94] Although the UOC insisted that it had broken ties with Moscow, by April 2023 Ukrainian authorities had opened over 60 criminal cases against its clergymen, and UOC branches were expelled from several places of worship in Kyiv.

In June, the Kyiv Regional Council called on the Verkhovna Rada to adopt legislation banning the UOC altogether, alleging that it was 'controlled by the aggressor country'.[95]

In Russia, an interview with Patriarch Kirill aired on TV's Rossiia 1 on 7 January 2023 revealed more about his Church's position on the war in Ukraine. He implied that Russia represents Christian values and moral principles, while Europe and the West do not. Grumbling that Russian Orthodoxy is suppressed in Ukraine, Kirill complained that 'in the centre of Europe a nasty persecution of the Church is really unleashed – under the slogans of democracy, freedom, and so on'. He then switched to a condemnation of 'sex change' as part of the 'de-Christianization of Western society'. He insisted, too, that Russians and Ukrainians must not become enemies, that there must be 'no cultivation of hatred' and that the Orthodox Church is the one force that can keep them all together. The political leadership of Ukraine, not the people, and the West are forces trying to divide the 'one nation that emerged from the Kyiv Baptismal font, spread from the White Sea to the Black Sea', he said. In this way, Kirill justified war against the regime in Kyiv, echoing secular mantras espoused by Putin in spiritual terminology.[96] Equally hypocritically.

Questions of Citizenship

We have seen that shortly after Putin's administration orchestrated referenda and the subsequent annexations of territories in Ukraine, the State Duma adopted a series of laws designed to Russianize the newly seized lands. Citizenship laws were amended to facilitate a rapid transformation of citizens of Ukraine into citizens of Russians. At about the same time, Putin submitted laws to the Duma that extended protocols for depriving people who were already Russian of their citizenship.

Existing legislation allowed the state to withdraw citizenship from people who commit terrorist acts, forge documents or traffic in drugs. These were amended to take into account people who acted on behalf of an 'undesirable' foreign NGO, distributed false information about Russia's Armed Forces, made public statements that challenged Russia's territorial integrity, or discredited 'the use of the Armed Forces of the Russian Federation in order to protect the interests of the Russian Federation and its citizens, maintain international peace and security, or exercise their powers by state bodies of the Russian Federation for these purposes' (Criminal Code amendment, 280.3).[97]

Commissioner for Human Rights Tatyana Moskalkova urged the government to grant children of Russian citizens from mixed marriages (i.e. a Russian and a Ukrainian) citizenship if only one parent granted permission. Earlier, in September, the Federation Council approved a law granting citizenship to foreigners who took up contracts to serve in Russia's Armed Forces and served for at least six months.[98] This law was amended in January 2024 to make it even easier for foreign contract soldiers to become citizens. At that time, Putin signed another law granting the right of any Ukrainian born before 18 March 2014 and permanently living in Crimea or Sevastopol to obtain Russian citizenship.[99] In this way, Moscow could augment its Armed Forces, if only slightly, perhaps avoid further conscription orders and also tighten its hold on Crimea.

War Crimes Conundrum

When the UN Independent International Commission of Inquiry on Ukraine delivered its report on investigations of 'events' in Kyiv, Chernihiv, Kharkiv and Sumy to the UN General Assembly on 18 October 2022, it provided evidence that there was an 'undeniable need for accountability for an array of war crimes, violations of human rights and international humanitarian law committed in Ukraine'. Although, as we have seen, Russian forces were responsible for the 'vast majority' of these crimes, the horrendous Bucha revelations serving as the report's starting point, Ukrainian forces were not innocent of brutalities. Western media and Ukraine reported on Russia's misdeeds; the Russian media reported on Ukrainian misdeeds. Separating fact from fiction was not always straight forward in either case.[100]

As the conflict settled into its attrition mode in December 2022, the Ukrainian Prosecutor General's office reported that it had recorded 51,161 war crimes and crimes of aggression in Ukraine since the start of the war. The list included 'breaking the laws and customs of war', 'planning, preparing for or starting and waging an aggressive war' and 'propaganda of war'. A second category registered 18,585 crimes against national security, especially acts of treason, sabotage and collaboration with the enemy by Ukrainians. The scope of these criteria meant that the state could label almost any action a war crime.[101]

The question of war crimes became more substantive in January 2023, when the European Parliament passed a resolution to set up a special international tribunal to prosecute Russia's leadership for its crime of 'aggression against Ukraine'.[102] The resolution referred to outrages committed in Bucha and Irpin specifically, and named Putin, 'the political and military leadership of Russia, but also Alyaksandr Lukashenka and his cronies in Belarus', as subjects to be investigated.[103] The resolution had little opposition, perhaps because it came shortly after civilian residences were bombed in Dnipro.

In March, the International Criminal Court (ICC) opened two cases against Russian officials, having to do with the abduction of Ukrainian children and deliberate targeting of civilian infrastructure.[104] At about the same time, major Western media were headlining statements by the UN team investigating human rights violations in Ukraine that Russian authorities had committed a 'wide range of war crimes', emphasizing the deportation of Ukrainian children. Less attention was paid to a further admission that UN investigators had not yet found any evidence of genocide within Ukraine, though the term was used often by politicians on both sides.[105]

The ICC took its investigation further by issuing a symbolic arrest warrant for Putin, saying that he was 'allegedly responsible for the war crime of unlawful deportation of (children) and that of unlawful transfer of population (children) from occupied areas of Ukraine to the Russian Federation'. The warrant went on to proclaim that there were 'reasonable grounds to believe that Mr. Putin bears individual criminal responsibility for the aforementioned crimes'. The court also issued a warrant for the arrest of Maria Lvova-Belova, the presidential commissioner for Children's Rights. Russia immediately rejected the warrant as unacceptable, noting that Russia does not recognize the ICC's jurisdiction. Lvova-Belova protested that they moved the children, mostly orphans, out of war zones and created safer conditions for them.[106] Russia's envoy to the UN, Vassily Nebenzia repeated her defence: 'We are talking about evacuation from a war zone in full compliance with obligations under international humanitarian law, as well as the Convention on the Rights of the Child'. Saying also that the evacuations were temporary, that where possible the children were placed with family members in Russia and that the children had a full right to communicate with relatives or friends for reunification.[107] This assertion could not be verified easily, but seemed unlikely in practice.

At the end of August 2023, Lvova-Belova acknowledged that thousands of Ukrainian children had come to Russia since February 2022 but claimed that the vast majority of them were accompanied by their parents or their relatives as part of the 4.8 million refugees from Ukraine who migrated to Russia. Only about 1,500 orphans were evacuated and 380 of those have been adopted by Russian parents, her Children's Rights report asserted. According to Kyiv's database 'Children of War', of 19,546 Ukrainian children 'deported' to Russia by September 2023, 386 had been returned.[108]

Russia did not own a monopoly on alleged war crimes. Tactics and weaponry also came under scrutiny. From time to time, an international body questioned Ukraine's use of banned anti-personnel 'Butterfly' landmines to stop Russian forces from returning to areas from which they had been forced out, among them Izium. According to Human Rights Watch, these small mines had injured up to 50 civilians, some of them children, to the time of the report in January 2023. While in no way excusing Russia from using landmines too, an HRW spokesman said that revelations of their use by Ukraine compromised its 'moral high ground'.[109] Ukraine had signed on to an international ban on land mines; Russia, the United States, China and other big players have not. These small mines can be distributed by mortar or rocket fire.

The HRW already had called out Ukrainian forces for killing a Swiss Red Cross worker with an illegal cluster bomb used against separatists in Donetsk in 2014, only to be ignored.[110] Human Rights Watch, Mines Action Canada and other human rights organizations vigorously objected to Washington's decision in July 2023 to send cluster bombs to Ukraine, in vain.

When in November 2022, Matilda Bogner, head of the UN Human Rights Monitoring Mission in Ukraine, released a study of the treatment of prisoners of war, she censured both sides for widespread abuse, torture and even execution of prisoners of war. Severe physical and psychological torture against captured Ukrainian and Russian soldiers, and very poor internment conditions (lack of food, poor hygiene, overcrowding), were themes common to both military camps.[111]

In the long run, of course, the question of war crimes may depend on the extent to which one side or the other takes civilian lives. In this respect, the SVO itself could be deemed a war crime and, to make certain of that, the International Centre for the Prosecution of the Crime of Aggression against Ukraine (ICPA) opened in The Hague in July 2023. Funded by the European Commission's Service for Foreign Policy Instruments and located at the EU's judicial co-operation agency, Eurojust, the Centre will provide research support for agencies investigating Russian acts of aggression, and help bring evidence to cases tried by the ICC.

Assigned an initial task of centralizing and storing evidence for use by whatever international court eventually hears cases, the ICPA's central mission is to examine aggression, which means it will deal only with Russian actions. Given that the Commission's start-up investigatory team is made up of representatives from the three Baltic states, Ukraine, Poland and Romania, one would have to wonder about its potential for bias. To be sure, the Ukrainian government's claim in November 2023 that it had collected evidence of 109,000 Russian war crimes may make the ICPA's task relatively simple. The list included cyber and environmental crimes. The dilemma, of course, is to decide which of these alleged war crimes are true and which are products of wartime propaganda.[112]

NOTES

1. 'Russia presidential rights body urged "not to upset" Putin with war questions – reports', *The Moscow Times*, 7 December 2022; 'Putin names war supporters to Russia's Human Rights Council', *The Moscow Times*, 17 November 2022.

2. Constant Méhéut, 'Russia is denied a seat on the U.N. Human Rights Council', *New York Times*, 10 October 2023; 'V OON ne izbrali Rossiiu v Sovet po pravam ccheloveka', *Vedomosti*, 10 October 2023.

3. 'Dvizhenie "Vesna"'. '"Vesnu" priznali "ekstremistskoi organizatsiei"', *Telegram*, 6 December 2022, t.me/vesna_democrat/4760.

4. 'Sudy obshchei iuridiktsii goroda Moskvy. '25 ianvaria 2023 goda Moskovskii gorodskoi sud . . .', *Telegram*, 25 January 2023, t.me/moscowcourts/1441; 'Russia's justice ministry seeks dissolution of Moscow Helsinki group', *The Moscow Times*, 21 January 2022.

5. Sakharovskii Tsentr, 'Zaiavlenie v sviazi s iz'iatiem pomeshchenii Sakharovskogo tsentra', 26 January 2023, sakharov-center.ru/article/zayavlenie-v-svyazi-s-izyatiem-pomescheniy-sakharovskogo-centra.

6. '"Freedom cannot be shut down": Defiance as Russia's Sakharov Centre holds last public event', *The Moscow Times*, 17 April 2023.

7. Po mneniiu 'sovy', 'Mosgorsud postanovil likvidirovat' Tsentr "Sova"', *Telegram*, 27 April 2023, t.me/sovacenter/179; 'Mosgorsud po isku Miniusta likvidiroval tsentr "Sova"', *Interfaks*, 27 April 2023; 'Moscow court orders closure of Sova Analytical Centre', *The Moscow Times*, 27 April 2023.

8. 'Miniust nachal proverku "Yel'tsin tsentra" na predmet deiatel'nosti inoagenta', *TASS*, 15 June 2023; '"Nezamedlitel'no ostanovit'": "Yel'tsin Tsentr" prizval prekratit' voennuiu operatsiiu na Ukraine', *E1.ru*, 25 February 2022, e1.ru/text/politics/2022/02/25/70471550/.

9. The Nobel Prize, 'Prize announcement; Ales Bialiatski, memorial, Center for Civil Liberties', 7 October 2022, nobelprize.org/prizes/peace/2022/prize-announcement/; 'Pravozashchitnyi tsentr "Memorial" poluchil Nobelevskuiu premiiu mira', *Vedomosti*, 7 October 2022.

10. Council of Europe, '2022 Vaclav Havel Prize awarded to imprisoned Russian opposition leader Vladimir Kara-Murza', *Strasbourg*, 10 October 2022.

11. 'Mosgorsud prigovoril k 25 godam kolonii zhurnalista Kara-Murzu za gosizmenu', *RAPSI*, 17 April 2023.

12. '"Small courageous steps": Memorial opposing oppression in Russia', *The Moscow Times*, 5 November 2022.

13. Obshchestvo Memorial, 'Priamo seichas po mnozhestvu adresov sotrudnikov Memoriala v Moskve prishli s obyskom: Vyzvany advokaty', *Telegram*, 21 March 2023, t.me/toposmemoru/2710; 'In Moscow, the security forces came with searches to the employees of "Memorial"', *OVD-Info*, 21 March 2023.

14. '"People are running from you, Mr. President: Can't you see?" The last word of Russian opposition Ilya Yashin in court: Full text', *Novaia Gazeta Evropa*, 6 December 2022.

15. Ilya Yashin, 'A message to the world from inside a Russian prison', *Time*, 10 February 2023, signed by Yashin from 'Detention Center No. 1, Udmurtiya, Russia'.

16. On this, see Andrei Kolesnikov, 'Russia's quiet riot', *Foreign Affairs*, 13 December 2022.

17. Federal'nyi zakon ot 14.07.2022, No. 255-F3 'O kontrole za deiatel'nost'iu lits, nokhodiashchikhsia pod inostrannym vliianiem', publication.pravo.gov.ru/Document/View/0001202207140018?index=37&rangeSize=1.

18. Vera Chelishcheva, 'Pugacheva's Rebellion', *Novaia Gazeta Evropa*, 22 January 2024. For her post to the Ministry of Justice asking to be included on its list of foreign agents, instagram.com/p/CipbuA9qzIe/.

19. 'The Ministry of Justice declared . . . as foreign agents', *Meduza*, 21 October 2022. For the ever-expanding list: minjust.gov.ru/ru/activity/directions/942/spisok-lic-vypolnyayushih-funkcii-inostrannogo-agenta/, which is currently inaccessible. For commentary, see Nina L. Khrushcheva, 'Russian culture is headed for the Gulag owing to Putin's war', *Globe and Mail*, 28 February 2013, and Paul Sonne, Alex Marshall, 'Russia's exiled music stars are persevering', *New York Times International Weekly*, 2–3 December 2023.

20. 'Russia seeks arrests of 2 animators, ex-lawmaker Gudkov', *The Moscow Times*, 26 December 2023; 'MVD ob'iavilo v rozysk sozdatelia animatsionnogo seriala Mr. Freeman Pavla Muntiana', *Mediazona*, 26 December 2023.

21. 'Putin podpisal zakon, uzhetochaiushchii administrativnuiu i ugolovnuiu otvetstvennost' dlia "inoagentov"', *OVD-Info*, 22 December 2022.

22. 'The Ministry of Justice included the bell, Rovshan Askerov and Mikhail Fishman in the register of "foreign agents"', *Meduza*, 9 December 2022.

23. 'Human rights activist Svetlana Gannushkina, Roskomsvoboda and feminist anti-war resistance were included in the register of "foreign agents"', *Meduza*, 23 December 2022.

24. See Daria Dergacheva, 'Every Friday, Russia labels new citizens and organizations as "foreign agents"', *Global Voices*, 8 February 2023.

25. 'Rossii ob'iavil "inoagentom" solista gruppy "Bi-2"', *Meduza*, 26 May 2023. For Ministry of Justice lists, minjust.gov.ru/ru/events/49542/. This site is no longer readily accessible.

26. 'The Ministry of Justice declared Natalya Sindeeva, the owner of the Bookmate book service and the founder of Dozhd, as "foreign agents"', *Meduza*, 28 October 2022.

27. 'The Ministry of Justice declared WWF and economist Sergei Guriev "foreign agents"', *Meduza*, 10 March 2023.

28. 'Priznannoe "inostrannym agentom": ekologicheskoe izdanie "Kedr" zakrylos' posle ugroz geroiam publikatsii', *Mediazona*, 8 January 2024; 'Russian environmental news outlet Keddr closes after "foreign agent" designation', *The Moscow Times*, 8 January 2023.

29. 'Miniust vnes kak minimum 861 cheloveka v zakrytyi reestr lits, "affilirovannykh" s "inoagentami"', *OVD-Info*, 15 June 2023; 'The Ministry of Justice of the Russian Federation has included more than 800 people in a closed register of persons "affiliated with foreign agents" – and this is only in a month', *Meduza*, 15 June 2023.

30. Genprokuratura Rossii, 'Genprokuratura Rossii priniala reshenei o priznanii . . .', *Telegram*, 6 March 2023, t.me/genprocrf/2448; 'Russia deems transparency international "undesirable" organization', *The Moscow Times*, 5 March 2023.

31. 'Istochnik: na sopredsedatelia dvizheniia "Golos" Mel'kon'iantsa zaveli delo', *RIA Novosti*, 17 August 2023.

32. 'The government approved a new type of "foreign agent" plate', *Meduza*, 22 November 2022.

33. Genprokuratura Rossii, 'Deiatel'nosti mezhdunarodnoi nepravitel'stvennoi nekommercheskoi organizatsii "Grinpis Interneshnl" (Niderlandy) priznana nezhelatel'noi na territorii RF', *Telegram*, 19 May 2023, t.me/genprocrf/2596; 'Genprokuratura priznala deiatel'nost' gruppy "Agora" nezhelatel'noi v Rossii', *RIA Novosti*, 19 June 2023; 'Russian Ministry of Justice declares blogger Ilya Varlamov and lawyer Pavel Chikov "foreign agents"', *Meduza*, 23 March 2023.

34. 'Putin prigrozil otvetit' na mokovskii terakt tem zhe "oruzhiem" i poruchil MVD uzhestochit' migratsionnuiu politiku', *iVazhnye istorii*, 2 April 2024; 'Russia's civil society in 2023: Beleaguered but not beaten', *The Moscow Times*, 28 December 2023.

35. 'Meduza has been declared an "undesirable" organization: Meduza continues to work. Keep reading us', *Meduza*, 26 January 2023.

36. 'Rasshirennoe zasedanie kollegii General'noi prokuratury', *Kremlin.ru*, 15 March 2023, kremlin.ru/events/president/news/70678.

37. General'naya prokuratura Rossiiskoi Federatsii, 'Novosti', 21 June 2023, epp.genproc.gov.ru/web/gprf/mass-media/news?item=88519899; 'The Russian prosecutor general's office of the Russian federation declared *Novaya Gazeta Evropa* "Undesirable"', *Meduza*, 28 June 2023.

38. 'Komissiia Gosdumy po rassledovaniiu vmeshatel . . .', *Telegram*, 24 January 2024, t.me/komisgd/693; 'Russia labels youth magazine DOXA "undesirable": – lawmaker', *The Moscow Times*, 25 January 2024.

39. 'Russia moves to ban foreign state-funded orgs as "undesirables"', *The Moscow Times*, 12 February 2024. For the Ministry list, minjust.gov.ru/ru/documents/7756/.

40. 'Arshak Makichyanm@MakichyanA, 'The FSB has issued my family a 50-year entry ban . . .', *Thread*, 22 March 2023, twitter.com/MakichyanA/status/1638533089725956099?s=20; 'FSB bans climate activist's family from Russia for half a century', *The Moscow Times*, 23 March 2023.

41. 'Miniust vkliuchil v reestr inoagenTov artista Slepakova i izdanie "Agentsvo"', *Vedomosti*, 14 April 2023.

42. 'V reestr "inoagentov" vnesli "Shkoly prizyvnika", "Advokatskuiu ulitsu", zhurnalistov i politikov', *OVD-Info*, 21 April 2023, minjust.gov.ru/uploaded/files/kopiya-reestr-inostrannyih-agentov-21-04-2023.pdf.

43. 'Avgustovskie inoagenty', *Aktual'nye kommentarii*, 31 August 2023; 'Russia brands novel winner muratov a "foreign agent"', *RFE/RL*, 1 September 2023.

44. 'Po predateliu v den', *Kholod*, 7 August 2023, holod.media/2023/08/07/po-predatelyu-v-den/; Pervyi otdel, 'Massovye proverki telefonov, pytki bez tseli, vse bol'she del o gosimene: advokat Yevgenii Smirnov o novykh repressivnykh trendakh. . . .' *Telegram*, 12 May 2023, t.me/deptone/5699; 'Russia's 2023 treason cases hit record high – NGO', *The Moscow Times*, 21 December 2023.

45. 'Zakon o pozhiznennom lishenii svobody za gosizmenu podpisan prezidentom', *RAPSI*, 28 April 2023.

46. 'Putin podpisal zakony, usilivaiushchie presledovanie "inoagentov"', *OVID-Info*, 24 July 2023.

47. 'On Boris Grebenshchikov, a protocol was drawn up on the "discredit" of the army', *Meduza*, 14 May 2023; 'Russia police raid opposition politicians' homes, detain activist', *The Moscow Times*, 27 October 2023; 'U soratnikov eks-deputata Gosdumu Ponomareva proveli obyski', *RIA Novosti*, 18 May 2023. See also 'Russian politicians, journalists targeted in police raids linked to ex-lawmaker Ponomaryov', *The Moscow Times*, 29 December 2022.

48. Mozhem ob'iasnit, 'Minobrnauki nachalo sbor lichnykh dannykh studentov i prepodavatelei, obshchavshikhsia v etom godu s inostrantsami. . . .', *Telegram*, 16 November 2023, t.me/mozhemobyasnit/16517. This post includes a copy of the letter distributed by MinJust; 'Russia tracks academics with foreign contacts as treason cases rise – reports', *The Moscow Times*, 17 November 2023.

49. 'Eye of the sovereign censorship', *iVazhnye istorii*, 8 February 2023, istories.media/stories/2023/02/08/oko-gosudarevoi-tsenzuri/; 'Anti-war historian fired from St. Petersburg European university', *The Moscow Times*, 5 March 2024.

50. For True Russia's website in English, see truerussia.org.

51. 'Russian journalist whose home address was posted online by lawmaker says she has left country "until better times come"', *Meduza*, 22 January 2024.

52. Viktoriia Nikiforova, 'Ulitskaya dala povbod k primeneniiu novogo zakona konfiskatsii imushchestva', *RIA Novosti*, 2 February 2024; 'Russia labels author lyudmila ulitskaya foreign agent', *The Moscow Times*, 1 March 2024.

53. 'Bolee 20% inostrannykh agentov v Rossii nakhoyatsya pod ugolovnym presledovaniem', *Verstka*, 28 February 2024; 'Criminal cases against "foreign agents" doubled in 2023 – Vyorstka', *The Moscow Times*, 28 February 2024.

54. 'Putin podpisal zakon o zaprete reklamu na resursakh inogentov', *Izvestiia*, 11 March 2024.

55. Aleksandr Tikhonov, Yana Surinskaya, 'Gosduma priniala zakon ob iz'iatin zagranpasportov u rossiian', *Vedomosti*, 23 May 2023.

56. 'The State Duma proposed to completely ban "propaganda of non-traditional relations"', *Meduza*, 11 July 2022; 'No laws will make gays and lesbians disappear', *Meduza*, 19 October 2022.

57. 'At hearings in the State Duma, the ban on "gay propaganda" was compared to "victory on the battlefield"', *Meduza*, 17 October 2022. On this generally, see Vasily Legeido, '"There are no homosexuals in this country": How Putin's embrace of homophobia echoes dictators of the past', *Meduza*, 21 October 2022.

58. 'Russian lawmakers vote in favor of "LGBT propaganda" expansion', *The Moscow Times*, 27 October 2022; 'Russian deputies want to expand the law on "gay propaganda" – and increase discrimination against LGBT people', *The Bell*, 25 October 2022.

59. 'Magaziny "Respublika" i "Chitai-gorod" sniali s prodazhi knigi s LGBT-tematikoi posle podpisaniia Putinym zakona o "propagande"', *Novaia Gazeta Evropa*, 5 December 2022; 'Russia bans books mentioning LGBT issues', *The Bell*, 6 December 2022.

60. '"LitRes" poprosit avtorov perepisat' teksty iz-za zakona on LGBT', *RBC.ru*, 5 December 2022; 'Choices narrow in Russian bookstores amid anti-LGBT law, wartime restrictions', *The Moscow Times*, 8 January 2023.

61. Aleksandr Khinshtein, 'UR State Duma deputy, letter on Telegram to the minister of internal affairs', *Telegram*, 10 January 2023, t.me/Hinshtein/3321; 'First probe opened into breach of Russia's new "LGBT propaganda" law', *The Moscow Times*, 10 January 2023.

62. 'Russia vows to defend "traditional values" against "gay propaganda"', *The Moscow Times*, 9 November 2022.

63. On this, see essays in 'Anti-LGBTQ discrimination and violence', *Russian Analytical Digest*, No. 300, 14 September 2023.

64. Ankush Kumar, 'LGBTQ group shut down by Putin is back from the dead', *The Daily Beast*, 7 January 2023; Dilya Gafurova, 'Russia's biggest LGBT+ group has been shut down: But we're going nowhere', *Open Democracy*, 22 April 2022, opendemocracy.net/en/5050/cf-sphere-russia-lgbtqi-shut-down/.

65. Elena Kostyuchenko, *I Love Russia: Reporting from a Lost Country*. Toronto: Random House, 2023. Translated by Bela Shayevich & Ilona Yazhbin Chavasse.

66. 'Poslanie Prezidenta Federal'nomu Sobraniiu', *Kremlin.ru*, 21 February 2023, kremlin.ru/events/president/news/705675.

67. 'Knigizhar', *Telegram*, 19 December 2022, t.me/bookngrill/5453; Vasilisa Kirilochkina, 'Books removed and movies banned under Russia's "LGBT Propaganda" law', *The Moscow Times*, 15 March 2023.

68. Yekaterina Kiniakina, Marina Tiuniaeva, 'Za demonstratsiiu netraditsionnykh seksual'nykh otnoshenii sostavleno 33 protokola', *Vedomosti*, 19 June 2023; 'Na "Kinopoisk" sostavili protokol o "demonstratsii LGBT" nesovershennoletnim', *Mediazona*, 20 June 2023.

69. Gosudarstvennaya Duma, 'Deputaty podderzhali popravki zaprete smeny pola', 14 June 2023, duma.gov.ru/news/57290/; 'Duma TV: Forwarded from

Viacheslav Volodin', 'Gosudarstvennaia Duma zapretila smenu pola v Rossii', *Telegram*, 14 July 2023, t.me/dumatv/4500. For the full law, duma.gov.ru/news/57524/.

70. '"Gosduma zapretit transgendernym i nebinarnyi liudiam absoliutno vse, poiavitsia podpol'nyi khirurgicheskii rynok" – pravozashchitniki', *The Insider*, 14 June 2023, theins.ru/news/262553.

71. Yana Surinskaia, Yekaterina Grobman, 'Chem obernetsia isk Miniusta o priznanii LGBT ekstremistskim dvizheniem', *Vedomosti*, 18 November 2023. See minjust.gov.ru/ru/events/49843; 'Russia moves to ban "international" LGBT movement'", *The Moscow Times*, 17 November 2023; 'Verkhovnyi sud ob'iavil "dvizhenie LGBT" ekstremistskoi organizatsiei', *Mediazona*, 30 November 2023.

72. 'Rosfinmonitoring vnes dvizhenie LGBT v perechen' terroristicheskikh i ekstremistskikh', *TASS*, 22 March 2024;

73. Pierre Emmanuel Ngendakumana, 'Moscow police raid gay clubs after high court labels LGBTQ+ "extremist"', *Politico*, 2 December 2023; 'Moscow police raid gay clubs after "extremist" ban on LGBT community', *The Moscow Times*, 3 December 2023.

74. 'Razrushenie traditsionnykh tsennostei i feminitivy: "Svobodnye novosti" publikuiut polnyi tekst resheniia Verkhovnogo suda RF o priznanii ekstremistskim "dbvizheniia LGBT"', *Svobodnye*, 18 January 2024, fn-volga.ru/news/view/id/219533' 'Pervoe delo o "demonstratsii simboliki ekstremistskoi organizatsii" za raduzhnyi flag: Onlain', *Mediazona*, 30 January 2024; 'Russian court jails woman for wearing "extremist" rainbow earrings', *The Moscow Times*, 31 January 2024.

75. 'Artist Yulia Tsvetkova left Russia', *OVD-Info*, 25 November 2022.

76. 'Queers as extremists: The assault on LGBTQ+ rights in Russia', *The Moscow Times*, 22 February 2024.

77. 'Mikhail Mishustin approved a new National Strategy of Action for women until 2030', *Posol'skaia zhizn'*, 8 January 2023, embassylife.ru/en/post/14580.

78. 'Ministry of Health of the Russian Federation is ready to discuss a possible ban on abortions in private clinics', *Interfax*, 18 July 2023; 'Esli gosudarstvo zalezlo zhenshchinam v postel', to vriad li ostanovitsia', *Vërstka*, 21 July 2023; Leyla Latypova, 'Russia edges closer to abortion ban in quest to preserve "traditional values"', *The Moscow Times*, 28 July 2023.

79. Putin, 'Videoobrashchenie po sluchaiu Mezhdunarodnogo zhenskogo dnia', *Kremlin.ru*, 8 Marcch 2024, kremlin.ru/events/president/news/73624.

80. Feministskoe Antivoennoe Soprotivlenie, 'Manifest feministkogo antivoennogo soprotivleniia', *Telegram*, 25 February 2022, t.me/femagainstwar/4.

81. 'Feministskoe Antivoennoe Soprotivlenie', *Telegram*, 9 March 2022, t.me/femagainstwar/368.

82. See, e.g. 'Feministskoe antivoennoe soprotivlenie', *Telegram*, 8 March 2023, t.me/femagainstwar/7493; 'Women's Day celebrations a lightning rod for a divided Russia', *The Moscow Times*, 8 March 2023; 'Tseremoniia vrucheniia goudarstvennykh nagrad po sluchaiu Mezhdunarodnogo zhenskogo dnia', *Kremlin.ru*, 8 March 2023, kremlin.ru/events/president/news/70653. For more from activist women's groups, see 'March 8 originated as a day of women's struggle for their rights: Here are nine problems women still face', *Meduza*, 8 March 2023.

83. 'Vos'maia initsiativnaia gruppa', *Telegram*, 8 March 2023, t.me/Femspb/1835.

84. 'Feministskoe Antivoennoe Soprotivlenie', *Telegram*, t.me/femagainstwar/1384, accessed 8 March 2023, cited in *Meduza*, 8 March 2023, op.cit., see endnote #17; SotsFem Al'ternativa (socfemalt), Instagram, 8 March 2023, instagram.com/socfemalt/; Miagkaia Sila, *Telegram*, t.me/myagkaya_sila_ru, as above.

85. *Zhenskaya Pravda*, femagainstwar.notion.site/femagainstwar/a35a3040b7ad42bb85d7d9c39ef76fa1.

86. 'Reporters detained at moscow protest by soldiers' Wives – AFP', *The Moscow Times*, 3 February 2024; 'White scarves and flowers: Wives and mothers of mobilized soldiers take resentment to the Kremlin', *The Moscow Times*, 17 January 2024.

87. For background, see 'The underground network helping Russians escape the draft', *RFE/RL*, 22 April 2023.

88. 'Are feminists the Kremlin's next target?' *The Moscow Times*, 3 May 2024.

89. '"Putin fighting sacred battle": Russian president's aide calls Ukraine "Satan", tears into West', *YouTube*, 8 November 2022; youtube.com/watch?v=4Tf9H2He4y0; 'Russia fighting "sacred" battle against Satan, Medvedev says', *RFE/RL*, 4 November 2022; '"Sacred goal": Russia paints Ukraine assault in spiritual terms', *The Moscow Times*, 6 December 2023.

90. 'Orthodox clerics call for stop to war In Ukraine in challenge to Russian government', *RFE/RL*, 1 March 2022; Elise Ann Allen, 'Russian Orthodox priests call for immediate end to war in Ukraine', *Crux*, 6 March 2022; Aleksandar Brezar, 'Ukraine war: Meet Father Grigory, Russia's most prominent anti-war priest', *Euronews*, 18 October 2022.

91. 'Obrashchenie sviashchennosluzhitelei Russkoi Pravoslavnoi tserkvi s prizyvom k primirennuiu i prekrashcheniiu voiny', available here in English as well, with list of signatories, docs.google.com/forms/d/1yOGuXjdFQ1A3BQaEEQr744cwDzmSQ1qePaaBi4z6q3w/viewform?edit_requested=true, accessed 12 February 2023.

92. On this, see Leyla Latypova, 'Russia's religious leaders who criticized the Ukraine war', *The Moscow Times*, 11 February 2023; 'Russia brands exiled former Moscow chief rabbi a "foreign agent"', *Times of Israel*, 2 July 2023.

93. 'Ekaterina Grobman, 'Monakhov Ukrainskoi pravoslavnoiu tserkvi vyseliaiut iz Kievo-Pecherskoi Lavry', *Vedomosti*, 10 March 2023; 'Ukraine urges UN to remain balanced on issue of Russian-backed church eviction', *Kyiv Post*, 27 March 2023.

94. Polina Khudiakova, 'Namestnika Kievo-Pecherskoi lavry khotiat otpravit' pod domashnii arest', *Vedomosti*, 1 April 2023; 'Russia-backed church leader under house arrest as Kyiv Lavra conflict intensifies', *Kyiv Post*, 2 April 2023.

95. 'Kyiv region calls for ban of Moscow-linked Orthodox Church', *Kyiv Post*, 10 June 2023.

96. Russkaya Pravoslavnaia Tserkov, 'Christmas interview of His Holiness Patriarch Kirill to the TV channel "Russia 1"', 7 January 2023, patriarchia.ru/db/text/5992951.html. For long excerpts in Russian, Yelena Yakovleva, 'Patriarkh Kirill: Bor'ba za nravstvennye printsipy, za sokhranenie very – eto bor'ba za budushchee

vsego chelovechestva: Za zhizn' mira ni mnogo ni malo', *Rossiiskaa Gazeta*, 8 January 2023.

97. Valentina Yegorova, 'Putin rasshiril krug prestuplenii, za kotorye mozhno lishit' priobretennogo grazhdanstva RF', *Rossiiskaia Gazeta*, 13 November 2022; 'Putin proposed to deprive acquired citizenship for discrediting the army', *RIA Novosti*, 13 November 2022; for the bill on citizenship, see sozd.duma.gov.ru/bill/49 269-8.

98. Dmitrii Goncharuk, 'Sovfed odobril zakon ob uproshchennom predostavlenii grazhdanstva inostrantsam, zakliuchivshim kontrakt o sluzhbe v VS', *Rossiiskaia Gazeta*, 21 September 2022; Yelena Yakovleva, 'Moskal'kova predlozhila davat' grazhdanstvo RF detiam ot smeshannykh brakov bez soglasiia supruga', *Rossiiskaia Gazeta*, 1 November 2022.

99. Lyubov Mikhedova, 'Putin razreshil davat' grazhdanstvo sluzhashchim v rossiiskoi armii inostrantsam', *Vedomosti*, 3 January 2024.

100. United Nation, Office of the High Commissioner for Human Rights, Report, 'A/77/533: Independent international commission of inquiry on Ukraine – note by the secretary-general', 18 October 2022, ohchr.org/sites/default/files/2022-10/A-77 -3737%20-ADVANCE-UNEDITED-VERSION.pdf; for a typical Russian response, 'Organ OON soobshchil o voennykh prestupleniiakh ukraintsev', *Vedomosti*, 18 October, 2022; and in the US, Zach Schonfeld, 'Russia committed "vast majority" of alleged war crimes in Ukraine – UN report', *The Hill*, 18 October 2022.

101. Ofis General'nogo prokurora, 'Zlochini vchineni v period povnomasshtabnogo vtorgnenia RF', *Telegram*, 4 December 2022, t.me/pgo_gov_ua/7830; 'Prosecutor General's office records over 51,000 Russian war crimes, crimes of aggression in Ukraine', *The Kyiv Independent*, 5 December 2022.

102. For background, see Oona A. Hathaway, 'Russia's crime and punishment: How to prosecute the illegal war in Ukraine', *Foreign Affairs*, 17 January 2023.

103. News. European Parliament, 'Ukraine war: MEPs push for special tribunal to punish Russian crimes', *Press Releases*, 19 January 2023, europarl.europa.eu/n ews/en/press-room/20230113IPR66653/ukraine-war-meps-push-for-special-tribunal -to-punish-russian-crimes.

104. 'International court to open war crimes cases against Russia, officials say', *New York Times*, 13 March 2023; 'ICC to open war crimes cases against Russians – report', *The Moscow Times*, 13 March 2023.

105. 'UN investigators say no findings yet of genocide within Ukraine', *Barron's*, 16 March 2023; 'Murder, torture and rape but no genocide – the UN's latest report on Ukraine', *Euronews*, 16 March 2023.

106. International Criminal Court, 'Situation in Ukraine: ICC judges issue arrest warrants against Vladimir Vladimirovich Putin and Marie Alekseyevna Lvova-Belova', *Press Release*, 17 March 2023; 'Ukraine latest: Kremlin says ICC's Putin arrest warrant is void', *Bloomberg News*, 17 March 2023.

107. 'U.N. Investigators: Russian deportation of Ukrainian children a "war crime"', *The Moscow Times*, 16 March 2023; Kevin Liffey, 'Ukrainian war zone children are in temporary Russian care, not adopted or abducted – envoy', *Reuters*, 31 March 2023

108. *Doklad o Deiatel'nosti Upolnomochennogo pri Prezidente Rossiiskoi Federatsii po pravam rebenka v 2022*, Moscow: 27 September 2023, pp. 117–126, deti.gov.ru/detigray/upload/documents/July2023/7JkHUTqLIsZL45JDp4Xl.pdf; 'Deti Voiny, 24 Fevralia 2022-31 Avgusta 2023', acccessed 31 August 2023, childrenofwar.gov.ua/ru/.

109. Human Rights Watch, 'Ukraine: Banned landmines harm civilians', 31 January 2023, hrw.org/news/2023/01/31/ukraine-banned-landmines-harm-civilians.

110. Human Rights Watch, 'Ukraine: Widespread use of cluster munitions: Government responsible for cluster attacks on Donetsk', 20 October 2014, hrw.org/news/2014/10/20/ukraine-widespread-use-cluster-munitions; for the killing of an International Red Cross worker by a Ukrainian cluster bomb, see J. L. Black, *Putin's Third Term as Russia's President, 2012–18*. Abingdon, UK: Routledge, 2019, p. 102.

111. United Nations, OHCHR, 'Ukraine/Russia: Prisoners of war', 15 November 2022, ohchr.org/en/press-briefing-notes/2022/11/ukraine-russia-prisoners-war; Andrew E. Kramer, 'Accounts of torture emerge from Kherson, Ukraine's "city of fear"', *New York Times*, 15 November 2022; 'Russia accuses Ukraine of executing at least 10 prisoners of war', *The Moscow Times*, 18 November 2022.

112. Maggie Miller, 'Ukraine says it has evidence of 109,000 Russian war crimes', *Politico*, 18 November 2023; 'History in the making – The International Centre for the Prosecution of the Crime of Aggression against Ukraine starts operation at Eurojust', *Eurojust: Press Release*, 3 July 2023; Margherita Capacci, 'The ICPA, new kid on the block in the world capital of international justice', *Justice.Info.Net*, 7 July 2023, justiceinfo.net/en/119061-icpa-new-kid-block-world-capital-international-justice.html. See also, eurojust.europa.eu/joint-investigation-team-alleged-crimes-committed-ukraine.

Chapter 7

International Considerations

Are Russians 'Isolated from the Civilized World'?

Unanticipated Ukrainian resistance forced Lavrov to admit, indirectly, that the original game was up. Speaking to the UN General Assembly (UNGA) on 24 September 2022, he drew new red lines by turning the SVO into a fountainhead for dreams of a new world order. The Russian foreign minister insisted that Russia had no choice but to launch military action, so as to help the world decide 'whether or not it is going to be the type of order with one hegemon leading it'. Complaining further that NATO had been using Ukraine to threaten Russia's security, he set out sides in a new version of Cold War by also defending China's stand on Taiwan.[1]

Closer to home, the war in Ukraine had an almost immediate effect on Moscow's status as umpire in its traditional near neighbourhood. It was unable to quell border clashes between Tajikistan and Kyrgyzstan, or prevent war between Azerbaijan and Armenia. Other former Soviet republics, Ukraine, Georgia and Moldova, are now more determined than ever to join either the EU or NATO, or both, and Kazakhstan has started to look for new trade partners.

Existing trade routes that bypass Russia, such as the Middle Corridor, have become more important.

Although personnel within the Ministry of Foreign Affairs (MID) kept their objections quiet, if they had any, Lavrov was embarrassed by Boris Bondarev, a senior diplomat with the UN who defected and published a scathing essay on Russia's foreign service in the prestigious American journal *Foreign Affairs*. Labelling himself a 'diplomat in exile' who jumped off the 'crazy train', Bondarev described how members of the Russian foreign service report anything to Moscow that fits the Kremlin's propaganda line, or they fabricate them. The MID, he said, is increasingly disconnected from reality, 'warped by its own propaganda', forced to 'embrace bombastic rhetoric' and defend Moscow's 'lies and non-sequiturs'. Even Lavrov merely tells Putin what he wants to hear, providing him with an 'echo chamber', Bondarev wrote. Pondering what might happen if Russia loses, he cautioned the West not to repeat its mistakes of the 1990s; that is, don't gloat, and instead help Russia recover so that its professional diplomats are able to make 'Russia a responsible and honest global partner'.[2] He was preaching to the converted in the West, and to the deaf and mute in the East.

Putin likewise turned to the 1990s and the dissolution of the USSR for sources of the present-day crisis, telling the truncated Valdai Discussion Club in late October 2022 that:

> The collapse of the Soviet Union also destroyed the balance of geopolitical forces. The West felt like a winner and proclaimed a unipolar world order in which only its will, its culture, its interests had the right to exist.
>
> Now this historical period of undivided dominance of the West in world affairs is coming to an end, the unipolar world is becoming a thing of the past. We are standing at a historic milestone, ahead of what is probably the most dangerous, unpredictable and at the same time important decade since the end of World War II. The West is not able to single-handedly manage humanity, but is desperately trying to do so, and most of the peoples of the world no longer want to put up with it. This is the main contradiction of the new era.[3]

The old 'iron curtain' based on competing messianic ideologies was gone only to be replaced by a more volatile geopolitical competition, fought out in intra-civilizational terminology. Moreover, it was clear after a half year fighting in Ukraine that Putin hoped to exploit his war and Russia's consequent pivot to the East to disrupt the existing world order and replace it with a multi-polar one characterized by conservative values. The new world order would grant standing to the rapidly developing Global South, a term that encompasses developing (or less-developed) countries in the Southern Hemisphere and often used in place of the old 'non-aligned' code name.[4]

After a year of the SVO, the latent distrust of Russians towards Western countries had hardened, reaching unprecedented levels towards the US and the EU, and their already positive opinions of China and India had grown more favourable. These attitudes tended to vary according to the age of those surveyed by the Levada Centre in February 2023, categories that usually also mirrored the respondents' main source of information, from state-TV for older groups and from social media for younger people (see table 7.1).

As the East-West rift grew wider, Russia began alienating countries that it might otherwise have considered 'friendly', or at least neutral, above all Romania, Moldova and Armenia.

Table 7.1. Public Attitudes in Russia towards Other Countries, February 2023

Q. What is your attitude towards . . . ?

Country	Percentages of Respondents		
	Good	Bad	Difficult to Answer
China	85	6	9
India	80	5	15
Turkey	61	22	17
EU	18	69	13
Ukraine	17	69	14
USA	14	73	13

Q. What is your attitude towards the USA, by age group?

All ages	14	73	13
18–24	27	57	16
25–39	20	65	15
40–54	13	72	15
55 and older	7	83	10

Source: Compiled by the author from 'Otnoshenie k stranam: Fevral' 2023 goda, Levada-tsentr, 3 March 2023, levada.ru/2023/03/09/otnoshenie-k-stranam-fevral-2023-goda/.

INTERNATIONAL DIVIDE

The EU's resolution naming Russia a state sponsor of terrorism had implications beyond simply punishing the country for its targeting of civilian infrastructure. Along with the restrictions to which Russia was already subject, the label overrides state immunity, making it possible to launch lawsuits in Europe against the Kremlin. It could also spell an end to diplomatic relations on such matters as climate change, cybersecurity, cyber space and even prisoner exchanges, matters in which the Russian population had a stake. The Biden administration failed to support the resolution, perhaps because several American citizens were still in Russian prisons at that time.

A tone was set for East-West relations for future decades when a motion in the United Nations Security Council (UNSC) to condemn the referendums in, and subsequent annexations of, occupied territories in Ukraine was vetoed by Russian ambassador to the UN, Nebenzia. Sponsored by the United States and Albania, the vote in the 15-member Security Council was 10–1 with China, India, Brazil and Gabon abstaining. Taken to the 193-member General Assembly on 12 October, the resolution condemning Russia's annexation of Ukrainian territory was adopted, 143-5-35. That was the fourth, and strongest, motion adopted by the UNGA in support of Ukraine and against Russia since the invasion. Countries partnered with Russia in the Shanghai Cooperation Organization (SCO) were among the abstainers, along with

BRICS member South Africa. Only Russia, North Korea, Belarus, Nicaragua and Syria voted 'no'.

Hailed in the West as a sign that Russia was increasingly isolated in the world arena, an ambition pushed in Washington since 2014,[5] the vote actually showed that it wasn't, quite yet. Members of the UNGA from countries that abstained represented about half of the world's population, and all of Eurasia. Besides working with Russia in the SCO and BRICS, China, India and Pakistan are purchasers of Russian energy and weapons. Non-aligned states in Africa, Latin America and Southeast Asia remained linked to Russia for a wide variety of reasons, not the least being self-interest and an intuitive distrust of the United States and European powers.

Symptomatic of its role as a pariah, Russia was not invited to the Munich Security Conference held in February 2023. The MID responded that the conference was no longer of any interest to Russia anyway. Because several Russian-born critics of the Putin regime living abroad (Garri Kasparov, Mikhail Khodorkovsky, Dmitry Gudkov) were asked to discuss 'the future of Russia', the MID had a point when it said that the conference had lost its objectivity.[6]

The over-arching opposition to Russia in the UNGA remained strong. On the first anniversary of Putin's launch of the SVO, it approved by large margins six non-binding resolutions calling for the Kremlin to stop warring on Ukraine. In April, Russia's candidacy for three important UN bodies, the Economic and Social Council, the executive of UNICEF, and the Commission on Crime Prevention and Criminal Justice, all failed. Russia did achieve membership by acclamation on two minor bodies, for example, the Commission for Social Development, from which the United States and the United Kingdom promptly disassociated themselves.

The perception in the West of Russia as 'isolated' means, of course, isolated from the West, and not from the larger remaining parts of the world. Discussion between Lavrov and South African foreign minister, Naledi Pandor, in January 2023, revealed that the BRICS group expected to expand. Among the 20 countries that have shown an interest in joining, 13 had made actual applications. These included Saudi Arabia, Iran, Egypt, Algeria, Bahrain, the UAE, Mexico, Argentina, Nigeria and Indonesia. As the agenda for an August summit took shape in May, a leading item other than expansion was the possibility of creating a BRICS currency as an alternative to the US dollar in inter-member trade. From Moscow's perspective, such a currency could help Russia by-pass Western-imposed sanctions. To date, no such currency has been agreed.

BRICS was placed on diplomatic alert in March 2023 when the ICC issued its arrest warrant for Putin. Preparing to host the August summit, South Africa was faced with the question of whether to arrest him if he attended, or suggest he not attend. Pretoria, which adheres to the Rome Statute on which the ICC is based, decided to ask that Putin attend virtually, not personally and, when Putin seemed determined to come, granted diplomatic immunity to all top-level attendees. Some senior South African officials proposed that the summit venue be moved to China; others said that the country wished to remain neutral in the Ukraine affair and refused to be pressured by the EU or the US.[7]

After much discussion, 'by mutual agreement' in mid-July, it was decided that Putin would participate in the BRICS summit by video conference, and Lavrov would represent Russia in person.[8]

Foreign ministers from the five BRICS members met in Cape Town in June, joined by 15 foreign ministers from other African countries, the so-called Global South and by a delegation from Saudi Arabia. Its 30-point joint statement called for further cooperation among members, expressed 'concern' about the use of 'coercive measures' such as sanctions, backed India, Brazil and South Africa for greater roles in the UN, called for reform in the UN and IMF, supported climate change environmental policies, and opposed the weaponization of space. In the one sentence devoted to Ukraine, they 'noted with appreciation relevant proposals of mediation and good offices aimed at peaceful resolution of the conflict through dialogue and diplomacy'.[9] That was not very helpful.

The question of the ICC warrant for Putin became a problem for other political-military blocs. Hungary, a member of NATO and the EU, announced that it would not arrest the Russian president if he travelled there. Armenia, a member of the Russia-led Collective Security Treaty Organization (CSTO), said that it would, and warned Putin not to visit. Yerevan began the process for becoming a signatory to the Rome Statute, and made it clear that it does not support Russia's war in Ukraine. Another member of NATO, Turkey, made it known in June 2023 that it planned to invite Putin for a state visit, though no dates were set.

The international agency that most worried Russia, of course, was NATO. The Alliance's expansion eastward, Russia's special bête noire, hit a bit of a stumbling block in January 2023, when Turkey's Erdogan said he would veto Sweden's application after right-wing Swedes burned a Quran outside the Turkish embassy in Stockholm. Long-time neutrals Sweden and Finland had applied for accession in May 2022 in response to the invasion of Ukraine. Given that admission must be agreed by all NATO members, Turkey's continued anger at Sweden for supporting Kurdish militias in Syria was awkward. Hungary was also reluctant to support Sweden and Finland's entry, but cautiously agreed under pressure and incentives from the EU and the US.[10]

A Permanent Joint Mechanism made up of Turkey, Finland and Sweden to deal with the matter convened for the third time in early March 2023, with

Stoltenberg as chair. Its purpose, to ameliorate Turkey's concerns, appeared to be successful. When, at the end of March, the Turkish parliament approved a go-ahead, Stoltenberg welcomed Finland to the Alliance as its 31st member and said he looked forward to Swedish accession 'as soon as possible'.[11] Russia warned that it would raise the military components on its side of the 1,300-km (810 miles) border it shares with Finland, the longest of any NATO country with Russia. In November, Finland closed its checkpoints on that border.

To make the optics worse for Russia, Ukrainian foreign minister Kuleba used Finland's membership as a sign that it was inevitable that Ukraine join as well. To explain why that should happen, he prepared an essay for *Foreign Affairs* titled 'Why NATO Must Admit Ukraine'.[12] Coupled with Zelensky's constant in-person and videoed presentations to Western governments and other organizations, such as NATO, the G-7 and the UN, Kuleba's paper fed the growing sense of Ukraine as an essential component of the West's collective security system. This assumption was granted credence at a summit of NATO foreign ministers in Brussels on 16 June 2023, where plans to establish a new NATO-Ukraine Council were outlined.[13]

NATO Ponders Ukrainian Accession

At the Ukraine Recovery Conference in London, in June, Prime Minister Shmyhal was left with the impression that his country would be fast-tracked into both the EU and NATO even though membership in each of them requires adherence to pre-conditions that normally take a long time to negotiate. France and the UK have supported Kyiv's fast-track into NATO, the United States and Germany have not. Shmyhal told journalists in London that Ukraine was already a 'de-facto NATO army', fighting with NATO weaponry according to NATO standards, against a de facto NATO enemy.[14]

As the important summit approached, the question of Ukrainian membership dominated all preliminary chatter. The United States and Germany remained cautious about allowing admission before certain criteria were met, among them democratization and curbing corruption, while the Baltic states and Poland favoured immediate entry. Repeating an old refrain, Russia promised a 'firm response' if Ukraine was admitted to NATO, calling it 'an absolute danger, a threat to our country'.[15] Pundits debated the pros and cons of Ukrainian accession while politicians focused on more immediate national and, with elections looming almost everywhere, personal interests in the subject.

In the end, NATO's 31-members promised only to admit Ukraine after all allies agreed and certain 'conditions' were met.[16] In one major concession, the Alliance eliminated the Membership Action Plan (MAP) stage for Ukraine. Guaranteeing further material and political support for Kyiv as long as the war continued, NATO and its G-7 members hoped to signal Russia that international backing for Ukraine would not falter.

NATO delegates also finalized a structure for the NATO-Ukraine Council, condoned the use of cluster bombs by Ukraine, and extended Stoltenberg's term as Secretary General for the fourth time. The gathering's final communiqué proclaimed that 'Russia bears full responsibility for its illegal, unjustifiable, and unprovoked war of aggression against Ukraine, which has gravely undermined Euro-Atlantic and global security and for which it must be held fully accountable'.[17]

Putin warned that Ukrainian membership 'will make the world much more vulnerable and increase tensions in the international arena'.[18] None of the pontification from either side was unexpected.

After nearly two years of rejection and negotiation, Erdogan agreed, one day prior to the summit, to send the accession protocol for Sweden to Turkey's national assembly. This action was taken after Erdogan gained significant concessions, among them the right to purchase 40 F-16s fighter jets from the United States, plus 80 modernization kits, and an agreement by Stockholm to stifle Kurdish groups in Sweden that Turkey label as terrorist. While Erdogan did not achieve his main goal, EU membership, this decision once again disrupted Ankara's relations with Moscow. Turkish legislators endorsed Sweden's membership in NATO on 22 January 2024. A month later, the Hungarian parliament voted to accept Sweden as a new member of NATO, this time in return for four Swedish-made Gripen jets and an AI research centre for Budapest opened by Saab.

Sweden officially became NATO's 32nd member in March 2024.[19] With the exceptions of Belarus and Ukraine, Russia's Western border was now entirely NATO.

The Group of 20 (G-20)

Putin did not attend G-20 sessions in Bali, Indonesia, in November 2022, again leaving Lavrov to take the heat. The G-20 comprises 19 of the world's wealthiest countries, plus the EU. Biden and Xi showed up and met separately the day before the actual meetings got underway. The Western contingent focused on matters of peace and security, while Lavrov's team tried to persuade delegates to shift attention to socio-economic issues. He was unsuccessful and Zelensky, whose country is not one of the '20', was able to address the body by video and urged members to help put a stop to Russia's aggression.

A few days before the G-20 summit, Lavrov attended a meeting of the 10-member ASEAN in Cambodia, where disagreement between non-members Russia and the United States on wording related to Ukraine spelled an end to a final communiqué. The week-long series of meetings in Phnom Penh saw the launch of a US-ASEAN Comprehensive Strategic Partnership that heralded a resurgence of US presence in the east-Asian region where it has been overshadowed by China and Russia.[20]

When G-20 foreign ministers met again in March 2023, in India, Lavrov and Blinken spoke to each other, briefly. The US representative told his Russian counterpart that Washington would stand by Kyiv and asked Lavrov to re-join the New START agreement. Lavrov said later that the Western countries 'only deal in blackmail and threatening everyone else'. The organization also failed to produce a closing joint statement when Russia and China refused to sign a document that demanded Russia's withdrawal from Ukraine.[21] Apparently, much of the time was taken up with Russian and Western representatives exchanging insults.

September's G-20 summit in India was unusual in that neither Putin nor Xi attended, though they sent representatives, leaving the floor to Western leaders. Perhaps to counter Russia's growing involvement in Africa, the G-20 decided to grant full membership to the African Union, raising the 55-member organization to the same level as the EU. It had been one of the designated 'invited' organizations.

Whereas the world economic leaders urged the resumption of grain, food and fertilizer export trade from Ukraine and Russia, its final communiqué called for an end to the 'cessation of military destruction or other attacks on relevant infrastructure', without mentioning Russia's invasion. In its one reference to the 'war in Ukraine', the G-20 demanded respect for the territorial integrity of all countries and said that the 'use or threat of use of nuclear weapons is inadmissible'.[22] Putin maintained this approach when he spoke by video link to a special session of G-20 called by India's prime minister Narendra Modi in November. After listening to criticism of the war from other members, he said only that 'we should think about how to stop this tragedy. By the way, Russia has never refused peace talks with Ukraine'.[23] By setting pre-conditions, Putin had already doomed any such talks before they could start. So had Zelensky.

That was a very busy week for Putin. As we have seen, he participated in a virtual summit of the BRICS, chaired by South Africa, in an attempt to find common cause in the Israel-Hamas war and attended a CSTO session in Minsk in person. The BRICS meeting, with additional invitees, Egypt, Ethiopia, Iran, Argentina, the UAE and Saudi Arabia, called for the release of hostages and a humanitarian cease-fire, but spoke strongly against any transfer of territory or 'deportation of Palestinians from their own land'.[24]

The CSTO agreed on upgrading security for the Eurasian region, noting specifically the absence of Armenia because of 'dissatisfaction' with the organization's security promises. Kazakhstan's Kassym-Jomart Tokaev outlined his country's priorities for 2024 when he would take over the chairmanship. These included greater administrative integration, a final framework for the CSTO's Rapid Reaction Force and tighter cooperation against terrorism. Putin urged unity.[25]

Indeed, in February 2024 Armenia formally suspended its participation in the Russia-led Alliance because, its prime minister said, the organization had not fulfilled its objectives.[26] In short, it abandoned Armenia in its time of need.

The Shanghai Cooperation Organization (SCO)

Russia's pivot away from the West politically and economically was underscored in September 2022 at a SCO heads-of-state summit in Samarkand. Leaders of member states, Russia, India, Kazakhstan, China, Kyrgyzstan, Pakistan, Tajikistan and Uzbekistan, joined with heads of Observer states, Belarus, Iran and Mongolia. Azerbaijan, Armenia, Turkmenistan and Turkey also sent senior officials. Putin held talks on the side-lines with China's Xi, India's Modi and Turkey's Erdogan.[27]

The meeting agreed that Iran should become a full member in 2023 and that the process to make Belarus a full member should begin. Especially important for Russia were discussions about the full accession of Turkey, a NATO member.[28]

Delegates signed memorandums of Dialogue partnerships for Egypt, Qatar and Saudi Arabia, and decided to launch procedures for granting similar status to Bahrain, Kuwait, the United Arab Emirates, Myanmar and the Maldives. The summit provided important relief for the Kremlin as its isolation from Europe grew. In the Samarkand Declaration, SCO members criticized the unilateral application of sanctions, agreed on broadening the use of national currencies in trade relations with each other and called for 'strengthened cooperation' in cultural matters and foreign affairs.[29]

The SCO meetings also demonstrated the rise of China as the organization's leading power. President Xi travelled there via Kazakhstan, where Beijing's Belt and Road Initiative (BRI) affords it a powerful presence. The BRI is a vast commercial and infrastructure project that links China to Central and Southeast Asia, Russia and Europe.[30] Xi and India's Modi, who took over the rotating presidency of the SCO for 2022–2023, voiced concerns over Putin's war on Ukraine, Modi less subtly than Xi, though they also continued to object to sanctions against Russia.

The decision to welcome a Saudi Arabian plan to join as a Dialogue Partner followed a reconciliation accord brokered by Beijing between Riyadh and Teheran by just a few weeks, and was likely also a result of Chinese diplomacy.[31] With its Full, Dialogue and Observer members, the SCO can claim a commanding position over the world's production of natural resources and their consumers. In July, Lukashenka signed a law on adhering to all SCO treaties, paving the way for Belarus to become a full participant in the organization.

Other international agencies with active Russian participation grew too. Egypt joined the BRICS's New Development Bank in March 2023. For Cairo, the link could help guarantee investments and continued access to Russian grains, where nearly 50 per cent of its grain imports originate, while BRICS members might gain preferential access to the Suez Canal.[32]

Russia also had to re-set relations with its Central Asia neighbours. Foreign ministers from Russia, China, Iran, Pakistan, Turkmenistan and Uzbekistan met in Samarkand on 13 April for the fourth Ministerial Conference of Afghanistan's neighbouring countries to discuss regional security. They agreed to continue coordinating their relations with the Taliban so as to counter 'threats of terrorism and drug trafficking'. Russia and China still have functioning missions in Kabul though they do not recognize the Taliban as the country's legitimate government, calling it an 'interim government'.[33] Lavrov and his Chinese counterpart, Qin Gang, met separately to discuss several matters of mutual interest, including Ukraine. These meetings were part of a two-day Commonwealth of Independent States (CIS) conference of foreign ministers with representatives from Azerbaijan, Armenia, Belarus and Kazakhstan also in attendance.

SCO defence ministers met two weeks later in India, where Shoigu raised objections to a US offer of military assistance to help Central Asian defend themselves against terrorism. Russia, he said, would deal with a growing threat from ISIS in Central Asia by raising the combat readiness of its bases in Kyrgyzstan and Tajikistan. Border-related tensions between India and China, and India and Pakistan complicated SCO relationships, and the Taliban's inability, or unwillingness, to curb ISIS in Northern Afghanistan posed problems for other members. The Russian delegates made it clear that they wanted to re-affirm its wide range of military-technical cooperation with India.[34]

United Nations Security Council (UNSC)

It was Russia's turn to take over the presidency of the UNSC for April 2023 as part of the monthly rotation among its 15 members. Western nations and Ukraine objected, but protocol gave them no room to prevent the change. The president has little influence on decisions, but controls the agenda. Lavrov set the tone in late April when he flew in to speak to the UNSC on 'The Defence of the Principles of the UN Charter'. Warning that the world was at a 'dangerous threshold' and blaming the United States for compounding crises around the world, he accused Washington of causing the war in Ukraine by encouraging the 'openly racist regime' in Kyiv. All this in support of multilateralism against 'the aggressive and volatile advancement of Washington's hegemony'.[35]

UN Secretary-General Guterres responded that Russia's invasion of Ukraine violated the UN charter, caused 'global economic dislocation' and massive suffering for Ukrainians.[36] Representatives of the US, the EU and Japan called Lavrov's speech hypocritical and cynical. An adviser in the Ukrainian president's office named it an April Fool's day joke. In short, Lavrov's speech in support of multilateralism and international consensus was primarily an exercise in shifting responsibility, and revealed how unlikely it was that either would be achieved.

BRICS Summit, August 2023

On the eve of his arrival in Johannesburg for the long-awaited BRICS summit, Lavrov published an essay in a South African magazine, *Ubuntu*. In 'BRICS: Course Towards a Fair World Order', he again criticized the 'colonial and racist' attitudes of Western leaders and boasted of the Global South and Russia's role in ending the 'domination by one country or even a small group of states' and replacing them with a 'fairer multipolar world order'. He referred to Russia as a 'state-civilization' and an advocate of raising Africa's profile in the new world order.[37]

The Russian approach had some resonance. Over 40 countries now expressed some interest in joining BRICS and 20 made formal applications. Among these were Iran and Venezuela, both dealing with sanctions imposed against them and political isolation; Saudi Arabia and the UAE in the Gulf region, and Nigeria and Ethiopia in Africa. These and other attendees made it clear that they wanted a greater voice in international financial and trade agencies, such as the WTO, the IMF and the World Bank. Russia sees the BRICS as a means to avoid the worst consequences of its isolation from the West.

BRICS countries and the Global South may share resentments about perceived Western diktats and a desire for de-dollarization, but the likelihood of them acting together without inter-state discord remained slim. Tensions between India and China may override decisions that must be made by consensus, and complications connected to the use of the renminbi (yuan), rupee or the rouble will keep the oil exporters (Saudi Arabia, Iran, Nigeria, Algeria, Venezuela, the UAR) and their Central Banks more on the side of the dollar and the euro. These considerations, and others, have to be agreed by the existing five members as they discuss criteria that applicants must meet to join.

One day after the BRICS leadership convened, South Africa's president Cyril Ramaphosa announced that Saudi Arabia, the UAE, Iran, Ethiopia, Egypt and Argentina would become full members as of 1 January 2024.

There were some cautionary tales to counter Moscow's excitement. The quantitative expansion may slow the qualitative strengthening of BRICS, because the organization still has no charter or permanent secretariat. Criteria for membership are undefined, differences among members can be explosive and individual members have asymmetrical relations with the United States and the EU.[38] Political whim was a factor also. In late December 2023, newly elected president of Argentina, Javier Milei, withdrew his country's planned entry to BRICS, saying he wished to change Argentina's foreign policy and introduce austerity economic plans.

The Commonwealth of Independent States (CIS)

In its immediate neighbourhood, Moscow's relationships stayed much the same or, as in the case of Poland and the Baltic states, grew testier. At an annual informal meeting with CIS heads of state in St. Petersburg on 26–27 December 2022, Putin and his counterparts from Azerbaijan, Armenia, Belarus, Kazakhstan, Kyrgyzstan, Tajikistan, Turkmenistan and Uzbekistan all lauded growing economic ties and none referenced the war in Ukraine – at least for public consumption. Putin noted the value of cultural exchanges and the things that bind CIS members together: a 'common history, spiritual roots, a deep interweaving of cultures and customs, values and tradition – and, of course, the Russian language as a unifying force'.[39] Circumstances being what they were in Central Asia and the South Caucasus, it was not clear how long this artificial euphoria would survive.

The CIS was tested in October 2023 when its next summit was held in Bishkek. Kyrgyzstan, an ICC member that has not ratified the Rome Statute, welcomed Putin, who marked his first trip out of Russia since the ICC issued the warrant for his arrest. This time, Armenia's prime minister did not attend. Putin outlined the mutual advantages of membership and also the organization's links with the BRICS, both of which were to be chaired by Russia in 2024, and urged further economic integration. During multiple bilateral talks, Putin offered to host peace negotiations between Azerbaijan and Armenia, and his deputy prime minister discussed the expansion of the Tikhoretsk-Baku oil pipeline with Azerbaijan's energy minister.[40] Although no one at the meeting said so, Moscow's preference for Baku was suddenly clearer.

INTERNATIONAL COMPLICATIONS

Grain Corridor

In the spring of 2022, the UN's Guterres initiated talks about the breakdown in the global food supply chain, referring to the inability of Ukraine to ship grains and fertilizers to areas that desperately needed them. These talks culminated in an agreement that allowed grain ships to sail from Odesa and two other Ukrainian ports previously blockaded by the Russian fleet. As of 22 July, ships were guided through mine fields by Ukrainian pilots and then inspected by UN teams of Russian, Turkish, Ukrainian and UN officials at a Joint Coordination Centre in Istanbul.

This system's slow but steady procedure worked until October, when Russia suspended its participation after its Black Sea Fleet at Sevastopol suffered a 'massive' attack by Ukrainian drones. By that time, over nine million tonnes of Ukrainian grain had been shipped under the agreement, which was due for renewal on 19 November.

While US Secretary of State Antony J. Blinken raged that Russia was 'weaponizing food', Turkey's Erdogan told a TV audience that he planned to sustain the delivery of Ukrainian grain to world markets. Peskov responded by citing a Ministry of Agriculture report that most of the grains were delivered to European states and not to the much more-needy regions the UN cited in support of the grain corridor. He also said that Russia was ready to compensate African countries for the lost volumes of grain.[41] Ships continued to leave and enter designated Ukrainian ports, but at a much slower rate than previously.

Negotiations on the Black Sea corridor conducted at UN offices in Geneva a week before its expiry resulted in a pact on exporting Russian grain and fertilizers. The agreement in question was a partner of the deal to allow the export of Ukrainian grains. The UN and Ukraine agreed to a four-month extension of the original grain deal, with Russia still hesitating until, in early March 2023, it finally agreed to a 60-day extension of the grain corridor.[42] Because Russia failed to achieve ways and means to facilitate payments, obtain shipping insurance or gain access to EU ports for its own grains and fertilizer, it stipulated that the next extension, if there was one, would depend on bank payments, transport logistics and insurance related to Russia's agricultural trade, and the 'unfreezing' of financial activities related to the Tolyatti-Odesa pipeline. Though sanctions were not yet imposed directly upon Russian agricultural products, they do prevent Russian ships carrying grains and fertilizers from entering relevant ports, and prohibit foreign ships from entering Russian ports to pick up the products.[43] Talks continued until

18 March, when the UN and Turkey declared that the 60-day extension was agreed.

The question grew more complex in April 2023, when Hungary and Poland imposed bans against grain and other food imports from Ukraine. While this unilateral action angered the rest of the EU, Warsaw and Budapest argued that the cheaper Ukrainian products tended to accumulate in their countries because of logistical and other bottlenecks and undermine domestic farm products. Similar bans, which included transit, were under consideration in Bulgaria and Slovakia.[44]

As it happened, one day before the expiry date of the 60-day extension, on 17 May 2023, Russia agreed to extend the grain and fertilizer supply arrangement for another two months.[45] The UN, Ukraine, Russia and Turkey all welcomed the news.

But the impediments did not fade away. Within a year of the original agreement, the movement of grain ships from Ukrainian ports was again stalled. Russia's envoy to the UN said that there were no reasons to maintain the agreement due to expire on 18 July, to which the EU responded that it might be willing to lift sanctions against the Russian Agricultural Bank so that it could manage payments for grain and fertilizer exports.[46] The record price of food and the dearth of supplies for parts of African and drought-plagued areas of the world made such exports from Russia and Ukraine essential to the international community.

Asked early in July about the apparent threat to the grain deal, Putin complained again that, while the deal was arranged originally to support the poorest countries, almost all of the grains exported from Ukraine went to 'well-fed, prosperous Europe'. This was partly true. According to the UN, 49 per cent of shipments from Ukraine went to developing countries, only 6 per cent to the most-needy countries and slight majority to developed countries. Putin's real concern was that promises related to insurance and movement of money to facilitate export of unsanctioned Russian agricultural products were not yet fulfilled.[47] Cards were on the table as the new deadline loomed.

On the final day of the extension, Peskov told journalists that, because the part of the arrangement related to Russia had not been implemented, the grain deal was de facto 'stopped'.[48]

Russian forces resumed bombing storage sites in Odesa and on the Ukrainian side of the Danube in August, destroying thousands of tonnes of Ukrainian grains.

Shipping talks were back on the table in September 2023, when Turkish foreign minister met with Russia's defence minister in Moscow and, a week later, Erdogan arrived in Sochi for a meet with Putin. These talks did not go well for the grain corridor. Putin again refused to allow Ukraine to export grain safely on the Black Sea unless Western countries lifted shipping and insurance obstacles against Russia's agricultural trade. He again argued that, since most of the Ukrainian grains went to developed countries, the blockade could not be causing starvation elsewhere. The West, he said, 'deceived us about humanitarian goals'.[49] Left unmentioned by the Kremlin were its real considerations: grain sales provided money for Kyiv's war effort; and the blockade made Russia's grains more valuable.

In time, Ukrainians created a new grain corridor of their own. Drone attacks on the Black Sea Fleet in Sevastopol forced the MoD to move military ships to Novorossiisk, and Ukrainian ships have been carrying grain from Black Sea and river ports since early October 2023. They sail along Ukraine's southwest Black Sea coast, hugging the territorial waters of Romania and Bulgaria, both NATO countries, to Turkey. The UK provides special insurance and, according to Ukrainian sources, unnamed allies have given warships to Ukraine to accompany the grain carriers.[50]

Spy Capers and Diplomatic Expulsions

In the diplomatic world, the new great divide was highlighted by dramatic shrinkage in Russian diplomatic missions in Europe and European missions in Russia, a process already advanced before 2022. Some of the downsizing was due to real and alleged spy catching, others as a result of economic or political disputes. According to one account, about 600 Russian officials were expelled from Europe between the spring of 2022 and the end of 2023.[51]

Norwegian security forces arrested several Russians, at separate times, in October 2022 and charged them with using drones to take illegal surveillance photos of planes and airports. While complaining of these arrests, Zakharova accused Norway of instituting a 'powerful anti-Russian campaign' and needlessly ramping up the combat readiness of its armed forces.[52] Norwegian prime minister Jonas Gahr Støre said earlier that the war in Ukraine placed his country 'in the most serious situation in terms of security policy in decades'. One of the detainees was Andrei Yakunin, co-founder of the Venture Investments & Yield Management fund and son of the former head of Russian Railways, Vladimir Yakunin.[53]

A pattern seemed to have been set. Calling Estonia 'Russophobic' in January 2023, after Talinn pledged more arms to Ukraine, Moscow gave its ambassador two weeks to leave. Estonia responded with tat-for-tat expulsions, and Latvia announced that it would downgrade the Russian embassy in Riga as a gesture of support for Estonia.[54]

A few days later, Austria gave four Russians working in the Embassy and Mission in Vienna a week to exit the country, after committing undefined acts 'incompatible with their status as diplomats'.[55]

Also in February, the Dutch government expelled 'a number' of Russian diplomats, alleging that they tried to smuggle spies into the country. Although the embassies of both countries stayed open, a Russian trade office in Amsterdam shut down and the Dutch consulate in St. Petersburg was closed in tit-for-tat actions. This was the second wave of mutual expulsions, the first coming shortly after Russia's invasion of Ukraine in 2022. A larger diplomatic shift came in the spring, when Germany and Russia expelled over thirty of each other's diplomats. These numbers represented about 40 per cent of embassy and mission personnel in both countries. Specific reasons were not made public.[56] Within the same two-week span, Norway expelled 15 more Russian diplomats and Sweden sent five people home, in both cases under the general caveat that their activities in the host country were 'incompatible with their status as diplomats'.

In the final week of May 2023, Russia followed up by shutting Sweden's consulate in St. Petersburg and expelling five diplomats; and Germany's foreign ministry announced the closure of four of the five Russian consulates operating in Germany.[57] The diplomatic presence of Russians in Europe and European presence in Russia shrank even further when, in July, Russia closed down a Polish consulate in Smolensk. This was retaliation for the seizure by Polish authorities of a building in Warsaw housing a secondary school for children of Russian diplomats. In what seemed to have become a monthly happening in Europe, North Macedonia jumped back on the persona-non-grata wagon and expelled three Russian representatives in September. This was the third such action by Skopje since February 2022.

Russia's worry about spies and its own 'snitching' protocols were ratchetted up in May when Putin blamed acts of sabotage and assassinations in Russia on Western spies helping Kyiv. He made this claim in April while accrediting new ambassadors to Moscow. Recently appointed envoys from the United Kingdom and the United States were in the line-up. FSB head Bortnikov accused the West of recruiting young Russians for the same purpose. In response, the administration of Penza State University issued a warning to its students: 'Important! Analyse your social circle, especially among high school students', because planned terrorist acts could attract young people from ages 15 to 21.[58]

Over a period of several weeks in the summer, police arrested 16 members of an alleged Russian spy ring in Poland, one of them a hockey player. They were charged in February 2024, about the same time that Ukraine's general prosecutor announced that the SBU had 'neutralized' an FSB spy operation in Kyiv. Five former and current Ukrainian intelligence officers were arrested for treason.

Within days of its formal admittance to NATO, Finland announced that it would banish nine Russians from the embassy in Helsinki for 'acting in an intelligence capacity'. Shortly thereafter, Iceland suspended work at its embassy in Russia and called on the Kremlin to follow suit in Reykjavik. In this case, the Icelandic foreign ministry noted that since most economic and political ties had already been severed, there simply wasn't enough work for its diplomats in Moscow. In July, Helsinki withdrew its consent for Russia to operate a consulate general in Turku.

Romania came next, ousting 11 diplomats and 29 Russian embassy employees in July, cutting the staff roster by more than half. The Romanian foreign ministry made it plain that the slash was a direct result of deteriorating relations caused by Russia's 'war of aggression against Ukraine'. As a result of 'numerous unfriendly actions', Romania's neighbour Moldova followed suit. In late July, its government gave 40 Russian diplomats and embassy staff two weeks to leave Chisenau, leaving only 10 Russian diplomats operating in the country.[59]

Bulgarian authorities went a different route in September 2023, by expelling the head of the Russian Orthodox Church in Sofia, Archimandrite Vassian, along with two Belarusian priests following accusations that they acted in the interests of the Kremlin. The Russian MID called it a 'blatantly unfriendly act' but did not send a corresponding Bulgarian prelate home from Moscow.[60]

Aborted Mutiny in Russia

The march on Moscow by Wagner PMC troops in June sent a shiver through the international community. Western leaders with no sympathy for Putin had even less liking for Prigozhin. Attempting to forestall accusations from the Kremlin that Washington and its allies promoted the insurrection, Joe Biden and the US State Department made a point of informing Russian diplomats and the American public that they had nothing to do with the affair. As it happened, Putin did not immediately blame the West, although he pointed out that the West delighted in Russia's problem. On the other hand, the head of Russia's National Guard, Viktor Zolotov, hinted that 'Western special services' were involved: 'The rebellion was inspired by the West and was superimposed on Prigozhin's ambitions', he told an interviewer on 26 June.[61] This then became the party line. Although all governments search frantically for scapegoats when there is a crisis, Moscow's refusal to look inwards for cause, ever, has become a national characteristic.

INTERNATIONAL SPORT

Putin's war in Ukraine had devastating consequence for Russian and Belarusan athletics, especially for teams, but also for individuals. Their isolation from important international athletic matches was underscored in November

2022 when the FIFA World Cup events got underway in Qatar. Russia had hosted the world's most widely watched sport extravaganza in 2018, but this time was banned from competing.[62] Its women's football (soccer) team was barred from the Euro 2022 competition and Spartak Moscow was dumped by the Europa League.

At the professional level, the National Hockey League (NHL) and its Players' Association (NHLPA) postponed World Cup of Hockey events in 2022, and decided not to hold them in 2024. The last of these events, in which hockey's best players from all leagues were invited to play, were held in 2016 with Team Canada the winner.[63]

No Russian or Belarusan team appeared in the International Ice Hockey Federation's (IIHF) under-20 tournament held in Canada's Nova Scotia and New Brunswick in December–January 2022–2023. When the IIHF met in March 2023, bans on Russian and Belarusan teams were extended for the next two years, as much for security reasons as for punishment. Russian players were also excluded from the women's world championships planned for play in American cities in March or April 2024 and from the men's events scheduled for the Czech Republic. Russia and Belarus were left out of the 2024 World Junior Championship in Goteborg, Sweden.

Further isolation of Russian athletes came in mid-November 2022, when an Extraordinary General Assembly of the International Paralympic Committee (IPC), meeting in Berlin, suspended the National Paralympic Committees (NPCs) from Russia (64–39) and Belarus (54–45). Their teams had been banned from the Beijing Winter Olympics earlier in the year, but that was for a specific event. The more recent action was for all events registered with the IPC and might have kept Russian and Belarusan athletes out of the 2024 Summer Games in France.[64] Both NPCs appealed.

Complications arose again in February 2023, when Latvia threatened to boycott the Summer Games if Russian athletes were allowed to compete. Poland and the other two Baltic states supported Latvia. Under the current IOC rules, set after the 2018 doping scandal, Russians are permitted to participate under a neutral flag and no national anthem. They cannot actively support the war in Ukraine.

Shifting the Playing Field

Whereas the International Olympic Committee (IOC) wavered and continued to consider ways in which Russia and Belarusan athletes could compete in the summer events in Paris 2024 as neutrals, World Athletics took a somewhat different approach. While lifting its doping ban on the Russian Track and Field Federation that had been in place since 2015, it still barred Russian and Belarusan athletes from international competitions, even as neutrals, because of the actions of their government in Ukraine.[65] Changing the rules again in June 2023 by agreeing to allow Russians to compete in the Paris Olympics under strict neutral conditions, IOC president Thomas Bach criticized Ukraine for not allowing its athletes to participate with Russians present no matter the conditions. This remained a dilemma for the IOC to work out, which they did in the spring of 2024 when its members and those of the International Paralympic Committee agreed that individual Russians could participate as neutrals and that Ukrainian athletes need not stand next to them or shake their hands.

World Athletics continued to keep all Russians out. World football (soccer) bodies FIFA and UEFA maintained their bans against Russian teams in international competitions.

Russian and Belarusan athletes continued to compete in international tennis, though without personal or TV flag displays. There was discomfort in some circles when Belarusan Aryna Sabalenka won the women's trophy at the Australian Open in January 2024, and the father of male winner, Serbian Novak Djokovic, waved a Russian flag in the stands.

Wimbledon was the only one among the four Grand Slam tournament sites to bar Russian and Belarusan players altogether in 2022. It relented somewhat in 2023, allowing them to contend, but only after they signed a declaration of neutrality and agreed not to support the war or accept funding from their governments. Competitors were permitted to wear blue-and-yellow ribbons in support of Ukraine. These changes made it possible for women's number two in the world, Sabalenka, and men's number three, Russian Danil Medvedev, to participate. Organizers must have heaved a sigh of relief when neither athlete won.

The International Boxing Association (IBA) allowed Russian and Belarusan boxers to compete in the men's and women's world boxing championships in 2023. In response, the United States, Canada, the United Kingdom, Czechia, Ireland and other countries boycotted the women's matches in India (March) and men's in Uzbekistan (May), while the IBA offered to support boxers who wanted to compete in spite of their national federation's boycott decisions.[66]

When the World Aquatics governing body decided to allow Russian and Belarusan participation in its international events including the Paris Olympics, it set unusual criteria. Besides the existing guidelines about them taking part as neutrals (no flag, no anthem, no logos), individuals are not allowed to talk to the media and, because they cannot be part of a team, they are excluded from relay, artistic swimming, synchronized diving and water polo.[67] Swimmers who express support for Russia's war in Ukraine will be banned.

In more dramatic shifts, the IPC changed its mind September 2023 and agreed that Russian athletes could compete in the Paris Paralympic competition. Russian junior teams were re-admitted to international competitions organized by the Union of European Football Associations (UEFA). In both cases Russian athletes will have to compete without national flags, team colours or emblems.[68]

That respite was brief. After pressure from countries that refused to compete with Russian teams in the mix, the UEFA changed its mind in October 2023 and Russian athletes were disqualified from the Under-17 European Championships scheduled to begin that month. A senior vice-president of UEFA, a Swede, was forced to resign because he had supported Russian participation. Shortly thereafter, the IOC suspended the Russian Olympic Committee (ROC) because it had incorporated Olympic councils from territories annexed from Ukraine. While independent Russian athletes still may compete, the ROC will lose access to valuable funding from the IOC in Switzerland.

There was good news for some Russian athletes, however. In December, the IOC decided to allow individuals from Russia and Belarus to compete as neutrals if they qualify for the summer Olympics in Paris. Disqualifying conditions still include active support for the war in Ukraine.[69] Russian and Belarusan competitors will not be allowed to participate in the opening and closing day parades. Russia sent over 300 athletes to the 2021 Summer Games (Tokyo), but the Paris competitions are likely to see far fewer. Ukraine and several other national teams threatened boycotts over this decision.

Some Russian athletes went so far as to switch citizenship so they could participate. The Ministry of Sports announced in the fall of 2023 that 55 athletes in Olympic sports had changed their citizenship. The number went over 100 if non-Olympic sports are included. Other sources claimed that the number was over 200, a large percentage of them chess players. Five tennis pros switched, and so did rhythmic gymnast Elizaveta Lugovskikh, now competing for Montenegro, European biathlon champion Daria Virolainen (Finland), Russian champion in the marathon Sardana Trofimova (Kyrgyzstan), figure skaters Diana Davis and Gleb Smolkin (Georgia), and so on.[70]

Meanwhile, at home Putin called for proposals on the revival of Soviet-style Athletes Parades on Red Square. He also commanded the Presidential Council for the Development of Physical Culture and Sports to submit plans for gradually reducing dependence on imported equipment for elite and professional sports, using gambling revenues to develop sports for people with disabilities and develop the domestic video game market. Thus, the isolation of the Russian sport sector from the international scene deepened.[71]

As the EURO 2024 football (soccer) tournament got underway in June 2024 with no Russian teams participating, and the Paris Olympics coming up with only a few dozen individual Russians allowed to participate as neutrals (and some of those declined the invitation), Russian sports officials tried to appease the huge Russian sporting community by hyping up an alternative. The annual BRICS Games, this year in Kazan, generated very little excitement. Tens of thousands of Russian athletes and sport enthusiasts felt another kind of pain brought on by the war.

RUSSIAN FOREIGN POLICY CONCEPT, 2023

On the last day of March 2023, Putin approved a new 'Foreign Policy Concept of the Russian Federation'. Called a strategic planning document bearing the basic principles and strategic goals of the country's foreign policy, the Concept challenged what it called the 'global domination and neo-colonialism' of Western countries. It accused them of multiple illegal tools and coercive measures, above all 'the imposition of destructive neo-liberal ideological attitudes' to sustain their dominance. It blamed the United States 'and its satellites' of exploiting Ukraine in a new kind of hybrid war to weaken Russia.

To achieve the new world order outlined in the Concept, the Kremlin urged its allies to strengthen the international role of the BRICS, the SCO, the CIS, the Eurasian Economic Union (EEU), CSTO, RIC (Russia, India, China) and any other international organization in which Russia plays a significant role. Praising the roles played by China and India in re-shaping the world order and helping Russia integrate Eurasia into a single mutually self-supporting group of nations, it cited the ASEAN and China's One Belt-One Road Initiative as keys to success. Africa, the Middle East and Latin America were raised ahead of Europe as partners to be valued. Ironically, the document proclaimed that 'the use of military force in violation of international law' increases the risk of clashes between large states' (Section 1, Art. 11).[72]

In contrast to its 2016 predecessor, which expressed a desire to cooperate with NATO and the EU, the new Concept resonates with the old Soviet vision of a world divided between two immutably hostile camps. Although the conflict in Ukraine is mentioned only once (II, 13), and that indirectly, such terms as 'Russophobia' and the 'collective West' appear several times and 'neo-Nazis' more often. All in all, the Concept echoed an earlier age and ignored the reality that it is the Kremlin, not the West, that is now undermining Russia's place in the world.

MORE PEACE PLANS

It was in the fall of 2023 that Lavrov, Gerhard Schröder (Germany), Naftali Bennett (Israel) and Ukrainian presidential adviser David Arakhamia, all finally acknowledged that a peace plan acceptable to both sides might have been achieved in March 2022, if the United States, the United Kingdom and their European allies had not prevented it.[73]

Diplomats and national leaders are still trying to achieve a settlement. Macron claimed to have told Xi that he should strive to 'bring Russia to its senses' during meetings in Beijing, where on 5 April 2023 he and the President of the European Commission, Ursula von der Leyen, arrived. At the time, Zelensky was in Warsaw, receiving the Order of the White Eagle. Germany's Olaf Scholz and Spain's Pedro Sanchez preceded Macron to Beijing and also claimed to have put pressure on Xi to help stop the war in Ukraine.[74] Given that that the EU is China's leading trade partner, their worries may have had some backroom influence on Xi's discussions with Putin, but nothing noticeable in public.

Diplomatic activity in April related to Ukraine seemed frantic in nature. Prior to his own meeting with XI the next week, Brazil's Lula da Silva suggested that peace could be achieved if only Ukraine would give Crimea up to Russia, and Russia withdrew from other occupied territories. Brazil's top foreign policy adviser, former foreign minister, Celso Amorim, was in Moscow earlier in the month to discuss peace possibilities with Putin, and Lavrov arrived in Brasilia on 17 April. Amorim talked also with Macron before the French president flew to Beijing. Brazil, a partner of both Russia and China in the BRICS, condemned Russia's invasion of Ukraine, but refused to participate in sanctions regimes or send weapons to Ukraine.[75]

Germany's foreign minister Annalena Baerbock flew into Beijing three days later to meet with her counterpart and, she said, also to urge China to influence Russia to end its war. She was expected to remind Beijing of how important the EU was to China's economy and to make it plain that the EU was united in its position on Ukraine.[76]

Zelensky's 10-point peace plan was on the table, with the EU's support, when China's special envoy to Ukraine arrived in Kyiv on 16–17 May. The envoy, former Chinese ambassador to Russia Li Hui, then flew to Russia, Poland, France and Germany to discuss possible peace settlements.[77] Li met with Zelensky, Ukraine's foreign minister and several other senior officials and said afterwards that there was no obvious panacea to the conflict, that China would be willing to arbitrate but that all protagonists would have to make compromises.[78] Neither combatant was interested in compromise.

Adding to the diplomatic muddle, South Africa's Ramaphosa informed reporters that Putin and Zelensky had agreed to meet a group of African leaders to discuss their peace proposals. He added that the UN Secretary General, the United States and the United Kingdom had offered 'cautious' support for this initiative.[79] Other countries in this project were Zambia, Senegal, Congo, Uganda and Egypt. Neither specifics of the plan, nor dates of the proposed meetings were revealed at that time. Moreover, when African leaders convened with Zelensky in Kyiv, the Ukrainian foreign minister said that Russian Kinzhai hypersonic missiles and Kalibr cruise missiles were intercepted over the city region. Ramaphosa's spokesperson at first called the statement false and, though he later changed his tune, that statement undermined assertions that the delegation was neutral.[80] Nothing of substance emerged from the meeting.

In St. Petersburg on 17 June, Ramaphosa told journalists that the war had to be settled through negotiations and diplomatic means, using the word 'war' several times though it was still taboo for Russians. The African delegation again presented its 10 principles which included de-escalation, the recognition of national sovereignty, security guarantees for all countries, unimpeded grain exports through the Black Sea and sending prisoners of war and children back to their countries of origin.

Although Peskov said that Putin had 'shown interest' in the plan, neither side demonstrated any flexibility on questions related to territory. At one point in the talks, Putin presented a draft proposal titled 'Treaty on Permanent Neutrality and Security Guarantees of Ukraine' that, he said, was prepared in Istanbul in 2022 but rejected by Kyiv. He again accused Ukraine of starting the conflict with the 'bloody coup' of 2014.[81] Ramaphosa offered to mediate peace negotiations, and told journalists that both leaders had agreed to further diplomatic engagement. Neither president agreed to speak with the other.

Before that, in May, Zelensky was a guest at an Arab League summit in the port of Jeddah, Saudi Arabia, and, on the 21st, attended the G-7 Summit in Hiroshima, where he negotiated weapons deliveries and observed the new wave of sanctions against Russia rolled out by G-7 leaders. Although Ukraine was the centre-piece of that summit, its attendees also pondered climate change issues, economic stability, world poverty levels and AI. A joint communiqué cautioned China not to undermine 'the integrity of our democratic institutions and our economic prosperity', re-affirmed the G-7's support for Ukraine 'for as long as it takes in the face of Russia's illegal war of aggression', and committed its members to work towards a world without nuclear weapons. In that connection, G-7 leaders and their guests (Ukraine, Australia, Brazil, the Cook Islands, Comoros, India, Indonesia, South Korea and Vietnam) would have been relieved, somewhat, to learn that a Levada Centre survey conducted over the last week of April showed that only 29 per cent of Russian respondents said that using nuclear weapons against Ukraine could be justified and 56 per cent said that they could not.[82]

The Russian MoD labelled the G-7 summit a 'propaganda show' aimed at 'whipping up anti-Russian and anti-Chinese hysteria'. Russia was probably more concerned about the emphasis on cooperation with southeast Asian countries and ASEAN, and the invitations to BRICS members Brazil and India, while excluding South Africa.[83] An irritated China welcomed Russia's Mishustin in Shanghai just two days after the G-7 summit, and the next day in Beijing, where they confirmed political and economic ties in the face of hostility from the West. The fact that von der Leyen had said that the G-7 also supports Taiwan unconditionally, served as an incentive for closer China-Russia cooperation.[84]

Peace Plans – Fact or Fantasy?

Peace propositions kept cropping up. The Pope's envoy for peace in Ukraine, Cardinal Matteo Maria Zuppi, showed up in Moscow in late June to converse with Putin's adviser on foreign policy, Yuri Ushakov, and Patriarch Kirill. He urged them to make a 'humanitarian gesture' by repatriating Ukrainian children. Zuppi had been in Kyiv for two days earlier in the month.[85]

Whatever the intent of these new discussions, Dmitry Medvedev threw cold water on them in an article for the official government gazette, *Rossiiskaia Gazeta*. In it, he said that nuclear war was 'quite probable' and that the Russian 'operation' in Ukraine could go on forever. Adding that Russia is not isolated, its economy is not 'falling apart' and that Moscow did not object to Finland and Sweden joining NATO, but wants only to prevent Ukraine from doing so, he accused the West of whipping up Russophobia by claiming otherwise. His list of 'wants' to ensure peace included: 'the Kyiv Nazi regime must be annihilated'; an over-arching peace treaty must be signed, and the UN re-organized. Here he cautioned that he was 'not talking about the fate of the current international freaks like the ICC, the Council of Europe or the OSCE. They are already in the stinking garbage heap of world development'. Concluding by stating the obvious, 'I am not an optimist', Medvedev was well aware that his criteria for peace were out of reach.[86] One can only wonder how the harangue was received by Russian readers.

Just as drones and cruise missiles heated up the war of attrition in Ukraine, national security advisers from about 40 countries showed up in Jeddah, 5–6 August 2023, for the second round of a Kyiv-organized peace conference – with no Russian participation.

Along with host Saudi Arabia and several other oil-rich countries, the roster of invitees to Jeddah named delegates from Brazil, China, India and South Africa from the BRICS. The US and EU members were represented. The agenda included ten topics related to the war, among them food and energy security, prisoner exchanges, environmental security and the possibility of a war crimes tribunal. Zelensky's representative, Podolyak, held firm to the Ukrainian positon that peace was not possible until Russia withdrew from all occupied Ukrainian territory.

Whatever that two-day session concluded, Peskov had already informed a *New York Times* interviewer that the Kremlin had little interest in any peace deal that involved the return of annexed territories to Ukraine. Zakharova chimed in by proclaiming that Russia's partners in the BRICS would 're-affirm our [Russia's] position on the so-called "peace formula" of Zelensky'. She added that, in Moscow's opinion, any agreement must restore the initial features of Ukraine's sovereignty, neutrality, non-bloc and non-nuclear status.[87] The 'peace plans' still represented more fantasy than fact.

Eleventh Moscow Conference on International Security, 15 August 2023

There was not much peace talked at the gathering of defence ministers in Moscow in August, at least not by Russian participants. According to TASS, 26 defence ministers joined chiefs of general staffs and other officials from 75 countries and six international organizations. BRICS, the SCO, the EEU, CIS and CSTO member-states were well represented, along with Egypt, Turkey and several nations from the Global South. Putin spoke to the meeting via video, while Lavrov, Shoigu and Foreign Intelligence Service (SVR) head, Sergei Naryshkin addressed the audience in person. No longer an invitee to the Munich Security Conference held annually since the late 1960s, Moscow relied on this conference to bring its wavering affiliates back to the fold.

Lavrov's long address re-stated the Kremlin and the MID's standard narrative about the war in Ukraine, adding accusations about Ukraine conducting 'terrorist acts' against Moscow and the Kerch Bridge, while failing to mention Russian missiles hitting Ukrainian cities.[88] Putin's welcoming speech by video included an invitation for everyone present to visit the International Technical-Military Forum that was taking place in three separate venues in Moscow over the entire week of 14–20 August. There, he boasted, they could observe various 'cutting-edge weapons of almost all types – advanced control systems, intelligence systems, high-precision weapons, and robots', exhibited by 1,500 Russian and 85 foreign defence industry companies. According to an Indonesian report, Putin was calling on his audience to help form global technical-military partnerships to counter, if not fight against, NATO.[89]

Kyiv's Peace Plan – Third and Fourth Rounds

The two 'sides' continued to operate in fully separate spheres. The third round of Ukraine's meetings with international security advisers in 2023 gathered in Malta in late October. This time more than 65 delegates showed up, with Russian again uninvited. The agenda listed half of Ukraine's 10-point plan: nuclear safety, energy security, food security, prisoner releases and restoration of Ukrainian territories. Although no peace settlement could be expected from these two-day sessions, they helped sustain support for Kyiv and also to forestall loss of interest as Western media attention shifted to the Israeli-Hamas war.

Organizers need not have worried about diminishing attention to the Russia-Ukraine war, because Dmitry Medvedev jerked eyes back to Russia with a blistering verbal attack on Poland. In another essay for *Rossiiskaia Gazeta,* the day before Russia's National Unity, 4 November, he called Poland 'one of the most frantic members of NATO and the EU' working hard to 'deepen the Ukrainian crisis'. Accusing the Polish leadership of trying to regain territories lost in 1945, he called the country an 'historical loser' driven now by Russophobia, racism, anti-Semitism, 'unbridled selfishness' and megalomania. Medvedev predicted that the modern-day Poland would collapse of its own internal weaknesses. Officials in Warsaw termed the diatribe 'typical of the Kremlin's propaganda' and the Ukrainian media dubbed it a 'rant', but dangerous.[90]

The fourth round of national security advisers was held in Davos, Switzerland, on 14 January 2024, just prior to the annual World Economy Forum, with the specific purpose of discussing Ukraine peace formula. Ukraine stuck to its 10-point plan, the central articles of which were that Russia must leave all occupied territories and be held accountable for war crimes. This time, more than 80 delegations showed up, 18 of them from Asia and 12 from Africa. India, Brazil and Saudi Arabia were represented. Leader of the Ukrainian group, Andriy Yermak, took this as a sign that support for Ukraine was growing. But China decided not to attend and Russia was not invited. It was left to the Swiss foreign minister to suggest that discussion of Ukraine's peace plane without Russian presence was a pointless exercise.[91]

During his lengthy interview with Tucker Carlson in February 2024, Putin claimed that Russia was 'willing to negotiate' and suggested that the US government should persuade Kyiv to come to the table. Only Carlson took this statement seriously.[92]

RUSSIA LOOKS TO THE 'GLOBAL MAJORITY'

Speaking on the domestic media on 28 December 2023, Lavrov said that 'the overwhelming majority of states, the World Majority, have not joined the sanctions' but have been too afraid of the United States to speak out against them. That reluctance is wavering, he alleged, and the 'Global Majority . . . are ready to work with us'. He referred to the growing BRICS and the SCO as signs of this change in international relationships, and by 'majority' he meant also the Global South.[93]

The 'global majority' theme had already become part of the lexicon used by Russian foreign affair pundits, who predicted the collapse of the alleged hegemony held by the US and EU over the world's economy and politics. Sergei Karaganov, for example, wrote in earlier in December that the SVO had proven to be a 'turning point' leading to the emergence of the World Majority 'as a clearly defined phenomenon in international relations'. This new reality will lead to a new world order in which Russia will be a major player, whereas the West will be contained and aggression will be curtailed. Russian threats to deploy nuclear weapons will hasten that process, Karaganov concluded.[94] Other prominent Russian specialists on foreign policy, such as Dmitrii Trenin, spread similar hypotheses.

As president of the BRICS for 2024, the Russian MID has an opportunity to influence countries of the so-called Global South, or what Moscow now calls the 'world majority', most of which do not blame Russia for the war in Ukraine. The recently expanded BRICS can claim in 2024 to have a 24 per cent share of the world's GDP (IMF data) and 45 per cent of its population (World Bank data). According to Angela Stent, Moscow's influence in these parts of the world is predicated on an intuitive scepticism about the West generally, and about the United States particularly. Many of these areas still rely on Russia for hydrocarbon and nuclear energy, fertilizers, grains and weapons.[95]

Thus, they provide Lavrov and Putin with an ideological and practical framework for propaganda aimed at the Africa, Latin America, large parts of Asia and southeast Asia, and even central Europe. And also votes in the United Nations General Assembly. Western leaders, politicians and pundits intoned in a variety of ways that Russia and Russians should be isolated from the 'civilized' world, by which they rather arrogantly meant the West. Yet by 2022, Putin and Russia may have been pariahs in large parts of the world, and the millions of Russians who believed themselves 'European' must have felt that they had no friends left – but 'isolated' they were not.

NOTES

1. General Assembly of the United Nations. General Debate. Russian Federation, 'Mr. Sergey Lavrov, minister for foreign affairs', 24 September 2022, gadebate.un.org/en/77/russian-federation.

2. Boris Bondarev, 'The sources of Russian misconduct: A diplomat defects from the Kremlin', *Foreign Affairs*, November/December 2022.

3. Putin, 'Zasedanie Mezhdunarodnogo diskussionnogo kluba "Valdai"', *Kremlin.ru*, 27 October 2022, kremlin.ru/events/president/news/69695.

4. On this, see Michael Kimmage, Hanna Notte, 'How Russia globalized the war in Ukraine', *Foreign Affairs*, 1 September 2023; Stewart Patrick, 'The term "Global South" is surging: It should be retired', *Carnegie Endowment for International Peace*, 15 August 2023; Comfort Ero, 'The trouble with "the Global South"', *Foreign Affairs*, 1 April 2024.

5. See, e.g. Russell Berman, 'US moves to isolate Russia from "community of nations"', *The Hill*, 3 March 2024; Zeke J. Miller, 'Obama: U.S. working to "isolate Russia"', *Time*, 3 March 2024.

6. Igor Dunayevsky, 'Miunkhenskuiu konferentsiiu prevratiat v antirossiiskii shabash s priglasheniem begloi oppozitsii iz RF', *Rossiiskaia Gazeta*, 1 December 2022; 'Munich security conference Snubs Moscow', *RFE/RL*, 22 November 2022.

7. Amana Khoza, Andisiwe Makinana, Sibongakonke Shoba, 'SA's quiet push for "virtual" Putin visit to solve ICC arrest warrant dilemma', *Sunday Times* (SA), 30 April 2023; Paul Richardson, Paul Vecchiatto, 'S. Africa grants BRICS-meeting immunity after Putin invite', *Bloomberg*, 30 May 2023.

8. The Presidency. Republic of South Africa, 'South Africa finalises 15th BRICS Summit format', 19 July 2023; Gurlan Gadymov, 'Vladimir Putin primet uchastie v sammite BRIKS, no po VKS', *Vedomosti*, 19 July 2023.

9. Russian Ministry of Foreign Affairs, 'Joint statement of the BRICS ministers of foreign affairs and international relations, Cape Town, South Africa, 1 June 2023', 2 June 2023, mid.ru/en/foreign_policy/news/1873948.

10. 'Orban says Hungary to approve Finland and Sweden's accession next year', *RFE/RL*, 25 November 2022; 'Turkey "wants things we can't give", says NATO hopeful Sweden', *Euronews*, 8 January 2023; Jack Detsch, 'Turkey's still got beef with NATO aspirants', *FP* (Foreign Policy), 26 January 2023.

11. 'NATO secretary general hosts meeting of senior officials from Türkiye, Finland and Sweden', *NATO Update,* 9 March 2023; 'Statement by the secretary general on Finland's membership in NATO', *NATO Update*, 31 March 2023; 'Finland joins NATO as 31st Ally', *NATO Update*, 4 April 2023.

12. Dmytro Kuleba, 'Why NATO must admit Ukraine: Kyiv needs the alliance and the alliance needs Kyiv', *Foreign Affairs*, 25 April 2023.

13. 'NATO defence ministers conclude two days of meetings, pledging increased support for Ukraine', *NATO Update*, 16 June 2023.

14. Reports from the Ukraine Recovery Conference: Paul Waldie, 'Ukraine PM confident in EU, NATO bid', *Globe and Mail*, 23 June 2023; 'Ukraine in EU and NATO, a matter of coming years: Ukrainian PM', *TVP World* (Poland), 22 June 2023; 'Denys Shmyhal voices four key messages of Ukraine Recovery Conference in London', *Ukraine Government Portal*, 22 June 2023, kmu.gov.ua/en/news/denys-shmyhal-ozvuchyv-chotyry-vazhlyvykh-mesedzhi-konferentsii-vidnovlennia-v-londoni.

15. Aisel Gereikhanova, 'V Kremle rassmatrivaiut vozmozhnoe vstuplenie Ukrainy v NATO kak absoliutniu ugrozu dlia Rossii', *Rossiiskaia Gazeta*, 10 July 2023.

16. For opposing opinions, see, e.g. Justin Logan, Joshua Shifrinson, 'Don't let Ukraine join NATO: The costs of expanding the alliance outweighs the benefits', *Foreign Affairs*, 7 July 2023; Dr. Philip Dandolov, 'Imperialist red herring? NATO expansion and the Ukraine war', *Geopolitical Monitor*, 5 July 2023.

17. NATO, 'Vilnius summit communiqué', *Press Release 001*, 11 July 2023.

18. Putin, 'Otvety na voprosy predstavitelei SMI', *Kremlin.ru*, 13 July 2023, kremlin.ru/events/president/news/71667.

19. 'Sweden officially joins NATO', *NATO Update*, 7 March 2024.

20. The White House, 'Fact sheet: President Biden and ASEAN leaders launch the U.S-ASEAN comprehensive strategic partnership', *Briefing Room Statement*, 12 November 2022.

21. See the conference website: g20.org/en/; and YouTube, 'G20 meet 2023 live: Russia, West take strong positions as Ukraine war takes centre stage at G20 meet', *WION*, 3 February 2023, youtube.com/watch?v=t34dL8uA6dI.

22. 'One Earth: One family: One future', *G20 New Delhi Leaders' Declaration, 9–10 September 2023*, No's 8, 11.

23. 'Vneocherednoi sammit "Gruppy dvastsati"', *Kremlin.ru*, 22 November 2023, kremlin.ru/events/president/news/72790.

24. Lindsey Chutel, Matthew Mpoke Bigg, 'At BRICS summit, countries diverge slightly on Israel and war in Gaza', *New York Times*, 21 November 2023.

25. Daria Snegova, 'O chem zaiavili lidery stran ODKB na sammite v Minske. Glavnoe', *Vedomosti*, 23 November 2023; 'Sammit ODKB', *Kremlin.ru*, 23 November 2023, kremlin.ru/events/president/news/72800.

26. 'Armenia says "Froze" participation in Russia-led security bloc', *The Moscow Times*, 23 February 2024.

27. Yelena Mukhametshina, 'Putin provedet vstrechi s liderami Kitaia, Indii, Turtsii i Azerbaidzhana na sammite ShOS', *Vedomosti*, 14 September 2022.

28. Baris Balci, Selcan Hacaoglu, 'Turkey seeks to be first NATO member to join China-Led SCO', *Bloomberg*, 17 September 2022. For background, see special issue of *Perceptions. Journal of International Affairs*, Vol. 23, No. 2 (Summer 2018), for essays on Russia-Turkey relations.

29. For the Samarkand Declaration, see the SCO website, eng.sectsco.org/; 'SCO summit 2022 LIVE', daily reports in First Post, firstpost.com.

30. See Zachary Fillingham, 'Belt and road at 10: A paradigm shift in development finance?' *Geopolitical Monitor*, 1 November 2023.

31. 'Saudi Arabia to partner with China-led security bloc', *VOA*, 29 March 2023.

32. Ilya Lakstygal, Nurlan Gasimov, 'Kak izmenit BRIKS vstuplenie Egipta', *Vedomosti*, 15 June 2023.

33. Ministry of Foreign Affairs of the People's Republic of China, 'Joint statement of the second informal meeting on Afghanistan between foreign ministers of China, Russia, Pakistan and Iran', 14 April 2023, fmprc.gov.cn/mfa_eng/zxxx_662805/202304/t20230414_11059063.html.

34. Vladimir Kulagin, 'Ministry oborony SHOS v Indii nashli povodu dlia sotrudnichestva i kritiki', *Vedomosti*, 28 April 2023.

35. 'Watch: Russian Foreign Minister Lavrov attends U.N. Security Council meeting on peace', YouTube, *PBS Newshour*, 24 April 2023, youtube.com/watch?v=XTYTx7bzwi0.

36. United Nations. Secretary-General, 'Multilateral cooperation "beating heart" of United Nations, secretary-general tells security council, urging all member states to recommit to charter', *Press Release*, 24 April 2023, press.un.org/en/2023/sgsm21773.doc.htm.

37. MID RF, 'Stat'ia Ministra inosstrannykh del Rosssiiskoi Federatsii S.V. Lavrova dlia iuzhnoafrikanskogo zhurnala "Ubuntu", 21 Avgusta 2023 goda', 21 August 2023, mid.ru/ru/foreign_policy/news/1901054/.

38. See, e.g. George Monastiriakos, 'The BRICS is not a strategic threat to the United States', *Geopolitical Monitor*, 7 September 2023; 'Can Russia and China breathe new life into BRICS?' *FP* (Foreign Policy), 18 August 2023.

39. 'Neformal'nyi sammitt SNG', *Kremlin.ru*, 26 December 2022, kremlin.ru/events/president/news/70189.

40. Daria Savenkova, Vasily Milkin, 'Rossiia i Azerbaidzhan obsudili rasshirenie nefteprovod', *Vedomosti*, 14 October 2023; Yelena Mukhametshina, 'Chto govoril Vladimir Putin na zasedanii soveta glav gosudarstv SNG', *Vedomosti*, 14 October 2023.

41. 'V Kremle sochi nerealizuemoi zernovuiu sdelku bez uchastiia Rossiia', *Vedomosti*, 31 October 2022; 'Blinken: Russia "weaponizing food" by suspending grain exports', *VOA*, 30 October 2022.

42. Tweet, Volodimir Zelens'kiy @ ZelenskyyUa, 'Grain deal will be prolonged . . .', 17 November 2022, twitter.com/ZelenskyyUa/status/1593147550672224256; Dar'ia Mosolkina, 'Pochemu Rossiia soglasilas' na prodlenie zernovoi sdelki', *Vedomosti*, 17 November 2022; Michelle Nichols, 'UN secretary general says Black Sea grain deal extended', *Financial Post*, 17 November 2022.

43. 'Russia agrees to 60-day Black Sea grain deal extension', *The Moscow Times*, 13 March 2023; Aine Quinn, Megan Durisin, Aliaksandr Kudrytski, 'Ukraine rebuffs Russia's offer of a 60-day extension on grain deal', *Bloomberg*, 13 March 2023; 'Budet li prodlena zernovaia sdelka: pozitsii storon', *Aktual'nye kommentarii*, 13 March 2023.

44. 'Hungary bans agricultural imports from Ukraine', *Ukrinform*, 16 April 2023; Alan Charlish, Pavel Polityuk, Jan Strupczewski, 'EU warns against unilateral action after Poland, Hungary ban Ukrainian grain', *Globe and Mail*, 17 April 2023; '"Not acceptable": EU decries bans on Ukrainian grain imports imposed by Poland and Hungary', *Euronews*, 17 April 2023.

45. 'Rossiia podtverdila prodlenie "zernovoi sdelki" na dva mesiatsa', *Interfaks*, 17 May 2023.

46. Yevgeniia Chukalina, 'Zernovaia sdelka vyrodilas' iz gumanitarnogo proekta v kommercheskii"', *Izvestiia*, 3 July 2023.

47. Putin, 'Otvety na voprsoy predstavitelei SMI', *Kremlin.ru*, 13 July 2023, kremlin.ru/events/president/news/71667; Paula Dupraz-Dobias, 'Where are Ukraine's grains actually going across the world?' *PassBlue*, 8 May 2023. *PassBlue* is a non-profit news outlet for women's issues, human rights and UN activities.

48. 'Peskov stated that on Monday the grain deal was actually terminated', *Interfax*, 17 July 2023.

49. Anastasiia Shvetsova, Anna Naraeva, 'Vystuplenie Putina po itogam peregovorov s Erdoganom, Glavnoe', *Vedomosti*, 4 September 2023; 'Rossiisko-turetskie peregovory', *Kremlin.ru*, 4 September 2023, kremlin.ru/events/president/news/72184.

50. 'Ukraine to receive warships to help protect its Black Sea grain corridor', *The New Voice of Ukraine*, 25 November 2023; Eric Reguly, 'How Ukraine's crop exports rebounded from war's devastation', *Globe and Mail*, 15 February 2024.

51. Andrei Soldatov, Irina Borogan, 'The rebirth of Russian spycraft', *Foreign Affairs*, 27 December 2023.

52. 'Norvezhsskaia politsiia zaderzhala rossiianina iz-za dronov v bagazhe', *Vedomosti*, 15 October 2022; Yevgeniia Dubrovina, 'Zakharova rastsenila deistviia Norvegii kak eskalatsiiu napriazhennosti', *Vedomosti*, 2 November 2022.

53. Jonas Støre quoted in, 'Norway has raised the level of readiness of the armed forces because of the special operation', *RIA Novosti*, 31 October 2022.

54. Vasilii Koshkin, 'MID RF soobshchil o ponizhenii urovnia diplomaticheskikh otnoshenii s Estoniei', *Rossiiskaia Gazeta*, 23 January 2023; 'Moscow expels estonian ambassador as tallinn pledges more arms to Kyiv', *The Moscow Times*, 23 January 2023.

55. MFA Austria @MFA_Austria, 'Statement of the Austrian foreign ministry on four Russian diplomats in Vienna', *TWEET*, 2 February 2023, twitter.com/MFA_Austria/status/1621054531931934720?s=20&t=QldF-gIjDUGh_UKYWrx-gA.

56. Nikolaus Harbusch, Luisa Volkhausen, 'Deutschland weist russische Diplomaten aus', *Bild*, 22 April 2023; Maksim Tsulanov, 'Rossiia i Germaniia reshili obmeniat'sia vysylkoi diplomatov', *Vedomosti*, 22 April 2023.

57. Gleb Sotnikov, 'Shvetsiia vysylaet piat' rossiiskikh diplomatov', *Rossiiskaia Gazeta*, 25 April 2023; 'Sweden says expelling 5 Russian diplomats', *The Moscow Times*, 24 April 2023; 'MID, 'Ob otvetnykh merakh v otnoshenii Shvetsii', *Soobshchenie dlia SMI*, 25 May 2023, mid.ru/ru/foreign_policy/news/1872247/; 'Germany tells Moscow to close 4 consulates', *The Moscow Times*, 31 May 2023.

58. Penzenskii Gosudarstvennyi Universitet, 'Vnimanie! Bud'te bditel'ny!', 11 May 2023, pnzgu.ru/news/2023/05/11/21165085; 'Russia accuses Ukraine, West of recruiting youth for "sabotage"', *The Moscow Times*, 11 April 2023; 'Vladimir Putin prinial veritel'nye gramoty semnadtsati poslov inostrannykh gosudarstv', *Kremlin.ru*, 5 April 2023, Kremlin.ru/events/president/news/70868.

59. Daniel Bellamy, 'Romania expels 40 Russian diplomats and embassy staff', *Euronews*, 31 July 2023.

60. Ministerstvo inostrannykh del RF, 'Kommentarii ofitsial'nogo predstavitelia MID Rosiia M.V. Zakharovoi v sviazi s vysylkoi iz Bolgarii sviashchennikov RPTs', 21 September 2023, mid.ru/ru/foreign_policy/news/1905499/?lang=ru.

61. 'Zolotov nazval dve prichiny miatezha Prigozhina', *MKRU* (Moskovsky komsomolets), 27 June 2023.

62. See Graham Dunbar, 'FIFA warned court of World Cup chaos if Russia played', *AP News*, 12 April 2022; 'Former host Russia frozen out as World Cup begins in Qatar', *AP*, 14 November 2022.

63. 'NHL, NHLPA announce World Cup of Hockey delayed from 2024 to "hopefully" 2025', *The Athletic*, 11 November 2022.

64. International Paralympic Committee, 'NPC Russia and NPC Belarus suspended at IPC extraordinary general assembly', 16 November 2022, paralympic.org/news/npc-russia-and-npc-belarus-suspended-ipc-extraordinary-general-assembly.

65. Luke Phillips, 'World athletics doping ban on Russia lifted, but Russians still suspended', *Barron's*, 23 March 2023.

66. International Boxing Association, 'IBA offers support to boxers whose national federations boycott to take part in IBA's 2023 women's and men's championships and will pursue strong sanctions against participating officials', 10 February 2023.

67. David Rieder, 'World aquatics to allow Russian and Belarusan athletes to compete as 'individual neutral athletes': Paris still uncertain', *Swimming World*, 4 September 2023.

68. 'Eks-glava RFS ob'iasnil prichiny dopuska do turnirov iunosheskikh sbornykh Rossii', *RIA Novosti sport*, 26 September 2023; Sergei Podgornov, '"Nashi sbornye khotia by nachnut igrat: Dlia nas rebiata vse ravno russkie, my eto znaem" – Radimov o predlozhenii UEFA po dopusku sbornykh U-17', *Match!* 26 September 2023.

69. Andrew Daw, Tariq Panja, 'Athletes from Russia and Belarus are cleared to compete at Paris Olympics', *New York Times*, 8 December 2023.

70. Kirill Soskov, 'Trend goda: Rossiiskie atlety meniaiut sportivnoe grazhdanstvo radi top-turnirov', *Vedomosti*, 29 December 2023.

71. 'Perechen' poruchenii po itogam zasedaniia Soveta pri Prezidente po razvitiiu fizicheskoi kul'tury i sporta', *Kremlin,ru*, 18 December 2023, kremlin.ru/acts/assignments/orders/73070.

72. 'Ukaz ob utverzhdenii Kontseptsii vneshnei politiki Ropssiiskoi Federatsii', *Kremlin.ru*, 31 March 2023, kremlin.ru/acts/news/70811.

73. See chapter 1, here, and '*Russian analytical report*, Nov. 20–27, 2023', *Russia Matters*. Belfer Center, Harvard Kennedy School.

74. Tessa Wong, 'Macron and von der Leyen: Europe's good cop and bad cop meet Xi Jinping', *BBC News*, 7 April 2023, bbc.com/news/world-asia-china-65186222; 'Takeaway from Macron's diplomatic mission to China', *Kyiv Post*, 8 April 2023.

75. Catherine Osborn, 'Can Brazil negotiate an end to the war in Ukraine?' *FP* (Foreign Policy), 7 April 2023.

76. See, e.g. Hans von der Burchard, Gabriel Rinaldi, 'Germany aims to "set the record straight" on China after Macron's Taiwan comments', *Politico*, 12 April 2023.

77. 'Chinese envoy to arrive in Kyiv on Tuesday', *Kyiv Post*, 15 May 2023; 'Top Chinese envoy to visit Ukraine, Russia on "peace" mission', *RFE/RL*, 14 May 2023.

78. Foreign Ministry of the PRC, 'Li Hui, special representative of the Chinese government for Eurasian affairs, visits Ukraine', 18 May 2023, fmprc.gov.cn/wjdt_67

4879/sjxw_674887/202305/t20230518_11079396.shtml; 'Kitai zaiavil ob otsutstvii panatsei dlia uregulirovaniia konflikta na Ukraine', *Vedomosti*, 18 May 2023.

79. 'Prezident IuAR zaiavil o razgovore s Putinym i Zelenskim', *RIA Novosti*, 16 May 2023.

80. 'Missile strikes over Kyiv as African leaders visit', *The Moscow Times*, 16 June 2023; 'Six hypersonic missiles downed over Kyiv during latest Russian attack', *Kyiv Post*, 16 June 2023.

81. Aisel Gereikhanova, 'Kak proshli peregovory Vladimira Putina s liderami afrikanskikh stran po uregulirovaniiu situatsii na Ukraine', *Rossiiskaia Gazeta*, 17 June 2023; 'South Africa's Ramaphosa tells Putin Ukraine "war must be settled"', *The Moscow Times*, 18 June 2023; 'African delegation presses Putin to seek "path to peace" in Ukraine, offers mediation', *RFE/RL*, 17 June 2023.

82. 'Vozmozhnosti primeneniia iadernogo oruzhiia v ukrainskom konflikte', *Levada-tsentr*, 12 May 2023, levada.ru/2023/05/12/o-vozmozhnosti-primeneniya-ya dernogo-oruzhiya-v-ukrainskom-konflikte/; The White House, 'G7 Hiroshima Leaders' Communiqué', 20 May 2023.

83. 'Zelensky's participation in G7 summit turned it into a propaganda show – foreign ministry', *TASS*, 21 May 2023.

84. European Commission, 'Statement by President von der Leyen at press conference with President Michel ahead of the council of Europe, G7 and EU-Republic of Korea summits', *Statement*, 15 May 2023; 'In Beijing, Russian PM says Western pressure strengthening ties with Russia', *RFE/RL*, 24 May 2023.

85. Devin Watkins, 'Cardinal Zuppi to visit Moscow as Pope Francis' peace envoy', *Vatican News*, accessed 27 June 2023.

86. Dmitry Medvedev, 'Epokha protivostoianiia', *Rossiiskaia Gazeta*, 2 July 2023. See also Michael Kimmage, Maria Lipman, 'Will Russia's break with the West be permanent?' *Foreign Affairs*, 19 June 2023.

87. Maksim Tulanov, 'MID ozhidaet paskrytiia detalei konsul'tatsii po Ukraine v Dzhidde', *Vedomosti*, 7 August 2023; 'SMI: Saudovskaia Araviia soobshchit Rossii itogi vstrechi po Ukraine', *Vedomosti*, 4 August 2023; for Peskov's comments, see Roger Cohen, Nanna Heitmann, 'Putin's forever war', *New York Times*, 6 August 2023.

88. 'Foreign Minister Sergey Lavrov's remarks at the 11th Moscow conference on international security, Moscow, August 15, 2023', 15 August 2023, mid.ru/en/foreign_policy/news/1900527/; 'Conference on international security ends in Moscow', *TASS*, 15 August 2023.

89. Putin, 'Video address to the participants and guests of the 11th Moscow conference on international security', *Kremlin.ru*, 15 August 2023, en.kremlin.ru/events/president/news/72040; FX Laksana Agung Saputra, 'Putin invites countries to establish defense cooperation with Russia', *Kompas*, 15 August 2023, kompas.id/baca/english/2023/08/15/en-putin-buka-pintu-kerjasama-militer.

90. Dmitry Medvedev, 'Rossiia i Pol'sha: zametka k 4 noiabr', *Rossiiskaia Gazeta*, 3 November 2023; 'Polish security official slams Putin ally's warning', *Polskie Radio*, 3 November 2023, polskieradio.pl/395/9766/artykul/3273504,polish-security-official-slams-putin-ally%E2%80%99s-warning; 'Medvedev is again drawn to

threaten Poland', *Ukrainska Pravda*, 3 November 2023, pravda.com.ua/eng/news/2023/11/3/7426977/.

91. 'No peace without Russia's word, says Swiss foreign minister at Davos', *SWI. Swissinfo.ch*, 14 January 2024.

92. 'Interv'iu Takeru Karlsonu', *Kremlin.ru*, 9 February 2024, kremlin.ru/events/president/news/73411; Michael Crowley, 'U.S. rejects Putin's latest call for Ukraine negotiations', *New York Times*, 9 February 2024.

93. 'Foreign Minister Sergey Lavrov's interview with RIA Novosti and Rossiia 24 TV . . .', 28 December 2023, mid.ru/en/foreign_policy/news/1923676/.

94. Sergei A. Karaganov, Aleksandr M. Kramarenko, Dmitrii V. Trenin', 'Politika Rossii v otnoshenii Mirovogo bol'shinstva', *Rossiia v Globalnoi Politike*, Mosccow 2023, globalaffairs.ru/wp-content/uploads/2023/12/doklad_politika-rossii-v-otnoshenii-mirovogo-bolshinstva.pdf.

95. Angela Stent, 'Russia, the West and the "world majority"', *Russia Matters*, 25 January 2024, russiamatters.org/analysis/russia-west-and-world-majority.

Chapter 8

The Russian Economy Pivots to the East

On 10 November 2022, the United States decided to no longer recognize Russia's economy as a 'market economy', citing 'wide interference' by the government in the national economy as its reason.[1] This move gave the US Department of Commerce legal allowance to apply anti-dumping laws to Russian goods, and to undermine Russia's place in the World Trade Organization (WTO). The Russian Ministry of Economic Development challenged the decision in the WTO, explaining that the increased involvement of the Russian government in the national economy was precisely because of wide-ranging sanctions imposed by the United States and other WTO countries.[2] The challenge failed.

The American action was but one of a series of financial hits taken by the Russian economy since February 2022. Ever-accumulating impositions against Russia's energy and financial sectors by the United States, EU members, Canada, Japan and Australia, including freezing about half of its foreign exchange reserves of $640 billion, took a toll. By November, tax revenues from the non-oil and gas sector were falling and, even though increased sales of oil to India and China kept the volume of energy sales up, they came at the cost of large discounts. The government's restriction on gas supplies to Europe caused gas production to drop by up to 20 per cent, and Russian banks saw nearly $15 billion in withdrawals in the fall of 2022. The Central Bank (CB) predicted a 7.1 per cent contraction in the Russian economy for the fourth quarter that year.[3]

Making prospects worse, during the first six months of 2022 more than 1,000 western companies suspended or cancelled their Russian operations. Tens of thousands of private citizens also left the country because of the war, mainly young well-educated people, and the monetary, material and human costs of the war itself were felt, but not yet calculated. In December, the annual Gaidar Economic Forum scheduled for January 2023 was postponed without a re-set date.[4]

The most morbid predictions made in 2022 did not come to pass, however. In January 2023, the International Monetary Fund (IMF) reversed an earlier negative prediction and forecast a slight, 0.3 per cent, growth for the Russian economy in 2023 and 2.1 per cent in 2024.[5] Putin gave at least one explanation for the turnaround when, in his 2023 address to the Federal Assembly, he said that Russia was actively seeking new or expanded markets in Southeast Asia and the Asia-Pacific region, thereby making the 'pivot to the East' slogan of the post-2014 era a specific policy.[6]

Meanwhile, in November 2023, reports from a variety of sources suggest that, after 20 months of war, life went on as usual in Moscow and other urban centres in Russia, with an almost casual indifference to the conflict in Ukraine. In Moscow, the government fed this 'life goes on' attitude by opening a vast Exhibition of Achievements of the National Economy (Vystavka dostizhenii narodnogo khoziastva) to highlight Russian economic and cultural accomplishments. Pavilions at the permanent trade show and amusement park carried presentations from all regions of Russia, including from Luhansk and Donetsk. They hailed national unity and featured characteristics purported to represent Russian civilization and values, often contrasted with pejorative images of the West.

The sanctions noted above were expected to undermine Russia's economy to the extent that it could no longer finance Putin's war. After more than two full years of brutal fighting it still was not clear when, or even if, that would happen.

MANAGING THE ECONOMY IN WARTIME

Shortly after his war in Ukraine passed its first half year, Putin chaired a gathering of senior officials in charge of the economy: the prime minister, several deputy prime ministers and heads of all the economic-related ministries in Cabinet.

Opening the meeting, Putin declared that 'Russia is confidently coping with external pressure' and that the 'economic blitzkrieg' against their country was not working. He maintained as well that Russia's economy was doing better than the economies of most G-20 countries.[7] He may have been at least partly right, but the people around the table also knew that (a) Russia's traditional import and export patterns had shifted dramatically, (b) that the Russian economy would have to adjust without EU countries as partners, and (c) domestic inflation and goods shortages would have to be resolved if the status quo was to be maintained.

The government did not start creating agencies for the purpose of rallying the economy until the fall of 2022. A new Government Coordination Council to manage the supply of equipment and housing for newly called-up recruits was the first of several initiatives.⁸ Putin picked Mishustin to chair the Council, helped by Shoigu and Moscow's Mayor Sobyanin. Heads of law enforcement agencies and various government economic and finance departments filled it out. The Council soon began to shift resources around so as to place the entire economy on a war footing.

It set targets for manufacturers to accelerate the production and delivery of weapons and supplies to the armed forces, monitor prices and suppliers, and build barracks and other military facilities. Its decisions are binding. Putin said that these adjustments were only for the duration of the SVO. But they had a permanent feel to them.⁹ It was now up to the civilian bureaucracy to provide the MoD with sufficient supplies of weapons, ammunition, medicines and rations.¹⁰

Sanctions and Counter-Sanctions

As of 12 January 2023, Russia had been subjected to 13,596 international sanctions, by far the highest number of any country.¹¹ That number continues to grow.

Putin's optimism notwithstanding, in August 2022 the Russian Ministry of Finance reported that its Eurobonds worth ₽563 billion had been frozen abroad, and that securities owned by Russians blocked in the National Settlement Depository amounted to about six trillion roubles (circa US$93 Bln). In addition to the frozen billions in international reserves, Russian banks were cut off from the Society for Worldwide Interbank Financial Telecommunications (SWIFT) and from access to international financial software. None of this boded well for the future of Russia's economy. Although Mishustin still insisted that Russia had enough resources to resume development, production in mining and manufacturing, electricity, natural gas and oil, coal and metal sectors was declining. The only important increases came in the medical supply, clothing and textiles sectors.¹²

On the other hand, in February 2023 the CB reported that its volume of international reserves had risen to $597.7 billion separately from the above-mentioned frozen assets. Russia also recorded a current account surplus of $227.4 billion in 2022.¹³ These came mainly from hydrocarbon sales, aided by existing large reserves of gold, yuan and euros.

In the world of energy supply, as its European market faded away, Russia gained a near equivalent market in the East, at least in volume. For example, Gazprom closed down gas flows to Europe from Nord Stream-1 in September 2022 and sold a record-breaking $8.3 billion in oil products to China.¹⁴

Western analysts continued to predict that Russia's apparent resistance to the ever-spreading sanctions regimes would soon break down – it didn't.[15]

More restrictions were levelled against Russia in late September, when the EU released its eighth wave of constraints as punishment for referendums in occupied Ukraine. Accusing Moscow of an 'illegal attempt to grab land', the EU added more names to its already lengthy black list and set new import bans calculated to deprive Russia of revenues. The roster of items that could not be sold to Russia expanded as well, to cover aviation technology, electronic components and specific chemical substances.[16]

Putin's reaction to talk of oil price ceilings in October was to insist that no country could force Russia to sell energy at prices below profits: 'We will only have one thing left to say, as in a well-known Russian fairy tale: freeze, freeze, wolf tail'.[17] A month after that, Russia extended its own list of items that it would not export to any country other than members of the Eurasian Economic Union (EEU). Though the Russian list contained more than 1,500 types of goods, it is not clear that any of them were in demand in Europe.[18]

When the annexations from Ukraine became de facto, the United States and the G-7 expanded their registry of sanctioned individuals and entities to any country that provide political or economic support for Russia's absorption of the occupied territories. Targeted were shell companies formed to avoid existing sanctions (14 international suppliers), family members of previously sanctioned individuals and most members of the State Duma and Federation Council. The US Department of Commerce added 57 entities to its export controls inventory.

Canada re-joined the parade on 28 October by imposing sanctions on more Russians and issuing bonds that individuals can purchase in support of the Ukrainian government. Norway took action on the same day by adopting the EU's sanctions into law for its own country and adding 30 names and seven entities to its embargo list.[19]

By that time the EU had sanctioned over 1,200 Russian individuals, 155 companies, and 1,000 categories of products, freezing assets and blocking entry into the bloc's market. But, according to one report, there were still special exemptions: Belgium maintained trade in Russia's diamonds; Greek tankers shipped unlimited amounts of Russian oil to non-European ports; France, Slovakia, Hungary, Finland and other countries imported Russian uranium for their nuclear power generators.[20]

According to a presentation by Russia's Trust Technologies, requested by the Audit Chamber in November 2022 sanctions cost Russia nearly 20 per cent of its non-commodity export sales, about 80 per cent of which had been going to the EU. The Chamber qualified its doomsday report by predicting that the losses would be made up by 2030, mostly on the basis of increased deliveries to CIS countries and the Middle East (esp. Turkey and Iran). Some commodity will be redirected to Asia and Latin America; Brazil will purchase fertilizers; China, India and Vietnam will take up the slack in metallurgical product exports.[21]

In this connection, reports suggest that Russia sent India an itemized record of some 500 products it can no longer purchase from Europe, hoping that India would provide them instead. High on the list were parts for cars, aircraft and trains. Presumably, these were on the table when India's foreign minister visited Moscow in November to co-chair a meeting of the India-Russia Intergovernmental Commission on Trade, Economic, Scientific, Technical and Cultural Cooperation.

At that meeting, Jaishankar made it clear that quid pro quos were in order. His country needed to balance its bilateral trade with Russia because of a growing deficit caused by increased oil purchases.[22] Russia had little choice but to comply, for it and the West had shut each other out. But that was not all. Even non-sanctioned goods were not always available, because some international container shipping companies refused to deliver to Russia; payments in euros and dollars became much more complicated, and could be blocked; and banks everywhere were hesitant about opening accounts for Russian companies or correspondent accounts for Russian banks.[23] Still, over two-thirds of the world's population lived in countries not sanctioning Russia.

As of 5 February 2023, sanctions levelled by the EU against Russian crude oil two months earlier were expanded to cover supplies of diesel fuel and gasoline. By then, Russia was almost completely cut off from its previously most significant energy export market, and needed to seek out new consumers, perhaps even in West Africa.[24] Established European consumers of some important Russian products, such as diesel fuels, had to look elsewhere as well. Thus, traditional global trade patterns shifted still further.

In April 2023, the Russian government began seizing temporary control of foreign assets in Russia; for example, Germany's Uniper SE's Russian division and Finland's Fortum Oyj. Shares in these entities were placed with Rosimushchestvo, the government's agency for state property management, on the assumption that they would be returned when penalties were lifted. Some foreign-owned service industry businesses bought by new Russian owners re-opened. In 2022, McDonalds sold all its business in Russia to a Siberian oligarch, who re-opened it as Vkusno-i-tochka. A Russian consortium purchased the Russian KFC chain, which had over 1,000 restaurants in Russia before the war, and re-branded it as Rostic's.[25] Another Russia-based conglomerate took over the Russian assets of tech giant Yandex in January 2024 replacing its holding company in the Netherlands, where an international branch remains. The new MKAO Yandex, for which Russian investors paid $5.2 billion, is now registered in Kaliningrad, where it will pay less taxes.[26]

Losing Markets

When Gazprom first shut down the Nord Stream-1 pipeline that carried natural gas to Germany under the Baltic Sea, it claimed that gas leaks needed to be found and repaired. Most analysts assumed the shutdown was a response to a G-7 decision to cap prices for Russian oil and an EU proposal to do the same thing for Russian gas.[27]

Earlier, Germany had ended its partnership with the long-planned and finally completed Nord Stream-2 project, agreed to cut Russia off from SWIFT and, in September, placed two of Rosneft's refineries under the trusteeship of its electricity and gas regulator, the Federal Network Agency. Rosneft's oil processing subsidiaries accounted for about 12 per cent of Germany's oil refining capacity. Earlier, the Agency had taken over management of Gazprom's subsidiary, SEFE GmbH (formerly Gazprom Germania). These actions were set for six month terms.[28] In November, the EU approved the allocation of €226.6 million to make the German state the sole owner of SEFE GmbH.[29]

The Nord Stream pipelines were back in the news in late September 2022 when, according to Swedish seismologists, four separate pipeline leaks in the Danish economic zone of the Baltic Sea were the result of underwater explosions.[30] Government officials in Poland and Ukraine, and several German legislators, immediately blamed Russia; Russia immediately blamed the United States, Ukraine and the CIA and announced that it would take the matter to the UNSC. Presidential adviser in Kyiv, Podolyak, accused Russia of planning a 'terrorist attack' against the EU; Peskov called the charges 'predictably stupid and absurd'.[31] In a matter of days, almost all European countries had reached an evidence-free consensus that it must have been Russia's doing.

Russia's gas supplies to Europe were not affected at that time because Nord Stream-2 was never put into operation, though it contained gas, and Nord Stream-1 had been shut down for repairs. Nevertheless, the incident exposed the vulnerability of pipeline deliveries. While mutual blame-casting continued, stable pressure was achieved within a week and Gazprom said it was technically possible to repair the damage, but had no idea when and if that would be done.[32]

Speaking to his Security Council on 10 October, Putin expressed regret that Russia was not allowed to participate in the investigation of the Nord Stream explosions, because 'we are all well aware of the ultimate beneficiary of this crime' – meaning Washington.[33] Indeed, Sweden, whose investigators were working with their Danish counterparts on the investigation, refused to share with Russia its findings on the explosions that took place in its economic zone.

A few days later, Putin announced at the Russia Energy Week forum that Russia would not sell energy to countries that capped prices ('cheating tricks and shameless blackmail') and that gas could still be delivered through undamaged parts of Nord Stream, and that the pipeline would be repaired, only if it was economically justified. 'Russia is ready to start such deliveries. The ball is in the European Union court', he said, and again hinted that the United States was behind the pipeline 'sabotage'. He went on to warn that Russia could close down the Nord Stream lines permanently and make Turkey the largest hub for gas supplies to Europe. Erdogan announced just such an agreement a week later.[34]

In the meantime, EU members at an energy summit argued about the imposition of a cap on gas prices. Germany and the Netherlands opted for a delay while France and most others preferred to act immediately. After much dispute, a 'roadmap' towards further talks was agreed.[35]

Western Companies Flee Russia – or Did They?

Although over 1,000 international companies exited Russia in the first few months after the invasion, the shift for others was slow, difficult or impossible. Many multinationals postponed their withdrawal, finding the process too complicated or, in some cases to avoid the threat of nationalization. In October, the French company Danone announced plans to abandon its business in Russia and, after seven months of negotiations, Exxon Mobil Corps bailed completely after Putin signed a decree expropriating its shares in Sakhalin-1.[36] After seven months of suspended operations, Ford Motor company and Mercedes-Benz finalized sales of their Russian properties and departed the country altogether in late October. Nokian Tires sold its Russian business, and Mazda pulled out. Japan's Bridgestone tire manufacturing company announced that it was looking for a local buyer in Ulyanovsk, where it had suspended its business.[37] Nissan, Renault and Toyota were already gone. Most of the big automotive companies continued to pay their staffs for a year and kept a clause in their deals allowing them to buy their assets back within the next six years.

The Canadian manufacturer of outerwear and sportswear and other sports equipment, Helly Hansen, whose brand is owned by Canadian Tire, wound down its business in Russia for almost no remuneration. New Russian owners changed the name to Retail RC. Other big international brands kept their hand in while publicizing withdrawals, some simply by changing their names: Reebok transferred its business to a Turkish holding company (FLO Retailing) and changed the brand to Sneaker Box; Coca-Cola is now Kind Kola (Dobraia Kola) in Russia.[38]

It was also the case that a number of Western companies that announced in 2022 they would leave or suspend activities in Russia were still there and making huge profits in 2023. For example, the energy giants, Total (France) and BP (UK), banks (Austria's Raiffeisen); IT enterprises (Cloudfare – USA); biotech (Bayer – USA); engineering (Bosch – Germany); service establishments (Mariott, Hyatt, Hilton), Burger King, Philip Morris, and many more. Some found it difficult to move because of Russian legislation; other explained that they had to protect their employees and customers; and even others claimed that they were threatened with nationalization.[39]

Companies withdrawing unilaterally from Russia did at considerable cost to themselves. Russian business tycoons were able to purchase assets of over 100 such companies at bargain-basement prices. The Russian government added to the confusion by seizing properties in Russia of several large international firms, such as Baltika brewery (Denmark's Carlsberg), Danone Rossiia food company (France); utilities companies, Uniper (Germany) and Fortum (Finland) and banks (Italy's Intessa). The Dutch brewer Heineken sold its operation in Russia to the Arnest Group, Russia's largest manufacturer of cosmetics, household goods and metal packaging, for one euro. Months later, Arnest rebranded the brewery by changing its logo and name to rid it of any foreign hue.[40] According to the Yale School of Management, by July 2023, 523 companies had left entirely, 503 had suspended operations and over 400 internationals were still doing business in Russia.[41]

In February, the British bank HSBC finally was allowed to sell 100 per cent of its stake in Russia to Expobank, a privately owned Russian commercial bank. Germany's Siemens closed down its business operations in Russia early in 2024, its revenues having dropped by half in 2023, and the German truck manufacturer, Daimler, sold its 15 per cent in KamAZ.[42]

In January 2024, *Vedomosti* published a report that showed 9,600 companies with foreign associations withdrew from Russia during the nearly two years of the SVO. This loss was partially made up for by new jointly owned companies with co-founders in China (25 per cent) and former Soviet republics (59 per cent). Turkey, India and even some 'unfriendly' countries provided the rest. Over-all, however, companies with non-resident participation in Russia declined by nearly 40 per cent.[43]

The Russia tourism industry suffered enormous losses. Already set back by the pandemic in 2020–2021, the flow of tourists to Russia was disrupted further by the difficulty in obtaining electronic visas, inability to make payments with foreign credit cards and the lack of flights from most European countries and North America. North American, European and Japanese tourists not inclined to visit Russia anyway. The Federal Tourism Agency, Rostourism, was abolished in October and its tasks were taken over by the Ministry of Economic Development.[44]

Wood exports suffered too, especially after the Forest Stewardship Council suspended its certification of suppliers of wood from Russia and Belarus.

Among other things, that meant that IKEA stopped purchasing wood from Russia and turned instead to the Baltic states, Poland and Germany. IKEA's four factories in Russia were closed in March 2022, and put up for sale.

Competition for Gazprom

The grand opening on 1 October of a natural gas pipeline linking Greece and Bulgaria was yet another nail in the coffin of Europe's reliance on gas from Russia. The new pipeline, partially funded by the EU, carries gas that originates in Azerbaijan. It flows across Turkey via the Trans-Anatolia Pipeline (TANAP), then across Greece in the Trans-Adriatic Pipeline (TAP) to Albania and from there under the Adriatic to Italy. Now it is connected to Bulgaria and may eventually be available to Moldova and Ukraine. European Commission president von der Leyen spoke at the ceremony and told her audience that the project meant freedom from domination by Russian energy.[45]

In the interim, the EU expanded its efforts to find alternate sources of energy. Germany inaugurated its first LNG terminal in December, 2022, while leaders of Hungary, Romania, Georgia and Azerbaijan finalized an agreement on an undersea electricity connector that will serve as a new power source for the EU. The electricity will originate from Azerbaijan's offshore wind farms, flow to Georgia and from there to Europe via a cable under the Black Sea to Romania and Hungary.

Gaining New Markets

After struggling with limited success to persuade European countries still buying gas from Russia to pay in roubles, Gazprom had a breakthrough in September 2022 when Turkey agreed to pay for 25 per cent of its gas import in the Russian currency. A few weeks before that, China announced that payments for gas via the Power of Siberia pipeline would be conducted in roubles and yuan in equal proportions.[46] The great increase in exporting oil products to China was matched by jumps in sales of Russian LNG, pipelined gas and coal. China was cautious, however, and refrained from new investments in Russian energy companies and from signing new long-term contracts. Beijing wanted the best of both worlds: buy cheaply from Russia and avoid challenging the sanctions regimes.[47]

In 2022, Russian companies producing petroleum products nearly doubled their exports over the previous year to countries that did not impose sanctions, mostly in the Middle East and Asia.[48]

In the Middle East, Saudi Arabia proved to be a more important customer. During the summer of 2022, Riyadh doubled its fuel oil purchases from Russia so that its own crude could be used for export and, in September, persuaded OPEC to reduce output so as to raise world oil prices. Saudi Arabia also increased its investments in Russian energy consortia. In these actions, the Saudis directly opposed Washington.[49] A second cut in production caused Biden to accuse OPEC of colluding with Russia, when Saudi Arabia was in reality conducting business in the way that benefits it the most; that is, slow production, keep prices up, make more profit in a year when Riyadh was having difficulty balancing its books.

During the first week of September 2023 Saudi Arabia and Russia agreed to extend voluntary oil production cuts through to the end of the year. Soon afterward the price of crude rose above $90, an important incentive for Russia, which said it would maintain its 300,000 barrels per day cut.[50] On 4 November, OPEC+ confirmed that the limits it placed on supplies in June would continue to 2024.

As its pipelined flow of gas to Europe dwindled to a trickle, Russia's LNG exports increased. Not yet subjected to sanctions, LNG sales to Belgium, France and the Netherlands multiplied. Japan's import of Russian LNG was the highest ever in December 2023 even though the volume of its purchases had dropped by about 10 per cent that year.[51] Trade with Japan was eclectic. Ore exports to Japan increased, while Russian imports from that country decreased by one quarter. Japan joined the Western sanctioning regimes and cut its purchases of oil from Russia by about 20 per cent, and coal by 30 per cent. Russian purchases of computers from Japan doubled, while in January, 2023, Tokyo banned the export of medical equipment and robots to Russia.[52]

At first glance, Russia's lucrative arms sales market seemed not to suffer. For example, an India (50.5 per cent)-Russia (49.5 per cent) joint venture accelerated plans to sell nuclear capable supersonic cruise missiles made in India to southeast Asian countries. In January 2023, the company BrahMos Aerospace celebrated its first sale to the Philippines ($375 million).[53] India now manufactures MiG fighters and SU-30 jets under Russian licence and, in the fall of 2023, entered into discussion with Vietnam, Malaysia and Indonesia for similar sales. However, as Russia consumed more and more of its own armament production, its exports under contract to India and elsewhere met with delays. For instance, in March 2023 India reported that it had not received its final deliveries of S-400 air defence systems, nor parts for its Russian-built fighter jets.[54]

The most important change was the fact that by 2023 China had become Russia's largest trading partner and its most important energy customer. Trade between the two countries had reached $190 billion in 2022 and was projected to be much higher in 2023–2024.[55] When Mishustin travelled to Shanghai in May 2023 for a Russian-Chinese Business Forum, he took with him oligarchs from the fertilizer, steel and mining sectors. Most of them subject to Western sanctions. Deputy Prime Minister Novak, CEO of Sberbank, German Gref and Economic Development Minister Maksim Reshetnikov joined them. They all moved on to Beijing, where they presented a common front against Western economic pressure. Novak predicted that Russian energy supplies to China would increase by 40 per cent before the year was out. It did.

Moscow's projections about increased trade in non-commodities with Beijing also were borne out. The import substitution project was rewarded by more than five times the usual quota of machinery imported from China during the first quarter of 2023. These included dump trucks, buses, loaders, tractors, cranes and other 'priority goods', most of which traditionally had come from Europe, above all from Germany. Trade turnover between Russia and China grew by 26 per cent in 2023 and reached a record value of $240 billion.[56]

Typical was the loss of a market for LPG (a motor fuel mixture of propane and butane) in Europe in 2022, subsequently offset by more than double the supply requested by Turkey and Asian countries in 2023.

The East was not Russia's only economic target. In December 2023, Russia's Uranium One Group signed a $450 million deal with Bolivia to produce battery and electric vehicle components. The project involved a substantial Russian investment in a lithium plant in Bolivia, which has huge lithium reserves.[57]

All-in-all, the Russian economy appeared to be stable, if not booming, by the end of 2023, and this appeared to be still the case over the first quarter of 2024.

BUDGETS FOR 2023–2026

Draft federal budgets submitted to the Duma in 28 September 2022 projected deficits for each of the next three years, dropping from two per cent of GDP in 2023 to less than one per cent in 2024. The prime minister foresaw strong economic growth for 2024.[58] Given the costs of war fighting and the potential for domestic crises related to healthcare, climate change, labour shortages and trade disruptions connected to sanctions, Mishustin's projection seemed unrealistic at that time.

To help cover the deficit and balance the budget for 2022, Mishustin ordered that one trillion roubles (approx. US$20Bln) be allocated to the National Welfare Fund. According to the Ministry of Finance, these monies were to be used to cover social obligations to citizens, replace government borrowing, help pay off public debt and provide budget loans to Russia's regions.[59]

By 2023, budget expenditures were driven, of course, by war. For the first time, allocations for national defence began surpassing allocations for social policy. The government projected a six per cent expenditure of the country's GDP on the military in 2024 – the highest in post-Soviet history. Although the Ministry of Finance predicted that this trend would reverse by 2026, the long-term costs of re-building and defending annexed territories, if they remain occupied by Russia, will make that also unlikely.[60]

The government had some reasons for optimism, however. One of these was its bumper grain harvest in 2022 and another was that legislation to enhance pensions, the minimum wage and general salaries kept pace with inflation – or so Moscow proclaimed. There can be no doubt that the foreign impositions hurt the Russian economy, but the damage was not as severe as western pundits foretold. 'Getting around the sanctions' became a relatively successful side industry.[61]

Speaking at a meeting of the Council for Strategic Development and National Projects on 15 December 2022, Putin acknowledged that Russia's GDP was projected to decline and that there would be deficits over the next two years. But the sanctions had failed, he declared, and the economic situation in Russia had stabilized. This was before EU confirmed its ninth round, and other new embargoes from the United States and Canada came into force.[62]

Ninth Round of EU Sanctions

Almost immediately after the EU approved an eighth batch of sanctions in October 2022, Russian authorities and economic planners began bracing for a ninth round, and also for the price cap on Russia oil.[63] Having finally decided to set a cap, the EU pondered what it should be, as the market price at that time was around $85 per barrel. Along with Australia, the United Kingdom, Canada, Japan and the United States, the 27-member EU finally agreed on $60, with a mechanism to review the price every two months. That level was higher than the $40–$45 that the Russian government usually relied on for its annual budgeting.[64]

The cap was accompanied by an embargo on shipments of Russian crude by sea to the EU, that is two-thirds of the bloc's imports from Russia. The problem remained that, whereas Poland and the Baltic states lobbied for a much lower price, much of Europe needed to ensure that Russia kept producing oil. If Russia were to cut production deeply, oil-importing countries would suffer recessions. Peskov told domestic news agencies that Russia would not accept the price cap and would stop delivering oil to countries that did, even though it had earned 67 billion euros ($71 billion) from oil sales to the EU since February, 2022.[65] It was not clear if the cap would slow the course of the war in Ukraine.

When the ninth round was finally introduced, it imposed restrictions on nearly 200 individuals and a wide range of legal entities in Russia. They fell on the Russian military, defence industry enterprises, State Duma deputies and senators, ministers, governors and political parties. Three more Russian banks were sanctioned, as were four more TV channels, so as to combat the 'Russian propaganda machine'.[66] In contrast to its earlier responses to sanctions, the CB voiced concern that the price cap and the EU's ban on seaborne Russian crude could 'significantly reduce' Russia's economic activity.[67]

Achieving final agreement on the ninth round was slow. On the one hand, some EU members, such as Germany, France, Spain and Italy, wanted permission to unfreeze assets of sanctioned individuals, to use them for reparations in Ukraine; others wanted to unlock holdings of Russian agricultural companies so as to keep grain shipments moving. On the other hand, Hungary urged members to lift restrictions against Russian cabinet members; Sweden opposed sanctions against Roskomnadzor, and so on. 'Make Russia pay' for reconstruction in Ukraine was a rallying cry for many EU member-states, but not all of them.[68]

As Western politicians became more open to confiscating the $300 billions of locked-in Russian assets to assist Ukraine, analysts cautioned about what kind of precedent that would set. Russia could retaliate by confiscating Western holdings in Russia, and the seizures could be challenged on basic principles of international law and free markets. Some would say that it would be a simple matter of theft.[69]

The increased focus on sanctions had consequences even before they were made official. For example, in December oil tankers queued up for as long as a week before the government in Ankara allowed them to pass through the Bosporus and Dardanelles straits. Turkish authorities demanded documented proof of insurance against spills before the ships could proceed. Sanctioning countries now turned to maritime protection and indemnity (P&I) insurance clubs so as to undermine Russia's shipping capacity. European P&I clubs cannot offer insurance to ships carrying Russian oil whose price is higher than $60 per barrel. Between February and June 2022, new targets for sanctions had been as follows, approximately: firms, 537; legal entities, 276; and organizations, 3,369.[70] The ninth round added many more.

Once again, the Russian foreign ministry shrugged off the new wave of restrictions, saying that they exacerbated 'socio-economic problems in the EU itself' and that Russia would simply expand its trade with new partners. Emphasizing this point, Putin boasted during a video-conference with XI in December 2022 that Russia and China had reached record-high growth rates of mutual trade.[71] Four months later, presidential aide Maksim Oreshkin told an economic conference that trade between Russia and China had increased by 29.3 per cent in 2022, far surpassing trade with the EU, and that the share of trade between them in national currencies was close to half.[72]

ENERGY SIDE ISSUES

Gas

In late December 2022 as EU countries prepared to receive gas via routes that by-passed Russia, deputy prime minister in charge of the fuel and energy complex, Aleksandr Novak, told state media that Gazprom was prepared to resume gas supplies to Europe using the recently closed down Yamal-Europe pipeline. He appeared to be talking to himself.

Gazprom announced also that work had started on implementing the earlier project to turn Turkey into a gas hub, with Turkish Thrace as the distribution centre for natural gas pipelined under the Black Sea.[73] During conversations about gas on 5 January 2023, Putin and Erdogan also discussed the NPP at Akkuyu, the first power unit of which was expected to be commissioned that year, and Russia's promise to supply agricultural products to the poorest countries via Turkey.[74]

With the European gas market now dead, Gazprom benefitted from Putin's visit to China in October 2023 for a celebration of the tenth anniversary of China's Belt and Road project and a meeting of the Russia-Chinese forum. Gazprom's CEO travelled with him and arranged extra sales to both China and Hungary above and beyond contracts already signed.[75]

Another important breakthrough came when Gazprombank was named the preferred investor to re-open a gas refinery in Mossel Bay, South Africa, valued at about $260 billion. Even though the Russian bank is sanctioned by the US, South African officials explained the deal as part of its role in BRICS.

Oil

At that same time in December 2022, Putin finally signed the expected decree forbidding sales of oil and oil products to any country that enforces a price cap. The EU, G-7 and Australia's price ceiling of $60 per barrel had come into force on 5 December, and the Russian decree went into effect on 1 February 2023 – for five months. The decree has a clause that allows Putin to overrule the ban in special cases.[76] As it happened, Germany and Poland extended their self-imposed deadlines to stop buying Russian oil by the end of 2022. They joined the EU ban on most seaborne imports from Russia, but found it hard to replace sources for oil received via the Druzhba pipeline and used by refineries in eastern Germany and plants in Poland. These flows were not subject to embargoes, so Poland and Germany said that they needed sanctions to relieve them from contracts, and required subsidies to make up for their loss.

Oil prices fell from $133 in the spring of 2022 to $87 a year later. That would still have been a good profit margin for Russia except that Russia had to sell at large discounts to India, Pakistan and China. Energy revenue losses left big gaps in the Russian budget.[77]

Growing closer to Saudi Arabia helped. With the Saudis joining the SCO as a Dialogue Partner and, on 1 April 2023, OPEC+ pledging to cut production by more than one million barrels per day, Russia's oil sales seemed secure again. Indeed, Russia exported a record amount of oil products in March 2023 even though G-7 members, the EU and Australia all stopped buying Russian petroleum products. Although the EU set additional price caps for diesel and fuel oil, it lifted price caps on Russian-extracted oil items that are produced outside the country and mixed with other suppliers' oil goods. EU members Greece and Malta took over half of Russian oil product exports in the spring of 2023; Turkey, Brazil, Libya and Morocco bought up much of Russia's diesel export; fuel oil went to India, the UAE, Nigeria and Singapore. Russian oil merchandise still could be re-exported from the European Mediterranean, North Africa and the Middle East to the Asia-Pacific region.[78]

In May 2023, Pakistan finalized its first purchase of discounted Russian crude, rather than refined fuels, as part of a deal that could reach about 100,000 barrels per day delivered by ship. Gazprom further improved its sales potential by arranging with Kazakhstan to supply Uzbekistan with natural gas and oil. The three-way agreement, which involves shipping oil by train and gas via pipelines will benefit all parties: Kazakhstan with transit fees, Uzbekistan with fuel for winter and Gazprom with new revenues.[79]

Oil supplies from Russia to China increased by 13 per cent during the first quarter of 2024.[80]

NPPs

After all the sanctioning impositions, there remained one last untouched energy source of revenue for Russia – nuclear fuels. Russia still provides over 40 per cent of the global market for nuclear fuels. European countries and even the United States continued to purchase nuclear products from Russia to the tune of €1.5 billion. In 2022, for example, Europe bought about 17 per cent of its enriched uranium from Russia, and the United States about 12 per cent.[81] In fact, the United States was still the biggest single consumer of Russian uranium until June 2024, when Washington banned such imports. Rosatom opened an NPP in Belarus at the end of 2023 and, in February 2024, signed a contract to sell nuclear fuel components for a research facility in Egypt.[82]

Russian energy sectors have survived sanctions levelled against companies, individuals, technologies and investments. Oil production and revenues have actually grown, but that success was accomplished in large part by increasing exports to China and India at bargain basement prices. That will change. In the long run, the sector will suffer from lack of major investments and access to state-of-the art technology, and the discount cannot be permanent. The same could be said for natural gas and gas exports, where Russia has to make major adjustments by changing the export flow from west to east. Traditional pipelines are used less and newer lines, Power of Siberia, Far Eastern Route and Mongolian Transit Route are used more often. LNG exports are growing and are not sanctioned, but technology transfer will be a problem in that sector as well.

INTERNATIONAL ECONOMIC ASSOCIATIONS: EEU, BRICS, SCO

The EEU was shaken by the war in Ukraine. Its full members outside Russia and Belarus, that is Armenia, Kazakhstan and Kyrgyzstan, and Observer states Cuba, Moldova and Uzbekistan, all had to revisit their economic dependence on Moscow and, indeed, their place in what was shaping up to be a major East-West economic duel. Wide-ranging sanctions made further integration with Russia risky and provided China with an opportunity to expand its economic influence over Eurasia.[83]

These issues dominated a meeting of the EEU's Supreme Economic Council when it met in Bishkek in December 2022. We have seen that Putin was there to shore up bilateral political and diplomatic relations, but economic decisions were important as well. The group confirmed that trade between members had not been interrupted and that energy prices for consumers in the organization remained lower than for their counterparts in the West. The Council removed more customs and administrative barriers between affiliates. Members agreed to create new mechanisms for financing industry, collecting indirect taxes in the EEU and broadening the list of service sectors in the single market space. They also established a new commission made up of heads of official agencies in the energy sector to assist in the eventual formation of a common energy market.

Scheduled to take over the EEU chairmanship in 2023, Russia announced that its focus would be on the development of scientific, technical and educational contacts, and also a single gas market. The EEU agreed to begin negotiations on a free trade agreement with the UAE.[84]

How to achieve all these ambitious plans was the problem. The organization's central dilemma was illustrated by decisions made by Kazakhstan in March 2023. Introducing an on-line system to track all goods that cross its borders, entering or leaving, Astana made certain, or fairly certain, that it would not become a platform through which other countries might circumvent embargoes against Russia. Kazakhstan did not restrict its own trade with Russia, its largest trading partner, but hoped not to facilitate sanction-breaking activities by other parties.[85]

It was left to the BRICS to form Russia's most stabilizing economic association in the 2020s. None of the organization's membership in 2022 supported the sanctions regimes. In addition to occupying about 30 per cent of the globe's dry land and more than 40 per cent of the world's population, the original partners (Brazil, Russia, India, China and South Africa) also account for almost half of the world's wheat and rice production and about 15 per cent of the world's gold reserves. Coupled with the much larger SCO membership, Russia is not short of trade partners. Talk in October 2022 of Saudi Arabia joining the BRICS, thereby linking the organization indirectly with OPEC, worried the West.

SCO Summits, 2022–2023

At a July 2022 meeting, the SCO had set out mechanisms for Economic Cooperation Zones, the first of which was established in the Jiaozhou area of Qingdao on China's East Coast. Their purpose was to allow SCO businesses to share technology, expertise and investment in one location.[86] To date (July 2024), no other such zones have followed.

Meeting a year later by video-conference in Samarkand, shortly after the St. Petersburg International Economic Forum (SPIEF), the SCO leaders touted China's Belt and Road Initiative and gave Putin another podium from which he could pretend on behalf of the Russian economy. He insisted that Russia had countered Western sanctions and emerged even stronger than before. Joining China in urging members to conduct inter-regional trade in roubles and yuan, he also assured them of his own hold on power at home.

The meeting signed 14 joint documents, agreed on a wide variety of general principles and completed procedures for new members (Iran, Belarus), but made little progress on specific economic projects.

WEAR AND TEAR

As the war of attrition in Ukraine neared its first anniversary, its costs and consequences began seeping deeper into the Russian economy. According to some Russian reports, the Finance Ministry began dipping into the National Wealth Fund at a rate that could drain it by 2025.[87]

The sudden absence of young men from the labour market because of military mobilization and emigration was another complication. Although this meant a very low unemployment rate (3.9 per cent in December 2022), it also caused a shift of workers from commercial and private construction, transport, processing and service industries to the higher-paid state sector, thereby skewing the labour market.

According to a RBC.ru report, up to 42 per cent of Russian industrial enterprises, plus manufacturing, mining and transportation, were short of workers in July 2023, a new high.[88]

Ever optimistic in public, Putin told a meeting of Russia's economic and financial ministers in January that year that the economy was doing better than expected; that is, the GDP fell by only 2.5 per cent in 2022 and not by the larger figure predicted by Russia's own economists. The military-industrial complex played an important role in the new economy, he said, but industries that relied heavily on foreign markets have to find new customers both abroad and at home. The federal budget deficit was low compared to other G-20 countries, inflation was dropping and both housing construction and road building were on schedule, especially in the regions – or so the president boasted. Putin ordered the government to raise the minimum wage and average monthly salary to keep ahead of inflation, which had reached 11.9 per cent by the end of 2022.[89]

According to the CB, inflation fell to between 4.6 and 6.5 per cent a half year later. That said, Russia's National Wealth Fund continued to shrink. In June, hoping to bring inflation down further, the CB extended its interest rate to 7.5 per cent per annum and the next month brought it up to 8.5 per cent. In July, the bank reported that inflation had dropped again, to 3.6 per cent. Several Western economists challenged this latter number and maintained that Russia's real inflation rate was much higher, caused mainly by the rouble in free-fall.[90] Whatever the reality, Russia's economy doubtless was not as strong as Putin regularly proclaimed.

By mid-August 2023 the rouble had crashed again, to 100 to the US dollar, compelling the CB to raise the interest rate to 12 per cent. A month later, as prices rose again and labour shortages drove wages up, Nabiullina hiked the rate another one per cent.[91] The government's projection of a 4.5 per cent inflation rate by 2024 seemed unrealistic given increased federal spending, the weakening rouble and rising tariff rates. Labour shortages, higher wages and more disposable income also combined against lower inflation.[92]

Warning in October that 'inflationary pressures had significantly increased to a level above the Central Bank's expectations', Nabiullina raised interest rates to 15 per cent, the fourth such hike in a row. Upping the key interest rate to 16 per cent in December, she promised the 'end of the rate increase cycle'.[93]

Tenth Round of EU Sanctions

On the one-year anniversary of the SVO, the EU levelled a tenth round of sanctions against Russia. These fell on trade in anything that might benefit the Russian military (technology, components, heavy vehicles and electronics). Synthetic rubber imports were banned. Sputnik radio and RT Arabic TV were prohibited. The EU added 121 individuals, several banks (e.g. Tinkoff, Alfa-Bank, Rosbank) and legal entities to its existing blacklist. As much as possible, it cut off attempts to use third country re-suppliers to avoid sanctions.[94]

In separate actions, the U.S. Treasury Department also pledged to clamp down on third-country facilitators, and announced a new series of sanctions on Russian companies, banks, manufacturers and individuals, 250 entities in all: visa restrictions on 1,219 members of the Russian military, increased tariffs on Russian metals, and on about 90 companies considered to be sanctions evaders. The latter targets were located in Italy, Turkey, China and the UAE. Washington coordinated its new sanctions with other G-7 countries.[95] By that time, more than 30 countries had levelled sanctions against Russia.

Somewhat slower off the mark, in March 2023 Canada banned the import of Russian steel and aluminium, and in June seized a huge Russian cargo jet (Antonov 124) that had been grounded in Toronto since the start of the war.[96]

Relying on China

Data released during Xi Jinping's state visit to Moscow in March 2023, illustrated the degree to which China had become vital to Russia's economic survival. During a meeting with Mishustin, the portfolio of the Intergovernmental Russian-Chinese Commission on Investment Cooperation (est. 2014) revealed 79 major projects worth over $165 billion. Both parties assumed that the list would grow. To bolster their links, Putin told Xi that Russia was prepared to switch to the yuan in trade with countries in Asia, Africa and Latin America.[97]

In his welcoming address, Putin stressed the gains in gas sales to China via the Power of Siberia pipeline. Supply had increased by nearly 50 per cent, he said, while failing to mention that, at that time, Gazprom was selling the commodity to China at a 70 per cent discount. Adding that plans to complete the Power of Siberia-2 through Mongolia were well underway, he was jumping the gun, for final agreements had not yet been achieved.[98] Negotiations over who was to construct the 2,600-km pipeline and who would set the price of the gas continued, with China holding the upper hand.

Russia now buys everything from computer chips and cars from China. With 553,000 car sales to Russia in 2023, China overtook Japan as the world's largest automobile exporter.

Downturn?

Rosstat released data in March 2023 that showed a record low unemployment rate of 3.5 per cent, but qualified this good news by acknowledging that in some regions and in some economic sectors, unemployment was much higher than the national average and that a growing percentage of the work force was on part-time employment.[99]

Although the IMF predicted growth in Russia's GDP for 2023, seeds of future problems were obvious. We have seen that the military-industrial complex was scooping up workers and commandeering industries, leaving the consumer economy depleted. This situation worsened as spending on consumption fell.[100]

Difficulties in accessing parts for its commercial airline and automobile industries, high-tech software or to attract foreign investment to its natural resource sectors, did not bode well for Russia's economic future. Even though Russian airlines were able to import essential parts for its Western aircraft (Boeings, Airbuses) through third parties, such as China, Turkey, the UAE and several Central Asian countries, these were not permanent fixes.[101]

The automotive sector began a tentative comeback in June 2023, when AvtoVAZ signed an agreement with Chinese partners to produce a new line of Ladas in 2024. Factories in St. Petersburg, Izhevsk and Togliatti, one of which had been a Nissan plant, will be the sites of production. This new venture may make up in part for the departure from Russia of Western car manufacturers.[102] The industry received a boost from Putin when he told the heads of manufacturing enterprises that all Russian officials must drive cars produced in Russia.[103]

According to *Business Insider*'s market analysis in April 2023, Russia's private sector economy is worse than the official figures show because military spending covers up massive losses in retail sales and stagnation in the housing market. The same sources say that Russia's federal budget had lost up to $15 billion in oil and gas revenues due to the EU's price cap and discounts to Asian consumers. Moscow's up-ticked dependence on China and the yuan seemed likely to intensify as the EU announced that it would set out its eleventh package of sanctions in May.[104]

Outwardly, however, economic and social conditions in Russia appeared to be relatively normal. Shelves remained full at super stores, though the percentage of products and goods in them from Russia, Belarus, China and other 'friendly' countries had risen dramatically. Even after the initial outflow, many foreign companies continued to function as they were with Russian owners and Russian names. While war raged in Ukraine in the spring and summer of 2023, bars in Russian cities were filled at nights. Luxury goods from Europe still found their way to the homes of Russia's elite. By that time, companies that left had to pay a 10 per cent exit tax, so many decided to stay (e.g. Germany's Metro AG and Bayer AG), both to maintain profits and, they claimed, to protect their thousands of employees.¹⁰⁵

As Russia posted a first quarter deficit of some ₽2.4 billion in 2023, the government imposed a one-shot windfall tax on large companies earning profits over ₽1 billion. The tax helped make up for falling energy revenues.¹⁰⁶

SPIEF 2023

The fact that very few representatives of Western economies turned up at 2023's SPIEF was not the only difference from previous such gatherings. Its agenda had a completely new look. Traditionally a major event for both domestic and international business leaders with prominent Western officials delivering keynote statements, the 2023 Forum banned the Western press and presented a programme that had less to do with business and more to do with domestic development. Of the nearly 150 events, more than half had to do with Russian sovereignty, the diaspora, 'ethnic conservatism', drug safety, youth programmes, sports and even healthy eating habits.¹⁰⁷

The closing session had Putin and Algerian president Abdelmadjid Tebboune as speakers. Putin delivered the usual glowing picture of Russia's economy, but then veered off in the Q&A, to wit: the economy has survived the imposition of sanctions, and is growing; we [Russians] are trying to stop the 'war in Ukraine' that has been going on since Kyiv started it in 2014; we will de-Nazify occupied territories; Ukraine's counter-offensive is failing; 'Zelensky is not a Jew. He is a disgrace to the Jewish people', equating him with Bandera, 'an anti-Semite, a neo-Nazi'.¹⁰⁸ Putin was beginning to sound a little desperate.

The absence of Western investors and the over-riding political tenor of SPIEF 2023 didn't mean that no contracts were agreed with foreign companies, though they were fewer than usual. Gazprom and Rosatom signed off on potentially lucrative deals, the latter to build an NPP in Sri Lanka. Kazakhstan and China arranged with Russian entities for oil transit and methanol plants. Most major deals, however, were internal.¹⁰⁹ According to Russian reports, 17,000 people from 130 countries and territories took part.¹¹⁰

It was only a few weeks later, at the Russia-Africa Summit, that Russia agreed to construct an NPP in the West African country of Burkina Faso.

Eastern Economic Forum (EEF)

Putin served as co-host with the vice president of Laos, Pani Yathothu, for the ninth Eastern Economic Forum held in Vladivostok, 10–13 September 2023. China was represented by the vice premier of its State Council and India by its minister of trade and ports. The forum's website claimed that more than 7,000 participants represented 68 countries, about 1,700 businesses and 700 companies; and that 296 economic agreements were reached. Russia, India, China, South Korea, Mongolia, Myanmar and Armenia sent the largest delegations.[111]

In his rambling address to the Forum, Putin again touted Russia's economic 'successes', especially in the Far East, and outlined plans for further development of that region, with financial support for eco-tourism, national parks, industry fairs and free plots of land. He denied that his government planned to nationalize private enterprises – a denial that was already proving to be untrue.[112] His grandiose promises for Russia's Far East had been heard before.

Putin also harshly criticized oligarchs who left the country (e.g. Chubais) and those who failed to repatriate their overseas assets.[113]

COSTS OF WAR

More is lost in war than lives, limbs and livelihoods. Although the Russian economy survived the first rounds of economic punishments, the fact that the needs of war caused the state to play a much greater role in the private sector will have long term consequences. As one analyst put it in May 2023, the pre-war emphasis on technological development, getting out from under dependence on natural resources and the free movement of capital were quickly replaced by 'capital controls, the labelling of countries as either friendly or hostile, the yuanization of payments, and the militarization of budget spending'.[114] These changes may be very costly in the long run.

The danger of Russia slipping into a period of stagnation if its 'pivot to the east' for markets and sources of investment (China, India, Vietnam, ASEAN) does prove profitable is real. Aware of this possibility, while predicting some growth in 2023 fuelled by deficit spending, the IMF forecast a reduction in the Russian economy of about seven per cent by 2027.[115]

Over all, the greatly increased level of public spending by the government, both by financing war production and pouring funds from national reserves into subsidies for higher pensions, salaries, benefits and even mortgages kept the economy growing, if slowly. Soldiers' wages, which are much higher than regional salaries, pumped some money into the economy. In the future, however, declining energy revenues, labour shortages, and inflation may prove to be too hard to overcome.

Eleventh and Twelfth Rounds of EU Sanctions

An eleventh round of sanctions adopted by the European Commission in June 2023 levelled penalties against 70 more Russian individuals and 30 entities, and instituted a ban on trailers entering EU space from Russia. Its main thrust, though, was to prevent circumvention of existing trade sanctions. The list revealed by von der Leyen in Kyiv still did not preclude imports of Russian diamonds, natural gas, LNG, cast iron and ferroalloys, or nuclear energy cooperation. Among the steps to close loopholes were an up-grade of road transit bans, especially on advanced tech products and aircraft parts to Russia via third countries, tighter embargoes on countries suspected of avoiding sanctions against Russia (e.g. Central Asian and Caucasus nations, China, Turkey and the UAE), and blacklisting specific companies in China.[116]

Early in January 2024, the EU added Russia's state-controlled diamond mining company Alrosa and its CEO to its sanctions list. Alrosa, the world's largest such company, accounts for 90 per cent of Russia's diamonds. Russian sources claimed that Alrosa had already been looking for new markets for their diamonds and that the sector was 'stabilized', though it was not clear who those buyers were, or if they even existed.[117]

With price caps and embargoes impacting its energy exports, tax revenues from oil and gas exports had fallen by about 36 per cent, and the rouble was still in freefall, refilling the current account was problematic. There were no reliable revenue-generating market substitutes in sight, except perhaps agriculture.[118]

Still, the Bloomberg Billionaires Index as of August 2023 placed 25 Russians among the world's 500 wealthiest people and noted that founders and CEOs of Lukoil, Novatek (gas producer) and NLMK (Steel) had increased their personal wealth by billions since the first of the year. Overall, Russian billionaires had augmented their existing fortunes by over $32 billion and, according to Forbes, their numbers had risen from 110 to 125 by January 2024.[119] They stayed quiet about the war and grew richer.

The EU's proposed twelfth round included new import and export bans, among them Russia's export of diamonds, and tightened the oil price cap. It introduced stronger measures against third country avoidance of sanctions against Russia, again. Borrell sent these propositions to each of the EU's 27 members in November 2023, and they were adopted in December. None of that prevented Russia from selling oil at above the price cap by using a large 'shadow fleet' of oil tankers, that is ships with unclear or false identities.[120]

The push by some or most of the EU membership for more stringent enforcement was driven by evidence that their previous impositions were still not working very well, and that enforcement was lax. Russia was receiving high-priority items, such as semi-conductors used by arms manufacturers, through trade diversion practices, that is via countries in Central Asian or Transcaucasia. Moreover, Russia had increased its exports to Europe in some products. Supplies of cast iron, for example, grew by 40 per cent over 2022, and pig iron by over 70 per cent. As 2023 wound down, it was plain that the EU's sanctions against Russia had been more porous than those levelled by the United States. That may have been because European exporters have much more to lose than their American counterparts.[121]

The twelfth round of sanctions brought the EU total of black-listed individuals to 1,645 plus 335 legal entities.[122] As the new series came into force, the EU finally decided that it would confiscate proceeds from frozen Russian assets to help pay for reconstruction in Ukraine. Most of these assets are held in Belgium's Euroclear, a central security depository. Incomes from those funds (circa €200 Bln) will be managed by the European Council.[123]

As a result of sanctions, Russia's exports to Europe were down by 68 per cent in 2023, to $84.9 billion, while its exports to Asia rose by 5.6 per cent, to $306.6 billion. Russia's trade balance was still positive, but the gap was narrower than in the previous year.[124]

More Sanctions

The unexplained death of Aleksei Navalny in February 2024 triggered another wave of sanctions from the United States against more than 500 Russian individuals and entities. These included a military drone manufacturer, the Mir payment system used by the CB and multiple other companies. The metals industry was left untouched. The newly sanctioned targets took in people and businesses in 11 countries besides Russia. The EU added more restrictions on foreign companies and on members of the Russian judiciary. Canada added 160 persons and entities to its list and the UK imposed penalties on everything linked to Navalny's incarceration and demise. Australia and Japan added new impositions as well.

AGRICULTURE

While the government struggled to keep food prices down, grain producers in Russia continued to do well in 2022–2023. Wheat shipments were at or near record highs in November and December 2022 and January 2023, increasing 24 per cent over the same three months a year earlier. Huge production levels over the last two years have helped Russia keep its export prices down, making purchases attractive even to EU countries, such as Spain, Italy and France, at the same time undercutting potential sales from Poland and other eastern EU countries.[125] Turkey was the leading consumer of Russian grains, followed by Egypt and Iran. Saudi Arabia, Algeria, Pakistan, Brazil and Mexico are among states that increased their grain purchases from Russia. Even with higher premiums paid for freight coverage, Russian wheat remained the least expensive internationally.

Minister of Agriculture Dmitry Patrushev reported that Russia exported over 60 million tons of grain during the agriculture year, 1 July 2022 to the end of June 2023. Record sales, primarily to 'friendly countries', earned about $41 billion, he said, noting as well that the Russian harvest had reached a high of 157.7 million tonnes in 2022–2023. A lesser, but still high, volume of 123 million tonnes was forecast for 2023–2024.[126]

Fertilizer shipments were stuck because of sanctions and were not improved by the grain corridor extension deal reached in March 2023. Wide-ranging sanctions also made it difficult for Russian producers to access foreign farm machinery, seeds, bull semen and pedigree livestock, all of which have been important imports in the past.[127]

Adding to these concerns, the Voronezh region in southwestern Russia suffered an anthrax outbreak in August. A large area had to be sealed off and authorities banned all export of meat, dairy product and feed from the region.[128] Less serious anthrax cases were reported earlier in the Siberian republics of Tyva and Chuvashia.

The weather change variable that affects agricultural production around the world may have greater consequences for Russia than previously because of loosening environmental protection regulation, lack of funding to combat drought, flood and fire, and shortages of Russian and migrant labour (see chapter 10).

NOTES

1. U.S. Department of Commerce, 'U.S. Department of Commerce revokes Russia's market economy status in antidumping proceedings', *International Trade Administration*, 10 November 2022.

2. 'Minekonomiki dopustilo obrashchenie v VTO iz-za SShA priznavat' ekonomiku RF rynochnoi', *Kommersant*, 11 November 2022; US International Trade Administration, 'U.S. Department of Commerce revokes Russia's market economy status in antidumping proceedings', 10 November 2022; Christine McDaniel, 'Another nail in the coffin of the Russian economy', *Forbes*, 10 November 2022.

3. See, e.g. Mark Gongloff, 'Putin, Russia can't escape the West's economic trap', *Bloomberg*, 23 November 2022; Huileng Tan, 'India and China are still snapping up Russian oil – but they are demanding huge bargains which is hitting Kremlin's war chest', *Business Insider: Markets*, 27 November 2022.

4. 'Gaidarovskii forum-2023 ne sostoitsia', *Kommersant*, 28 December 2022.

5. International Monetary Fund, *World Economic Outlook. Update. 2023 Jan.*, 31 January 2023, imf.org/en/Publications/WEO/Issues/2023/01/31/world-economic-outlook-update-january-2023.

6. 'Poslanie Prezidenta Federal'nomu Sobraniiu', *Kremlin.ru*, 21 February 2023, kremlin.ru/events/president/news/70565.

7. Putin, 'Soveshchanie po ekonomicheskim voprosam', *Kremlin.ru*, 12 September 2022, kremlin.ru/events/president/news/69336.

8. 'Ukaz o Koordinatsionnom sovete pri Pravitel'stve po obespecheniiu potrebnostei Vooruzhennykh Sil Rossiiskoi Federatsii, drugikh voisk, voinskikh formirovanii i organov', *Kremlin.ru*, 21 October 2022, kremlin.ru/acts/news/69657.

9. 'Soveshchanie s chlenami Koordinatsionnogo soveta pri Pravitel'stve po obespecheniiu potrebnostei VS RF', *Kremlin.ru*, 27 October 2022, kremlin.ru/events/president/news/69676.

10. On this, see Farida Rustamova, Maksim Tovkaylo, 'Amid Ukraine war, Putin is changing how Russia is governed', *The Moscow Times*, 1 November 2022; Pavel Luzin, 'The Kremlin's economic mobilization', *Eurasia Daily Monitor*, 31 October 2022.

11. 'Number of international sanctions imposed worldwide as of January 12, by target country', *Statista*, 17 January 2023, statista.com/statistics/1294726/number-of-global-sanctions-by-target-country/. The next highest after Russia was Iran, with 4,080 sanctions against its economy.

12. 'V Rossii zafiksirovano maksimal'noe snizhenie promproizvodstva za dva goda', *Kommersant*, 16 October 2022. For a chart, see rosstat.gov.ru/storage/mediabank/178_26-10-2022.html; Leonid Uvarchev, 'Bloomberg pereskazalo prezentatsiiu Minfina Rossii po ushcherbu finsektoru ot sanktsii', *Kommersant*, 14 September 2022; 'Mishustin: u Rossii dostatochno resursov dlia vozobnovleniia razvitiia', *Kommersant*, 14 September 2022.

13. Lusine Balasyan, 'Mezhdunarodnye rezervy RF uvelichilis' za nedeliu na $3,1 mlrd', *Kommersant*, 2 February 2023. See also 'Putin's got plenty of money to keep fighting', *The Bell*, 27 January 2023.

14. George Glover, 'China spent a record-breaking $8.3 billion on Russia energy in just 1 month as Europe shuns the supplies', *Business Insider*, 19 September 2022.

15. See, e.g. Phil Rosen, 'Russia's early resilience to sanctions is fading – its economy is on the back foot and Moscow could soon lose its place among the world's energy superpowers', *Business Insider*, 20 September 2022.

16. European Commission, 'Press statement by President von der Leyen on a new package of restrictive measures against Russia', 28 September 2022, ec.europa.eu/commission/presscorner/detail/en/STATEMENT_22_5856.

17. Quoted in Anna Narayeva, 'Sovet ES utverdil vos'moi paket sanktsii protiv Rossii', *Vedomosti*, 6 October 2022. The phrase was from a Russian/Ukrainian fairy tale, *Sister Fox and Brother Wolf*.

18. 'Pravitel'stvo prodlilo do 2024 goda zapret na vyvoz 1,6 tys. naimenovanii tovarov', *Kommersant*, 3 November 2022.

19. Canada. Prime minister of Canada Justin Trudeau, 'Prime minister of Canada announces new measures to support Ukraine', 28 October 2022, pm.gc.ca/en/news/news-releases/2022/10/28/prime-minister-announces-new-measures-support-ukraine; 'Norway adopts new sanctions against Russia', *NewsinEnglish.no*, 28 October 2022, newsinenglish.no/2022/10/28/norway-adopts-new-sanctions-against-russia/.

20. See Matina Stevis-Gridneff, 'As Europe piles sanctions on Russia, some sacred cows are spared', *New York Times*, 18 October 2022.

21. Anastasia Larina, 'RBK: sanktsii sokratili nesyr'evoi eksport Rossii na 19%', *Kommersant*, 10 November 2022.

22. For commentary, Rajeswari Pillai Rajagopalan, 'Indian foreign minister Jaishanker goes to Russia', *The Diplomat*, 11 November 2022.

23. On this, see Jennifer Sor, 'Russia's isolation from global markets is withering its economy and will wreck its status as an energy superpower, experts say', *Business Insider*, 26 December 2022; Alexandra Prokopenko, 'The cost of war: Russia's economy faces a decade of regress', *The Moscow Times*, 24 December 2022.

24. Robin Perkins, Rowan Staden-Coats, 'Europe still buying over quarter of diesel imports from Russia ahead of new curbs', *S&P Global: Commodity Insights*, 19 January 2023.

25. Tat'yana Shamanskaya, 'Gendirektor Rostic's: My sokhranim privychnyi uroven' servisa KFC i vkus bliud', *TASS*, 24 April 2023.

26. 'Aktsii "Yandeksa" podorozhali na 5% na novosti o registratsii bumag kompanii', *RBC.ru*, 25 December 2023; 'Rossiiskoe MKAO stalo vladel'tsem glavnogo iurlitsa "Yandeksa" v RF', *Interfaks*, 23 January 2024; 'Yandex NV strikes $5.2Bln deal with Russian investors', *The Moscow Times*, 6 February 2024.

27. 'Gazprom shuts its main gas pipeline to Europe', *The Bell*, 6 September 2022; 'Nordstream gas pipeline to Germany shut indefinitely – Gazprom', *The Moscow Times*, 2 September 2022; 'A price cap on Russian oil could cause a supply catastrophe', *Oilprice.com*, 15 September 2022.

28. 'Germany Seizes Russia's rosneft units to ensure energy supplies', *The Moscow Times*, 16 September 2022.

29. 'Evrokomissiia vydelit Germanii €225,6 mln dlia pogloshcheniia "dochki" "Gazproma"', *Kommersant*, 12 November 2022; European Commission, 'State aid: Commission approves €225.6 million German measure to support energy company SEFE GmbH', 12 November 2022, ec.europa.eu/commission/presscorner/detail/en/ip_22_6823.

30. 'State of emergency at the Nord Streams and the departing Russians. Peskov's briefing topics', *TASS*, 27 September 2022; 'Peskov did not rule out that the destruction on the Nord Stream could be due to sabotage', ibid.; Jorge Liboreiro, 'Sabotage fears after several gas leaks are identified in Nord Stream pipelines', *Euro News*, 27 September 2022, euronews.com/my-europe/2022/09/27/denmark-and-sweden-issue-navigation-warnings-over-nord-stream-gas-leaks.

31. For Peskov's Tweet, 'Kommersant' FM 93,6 @KFM926. See also, 'Explainer: What we know about the Russia-Europe Nord Stream pipeline leak', *The Moscow Times*, 28 September 2022, with photos of gas bubbling to the surface; Merlyn Thomas, Robert Plummer, 'Nord Stream: Ukraine accuses Russia of pipeline terror attack', *BBC News*, 30 September 2022, bbc.com/news/world-europe-63044747.

32. 'Nord Stream operator says repair of damaged strings of pipeline not ruled out', *TASS*, 28 September 2022.

33. Putin, 'Soveshchanie s postoiannymi chlenami Soveta Bezopasnosti', *Kremlin.ru*, 10 October 2022, kremlin.ru/events/president/news/69568; 'Vystuplenie Putina na soveshchanii s chlenami Sovbeza: Glavnoe', *Vedomosti*, 10 October 2022.

34. Putin, 'Plenarnoe zasedanie mezhdunarodnogo foruma "Rossiiskaia energetiocheskaia nedelia"', *Kremlin.ru*, 12 October 2022, kremlin.ru/events/president/news/69584; 'Erdogan anounces deal with Moscow to create gas hub in Turkey', *The Moscow Times*, 20 October 2022.

35. 'EU energy summit: European states agree "roadmap" to contain prices', YouTube, *France 24*, 21 October 2022, france24.com/en/video/20221021-eu-energy-summit-european-states-agree-roadmap-to-contain-prices.

36. Denis Kurenev, Margarita Sobol, 'Danone ob'iavila o planakh otkazat'sia ot biznesa v Rossii', *Vedomosti*, 14 October 2022; Diane Francis, 'Most multinationals remain in Russia and fund Putin's invasion of Ukraine', *Atlantic Council*, 18 September 2022; Irina Slav, 'Russia removes Exxon from major oil and gas project', Oilprice.com, 18 October 2022.

37. 'Ford exits sollers Ford joint venture in Russia following seven months suspension of operations', *Ford Media Center*, 26 October 2022; "Mercedes-Benz to sell off Russian assets to local investor', *The Moscow Times*, 26 October 2022; 'Proizvoditel' shin Bridgestone soobshchil o prodazhe aktivov v Rossii', *Vedomosti*, 31 October 2022.

38. Victor Davidoff, 'Are Western brands as serious about withdrawing from Russia as they appear?' *The Moscow Times*, 4 November 2022; 'Kanadskii proisvoditel' verkhnei i sportivnoi odezhdy Helly Hansen ushel iz Rossii', *Vedomosti*, 13 November 2022.

39. Mark Temnycky, 'The Russian tale: The Western companies helping underwrite Russia's war', *Kennan Institute, Wilson Center*, 23 March 2023; 'Western companies still operating in Russia were so profitable in 2022 that their corporate taxes contributed almost $4 billion to the country's revenues', *Business Insider*, 13 June 2023.

40. '"Khaineken" okonchatel'no ischez iz Rossii', *Vedomosti*, 4 December 2023.

41. Yale School of Management, 'Over 1,000 companies have curtailed operations in Russia – but some remain', 18 July 2023, som.yale.edu/story/2022/over-1000-companies-have-curtailed-operations-russia-some-remain; 'Russian businessmen snapped up $40 billion worth of Western company assets at bargain-bin prices amid the corporate exodus: Report', *Business Insider*, 18 July 2023; 'Putin allows the nationalization of Russia's largest Western-owned consumer companies', *The Bell*, 18 July 2023; 'Heineken exits Russia, sells operations for 1 euro', *The Moscow Times*, 25 August 2023.

42. 'Siemens in Russia', *Siemens*, 12 February 2024; 'Iz Rossii ushel poslednii zapadnyi proizvoditel' avtomobilei', *KorrespondenT.net*, 15 February 2024.

43. Anastasia Boyko, 'Za dva goda chislo kompanii inostrannym uchastiem sokratilos' pochti na 10,000', *Vedomosti*, 10 January 2023.

44. 'Putin abolishes rostourism, Russia's Federal Tourism Agency', *RusTourismNews*, 20 October 2022, rustourismnews.com/2022/10/20/putin-abolishes-rostourism-russias-federal-tourism-agency/.

45. 'Greece-Bulgaria pipeline starts operations to boost non-Russian gas flows', *Euronews*, 1 October 2022.

46. 'Putin: chetvert' postavok rossiiskogo gaza v Turtsiiu budet oplachivat'sia v rubliakh', *Kommersant*, 16 September 2022.

47. On this, see Erica Downs, 'A friend in need is a friend indeed? China-Russia energy relations in the wake of the war in Ukraine', *Journal of International Affairs*, 15 September 2022.

48. Dar'ia Sevenkova, 'Rossiia meniaet napravleniia postavki nefteproduktov', *Vedomosti*, 7 December 2022.

49. See, e.g. Clifford Krauss, 'Ostracized by the West, Russia finds a partner in Saudi Arabia', *New York Times*, 14 September 2022; Nayera Abdallah, Hadeel al Sayegh, 'Saudi prince made a $500 million Russia bet at start of Ukraine war', *Reuters*, 15 August 2022.

50. Michael Kern, 'Oil prices jump as Russia and Saudi Arabia extend cuts', *OilPrice.com*, 5 September 2023.

51. 'Yaponiia v dekabre importirovala iz Rossii rekordnye s 2017 goda ob'emy SPG', *RBC.ru*, 24 January 2024; Trade Statistics of Japan. Ministry of Finance, 'Value of exports and imports December 2023 (provisional)', accessed 24 January 2024, customs.go.jp/toukei/shinbun/trade-st_e/2023/202312ce.xml#pg20.

52. 'Iaponiia uvelichila import CPG iz Rossii na 211% po sravneniiu s 2021 godom', *Kommersant*, 15 September 2022. These numbers, and more, were drawn from the Japanese Ministry of Finance quarterly reports; 'Yaponiia s fevralia zapretit eksport meditsinskogo oborudovaniia i robotov v Rossiiu', *Vedomosti*, 27 January 2023.

53. Dinakar Peri, 'Philippines inks deal worth $375 million for BrahMos missiles', *The Hindu*, 28 January 2022.

54. 'India complains that Russia isn't delivering weapons it owes because it's throwing everything at Ukraine', *Business Insider*, 24 March 2023.

55. 'The federal customs service predicted an increase in trade turnover with China to $220 billion', *RBC.ru Economics*, 25 October 2023, rbc.ru/economics/25/10/2023/65379a1e9a7947d54437c488.

56. 'China-Russia 2023 trade value hits record high of $240 bln – Chinese customs', *Reuters*, 12 January 2024; 'Tovarooborot RF i Kitaia v 2023 godu dostig rekordnykh $240,11 mlrd', *Kommersant*, 12 January 2024.

57. Vasily Milkin, 'Rossiia pereorientiruet postavki SUG s Evropy na Aziiu', *Vedomosti*, 13 December 2023; 'Bolivia signs $450Mln lithium deal with Russia', *The Moscow Times*, 13 November 2023.

58. 'V Gosdumu peredan proekt federal'nogo biudzheta na 2023–2025 gody', *Kommersant*, 28 September 2022.

59. 'Mishustin poruchil napravit' iz FNB 1 trln rublei na pokrytie defitsita biudzheta v 2022 godu', *Kommersant*, 20 October 2022. The law is included here.

60. 'Russia plans huge defense spending hike in 2004 as war drags', *Bloomberg News*, 22 September 2023; Pavel Luzin, Alexandra Prokopenko, 'Russia's 2024 budget shows it's planning for a long war in Ukraine', *The Moscow Times*, 18 October 2023.

61. On this generally, see Alexander Hill, 'How the Russian economy is defying and withstanding Western sanctions', *The Conversation*, 20 November 2022.

62. 'Zasedanie Soveta po strategicheskomu razvitiiu i natsional'nyi proektam', *Kremlin.ru*, 15 December 2022, kremlin.ru/events/president/news/70086.

63. 'Deviatyi paket sanktsii protiv Rossii: kakimi budut novye organicheniia', *Aktual'nye kommentarii*, 22 November 2022; Essi Lehto, 'EU preparing new Russia sanctions package, von der Leyen says', *Reuters*, 24 November 2022; Jacob Hanke Vela, 'Brussels playbook: Russian oil price cap – Hungary's money – Kosovo woe', *Politico*, 22 November 2022.

64. Ewa Krukowska, Alberto Nardelli, Jorge Valero, 'EU agrees to set $60 price level for Russian oil exports', *Bloomberg*, 2 December 2022; Javier Blas, 'You say price cap, I say speed bump: Let's call the whole thing off', *Bloomberg*, 28 November 2022.

65. Andrei Sapozhnikov, 'V Kremle otkazalis' prinimat' soglasovannyi ES potolok tsen na neft', *Kommersant*, 3 December 2022; Andrei Saposhnikov, 'Postpred Ul'ianov: s etogo goda Evropa budet zhit' bez rossiiskoi nefti', *Kommersant*, 3 December, 2022; 'Russia denounces oil price cap agreed by EU, G7', *The Moscow Times*, 4 December 2022.

66. European Commission, 'Press statement by President von der Leyen on the ninth package of sanctions against Russia', 7 December 2022, ec.europa.eu/commission/presscorner/detail/en/statement_22_7568.

67. Bank Rossii, 'O chem govoriat trendu. Makroekonomika i rynka', *Biulleten*, No. 7, December 2022, p. 3; Dmitriy Grinkevich, Vasiliy Mil'kin, Lyubov Romanova, 'Vlasti podgotovoli tri varianta otveta na potolok tsen na neft, *Vedomosti*, 7 December 2022.

68. Jorge Liboreiro, '"Make Russia pay": EU moves ahead with confiscation of frozen assets, despite legal pitfalls', *Euronews*, 30 November 2022.

69. On this complicated issue, see Agathe Demarais, 'The unintended consequences of seizing Russian assets', *FP* (Foreign Policy), 27 November 2023; Ivan Timofeev, 'Mozhno li sprognozirovat' sanktsii na 2024 god? Da, vpolne', *RSMA* (Rossiiskii sovet po mezhdunaroifnym delam), 6 January 2024; 'Russian assets seized?' *Russia Analytical Report*, 9 January 2024; Dmitry Zhdannikov, Victoria Waldersee, 'Grabbing $300 billions of Russian assets is no panacea, West cautions in Davos', *Geopolitical Monitor*, 17 January 2024.

70. Minami Funakoshi, Hugh Lawson, Kannaki Deka, 'Tracking sanctions against Russia', *Reuters Graphics*, 7 July 2022.

71. 'Rossiisko-kitaiskie peregovory', *Kremlin.ru*, 30 December 2022, kremlin.ru/events/president/news/70303.

72. 'Oreshkin: Kitai oboshel ES po ob'emu torgovli s Rossiei', *Kommersant*, 25 April 2023.

73. 'Rossiia i Turtsiia pristupili k prakticheskoi realizatsii proekta gazovogo khaba', *Vedomosti*, 28 December 2022.

74. Denis Kurenev, 'Putin obsudil s Erdoganom sotrudnichestvo v energetike i Ukrainu', *Vedomosti*, 7 January 2023.

75. Charles Kennedy, 'Russia to boost natural gas supply to Hungary and China', *OilPrice.com*, 23 October 2023.

76. 'Putin bans oil sales to countries abiding by the price cap', *Offshore Energy*, 28 December 2022, offshore-energy.biz/putin-bans-oil-sales-to-countries-abiding-by-the-price-cap/; 'Russia to ban oil exports to countries with price cap', *The Moscow Times*, 28 December 2022.

77. See Tsvetana Paraskova, 'Russia's oil and gas revenues are in decline', *Oilprice.com*, 19 January 2023.

78. Darya Savenkova, 'Rossiia v marta postavila za rubezh rekordnyi ob'em nefteproduktov', *Vedomosti*, 5 April 2023; 'Russian oil exports to India surge 2,200% following European sanctions', *The Moscow Times*, 28 March 2023.

79. Daria Savenkova, Aleksandr Volobuev, 'Rossiiskaia neft' vytesniaet kazakstanskuiu s rynka Uzbekistana', *Vedomosti*, 9 October 2023; Isabel tag, 'Russia begins supplying gas to Uzbekistan via Kazakhstan', *World Pipelines*, 9 October 2023.

80. 'Postavki nefti iz Rossii v Kitai v pervom kvartale 2024 goda vyrosli na 13%, op. cit.

81. 'West lining Putin' coffers with nuclear fuel purchases', *Euronews*, 10 August 2023; 'Putin profits off US, European reliance on Russian nuclear fuel', *VOA*, 10 August 2023.

82. 'Rosatom has contracted . . . in Egypt', *Rosatom*, 8 February 2024, rosatom.ru/journalist/news/-rosatom-zakontraktoval-postavki-komponentov-topliva-dlya-issledovatelskogo-reaktora-v-egipte/; 'Second Belarus unit enters commercial operation', *WNN: World Nuclear News*, 2 November 2023; Lloyd Doggett, 'Russia's rosatom fuels Putin's war machine', *FP*, 9 April 2024.

83. See, 'How the war affects the Eurasian Economic Union', *Russian Analytical Digest*, No. 287, 30 October 2022.

84. 'Zasedanie Vysshego Evraziiskogo ekonomicheskogo soveta', *Kremlin.ru*, 9 December 2022, kremlin.ru/events/president/news/70058; Il'ia Lakstygal, 'Putin podvel itogi 2022 goda dlia EAES', *Vedomosti*, 10 December 2022.

85. Erdni Kagaltynov, 'Kazakhstan vvet sistemu monitoringa dlia predotvrashcheniia obkhoda sanktsii protiv Rossii', *Kommersant*, 23 March 2023; Joanna Lillis, 'Kazakhstan is ready to strengthen the verification of goods re-exported to Russia', *Eurasianet*, 22 March 2023.

86. 'Shanghai cooperation organization establishes economic cooperation zones', *Silk Road Briefing*, 16 June 2022.

87. 'FNB v ianvare umen'shilsia na 42,7 mlrd rub.', *Kommersant*, 5 February 2024.

88. 'Uroven' kadrovogo goloda v promyshlennosti ustanovil novyi rekord', *RBC.ru*, 3 August 2023, rbc.ru/economics/03/08/2023/64ca54369a7947ee430b0975?from=from_main_3; 'Russian factories face record labor shortages', *The Moscow Times*, 4 August 2023.

89. Anastasia Larina, 'Putin poruchil uvelichivat' MROT v 2023 godu vyshe urovnia infliatsii', *Kommersant*, 27 January 2023; 'Soveshchanie po ekonomicheskim voprosam', *Kremlin.ru*, 17 January 2023, kremlin.ru/events/president/news/70364.

90. Bank Rossii, 'Bank Rossii prinial reshenie sokhranit' kliuchevuiu stavku na urovne 7,50% godovykh', 9 June 2023, cbr.ru/press/pr/?id=39422; Bank of Russia, 'Bank of Russia increased key rate by 100 b.p., to 8.5% p.a.', 21 July 2023, cbr.ru/eng

/press/keypr/; Zahra Tayeb, 'Russian inflation is raging at 60%, not the reported 3.6%, thanks to the ruble's freefall", top economist Steve Hanke says', *Business Insider*, 24 July 2023.

91. Dmity Butrin, 'Avgust vzial rublem. Bank Rossii podnimet kliuchevuiu stavku dlia predotvrashcheniia chasto kursovoi paniki', *Kommersant*, 14 August 2023; 'Russia raises interest rate 20 134% amid inflation concerns', *The Moscow Times*, 15 September 2023.

92. 'Russia's wartime budget', *The Bell*, 30 September 2023.

93. 'Glava TsB Nabiullina zaiavila o skorom zavershenii tsikla povysheniia stavki', *Kommersant*, 15 December 2023.

94. Alberto Nardelli, 'EU sanctions aim to make banks divulge frozen Russian assets', *Bloomberg* 14 February 2023; 'EU to hit Russia with trade bans and tech export controls worth €11bn', *Financial Times*, 15 February 2023; 'Russia in review, Feb 10–17, 2023 – 4 things to know', *Russia Matters*, 20 February 2023.

95. US State Department, 'The United States imposes additional sweeping costs on Russia', Antony J. Blinken, *Press Statement*, 24 February 2023, state.gov/the-united-states-imposes-additional-sweeping-costs-on-russia/.

96. Government of Canada, Global Affairs, 'Canadian sanctions related to Russia', 9 March 2023, international.gc.ca/world-monde/international-relations-relations-internationales/sanctions/russia-russie.aspx?lang-eng.

97. 'Rossiisko-kitaiskie peregovory', *Kremlin.ru*, 21 March 2023, kremlin.ru/events/president/news/70748; 'Putin zaiavil o gotovnosti Rossii perekhodit' na iuani v torgovle s drugimi stranam', *Kommersant*, 21 March 2023.

98. 'Prezident Rossii i Predsedatel' KNR sdeli zaiavleniia dlia pressy', *Kremlin.ru*, 21 March 2023, kremlin.ru/events/president/news/70750.

99. Yaroslav Kostenko, Anastasia Boikpo, 'Pochemu Rosstat fiksiruet rekordno nizkuiu besrabotitsu i rost zarplat', *Vedomosti*, 31 March 2023.

100. Alexandra Prokopenka, 'Russia has too few workers', *The Bell*, 24 March 2023; 'Rabotnik dvadtsatipiatiletiia', *Kommersant*, 24 April 2023.

101. 'Russian airlines import $1.2Bln worth of Western parts despite sanction – Reuters', *The Moscow Times*, 23 August 2023.

102. '"AvtoVAZ" sovmestno s kitaitsami v 2024 godu zapustit sborku novykh modelei Lada', *Vedomosti*, 2 June 2024.

103. Anastasia Maier, Valeriia Merkulova, 'Vladimir Putin predlozhil vsem chinovnikam peresest' s inomarok na otechestvennye avtomobili', *Vedomosti*, 4 August 2023.

104. Zinya alfiti, 'Russia faces new sanctions to foil its effort to get around the old ones', *Markets Insider*, 14 April 2023; Phil Rosen, 'Russia's economy is worse than Moscow claims because military spending covers up how much the private sector is shrinking', *Markets Insider*, 13 April 2023; Zinya Salfiti, 'Russia's economy is hurting – and a new wave of EU sanctions aimed at crippling its "war machine" are coming. Here are 6 key developments in the past week', *Business Insider*, 16 April 2023.

105. David McHugh, 'Companies find that leaving Russia is not so simple', *Globe and Mail*, 26 May 2023; Kirill Ponomarev, '"Almost nothing had changed"; Anti-war Russians risk first trips home since invasion', *The Moscow Times*, 28 May 2023.

106. Minfin Rossii, 'Zakonoproekt o naloge na sverkhpribyl' dlia krupnykh kompanii odobren na zasedanii Praviteles'tva RF', 13 June 2023, minfin.gov.ru/ru/press-center/?id_4=38522-zakonoproekt_o_naloge_na_sverkhpribyl_dlya_krupnykh_kompanii_odobren_na_zasedanii_pravitelstva_rf; Huilen Tan, 'Russia has lost so much money due to the Ukraine war that it's now trying to raise $4 billion by slapping a windfall tax on its oligarchs', *Business Insider*, 14 June 2023.

107. 'Delovaya programma', *SPIEF*, accessed 14 June 2023, forumspb.com/programme/business-programme/?t=days&day=1&ref=en.thebell.io; 'The "Russian Davos" will debate "traditional values" and how to return Russians who fled abroad', *The Bell*, 7 June 2023.

108. 'Plenarnoe zasedanie Peterburgskogo mezhdunarodnogo ekonomicheskogo foruma', *Kremlin.ru*, 16 June 2023, kremlin.ru/events/president/news/71445.

109. 'Itogi PMEF-2023', *Kommersant*, 17 June 2023.

110. 'Kto prishel na PMEF', *Vedomosti*, 15 June 2023.

111. See the Forum's website: forumvostok.ru/en/about-the-forum/.

112. 'Chislo del po iskam prokurorov ob iz'iatii chastnykh aktivov previsylo 55', *RBC.ru*, 20 December 2023.

113. 'Plenarnoe zasedanie Vos'mogo Vostochnogo ekonomicheskogo foruma', *Kremlin.ru*, 12 September 2023, kremlin.ru/events/president/news/72259

114. Alexandra Prokopenko, 'How sanctions have changed Russian economic policy', *The Moscow Times*, 14 April 2023.

115. 'Economic "momentum" prompts IMF to raise Russia's growth forecast', *The Moscow Times*, 11 April 2023; see also Konstantin Sonin, 'Russia's road to economic Ruin', *Foreign Affairs*, 18 November 2022.

116. European Commission, 'Press statement by President von der Leyen with Ukrainian president Zelenskyy', 9 May 2023, ec.europa.eu/commission/presscorner/detail/en/statement_23_2661.

117. 'Evrosoiuz vvel sanktsii protiv "Alrosy"', *Vedomosti*, 3 January 2024; 'EU adds Alrosa and its CEO to sanctions list', *mining.com*, 3 January 2024; Alexandra Brzozowski, 'EU adds Russia's biggest diamond producer Alrosa to sanctions list', *Euractiv*, 3 January 2024.

118. On this, see Zahra Tayeb, 'Russia's economy has gone from bad to worse in a matter of months: Here's where the country is feeling pain the most', *Business Insider*, 16 July 2023.

119. 'Bloomberg billionaires index as of August 31, 2023', bloomberg.com/billionaires/, accessed 1 September 2023; 'Chislo rossiiskikh milliarderov vyroslo do rekordnykh 125 chelovek', *Forbes*, Russian edition, 2 April 2024.

120. 'Updated: Illuminating Russia's shadow fleet', *Windward*, accessed 30 June 2024.

121. Jack Schickler, 'EU policy: EU Russian sanctions stymied by complexity, poor enforcement', *euronews.business.com*, 20 November 2023; Alberto Nardellio, John Ainger, 'Some EU nations push to weaken Russian sanctions enforcement plan', *Bloomberg*, 25 November 2023; Georgy Kutuzov, 'Rossiiskie metallurgi na 40% uvelichili eksport chuguna v ES', *Vedomosti*, 27 November 2023.

122. Official Journal of the European Union, 'Council implementing regulations (EU) 2023/2875 of 18 December 2023', eur-lex.europa.eu/legal-content/EN/TXT/PDF/?uri=OJ:L_202302875.

123. Paola Tamma, 'EU agrees to set aside profits from frozen Russian assets', *Financial Times*, 29 January 2024; Vasily Tulupov, 'Sammit ES utverdil plan konfikatsii dokhodov ot zamorozhennykh aktivov Rossii', *Vedomosti*, 1 February 2024.

124. 'Russian exports to Europe down two-thirds in 2023', *Barron's*, 12 February 2024; 'Profitsit torgovogo balansa RF v 2023 godu upal na 58,5%', *Kommersant*, 12 February 2023.

125. 'Russia's wheat export pace overtakes 2021's despite challenges', *Fastmarkets*, 5 January 2023; Bartosz Brzezinski, 'Russia is winning the global grain war', *Politico*, 19 March 2024.

126. 'Rossiia v proshedshem sel'khozgodu eksportirovala rekordnye 69 mln toni zerna', *Kommersant*, 7 July 2023.

127. On this, see Stephen K. Wegren, 'Russia's not-so-secure food security', *Problems of Post-Communism*, 8 March 2023, On-line.

128. 'Administratsiia Paninskogo munitsipal'nogo raiona', *VK* (*VKontakte*), 20 August 2023, vk.com/panino_adm?w=wall-184508709_475; 'Russian region partially sealed off over anthrax outbreak', *The Moscow Times*, 21 August 2023.

Chapter 9

War of Words
Creating Young Patriots

In introducing a report on freedom of expression in post-Euromaidan Ukraine, chair of the PEN International Writers in Prison Committee Salil Tripathi wrote:

> In the fog of war, information gets distorted and misrepresented; lies are represented as truth, and assertions are made as facts. The one who controls the airwaves controls the discourse. Information becomes a valuable commodity, part of psychological warfare, deployed as a weapon, with the aim of undermining the spirit and will of the Other.[1]

These truths held fast in both the build-up to and the conduct of Putin's 'special military operation', the euphemism that the Kremlin used for the first two years of its aggressive war in Ukraine. Fabrications are by no means limited to statements from Moscow, though Russia wallows in them. All concerned governments have been blame-casting, fact-ducking and otherwise misinforming their citizenry in matters related to Ukraine since 2014. From February 2022, a war of words to encourage troops and citizens, inculcate patriotism at home and blacken the reputation of the enemy has intensified on both sides of the front line. Events are misrepresented, 'kills' are overestimated and the other side's successes are underestimated. Allies and associate countries aid and abet their 'side' with hyperbole to the extent that when the truth is told, it is not believed.[2]

To be sure, the distribution of false information about current events in Ukraine is asymmetrical, with Russia the top-heavy storyteller. This chapter deals primarily with Russian propaganda and self-deception, but the fact that all protagonists misinform their respective audiences in times of war should not go unmentioned. Deceits manufactured during a conflict may well determine the nature of the settlement when, and if, it comes.

In present day wartime falsehoods can reach much wider audiences than they could when, in 1928, Sir Arthur Ponsonby wrote that 'when war is declared, truth is the first casualty'.[3] Unprecedented mass communications technology now allows the distribution of both sophisticated and crude propaganda widely, quickly and believably. Protagonists pass on disinformation to receptive audiences with impunity, hoping that some, much or all of it will stick.

It is not always easy to keep false narratives consistent, and Russian state propaganda sometimes has had a hard time keeping up with events. For example, when in September 2022 the Ukrainian breakthrough in Kharkiv exposed untruths spouted by Russia's state-controlled media about Russian forces 'liberating' the area, state propagandists had to scramble to explain an obvious defeat. Prominent TV analyst Vladimir Solovyov went so far as to insist that Russia's losses were to American and British soldiers masquerading as Ukrainian soldiers. State media found it easier, however, simply to ignore the losses and focus instead on Russian military 'successes', namely missile strikes against Ukrainian infrastructure.[4]

As Ukrainian forces sustained their first counter-offensive, a Russian parliamentarian raged on television that Russia should launch nuclear strikes against the UK and Germany. His host suggested, jokingly one would hope, that a nuclear bomb on the UK during the Queen's funeral would be most effective because 'all the best people are there'. The host, Olga Skabeeva, appeared to agree with legislator Andrei Gurulyov that Russia could turn the UK into a 'Martian desert' with nuclear bombs. Joke or nor, there were no public persons left in Russia who dared to take umbrage at such outlandish commentary.[5]

As the tide turned somewhat on the battlefield, Russian state propaganda adopted a new tone. During a talk show televised on Rossiia 1, 28 November 2022, *RT*'s Simonyan justified Russia's continued strikes against Ukraine's infrastructure as 'the only thing we can do in this situation', implying that Russia might lose otherwise. Presenting Russia as victim, she proclaimed that 'God knows we didn't want this,' insisting that Russians are 'kind, polite and at times meek, . . . we are such softies, we are so kind. But should we be?' Her reference here was an apparently sarcastic one about unnamed members of Russia's 'higher circles' who, she said, were terrified of what The Hague would do to Russia if it lost the war. Such bombing 'every day' was necessary, she contended, because Ukraine was trying to take territory that is 'now ours'. Other state mouthpieces on the panel agreed with her.[6] This extraordinarily perverse vision of affairs was symptomatic of what Russian TV viewers absorb every day.

The number of topics made taboo in Russia grew exponentially as the war went on. Within weeks of the invasion, Putin signed a law forbidding all media from printing or airing what it called false information ('discrediting') about the armed forces. We have seen that among those 'falsehoods' were references to the SVO as a 'war' or an 'invasion'.[7] The list grew much longer on 4 November 2022, when the FSB issued an order banning public discussion of unclassified matters in a way that the information could be 'used by foreign states, organizations and citizens against Russia's security'. That order forbade public discussion of the structure and size of Russia's armed forces, its weapons, finances, deployments, morale, crimes, mobilization and civil defence, Roscosmos news, among others – in all 60 topics. Anyone sharing such information could be designated a 'foreign agent'. The law came into force on 1 December 2022, at the same time that the expanded 'foreign agent' label came into effect.[8]

Not surprisingly, in May 2023, Reporters Without Borders ranked Russia 164th of 180 countries in its annual world press freedom rankings. This drop of nine places from its 2022 rating was based on 'systemic censorship and the forced exodus of independent Russian and foreign outlets'.[9] True enough. The mainstream media in Russia was by that time exclusively an agency for disseminating information approved by the state. Ukraine was ranked seventy-ninth.

IMAGES OF THE ENEMY

Whatever the accuracy of Western image-making of Ukraine and Zelensky as the heroic 'good guys' and of Russia and Putin as the evil 'bad guys', such labelling leaves lasting impressions on their audiences. Zelensky appeared on the cover of *Time* magazine in January 2023 as 'Person of the Year' for 2022, and in December that latter year the European Parliament awarded the Sakharov Prize for Freedom of Thought to the people of Ukraine for their resistance to the Russian invasion. Imprisoned Russian dissident, Aleksei Navalny, earned the same cover image for January 2022 and also the Sakharov Prize for 2021. On the other hand, Putin as successor to the tsars, Lenin and Stalin, is an old cover story. Dark images of him have graced covers in the West since his very first year as Russia's president, repeatedly, on such widely read magazines as *Time, The Economist, Der Spiegel* and *Newsweek*.

Even as Russians came to see Putin as their saviour from the terrible 1990s, Western media looked for nits to pick. In later years, but still long before the crisis in Ukraine, they tended to turn to the most obvious Putinophobes for panel discussions to help shape their readers' impressions of Russia, often portraying it as a dictatorship about to implode. This practice was exemplified in January 2023, when the prestigious American quarterly, *Foreign Affairs,* published an essay by leaders of the pack, Garri Kasparov and Mikhail Khodorkovsky, who urged Biden to provide Ukraine with tanks and long-range weaponry. Putin, they said, was 'living on borrowed time' and 'if the West holds firm, Putin's regime will likely collapse in the near future'.[10] There was always much truth in their analyses, but they also suffered from some convenient amnesia driven by wishful thinking.

At any rate, it was not difficult for Putin and his team to persuade Russians that they were surrounded by a collective West preparing to denounce and pounce. In the case of Ukraine, the long-standing divisions between its majority ethnic Ukrainian and minority ethnic Russian citizens were greatly aggravated by the domestic political crisis of 2014 in Kyiv, Russia's annexation of Crimea, civil war in the Donbas, and the 'special military operation' in 2022, the latter of which a culmination of the earlier events. The West plays down, or even ignores, the fact that nationalists in Kyiv worked assiduously to suppress the Russian language and culture in Ukraine, thereby fuelling one of the storylines used by Putin to justify the SVO. The West shrugs off the prominent roles played in the 2014 and subsequent events in Kyiv by the neo-Nazi *Praviy sektor* (Right Sector) and its leader, Dmytro Yarosh, the political party *Svoboda* and extremist volunteer groups, such as the Azov Battalion. They saw nothing wrong with US and EU diplomats mingling with and openly supporting the Euromaidans, but would have been apoplectic if Russian diplomats were seen cheering on the mobs that surrounded Washington's Capitol Building in 2021. The Kremlin plays these incidents up.

Even after 20 months of war, Speaker of the State Duma, Volodin, used the eightieth anniversary of the liberation of Ukraine from German occupiers to complain that 'Nazi ideology has again become the state ideology of Ukraine' and pointed to the canonization in modern day Ukraine of Stepan Bandera, a Ukrainian nationalist who committed atrocities against Poles and Jews as an ally of Hitler in World War II.[11]

The Kremlin's team cherry-picks past and recent history to find justifications for present-day actions. Putin returned to this theme in December 2023, when in a reply to a journalist's question he said that the elevation of Bandera to 'national hero' in Ukraine was a manifestation of lingering Nazism, making de-Nazification still a Russian goal.[12] No matter how thin this oft-repeated rationalization was, it appeared to have been absorbed by its intended audience, the Russian people. Conflating the government in Kyiv and historic Nazism has been common practice by the Kremlin since the referendum in Crimea of 2014.

By framing the conflict that way, authorities nurture domestic perceptions of the SVO as a means to protect Russian identity and its historical legacies.

The Great Patriotic War analogy presented by history clubs and associations, and in school textbooks, documentary films, speeches and large public posters, encourage patriotism at all levels and render dissent more difficult on the ground.[13]

The most lasting personifications of permanent international division came just as the first full year of war wound down. Biden's quick visit to Kyiv on 19–20 February 2023 was marked by a resounding speech in which he talked of the war as a defence of democracy. Just hours later, Putin said in his annual address to the Federal Assembly that the war was a matter of defending Russian traditional values, and nationhood, against a collective West.[14] Battle lines in the war of words were set.

Meanwhile, according to the independent paper *Kholod* (Cold) in September 2023, the Kremlin ramped up its word-taboo campaign by requiring Russia's state-controlled media to no longer refer to Zelensky as 'president' of Ukraine; rather, they should use such terms as the 'Zelensky regime'.[15] As the Putinist version of events narrowed, independent observers could only wonder when, or if, public acquiescence might shift to scepticism and from there to disbelief.

The Kremlin's war against words accelerated throughout 2023, spreading far beyond phrases that appeared to re-define the SVO to prohibitions levelled against anything written or filmed that highlighted the LGBT community. In December, for example, major publishing house and booksellers suspended the printing and sales of well-known authors, such as Dmitry Bykov and Akunin, for their outspoken criticisms of the war even when their works of fiction or poetry had nothing to do with current affairs. AST Publishing House issued a statement that told the tale: 'Public statements by writers that have caused widespread public outcry require legal assessment. Until the situation is clarified, the release and shipment of books will not be resumed'.[16] There was no noticeable public outcry against this recommendation.

By that time, too, both sides were accusing the other of various forms of 'genocide'.

Putin as Hitler

Demonized in the West long before he initiated his war against Ukraine in 2022, Putin became the object of accelerated attempts to find commonalities between him and the Nazi leader. A popular derogatory sobriquet for Putin introduced by the CPRF as early as 2009, when it served as a real opposition voice, 'Putler', was taken up by Ukrainians and soon appearing on placards, posters and even T-shirts in the West.[17]

Whether or not serious analogies can be drawn between Putin and Hitler, it is true that the Kremlin's reliance on anti-Western conspiracy theories during the war created an ideological move further to the right throughout Russian society. A citizenry already susceptible to the notions that their country was surrounded by enemies and that the West was forever trying to weaken Russia by such phenomena as colour revolutions, cultural pornography and proxy wars, had been conditioned by 70 years of CPSU rule. Although important change was initiated during the Gorbachev era in the late 1980s, old impulses die hard. The resurgence of American 'exceptionalism', Western triumphalism and indifference to Russia's legitimate security interests in the 1990s helped keep the distrust alive, or at least gave Putin's propagandists gratuitous fodder to play with.

That entire Yeltsin decade, which many in the West wrongly see as one in which the seeds of democracy were sewn in Russia, was a time of wild and open corruption on a grand scale during which newly minted Russian capitalists looted the country's assets and the 'shock therapy' recommended by Western economists plunged 40 per cent of its population into poverty. It wasn't difficult for nationalists to persuade Russians that the horrors of the 1990s were by-products of Western liberalism. The expansion of NATO eastward merely served as further 'proof' that the West, and especially Washington, wanted to keep Russia weak and degraded. True or false, it is the perception that counts. Putin did not have to look hard to find home-grown fountainheads of distrust of the West.

The move to the right was by no means unique to Russia, for it had become a global phenomenon long before Russian invaded Ukraine. In Russia, however, the state's barrage of top-down propaganda underscoring patriotism, family 'values' and defence of Russian 'tradition', and sometimes a Russian 'civilization' (Russkiy mir), created an anti-liberal atmosphere that is not likely to fade very much after the war fighting ends. Recall that Lavrov began speaking of Russia as a 'state-civilization' in mid-2023. Earlier, Medvedev referred to the West as 'satanic' and Patriarch Kirill resurrected the 'Third Rome' doctrine and the idea that Russia had a mission 'to defend and spread its traditional values and spirituality in the world'. These notions were returned to Russian school curricula in September 2023.[18]

To be sure, there are thousands of Russians, perhaps millions, who think progressively, but their leading spokespeople have fled the country, reside in prison, or are compelled to keep quiet. Government repression, snitching and public shaming leave long-lasting scars and personalized enmities, especially when oppositionists have no forums left in which to voice their opinions openly.[19] Moreover, Russians are like people everywhere – they believe what they want to believe, and reject uncomfortable information.[20]

Atrocity Stories

Repeated stories about Russian soldiers raping women, boys and grannies, and torturing prisoners, filled the Ukrainian air waves, as did the more realistic charges that Russian organizations were kidnapping Ukrainian children, taking them to Russia and sending them out for adoption. Many of the horror stories were picked up and repeated without much questioning by the Western media. More cautious about fabricating tales of Ukrainian atrocities, perhaps because it did not wish to scare off recruits, Russian TV denigrated everything else Ukrainian instead, often referring to Ukraine as an unnatural country whose modern borders were created by the Red Army in 1945, and by Khrushchev in 1954. The Russian media was by no means free of atrocity tales, however: one presenter for *RT* was suspended after he claimed to have advocated 'drowning or burning' Ukrainian children who saw Russia as an occupying power in the 1980s. He also joked about Russian soldiers raping appreciative 'grannies'. Even Simonyan called the remarks 'wild and disgusting'.[21]

When confronted with stories of brutalities that could not be readily verified, each side spun them against its enemy. For example, after dozens of recently called-up Russian troops surrendered in Luhansk, accounts of their plight and complaints about lack of training, weapons and food when they were recruited leaked back into Russia via Telegram, with photos. Versions issued by Ukraine's foreign ministry went to Twitter, YouTube, TikTok and other outlets. The Ukrainian side used the photos and unverifiable complaints to demonstrate how badly the Russian MoD treated its conscripted soldiers. The Russian side used the same photos to demonstrate how harshly Ukrainian forces treated its prisoners.[22]

That doesn't mean that atrocity stories were not true – many were. Russian soldiers left a trail of brutal acts behind them as they withdrew from Kherson, and Prigozhin approved the execution by sledgehammer of a purported deserter from the Wagner Group. The victim, a convicted felon recruited from prison, had been taken prisoner by Ukrainian forces, was videoed by them saying bad things about conditions in the Russian army (and Wagner), and was then sent back as part of a prisoner exchange, to his death.[23] Nonetheless, without verification some of the atrocity stories served politicians with an excuse for public posturing and journalists with eye-catching headlines.

There was no need to feign horror when information about barbarisms at Bucha began seeping out. Photographs and videos of graves and bodies discovered after Russian forces were driven out of a city they had captured during the first march towards Kyiv shocked the world. Evidence of massive civilian casualties and deaths, tortured Ukrainian POWs, summary executions and first-hand stories of rapes and beatings were verified by the UN

High Commissioner for Human Rights. Russian officials denied the obvious and called substantiation of the atrocities 'fake news', or even 'false flag' operations, and the subject was placed off limits in Russia.

In other cases, videos shown on Ukrainian TV to demonstrate their forces capturing and appearing to kill Russian troops were claimed by Moscow to be films of Russian prisoners of war 'massacred' by Ukrainian forces. The UN promised an investigation; the State Duma adopted a resolution in which it labelled the alleged executioners 'Ukrainian Nazis' and called on the West to condemn the act.[24] The *New York Times*, which authenticated the videos, called them 'grisly' but could not confirm the circumstances under which the soldiers were killed. 'Ultimately', it said, 'they leave a mystery that had been used by both sides in the online battle for hearts and minds'.[25]

The issue of atrocities came up again in March 2023, when the UN Human Rights Monitoring Mission in Ukraine stated that it was 'deeply concerned' about reports of summary executions of prisoners of war by both Russian and Ukrainian forces on the battlefield. In this instance, head of mission, Matilda Bogner, said her mission had documented evidence of 25 Russian and 15 Ukrainian POWs executed by their captors. She also referenced numerous cases of 'enforced disappearances' and acts of sexual violence committed by both sides, though Russian forces were guilty in greater numbers.[26] A week later, the UN High Commissioner for Human Rights, Volker Türk, told the UN that more than half of the Russian POWs were 'subjected to torture or ill-treatment' while in Ukrainian hands. He added that UN officials reported cases of executions of prisoners by Ukrainian armed forces, and said that many civilians also suffered torture and sexual violence at the hands of Ukrainian personnel, and that 91 cases of enforced disappearances and arbitrary detentions were recorded.[27] These data failed to attract the attention of Western media. The point here is not that the blame attribution is symmetrical, rather, it is that there are lots of kettles calling lots of pots black.

On the other hand, when videos circulated in April purporting to show Russian soldiers cutting off the head of a Ukrainian prisoner of war the world was rightly horrified. Oddly, this and other such grizzly videos were distributed first by pro-war bloggers in Russia who revelled in such acts, among them Vladislav Pozdyankov, founder of the aggressively misogynist hate group Male State (Muzhkoe gosudarstvo) that was labelled 'extremist' by the Kremlin in 2021. Although his group was banned, Pozdyankov maintained a channel on Telegram on which at least one of these horror videos appeared. Kyiv was able to exploit the unauthenticated videos as if they were true, as some but likely not all presumably were, while the Western media spread the stories and Peskov called them fake.[28]

Still, drone footage has shown Russian soldiers executing surrendering prisoners in the Bakhmut, Zaporizhia and Avdiivka theatres.[29]

Adding to the babble, both sides make a habit of exaggerating the number of military deaths they inflict on the other side. For example, on 4 December 2022 the Ukrainian General Staff announced that its Armed Forces had 'eliminated' about 91,150 Russian 'invaders' since the beginning of the war. Two days later, Shoigu told an MoD conference that Russia's Armed Forces had killed 8,300 Ukrainian 'militants' in the month of November alone. They both listed huge numbers of tanks, aircraft and other enemy weaponry they had destroyed.[30] Most of these numbers were treated with scepticism by professional military analysts.

Similar messages appeared in 2023. We have seen that in October that year the Ukrainian General Staff claimed on Facebook that Russia's military personnel death toll since February 2022 surpassed 300,000 (see table 3.1), while materiel destruction included over 5,000 tanks, 320 aircraft, 324 helicopters and much more. With no means for verification, these numbers seem hyperbolic.[31] The Russian MoD exaggerated Ukrainian losses in military personnel and materiel one battle at a time, perhaps not wanting to alert Russians to natural conclusions about the scale of civilian lives lost and civilian centres destroyed. By October, the MoD still had not released new numbers of its own dead and wounded, though in July that year reports from *Mediazona* and *Meduza* placed the total at around 50,000.[32]

Studies by researchers with the European Consortium for Political Research (ECPR) concluded that, while Russia suffered a much higher toll of military deaths (excluding civilians), both sides overestimated their opponents' losses. Numbers are manipulated to shape public opinion, raise troop morale and persuade allies of their effectiveness in battle.[33] As it ever was.

Russia Changes Its Message

Regular pronouncements from the Russian MoD and the Kremlin about Russia's military successes and Ukraine's fatal weaknesses came up against harsh reality in late April, early May 2023. A leaked set of guidelines produced by the Kremlin for journalists revealed that the Russian leadership believed that an impending Ukrainian counter-offensive might be effective. The media was told how it should treat that possibility. Firstly, the Ukrainian offensive should not be underestimated, because it has full NATO support and, secondly, whatever triumphs Ukrainian forces might achieve should be played down as modest. The change in approach was marked as well by ever-increasing declarations that Russia's Armed Forces were defending their 'state civilization' against NATO and the collective West.

The media were told also not to mention how much reconstruction in occupied territories might cost in terms of government budgeting for schools, healthcare, science and social benefits. In short, the Kremlin was laying the groundwork for explaining further military and economic hardships to the Russian public; that is, as part of its defence against attacks from the West, with emphasis upon NATO and the US.[34]

State-controlled distributors of information began highlighting anniversaries of moments in recent history when 'Nazis' ran amok in Ukrainian cities, such as the 'Odesa massacre' of 2 May 2014, when an anti-Yanukovych mob urged on by the *Praviy sektor* forced opponents of the Maidan into Odesa's Trade Union building and burned them to death. Because no one was punished and the Poroshenko government refused to act on evidence about known perpetrators in this and other such incidents in 2014, the Kremlin laid blame on 'Nazism' in Kyiv.[35] Going further, Putin even cast doubt on Zelensky's Jewishness, and accused 'Western curators' of placing 'an ethnic Jew' in office so as to cover up a genocide of Ukraine's native Russia speakers.[36]

The Kremlin continued to question Ukraine's very existence as an independent state. It was Medvedev who was most active in resurrecting and highlighting this old Russian trope. Exclaiming on Telegram that 'Ukraine is the Sannikov Land founded by Lenin. Was not for long and disappeared from the map. There is no such land. Whatever they think in the West and in the occupied Russian city of Kyiv'. Equating Ukraine with a ghost island purported to once have existed in the Arctic Ocean, Medvedev stated that the borders demanded by Zelensky, that is, those of 1991, were actually 'borders of regions of Russia and once the provinces of the Russian Empire, and not mythical Ukraine'. Russia's citizenry, battered by waves of historical propaganda, may well have believed Medvedev's extremes, or have become numbed into indifference to them.[37]

The official narrative was recapped in varying forms on a daily basis by Russia's presidential administration (Peskov) and the Ministry of Foreign Affairs (Zakharova), who also consistently characterized attacks on Russian soil by Ukrainian operatives or regular forces as 'terrorist' acts. Given that Russian forces were pounding targets all over Ukraine, Western commentators wondered at the hypocrisy of such labelling, forgetting that Russian government spokespersons were speaking above all to a Russian audience, not to the West. Since the official narrative continued to treat the war as a 'special military operation', it could not describe drone and other attacks on Russian soil as acts of war. The Kremlin's messengers were trapped by their own falsehoods.

Apparently, however, a huge percentage of the population (circa 40 per cent) still was not paying much attention even as late as the end of October 2023. Over 60 per cent of respondents to a Levada Centre survey thought the SVO was progressing successfully (21 per cent thought not), and the original reasons for the SVO still held, though not very firmly: 25 per cent believed that Putin launched the 'operation' to protect Russians in the Donbas; 14 per cent that it was to eradicate fascism and Nazism in Ukraine. Only 13 per cent believed that the SVO's main purpose was to defend Russia from Western and Ukrainian aggression, 10 per cent believed that the purpose of the SVO was to return historical Russian lands and people to Russia; and a few (6 percent) blamed NATO in a variety of ways.[38]

The Kremlin amended its war rhetoric again shortly after Putin's successful presidential election, when Peskov finally labelled the war a war. Mounting casualties, the militarization of the economy and accelerating indoctrination in schools, the arts and media rendered references to a 'special military operation' obsolete.

OPPOSITION MEDIA FIND NEW HOMES

We have seen that pressure against opposition media accelerated quickly after the SVO was launched, and stamping contrary attitudes out altogether became government policy. Russian entities and individuals registered as 'foreign agents' were coerced into an uneasy silence, muted by legislation against alleged fake (feik) news, and charged with 'disrespect' for the military. Critical media were forced to shut down or move abroad. Entire Russian news outlets, such as *Mediazona, Meduza, The Moscow Times* and iStories joined *Novaia Gazeta Evropa* and the TV channel *Dozhd* on the 'foreign agents' registry, but continued to feed accounts of the war and domestic politics to Russian audiences via social media from outside the country. It is not known how many Russians accessed them, but those that did risked punishments from the state and anger on the part of their neighbours. Information about atrocities could reach Russians only from illicit sources, among them *Mediazona,* which continued to spread harsh indictments of Putin in Russia via YouTube.[39]

Mediazona's founders, feminist activists Pussy Riot, were among the loudest voices raging against Putin from outside the country. They explained themselves to Russians on 24 December 2022 as follows: 'The music of our anger, indignation, disagreement, a reproachful desperate cry against Putin's bloodthirsty puppets, led by a real cannibal monster, whose place is in the infinity of fierce hellish flames on the bones of the victims of this terrible war'.[40] This YouTube video featured the horrors committed at Bucha and culminated with one member of the band, masked, relieving herself on a portrait of Putin.

In November 2023, Pussy Riot released another musical video harshly criticizing Russia's wartime propaganda and calling for the release of Ukrainian children, all to the tune of Chaikovsky's Swan Lake. At that time, the troupe was on month-long tour of North America, starting in Montreal and ending in Brooklyn, New York.⁴¹ While they were there, member Lyudmila (Lucy) Shtein was arrested in absentia for spreading 'fake news' about the Russian military. She had been living in Lithuania and has applied for citizenship in Iceland.⁴²

In spite of multiple obstacles, opposition views from abroad filtered through. *Novaia Gazeta Evropa's* Russian-language edition retained a small audience at home and *Dozhd* claimed to have 14 million unique viewers in Russia and up to 22 million worldwide. Both outlets operated out of Latvia. *Dozhd*'s audience rose quickly after the announcement of partial mobilization because, its editor-in-chief said, thousands of Russians who were indifferent to the war suddenly found it closer to home. If these and other cries from the wilderness were heard by only a few in Russia, they at least provided forums around which the diaspora could unite.

Presidential Sniping

The war of words between Moscow and Washington was encapsulated in orations delivered by Putin and Biden. In a speech of 21 September 2022, purportedly to offer reasons for the forthcoming referendums in occupied Ukraine and the partial mobilization, Putin opened with a standard, if already tired, explication for the 'war' itself; that is, 'to liberate it [the Donbas] from the neo-Nazi regime that seized power in Ukraine in 2014 as a result of an armed coup'. He proceeded from there to blame everything on the collective West led by the United States that was trying 'to weaken, divide and ultimately destroy our country'. His list of villainies orchestrated by the West was long, and included 'gangs of international terrorists in the Caucasus', ever-expanding NATO infrastructure 'close to our borders', cultivating 'hatred for Russia, primarily in Ukraine', and turning the Ukrainian people into cannon fodder to be used against Russia.⁴³

A few hours after Putin's soliloquy, Biden addressed the 77th Session of the UN General Assembly. Opening with an immediate reference to 'a brutal, needless war – a war chosen by one man, to be very blunt', he went on to name Putin who, he said, 'shamelessly violated the core tenets of the United Nations Charter' by invading a neighbouring country. Biden's list of 'outrageous acts' was also a long one and included sham referendums, attacks on schools, railways and hospitals. The war, Biden continued,

> is about extinguishing Ukraine's right to exist as a state, plain and simple, and the right of Ukrainians to exist as a people. He repeated the Washington refrain that the war is about freedom vs. tyranny and accused Putin of making 'overt nuclear threats against Europe and a reckless disregard for the responsibilities of the non-proliferation regime'.⁴⁴

These presidential images of the enemy were now carved in stone.

The Kremlin's war of words was also predictable. Every act of destruction committed by Russian forces in Ukraine was explained in Moscow by some version of 'the West/NATO made me do it'. All evidence to the contrary, Russia continued to insist that it targeted only military-related sites. Each side proclaimed that it was winning or would win the war. The Kremlin carried on referring to the Ukrainian leadership as Nazis, and Ukrainian territory as historically Russian.

The Prigozhin affair prompted a break in the Western storyline, temporarily shifting it to speculation about Putin's future and hopeful revisions in their image of him as a strongman. Kyiv and the West interpreted the mutiny and its 'resolution' as a sign of Putin's weakness – 'cracks in the system' were the most prevalent words of wisdom. Blinken pulled no punches, rejoicing on 28 June 2023 that the aborted attack on Moscow marked the beginning of Putin's downfall:

> That [Prigozhin affair], in a way, encapsulates the extent to which this aggression against Ukraine has been a failure across the board for Putin. And we see it by virtually every metric. Russia is worse off economically. It's worse off militarily. Its standing in the world has plummeted. It's managed to wean Europe off of Russian energy in the space of a little over a year. It's managed to help NATO become stronger, more united, and bigger. And of course, it's managed to alienate virtually every Ukrainian and also unite Ukraine as never before.[45]

Blinken's judgement may have represented a consensus of European and North American opinion, but months later there were still no evidence that his general premise was correct. Moscow interpreted Putin's handling of the Prigozhin affair with no bloodshed as a sign of his strength and, except for shuffling some command position changes on the field, no perceptible 'cracks' appeared on the Kremlin's windshield.

War on Russia's Wordsmiths

As Russian winners of international awards for art, drama, literature and human rights activities fled the country or were sent off to jail, pressure at home on prominent artists, comedians, theatre directors and writers intensified. The Kremlin's war against words spread beyond the streets and broadsheets into all corners of Russian cultural life. One of the escapees, actor and director Aleksandr Molochnikov, an award winner who produced for the Bolshoi Theatre, left for New York in 2022. He described life in Moscow for artists who opposed the war: 'It's unsafe and dangerous to express a negative opinion of what Russian authorities call a "special operation", and what the world calls an invasion'.⁴⁶ While this atmosphere is well-documented, the wide-ranging extent to which film and stage actors who opposed the war found themselves out of work and performers (opera, theatre, even stand-up comedians) their events cancelled is not generally recognized. Deputies in the State Duma even debated ways and means to remove those who had bolted the country from existing films, perhaps even naming them 'traitors' in film credits. Others proposed a black list of actors banned from TV and film, and recommended that their scenes be cut out of existing films.⁴⁷ 'Human and civil rights' joined 'war' and 'invasion' as bad words.

The capricious assault on Russian culture took on an institutional form in early 2024 when the Ministry of Culture began sending letters to all state-funded theatres informing them that they must move from 'quantitative to qualitative indicators' and from there to produce 'works aimed at traditional Russian spiritual and moral values'. These instructions, the letter said, were intended to defend Russian audiences from 'the activity of extremist and terrorist organizations, the actions of the United States and its allies, transnational corporations, from foreign non-commercial organizations'. Ironically, though the long list of values theatres were expected to project included the usual emphasis upon family, morality and patriotism, it also embraced 'the rights and freedoms of the individual'. The new instructions were based on the law signed by Putin in November 2022, 'On Approval of the Fundamentals of State Policy for the Preservation and Strengthening of Traditional Russian Spiritual and Moral Values'.⁴⁸ How theatre directors could produce scripts to defend 'rights and freedoms of the individual' while also censoring them posed an impossible dilemma. Failure to acquiesce, of course, meant loss of state funding – at the least.

INCUBATING PATRIOTIC CITIZENS

Falling back on the old Soviet classroom system of *vospitanie* (upbringing), by which schoolchildren were groomed to graduate from General (Secondary) School as good young communists, the new Putinist school syllabuses were designed to graduate patriotic young people prepared to defend the homeland. In keeping with that goal, the draft federal budget for 2024 proposed spending four times as much on 'patriotic education' as it had in 2022; that is, funds for youth movements, teachers involved in 'patriotic' instruction, flags and state symbols, and monitoring youth on-line.⁴⁹

The state had already orchestrated a patriotic campaign in the form of huge recruitment posters on walls or standing alone on high stanchions looming over streets in Russia's cities. These invariably depicted heavily armed heroic-looking soldiers declaring that they were defending their motherland, earning medals and had, in various ways, performed glorious deeds for Russia. By 2023, the country was filling up with memorials dedicated to Russian soldiers who had lost their lives in Ukraine. At least one account claimed that, by November 2023, there already were over 3,000 such memorials – among them statues, plaques, murals and engraved stone slabs. At the same time, apparently, monuments to the victims of Stalinist terror and the gulag were vandalized or taken down, especially if they were dedicated to Ukrainian, Polish or Baltic peoples.[50]

The most effective campaign to raise the level of patriotism to that of a national ideology came within the school system. As a first step, the Russian Ministry of Education introduced a new course for all General School classes. Titled 'Conversations About Important Matters' (Razgovory o vazhnom) and launched in the summer by Putin himself, the course opened the school day every Monday as of 5 September 2022. The obligatory extra-curricular weekly lesson follows the morning flag-raising ceremony and anthem singing, focusses on moments in history that led to national unity against outside threats, and 'explains' current events.[51] The Ministry of Education placed manuals on its website showing exactly how the lessons, or Conversations, should be presented. Beginning in February 2023, the course was aired on Channel One's regular morning show, also on Mondays, so that children who missed school that day and their parents could view it. The purpose of the Conversation was clear: instil patriotic sentiments everywhere in Russia.[52]

Previously fading cadet training was re-invigorated as well, along with a state-funded youth organization called Big Change (Bol'shaia peremena). The State Duma approved the latter organization, which absorbs several existing youth bodies and is modelled after the Soviet Pioneer programme, in May 2022.[53] In February 2023, the government allocated ₽18.6 Bln (circa $250 Mln) for 'patriotic' summer camps for children. Called the *Avangard* project, it re-creates Soviet-style Pioneer summer camps.[54] Expositions justifying the war in Ukraine as one against the West and Nazism appeared in existing Museums and featured in newly opened exhibitions; for example, displays of artefacts from Ukraine's neo-Nazi Azov Battalion (in 2014) and harsh presentations about NATO were added to Moscow's popular Museum of the Great Patriotic War, or Victory Museum (Muzei Pobedy), for children to ponder.[55]

Galleries dedicated to the SVO itself and offering special 'patriotic' events for children sprang up. One of these, opened in Saratov in July 2023, was set on fire by an anti-war activist in December. It displayed personal belongings of soldiers killed in action, that is, 'fallen heroes', war trophies and materials related to Nazism in the Second World War and alleged Ukrainian neo-Nazism in the 2014–2022 period.[56]

Military education for students in the upper grades, male and female, now includes instruction on how to use Kalashnikov assault rifles, throw grenades and administer first aid. Cadets hear lessons on the 're-integration' of Crimea, the SVO, and the consequences for Russia of Western sanctions. They learn how to use gas masks. Teachers' organizations objected, pointing out that such hands-on military modules were abolished in the 1990s for reasons of safety.[57] Their complaints were ignored.

Complementing the cadet programme was the Young Army, full title 'All-Russia Military Patriotic Social Movement "Yunarmiya"', a military youth organization launched by Shoigu in 2016 and funded by the MoD. While celebrating its sixth anniversary in May 2022, head of the group said plainly, 'The most important task on your shoulders is to preserve and increase the tradition of patriotic education'.[58] That is precisely what they do. Along with their para-military training, members of these units prepare documentaries and group photos in support of the war and are regularly subjected to speeches from officials encouraging patriotism. The organization accepts boys and girls from the age of 8 to 17. The Yunarmiya had some 540,000 members in 2019, spurted to 718,000 by August 2022 and reached nearly one and a half million by 2024.[59]

At the other end of the youth age group, the Eaglets of Russia (Orliata Rossii) programme provides activities for over two million primary school children to help them develop into young patriots. Minister of Education Sergei Kravtsov persuaded Putin to extend the Eaglets project to kindergartens; that is, to children as young as three. Even the Soviet Union's Octobrists, the Eaglets' predecessor, had not started the state's organized ideological education before the age of seven.[60]

To manage the new, morality-based education the Russian Children's Centre (Rosdettsentr) was tasked in 2023 with working out a philosophy of education for children. According to Kravtsov, the new 'philosophy' will provide a 'single educational space' that will instil 'a commitment to traditional values, respect for elders, and love for the Motherland' in young people. School curriculums are complemented by a well-funded state-run organization called Movement of the First (Dvizhenie Pervykh). Established in December 2022, it is especially active among 6 to 18-year-olds in the Russian-occupied territories of Ukraine and as of January 2024 had almost five million members across Russia. Maksim Oreshkin heads its board of trustees.[61]

Thousands of out-of-class patriotic clubs and organized activities blossomed after 2014 and then surged more specifically in conjunction with schools in 2022. In addition to Big Change, there were civilian clubs and associations to teach military skills, such as *Voin* (Warrior), and *Shkola Geroev* (School of Heroes) to train boys between ages 2 and 17 how to be war heroes.[62]

There was pushback. As schools launched the new required programme in September 2022 the Teachers' Alliance published templates for letters of protest their members and parents could send to local school directors and other authorities. One of these was written for mailing to the federal Ministry of Education, as follows,

> Teacher Application Template! Not only is teaching these lessons not the teacher's responsibility, it's against your employment contract! The teacher is obliged to comply with all restrictions imposed by the Federal Law 'On Education'. Therefore, we have prepared a letter template for notifying the director of the impossibility of conducting lessons.[63]

One of the templates was called 'We defend school children from propaganda. How to refute "Patriotic Hour"'.

It is not known how many teachers actually submitted one of the proposed letters, but resistance was strong enough to persuade the ministry to remove direct references to Ukraine, the 'war' and military propaganda from manuals on patriotism. The Russian law on education forbids political 'agitation' courses, so the initially prescribed lessons were replaced by more subtle modules on modern 'heroes', the greatness of Russia and how to 'serve the motherland'.[64] With this small victory, the Teachers' Alliance soon faded from the opposition camp, both because it had opened itself up to charges of anti-war activities and because it was originally funded by Navalny's FBK, which made it vulnerable to accusation of 'extremism'.

In late October 2022, first Deputy Chief of Staff of the presidential administration, Sergei Kiriyenko, propose that teachers who inculcated a 'feeling of patriotism and a sense of pride' in the 'heroes' of the special military operation should themselves be granted unspecified awards. Speaking to the All-Russian Forum of Class Teachers in Moscow, telling them that 'we are defending Russia, the territory of Russia, we are defending the culture of Russia, we are defending the history of Russia and the memory of the heroes that every Russian family has. And this is such a special task'.[65]

New Textbooks, New Learning

In December 2022, Putin authorized a list of instructions approved at a meeting of the Council for the Development of Civil Society and Human Rights. Proposals to prepare 'sets of textbooks and teaching aids' for the subjects of 'History' and 'Social Science' programmes in primary general, basic general and secondary general education topped the agenda.

New texts for the 10th and 11th classes (grades) on the history of modern Russia were ready by the end of April 2023. They cover 1914–1945 (Class

10) and 1945 to the present (Class 11). Although the history of Europe is still there, sections on Asia, Africa and Latin America are added. According to Kravtsov, the new history text for Class 11, the final year for Russian secondary school students, includes a chapter titled 'Russia Today. The Special Military Operation'. It 'explains the reasons for the start of a special military operation, the imposition of sanctions, and the entry of new regions into the Russian Federation'.[66]

The first full page of that chapter opens with material on Bandera and Ukrainian 'fascists' in the Second World War, followed by Stalin's occupation of East and East-Central Europe after the war that is described as a defence of the 'people's democracies' against American imperialism. When it reaches the current conflict in Ukraine, Washington is said to be its 'main beneficiary'. Echoes of Soviet propaganda are everywhere in the new texts.[67]

In the words of *Meduza* in October 2022, this practice was spreading to the university level, where an 'ideological discipline' was added to curriculums. Not unlike the 'scientific communism' made compulsory in higher education during the Soviet era, the course is monitored by curators and teaches that the West is decadent and that Russia, by protecting and projecting its conservative values, is the world's cultural leader of the future.[68] Putin announced the new course, 'Fundamentals of Russian Statehood' (Osnovy rossiiskoi gosudarstvennosti) in December that year and it was launched in universities in September 2023.

Russia's Public Chamber said that the unit's aim was to shape 'a sense of citizenship and patriotism', and to clarify the 'modern value orientations of Russian civilization, such as stability, mission, responsibility and justice'. It is taught to first-year students in all universities, and relies on films, games, group projects, debates and podcasts, with periodic lectures by politicians and statesmen. Programmes to recruit and train teachers were underway by the spring of 2023.[69] A panel of senior education administrators insisted that the course was not propaganda; rather, it explained how the state works and the legal nature of relationships between the people and the state. One panellist maintained that 'meaningful patriotism' is the basis of Russian statehood, whereas 'destructive indifference' is the basis of Western 'liberal ideology'.[70]

In October 2022, the Faculty of Journalism at Moscow State University announced that it would add military journalism to its curriculum.[71] Coupled with first Deputy Minister Valery Gerasimov's recommendation that the final two years of secondary school include 140 hours learning basic military skills, first aid and orientation, the new offerings on statehood, history and military matters, will load students at most levels with citizenship and ideological training to the same extent, or more, than the Soviet school system provided.[72]

To make sure that the incubation period for young patriots got off to a smooth start, Putin proclaimed in March that 2023 was the Year of the Teachers and Mentors, featuring a pilot educational programme called Mentor School. To launch the 'mentor' dimension of the proclaimed year, Kravtsov visited a school in Moscow to take part on the morning's Conversation about Important Matters. There he praised the role of mentors, whether it be teacher or parent, and warned against relying too much on social media.[73]

Not all instructors acquiesced. Some teachers resigned because they believed that schools should not serve as advocates of war, others left the profession rather than be accused of being unpatriotic by local pro-war groups. Dozens fled the country. School teachers and university professors lost their jobs if they expressed, or were deemed to have expressed anti-war sentiments. Some were 'snitched' on by their students, or parents of students. Still, the great majority acceded to the new curriculums, many of them because they wanted to, some because they had too few options.[74]

Orwell Foretold It All

The weaponization of history by the Kremlin was demonstrated bluntly in February 2024 when Putin opened his responses to spineless questions from Tucker Carlson with more than 20-minutes of homilies on Russian history. He even passed on a folder of historical documents to corroborate his points: Ukraine was always part of Russia, Ukrainians and Russians are the same people, and the borders of post-Second World War Ukraine were created by the Red Army. He hinted that Hungary, Poland, Romania and Slovakia might take back parts of Ukraine they lost during the war, while Russia re-claims its parts (Novorossiya), and complained again that collaborators with the Nazis such as Stepan Bandera and local SS groups have been made national heroes in Ukraine, allowed to hold parades and 'wave flags' as recently as 2021.[75] This is the historical message that now permeates every learning level in Russia. It was always present among Russian nationalists, but in post-Soviet Russia the message was but one among many alternative interpretations. Now there is only one.

Not satisfied with re-shaping General School and post-secondary school curricula, special classes were set up to teach migrants the Russian language with political content, and Federation Council Speaker Valentina Matviyenko urged officials to stop using foreign words in official communications. Analogues for such terms as 'moderator', 'deadline' and 'coffee break' should be used instead, she told a hearing on preserving and protecting the Russian language.[76] Recent events having to do with language, education and politics could not help but convince many Russians that they were living in a new dystopian society.

In that regard, long before Orlov's reference to it, Russian translations of George Orwell's *1984* (published in 1949) began showing up in shop windows much more often than prior to the invasion of Ukraine and was even distributed free on the street by dissenters. In fact, *1984* topped on-line book sales in Russia over 2022–2023, often coupled with Bolshevik Russia's own dystopian science fiction novel, *We* (My), written by Yevgeny Zamyatin in 1921 and banned then by the government in Moscow. By the end of 2023, *1984* held the dubious distinction of being the most stolen book from Russia's giant book dealer chain Chitai-Gorod and was also in the top ten of its most-bought books purchased from off the shelves.[77]

The skewed logic dominating life and society in Russia since February 2022 was represented unblushingly by MID spokesperson Zakharova. Responding to a query from a journalist in May 2022, she offered the extraordinary extrapolation that Orwell's *1984* was not about Soviet totalitarianism, rather it was about the decline of Western liberalism.[78]

Among Russian classics, Tolstoy's *War and Peace* suddenly became the most popular title downloaded in Russia during 2022.[79] Even Ponsonby would be startled at the degree to which the official narrative about events related to Ukraine overwhelmed public messaging and determined readers' choices in Russia. Neither Orwell nor Zamyatin would have been surprised.

NOTES

1. PEN International, *Freedom of Expression in Post-Euromaidan Ukraine: External Aggression, Internal Challenge*. London: PEN International, 2018, p. 1.

2. On this, see J. L. Black, 'Setting the tone: Misinformation and disinformation from Kyiv, Moscow, Washington and Brussels in 2014', in J. L. Black, Michael Johns, eds. *Return of the Cold War: Ukraine, the West and Russia*. London and New York: Routledge, 2016, pp. 163–194.

3. Quoted in Sir Arthur Ponsonby, *Falsehood in Wartime: Containing an Assortment of Lies During the Great War*. London: Garland, 1928, p. 11 of introductory material.

4. 'State-owned Russian media shrugs off Russia's Kharkiv defeat', *The Bell*, 20 September 2022; Julia Davis, 'Kremlin TV airs call for Russia to admit "serious defeat"', *Yahoo News*, 13 September 2022.

5. Mia Jankowiccz, 'Russia state media airs lawmaker's threat to nuke Britain and Germany', *Business Insider*, 20 September 2022.

6. For Simonyan's monologue live, see Julia Davis @JuliaDavisNews, *Tweet*, 29 November 2022, twitter.com/JuliaDavisNews/status/1597465482592153601. See also 'Fear of losing war bites Russian propagandists', *Kyiv Post*, 30 November 2022.

7. Human Rights Watch, 'Russia criminalizes independent war reporting, anti-war protests', 7 March 2022, hrw.org/news/2022/03/07/russia-criminalizes-independent-war-reporting-anti-war-protests.

8. 'Order of the federal security service of the Russian federation dated November 4, 2022, No. 547 "On approval of the list of information in the field of military, military-technical activities of the Russian Federation, which, if received by foreign sources, can be used against the security of the Russian Federation"' (Registered 11/17/2022 No. 70986), publication.pravo.gov.ru/Document/View/0001202211117 0017?index=10&rangeSize=1; 'Russia bans public discussion of army, strategy, troop morale, mobilization', *The Moscow Times*, 1 December 2022.

9. 'Europe – Central Asia: Press freedom in Europe overshadowed by the war in Ukraine', *RSF: Reporters without Borders, Analysis 2023*, rsf.org/en/classement/2023/europe-central-asia, accessed 4 May 2023.

10. Garry Kasparov, Mikhail Khodorkovsky, 'Don't fear Putin's demise', *Foreign Affairs*, 20 January 2023.

11. Viacheslav Volodin, '80 let nazad v etot den' nasha voiska zavershili osvobozhenie Kieva ot fashistskikh zakhvatchikov. . . .', *Telegram*, 6 November 2023, t.me/vv_volodin/714. For a general discussion, see Nicolae N. Petro, *The Tragedy of Ukraine: What Classical Greek Tragedy Can Teach Us About Conflict*. Boston and Berlin: De Gruyter, 2022.

12. 'Itogi goda s Vladimirom Putinym', *Kremlin.ru*, 14 December 2023, kremlin.ru/events/president/news/72994.

13. On this, see Jade McGlynn, *Memory Makers*: *The Politics of the Past in Putin's Russia*. London: Bloomsbury, 2023.

14. The White House, 'Remarks by President Biden and President Zelenskyy of Ukraine in joint statement', *Kyiv*, 20 February 2023; 'Poslanie Prezidenta Federal'nomu Sobraniiu', *Kremlin.ru*, 21 February 2023, kremlin.ru/events/president/news/70565.

15. 'Kreml' potreboval ot rossiiskikh SMI ne nazyvat' Zelenskogo prezidentom', *Kholod*, 18 September 2023; 'Kremlin orders state media to stop calling Zelensky – "president" – holod', *The Moscow Times*, 19 September 2023.

16. 'Zaiavlenie Izdatel'stva AST', 14 December 2023, ast.ru/news/zayavlenie-izdatelstva-ast/.

17. 'Vladivostok officials ban "putler kaput" slogan', *RFE/RL*, 6 April 2009.

18. 'Russia fighting "sacred" battle against Satan, says Medvedev', *RFE/RL*, 4 November 2022; Katherine Kelaidis, 'How belief in Moscow as "the new rome" explains Kirill's astonishing declaration that "Russia has never attacked anyone"', *rd* (Religion Dispatches), 9 May 2022. On this generally, see Andrei Kolesnikov, 'The end of the Russian idea', *Foreign Affairs*, 22 August 2023.

19. See essays in special issue titled, 'Ideological and conspiratorial underpinnings of Russia's war against Ukraine', *Russian Analytical Digest*, No. 299, 4 August 2023.

20. On this, see Anton Shirikov, 'Filtering the news: Why Russians prefer propaganda and shield themselves from independent reporting', *PONARS Eurasia Policy Memo*, No. 873, January 2024.

21. Margarita Simonyan, 'Vyskazyvanie Antona Krasovskogo diko i omerzitel'no', *Telegram*, 23 October 2022, t.me/margaritasimonyan/12361; Mia Jankowicz, 'Russian state TV host suspended after he said Ukrainian children should be drowned and burned in their "monstrous little houses"', *Business Insider*, 24 October 2022; 'Possible war crime as Russia holds thousands of children U.S. Report', *The Moscow Times*, 15 February 2023.

22. Pravda Gerashchenko, 7 November 2022, t.me/Pravda_Gerashchenko/50381?single; Iuliia Vitiazeva, 7 November 2022, t.me/vityzeva/72573; 'Svodki opolcheniia Novorossii Z.O.V. (DNR, JNR . . .)', 7 November 2022, t.me/swodki/187767; 'Dozens of recently mobilized Russian conscripts surrender in luhansk', *The Moscow Times*, 7 November 2022.

23. See interview of Prigoshin in 'Press-sluzhba kompanii "Konkord"', *Prigozhin's Press Service*, 13 November 2022, vk.com/concordgroup_official?w=wall-17742 7428_1442; 'Prigozhin welcomes wagner deserter's gruesome sledgehammer killing', *The Moscow Times*, 14 November 2022.

24. Gosudarstvennaia Duma, 'GD priniala zaiavlenie v sviazi s rasstrelom ukrainskimi natsistami rossiiskikh voennoplennykh', 22 November 2022, duma.gov.ru/news /55802/; 'Russian lawmakers urge west to condemn Ukraine over soldiers' "massacre"', *The Moscow Times*, 22 November 2022.

25. Katherine Tangalakis-Lippert, 'UN reviewing video of captured Russian soldiers who appear to have been killed at close range', *Business Insider*, 20 November 2022; Malachy Browne, Stephen Hiltner, 'Videos suggest captured Russian soldiers shot at close range', *New York Times,* 20 November 2022.

26. Krzysztof Janowski (OHCHR), 'UN human rights Ukraine released reports on treatment of prisoners of war and overall human rights situations in Ukraine', United Nations, *Press Release*, 24 March 2023, ukraine.un.org/en/224744-un-human-rights -ukraine-released-reports-treatment-prisoners-war-and-overall-human-rights.

27. 'The UN acknowledged the facts of ill-treatment of Russian prisoners of war in Ukraine', *RAPSI*, 31 March 2023.

28. Allison Quinn, '"It hurts, stop"; Russia warmongers celebrate beheading video of a still-alive POW', *The Daily Beast*, 12 April 2023; 'Gruesome video appears to show Ukrainian PoWs beheading', *The Moscow Times*, 12 April 2023; 'A new video of the brutal murder is circulating: On it, according to the SBU, the Russian military cut off the head of a Ukrainian prisoner of war', *Meduza*, 12 April 2022. On the Male State, see J. L. Black, *Eternal Putin?: Confronting Navalny, the Pandemic, Sanctions, and the War with Ukraine*. Lanham, MD: Lexington Books, 2023, p. 81.

29. See, e.g. 'Ofis General'nogo prokurora', *Telegram*, 9 February 2024, t.me/ pgo_gov_ua/21594; ISW (Institute for War), 'Russian offensive campaign assessment', February 10, 2024.

30. Ivan Petrov, 'Shoigu: V noiabre VSU poteriali bolee 8,3 tysiachi boevikov, piat' samoletov i 149 tankov', *Rossiiskaia Gazeta*, 6 December 2022; 'Russian military death toll in Ukraine exceeds 91,000', *Ukrinform*, 4 December 2022; for the full Ukrainian list, see Facebook, 'General'nii shtab ESU/General Staff of the Armed Forces of Ukraine', facebook.com/GeneralStaff.ua/posts/pfbid02uLfS11e7 EcyrfvsAtPSjvnvU6osEwi2AheTYfcUsa4D7nQG6yscVgFHudGu5SAA4l.

31. General'niy shtab ZSU/ General Staff of the Armed Forces of Ukraine, 'Zagal'ni boivi vtrati protivnika z 24.03.22 po 20.10.23 orientovno sklali . . .', *Facebook*, accessed 20 October 2023, facebook.com/GeneralStaff.ua/posts/pfbid02VRY hrQu2rhx5w712ZDctdMDK73ZrAjt6ctgKNeVAjnFGKejUEYadxrX6NZz183KWl; 'Nearly 1400 Russian troops, 55 tanks eliminated over past 24 hours', *The New Voice of Ukraine*, 20 October 2023.

32. 'At least 47,000 Russian soldiers killed in Ukraine: A data investigation by Mediaziona and Meduza', *Mediazona*, 10 July 2023.

33. 'Estimating troop losses on both sides in the Russia-Ukraine war', *The Loop*. ECPR's Political Science Blog, accessed 21 October 2023, theloop.ecpr.eu/estimating-troop-losses-on-both-sides-in-the-russia-ukraine-war/#:~:text=Our%20estimates% 20of%20losses,and%205%3A1%2C%20respectively.

34. '"If Ukraine achieves success and takes territories, their loss will be understandable": Meduza found out how Russian propaganda will prepare Russians for the Ukrainian conteroffensive', *Meduza*, 2 May 2023; 'Kremlin guidelines for media coverage of Ukrainian counteroffensive leaked', *The Moscow Times*, 2 May 2023. See also Mikhail Zygar, 'Putin's new story about the war in Ukraine', *Foreign Affairs*, 10 November 2023.

35. See, e.g. Pavel Dulman, 'Kak ubivali Odessu', *Rossiiskaia Gazeta*, 2 May 2023.

36. Meduza – LIVE. 'Putin – o Zelenskom: "Ethnicheskii evrei prikryvaet geroizatsiiu natsizma", . . .', *Telegram*, 5 September 2023, t.me/meduzalive/91003; 'Putin: West installed Jew to rule Ukraine to "cover up glorification of Nazism"', *The Jerusalem Post*, 5 September 2023; Lahav Harkov, 'Ukraine first lady condemns Putin comment on Zelensky's Jewishness – exclusive', *The Jerusalem Post*, 22 June 2023.

37. Dmitrii Medvedev. 'Zemlia Sannikova', *Telegram*, 2 July 2023, t.me/medvedev_telegram/346; 'Medvedev sravnil Ukrainu s nesushchestvuiushchei "Zemlei Sannikova"', *Vedomosti*, 2 June 2023.

38. 'Konflikt s Ukrainoi: Otsenki oktiabria 2023 goda', *Levada-tsentr*, 31 October 2023, levada.ru/2023/10/31/konflikt-s-ukrainoj-otsenki-oktyabrya2023-goda/.

39. 'Mediazona was blocked for covering the war: Editorial statement – and our plans', *Mediazon*a, 6 March 2022, zona.media/article/2022/03/06/mz-blocked; 'Russia labels Moscow times a "foreign agent"', *The Moscow Times*, 17 November 2023.

40. Pussy Riot video, 'Mama, don't watch TV' (Mama, ne smotri televizor), 24 December 2022, youtube.com/watch?v=zr0GN2llJaY; Naomi Clarke, 'Pussy Riot release Ukraine war song and call for Putin to be tried', *Bloomberg*, 24 December 2022.

41. For the tour of 22 performances, titled Riot Days, 1 November to 8 December 2023, see riotdays.com/#tour.

42. 'Uchastnitsu Pussy Riot Liusiu Shtein zaochno arestovali po delu o feikakh o VS RF', *TASS*, 7 November 2023.

43. 'Obrashchenie Prezidenta Rossiiskoi Federatsii', *Kremlin.ru*, 21 September 2022, kremlin.ru/events/president/news/69390.

44. The White House, 'Remarks by President Biden before the 77th session of the United Nations General Assembly', 21 September 2022, whitehouse.gov/briefing-room/speeches-remarks/.

45. U.S. State Department, Remarks, 'Secretary Antony J. Blinken in conversation with council on foreign relations president Richard Haass', 28 June 2023.

46. Alexander Molochnikov, 'The Kremlin cracks down on Moscow's artists: "The life we had before the war is over"', *Rolling Stone*, 13 November 2022.

47. 'V Gosduma predlozhili v titrakh preduprezhdat' zritelei o "predatel'stve" aktera', *Lenta.ru*, 9 January 2023, lenta.ru/news/2023/01/09/gusev/; Mikhail Shevchuk, 'How cancel culture works in Russia', *The Moscow Times*, 10 February 2023.

48. Redaktsiia [Editorial Office], 'Khronika: teatr vo vremia voevykh deistvii. Mesiats 23', *Teatr*, 25 December 2023, oteatre.info/hronika-mesyats-23/. On the law, see Elena Aldasheva, 'The fundamentals of state policy on Russian spiritual and moral values have been adopted', *Teatr*, 11 November 2022, oteatre.info/prinyaty-osnovy-gospolitiki/.

49. 'Finansirovanie proektov po patrioticheskomu vospitaniiu dostignet ₽46 mlrd', *RBC.ru., Ekonomika*, 9 October 2023; 'Russia to hike spending on "patriotic education" fourfold – RBC', *The Moscow Times*, 9 October 2023.

50. Leyla Latypova, 'Amid Ukraine war, a quiet battle of memorials unfolds in Russia', *The Moscow Times*, 4 December 2023; Leo Chiu, 'Russia replaces memorials to Soviet victims with pro-war monuments', *Kyiv Post*, 5 December 2023; 'Plaques commemorating Gulag victims disappear around Moscow', *The Moscow Times*, 7 July 2023.

51. '"You can't talk about the greatness of the country, sitting in offices that are about to fall apart". "Talk about the important" continues in schools. We discussed them with teachers and schoolchildren – and found out if they really stopped mentioning the war and the "Nazis"', *Meduza*, 12 September 2022.

52. 'Razgovory o vazhnom', *Telegram*, 16 February 2023, t.me/razgovory_o_vazhnom/705.

53. 'Chto izvestno o novom dvizhenii detei i molodezhi "Bol'shaia peremena"', *TASS*, 19 May 2022; Fred Weir, 'Kremlin pushes patriotism in class: Teachers and parents push back', *The Christian Science Monitor*, 11 October 2022.

54. For the Avangard Centre programme instituted in 2022, see J. L. Black, *Eternal Putin?: Confronting Navalny, the Pandemic, Sanctions, and the War with Ukraine*. Lanham, MD: Lexington Books, 2023, p. 290.

55. On this, see Anton Troianovski, Valerie Hopkins, 'Putin shapes his ideal Russia', *New York Times International*, 25–26 February 2023.

56. 'Muzei istorii spetsial'noi voennoi operatsii', *Pushkinskaia karta*, kul'tura.ru, culture.ru/institutes/93407/muzei-istorii-specialnoi-voennoi-operacii, accessed September 2023; Astra, 'V Saratove podozhgli "muzei SVO"', *Telegram*, 21 December 2023, t.me/astrapress/44371.

57. 'In photos: Russian high schoolers undergo basic military, first aid training', *The Moscow Times*, 7 April 2023.

58. Quoted in Allyson Edwards, 'Designing the "good Russian patriot": Indoctrination, education, and youth in Russia', *Russian Analytical Digest*, No. 309, 31 January 2024, pp. 8–12, here p. 8.

59. Atle Staalesen, 'A wave of war propaganda is gushing over Russian youth', *The Barents Observer*, 16 March 2022; Maj. Ray Finch, 'Young army movement: Winning the hearts and minds of Russia's youth', *Military Review*, September–October, 2019, Art. 16; Ian Garner, 'Putinism is set to live on in Russia's youth', *The Moscow Times*, 8 April 2024.

60. 'Propaganda in kindergartens', *The Bell*, 14 December 2023.

61. 'Rosdettsentr podelilsia novoe filosofiei vospitaniia detei', *Pobeda RF*, 6 September 2023, pobedarf.ru/2023/06/09/rosdetczentr-podelilsya-novoj-filosofiej-vospitaniya-detej/; Jade McGlynn, 'Russia is preparing the next generation to die for their country', *The Moscow Times*, 22 September 2023; 'Almost 5 million people joined the Russian "first movement"', *Interfax*, 30 January 2024.

62. 'Shkola Geroev, Sistema vospitaniia synovei (2–17 let)', *shkolageroev.rf*, accessed 21 September 2023.

63. Al'ians Uchitelei, 'Shablon zaiavleniia ot uchiletia!', *Telegram*, 7 September 2022, t.me/teachers_union/851.

64. Al'ians Uchitelei, 'Zashchitim shkol'nikov ot propagandy. Kak otkazat'sia ot "patrioticheskogo chasa"', *Telegram*, 30 August 2022, t.me/teachers_union/790; see also Elise Morton, 'How Russia is molding the minds of schoolkids to support its brutal invasion of Ukraine', *Business Insider*, 29 January 2023.

65. 'Kiriyenko predlagaet voznagrazhdat' uchitelei za vospitanie v geroiakh SVO chuvstva patriotizma', *RAPSI*, 22 October 2022.

66. Iuliia Borta, 'Dostovernaia istoriia. 11 klassy smogut uchit'sia po novomu uchebniku s sentiabr', *Argumenty i fakty*, 25 April 2023; Yelena Novoselova, 'Akademik Aleksandr Chubar'ian: S pervogo sentiabria v shkolakh Rossii istoriiu budut izuchat' po-novomu', *Rossiiskaia Gazeta*, 15 May 2023.

67. See Jade McGlynn, 'Russia's history textbook rewrite is a bid to control the future', *The Moscow Times*, 15 August 2023; Taras Kuzio, 'Putin weaponizes history with new textbook justifying Ukraine invasion', *Atlantic Council*, 22 August 2023; 'Books to boots: Critics say new Russian history textbook is propaganda, preparation for war', *RFE/RL*, 1 September 2023.

68. '"Young people should understand where Russia is heading" . . .', *Meduza*, 25 October 2022, meduza.io/en/feature/2022/10/25/the-west-is-in-decay-but-our-future-is-shining.

69. Yelena Mukhametshina, 'Kakim budet kurs "Osnovy rossiiskoi gosudarstvennosti" dlia vsekh rossiiskikh studentov', *Vedomosti*, 31 March 2023.

70. Tatiana Knyazkova, 'Vyzovskii kurs "Onovy rossiiskoi gosudarstvennost" budet adaptivnym', *Vedomosti*, 25 August 2023.

71. 'Military journalism course is being created at Moscow State University', *TASS*, 27 October 2022; 'V MGU poiavitsia kurs voennoi zhurnalistiki', *Vedomosti*, 27 October 2022.

72. Natal'ia Bashlykova, 'Vse v kurse: Minoborony podderzhalo vvedenie voennoi podgotovki v shkolakh', *Izvestiia*, 8 November 2022; 'Russian army endorses

return of Soviet-era school military training – report', *The Moscow Times*, 7 November 2022. For background, see Wayne Dowler, *A History of Education in Modern Russia: Aims, Ways, Outcomes*. New York: Bloomsbury Academic, 2021.

73. 'Launch of year of teachers and mentors', *Kremlin.ru*, 2 March 2023, en/kremlin.ru/events/president/news/70627; Yegor Governors, 'Ministr prosveshcheniia sprosil u shkol'nikov o kachestvakh "nastavnika" i "cheloveka s bol'shoi bukvy"', *Vedomosti*, 6 March 2023.

74. 'Uchitel'nitsa s Sakhalina rasskazala, chto ucheniki zapisali ee razgovor s kritikoi voiny; ee oshtrafovali za "diskreditatsiiu" armii i uvolili', *Mediazona*, 5 April 2022, zona.media/news/2022/04/05/Korsakov; 'Professora RGISI Konstantina Uchitelia uvolili iz vuza posle togo, kak provlastnyi telegram-kanal obratil vnimanie na ego postu o voine', *Mediazona*, 20 February 2023, zona.media/news/2023/02/20/uchitel; Alla Konstantinova, 'Mal'yshi begut ko mne: "Putin razviazal voinu!" Monolog uchitel'nitsu iz Permi, gde director i 10 pedagogo uvolilis' iz-za vizitov "veteranov SVO", *Mediazona*, 21 August 2023, zona.media/article/2023/08/21/perm; 'Flight of the teachers: Why are educators leaving Russia?' *RFE/RL*, 1 March 2023; Anastasia Tenisheva, '"Advocating for war is wrong": Russian teachers resign over refusal to allow Ukraine veterans in class', *The Moscow Times*, 7 September 2023.

75. 'Interv'iu Takeru Karlsonu', *Kremlin.ru*, 9 February 2024, kremlin.ru/events/president/news/73411.

76. 'Matvienko prizvala chinovnikov ispol'zovat' russkie analogi inostrannykh slov', *Vedomosti*, 14 November 2023.

77. Prarthana Prakash, 'George Orwell's dystopian novel "1984" about an autocratic regime that oppresses its citizens is now a bestseller in Russia', *Fortune*, 14 December 2022; 'Explainer: How Orwell's "1984" looms large in wartime Russia', *The Moscow Times*, 26 May 2022. See also Masha Karp, *George Orwell in Russia*. London: Bloomsbury Academic, 2023, Kindle edition.

78. 'Zakharova pro sravnenie Rossii s oruelovskii "1984"', *YouTube*, 22 May 2023, youtube.com/watch?v=vdvkDp6-fbY&t=6s; 'Orwell's "1984" named the most-stolen book in Russia', *The Moscow Times*, 27 December 2023.

79. '"Voina i mir" stala samoi populiarnoi tsifrovoi klassicheskoi knigoi v Rossii', *Rossiiskaia Gazeta*, 6 June 2023.

Chapter 10

Ripple Effects

In Lieu of a Conclusion

As the focus of this book concluded in the early spring of 2024, Putin was only recently confirmed for another six-year term as president and his 'special military operation' in Ukraine was proclaimed officially a war – against the collective West. The conflict has gone on for more than two years and there still is no foreseeable end in sight. Every attempt by third parties to reach a settlement has failed, in part because neither combatant is interested in peace other than on its own terms, and in part because their most important allies tend to fuel rather than defuse the hostilities.

But status quo on the battle field and in outward appearances, cannot hide the unintended ripple effects of Putin's war that have spread out over Russia, Ukraine, Europe and much of the world arena like metaphorical tidal waves. Although the cost of war in terms of lives, limbs and infrastructure for both antagonists are huge, disproportionately for Ukraine, our concern here has been Russia, where the public may never know accurately how many Russian soldiers lost their lives or were injured – or the degree to which their Armed Forces have destroyed the homeland of their neighbours, friends and relatives in Ukraine.

An authoritarian government in Moscow has mutated into a dictatorship and a relatively quiescent Russian public has broken up into segments of adamant supporters of the war, adamant opponents of it, and both from what may be a passive silent majority. All polls aside, the actual size of these portions of the population remain unknown. The Russian economy has survived, but changed into one more reliant on an industrial-military complex with far greater government intervention than previously, and one that looks eastward, not westward, for business.

The country's vibrant and brilliant cultural scene has become single-minded and flag-waving in its public presentations.

Within months of the election some serious adjustments were made in the administrative and military sectors. Shoigu lost his job to an economist, Andrei Belousov, presumably with both the economy and Prigozhin in mind. Some would say this was also an attempt at a more innovative and inclusive approach, driven by the course of the war itself and, finally, with the Russian public in mind. Military strategists may have learned lessons as well; for example, the overwhelming usefulness of drones for both surveillance and fighting, a phenomenon that may mark the end of tank warfare. They may also have learned that incessant lying to the public about 'victories', the effectiveness of Russian tactics and weaponry, the efficiency of command on the field, and other military matters has negative consequences for troops on the ground – for they know better.

Moreover, a second deadly assault by Islamic extremists, this time in Dagestan (June 2024), demonstrated that old enemies have not gone away and would have to be dealt with.

Limited territorially, so far, the war's consequences are nonetheless global. Major and minor powers seek new levels of military security, the world economy suffers from higher inflation and looming food insecurity, and valuable arms control treaties between Russia and the United States from the 1980s have vanished into the dustbin of history. Long-standing trade patterns have dissolved, new geopolitical alignments are taking shape, countries in Africa and Latin America are demanding their place in the sun, and the West's political and financial leadership in the world is under siege. The world has become much less stable than it was just a few years ago, and Russia and the United States have embarked on a new Cold War with China looking on, perhaps with trepidation, perhaps with glee.[1]

We may never know the extent of Russia's financial expenditures related to the war. We do know that funds for environmental issues, education and healthcare were diminished as budget percentages as a result of massive defence spending. We know that traditional labour patterns have shifted, that specific industrial and business sectors have suffered, and that foreign trade partners have been re-aligned.

The national psyche will also have suffered either a blow or a boost, but will not return to its pre-2014 relative state of certainty.

Whereas Putin's war brought high employment and higher wages to many Russians, it also brought militarization, political dictatorship and another six years of Putinism. Whatever its final outcome, the war in Ukraine will continue to shape all dimensions of Russian life.

LONG-TERM PRICE OF WAR FOR RUSSIA

War Dead and Injured

As the war evolved, both combatants and some of Ukraine's Western allies regularly posted numbers of war dead and wounded – for the other side. While most of these tallies could not be verified, and sometimes could not even be taken seriously, the casualty lists are nonetheless high. The Russian MoD released death tolls only three times in 2022 and never in 2023, the last being in September 2022 when Shoigu announced that Russian losses were just under 6,000.

In the spring of 2024, the BBC and *Mediazona* published data showing that Russian military deaths had passed 50,000 since the start of the war, not including militia deaths in areas occupied by Russia in Donetsk and Luhansk. These totals were based on specific death notices, obituaries, cemetery searches and other documented fatality lists. A joint project by *Mediazona* and *Meduza* came up with an even higher 'confirmed' figure.[2] They both said that the real figure was likely much higher. Russian authorities remained mute about this matter.

Reconstruction

Repairs to residences, schools, hospitals, office buildings, roads and other infrastructure are going to be vastly expensive no matter who occupies territories in north, east and south Ukraine. Clearing the land and sea of mines and unexploded ordnance will be an additional burden.

Several of Russia's oligarchic class were tapped by foreign governments for involuntary contributions to reconstruction in Ukraine. For example, Canadian authorities seized assets owned by billionaire Roman Abramovich in Canada and designated them for 'reconstruction' in Ukraine.[3] Seizures of companies, boats and planes were one thing, dipping into the billions in Russian financial reserves frozen in Western banks was another. The long-term implications of such seizures by Western governments remain to be seen, but doubtless they will face legal complications and retaliation in kind.[4]

One report in 2022 had Russia already losing about 15 per cent of its millionaires, either by exiting or the already abroad not returning.[5]

Along with payment for the devastation inflicted upon annexed territories in Ukraine, Russians will have to pay to re-build destroyed infrastructure in their own territory, even though it is far less extensive than ruins in Ukraine. Making Russia pay for the material damage it has done to Ukraine outside the occupied areas, and the overall distribution of final costs for restoration will depend on the nature of the war settlement.

Demographic Issues

The number of war dead and injured undoubtedly will place a spotlight on Russia's previously worrying population decline. The coronavirus pandemic, the mass flight of young men from mobilization and an outflow of writers, intellectuals and activists because of oppressive laws all leave unique gaps in the structure and nature of Russia's population that will not be easy to fill.

Rosstat reported that Russia lost half a million people in 2022, dropping the estimated population to 146.4 million a year later. Some Russian experts expect their country to lose up to four million people between the ages of 20 and 40 by 2030.[6] Rosstat data showed that the birth rate in April 2023 decreased by nearly four per cent compared to the same month in 2022.[7]

Doubtless, the war in Ukraine will make it very difficult to recover these lost citizen numbers, and that is not just a matter of the dead and injured. The mere fact of tens of thousands of young men going off to war will mean the normal number of children to be fathered will decrease, and single parent households will increase. Mass emigration, consequent labour shortages and an overall anxiety about the future brought on by war contribute to families planning to have fewer children, or none. Declining purchasing power also dictates smaller families. Legislation and appeals from Putin designed to encourage more children, and warnings from the Orthodox Church against abortion, seem not to have slowed the demographic decline.[8]

Some of the population losses will be made up by immigrants from Ukraine. According to reports summarized for TASS, over five million refugees arrived in Russia from Ukraine during the first year of the war. That number is disputed.[9] Although given incentives to stay, many of the refugees expect to return to Ukraine, or Donbas, when the war is over, but that will depend largely on who is in charge and, or, if they have a place to go. In short, immigrants from Ukraine may ease Russia's demographic problem – but not by much and not for long.

There was also the murky question of children evacuated, deported or kidnapped from Ukraine. Charges that Russian officials have been rounding up thousands of children in occupied areas of Ukraine (up to 20,000 according to official Ukrainian figures), and sending them to Russifying camps, or to adoption if they were orphans, continue to spread. Some of the accounts were confirmed by the OSCE and Human Rights Watch, but details are difficult to come by. It is clear, however, that Russia hoped to balance some of its demographic losses with children from Ukraine.[10] Even that hope faded after Russia began returning children to extended families in Ukraine, incrementally in 2024.

Science and Education

Gaping holes left in science and technology fields have implications for the future as well. The huge loss of IT personnel was but one of the problems related to a wide-ranging brain drain (see ahead). Cut off from necessary international collaboration, at least with partners in the West, many Russian scientists now must work in near intellectual vacuums, unable to attend important conferences or even correspond usefully with foreign colleagues. China cannot fill this intellectual hole. It is much more difficult now for Russian scientists, in all fields, to get the results of their research published in top-of-the line international journals, or sustain contact with the many prestigious institutions that previously cooperated with specialists in Russia. Most foreign scientists working in Russia have left and are unlikely to return because of the spate of spying accusations and 'foreign agent' labelling. Russian graduate students have lost access to scholarships in the West.[11]

The arrest in 2022 of a scientist who specialized in the theoretical field of hypersonics set the tone. Anatoly Maslov, senior researcher at the Institute of Theoretical and Applied Mechanics, of the Siberian branch of Russia's Academy of Sciences, was charged with treason, even though his actual 'crime' appeared to be participation in foreign academic conferences and international projects. In 2024 a court in St. Petersburg sentenced the 77-year-old to 14 years in prison.[12]

Novaia Gazeta Evropa reported in January 2024 that 2,500 scientists had left Russia since the beginning of the war. Another expert complained in 2023 that equipment shortages and isolation had set Russian science back a decade.[13]

In the field of general education, the most striking ripple effect of the war is the militarization of school programmes. The re-introduction of cadet training and military skills, and war-themed propaganda into required curricula in both Russia proper and Russian-occupied areas of Ukraine will have long-term consequences for Russia's youth – perhaps creating an entire patriotic but misled generation not unlike their Komsomol predecessors.[14] In fact, a poll of over a thousand Russians between the ages of 18 and 35 conducted by the Chicago Council on Global Affairs suggests that this is happening already. Over 80 per cent of respondents were proud to be Russian; a majority were positive about the future of their country and a slim majority believe that Russia is a functional democracy. Significantly, a larger majority of youth claimed indifference to political matters.[15]

If Putin did not want to re-create the USSR territorially, as he has often insisted, he is doing a good job of re-creating its political and cultural practices.

Uncertain Pivot to the East

Moscow's dramatic 'pivot to the East' for economic and political succour that started in 2014 and reached a peak in 2024 is now more than a stopgap. Initially a matter of expediency driven by Western sanctions, the turn eastward became essential for Russia's economic survival, and handed China and India the high cards. The degree to which this turn of events has become reality was signalled by the 'Russia Calling!' investment forum in Moscow in December 2023. Previously heavy with potential investors from the West, this annual meeting (since 2009), welcomed representatives from only 20 countries and featured China, India, Turkey, Iran, the Arabian Peninsula, Central Asia and Africa.[16]

The 'pivot' may not provide long-term stability. China, now Russia's leading trade partner, and India both have important economic associations with Western countries that they do not wish to jeopardize. While Russia's dependence on Asia for economic partnerships could be lasting, the political and military components of that pivot will remain shaky. Neither China nor India have offered unequivocal support for Russia's war in Ukraine, and their relationship with each other is unpredictable. They comply, for the most part, with Western sanctions. Moreover, domestic propaganda to the contrary, most educated Russians who are not ultra-nationalistic will continue seeing themselves as European, not products of some kind of unique Eurasian civilization, and certainly not as Asians.

THE ECONOMY

Russia is the most sanctioned country in the world, subject in the February 2024 to over 16,000 sanctions since 22 February 2022 – with more to come.[17] About 2,500 were in place before that. With the exception of Australia and Japan, the restrictions all came from the Western world (see table 10.1).

Although various Russian finance and development ministers express cautious optimism about their economy, they still face harsh limitations. Oligarchic assets overseas have been seized and bank deposits frozen, Russian planes, trains and trucks have little or no access to Western space, Russian industry struggles to import technology and Russian banks are banned from SWIFT and other international financial institutions.

Protected at first by large financial reserves built on tax revenues from energy exports and, after 2014, the turn eastward for trading partners, the post-2022 slowdown in gas and oil sales, plus discounts to remaining large-quantity purchasers began draining the well. Huge expenditures on war

Table 10.1. Sanctions against Russia since 22 February 2022. Includes Individuals, Entities, Vessels and Aircrafts, as of 12 February 2024

USA	3,585
Canada	2,765
Switzerland	2,403
EU	1,785
UK	1,749
France	1,731
Australia	1,326
Japan	1,243
	16,587

Source: Russia Sanctions Dashboard. Castellum.AI, castellum.ai/russia-sanctions-dashboard.

materiel, plus war-related health care and reconstruction, have added to costs generated by sanctions. Import substitution has been only partially successful and huge amounts of capital flight cannot be replaced easily, if at all.[18] Expanded export markets in Asia, Southeast Asia, the Middle East and the Global South have provided relief, but may be less reliable in the long run than Russia's previous markets in the EU.

In the short term, however, Russia posted a 3.6 per cent growth in GDP in 2023, or so TASS claimed. Wartime spending and the fact that Russia and China adopted a payment system called the Financial Message Transmission System (Systema Peredachi Finansovykh Soobshchenii, SPFS) as an alternative to SWIFT were important parts of the explanation for the Russian economy's apparent resilience.[19] To date (winter 2024), the IMF predicts that Russia's GDP will rise 2.6 per cent before the end of 2024. Industrial production expanded by 3.5 per cent in 2023 and Russia's banks generated many billions more than in the previous year, which may explain why over 70 per cent of respondents to a Levada Centre survey published in February 2024 believed that Russia was moving in the right direction.[20]

On the face of it, Russia's booming economic link with China and India are saving the day and, indeed, the outflow of Western companies was not as wholesale as early reports suggested. Sanctions evaders and the pivot to the East have kept Russia's economy down but definitely not out.

That bubble could burst if the economy gets so attuned to producing goods and services for the war effort that all other manufacturing and retail dimension of its normal economy wither away; if its shortage of labour clashes with a shortage of military personnel; if its weapons production and quality begins to lag behind the level of Western military aid to Ukraine; and if Russia's cosy economic ties with China go sour. These are big 'ifs' – they are possibilities, not probabilities.

Chapter 10

RUSSIA'S INTERNATIONAL STATUS

Having lost its important links with the EU, NATO and the G-7, and even threatened with losing its place in the UNSC, the Kremlin has had to look elsewhere for new economic and political associations. But finding new trade partners is not the same as finding 'friends', let alone allies. Many of the new ties will hold only so long as Russia's more recent partners enjoy better economic deals from Moscow than they might have from the West. If any of them become further involved in new or on-going conflicts of their own, China vs. Taiwan, India vs. Pakistan, Armenia vs. Azerbaijan, Iran vs. Israel (or even the US), coups and civil wars in Africa, Moscow could quickly be overwhelmed by zero-sum decision making.

Russia remains powerful in the military sector even as the prestige of its vaunted Armed Forces suffered a major, but probably temporary, humiliation. The MoD still has advanced air defence systems, supersonic missiles, sophisticated planes and submarines, powerful cyber and electronics capabilities, and a large nuclear arsenal. Russia also remains a world leader in nuclear energy and technology, and Rosatom still leads in constructing NPPs, supplying nuclear reactors plus equipment and fuel for them. These all provide status, of sorts, but no guaranteed long-term constancy.

NEW COLD WAR

The West as Enemy

The explanation reverberating across the country since Russian Unity Day, 4 November 2022, is 'the West made me do it'. At that time, Dmitry Medvedev led the charge with a raging anti-West piece on Telegram, just two days after he proposed re-instating the death penalty for wartime saboteurs. In 'Why Our Cause is Just', he characterized the Ukrainian leadership as 'a bunch of insane Nazi drug addicts, a nation drugged and intimidated by them, and a large pack of barking dogs from the Western kennel'. Regions occupied in Ukraine by Russian forces were 'sacred' parts of Russia's 'thousand-year history', he said, and would not be ceded to anyone. Russia's mission was to free the world from the grip of the West, 'masters of darkness, the slave masters and oppressors, who dream of their monstrous colonial past and yearn to maintain their power over the world'. Not taken very seriously at that time, Medvedev's message is now the Kremlin's party line.[21] It is not yet known how this extreme message is received in the Russian general population.

As the war in Ukraine forced new line-ups among nations, with side-takers and 'neutrals' clarifying their positions by deed or by statement, analysts began speaking of a new Cold War, the setting for which has the US, NATO and the EU on one bench, Russia, China and a mixture of client states on the other. Both sides claim to be protecting shared 'values' from external threat. They tend to use Cold War analogies and terminology to define their, and their enemy's, motivation. Politicians and media personnel in the United States are still influenced by assumptions about American 'exceptionalism' and find it difficult to separate current events from lingering euphoria over 'winning' the first Cold War and, for a while, reigning as the sole superpower. Russian politicians and media personnel see their country as victims of Western disregard for its national interests during the 1990s and now as the last bastion of conservative values against degenerate influences from abroad.[22] Major Power messianism is back, perhaps more dangerously than previously, when important unwritten rules of engagement helped keep the peace.

The 'Iron Curtain' also has returned to separate Russia from Europe, only now it is an economic curtain located much further eastward than its predecessor of the 1950s, and both client and satellites states are attached to their patrons more loosely this time. Ideological competition is but one defining feature of the current global struggle. Control of cyber space, outer space and, of course, geopolitical space – previously referred to as 'spheres of influence' – are others. Global financial leadership is on the table. Cold and potential hot wars in multiple theatres are not helped by the fact that the UN has lost whatever authority it might once have had in conflict resolution, and international law bares no teeth.[23]

A New World Order?

Putin probably had not intended to resurrect a Cold War style standoff; rather, he had hoped to speed up an evolution towards a multi-lateral new world order over which Russia, China and the United States serve as equal monitors. At least this is what he and China's Xi Jinping have said many times. To a certain extent, they have succeeded. The expanded BRICS, SCO and OPEC+ are eating away at the previously unparalleled wealth and military power of the West, which still rides high, but no longer easily.[24] The Global South, or 'world majority', is now rising in its own right.

In some calculations, Russia's war on Ukraine caused the EU to come together and even make room for the possible accession of Ukraine and Moldova. It may be, however, that new admissions will make the EU shakier than previously, especially if it suspends the rigorous standardization and practices it has imposed on other applicants; for instance, Turkey. Currently, the EU's unity is tested by scattered protests from farmer groups blaming cheap Ukrainian grain imports for lowering prices for producers. Higher energy costs put added pressures on European farmers, industries and politicians.[25]

Consensus will be increasingly difficult to reach. The same might be said for the growing NATO behemoth. With a better-armed Turkey on the Black and Mediterranean Seas and the addition of Sweden's sophisticated Gripen fighter jets and state-of-the-art submarines on the Baltic Sea, NATO has strengthened its military profile enormously, and Russia's war has made the search for unanimity less problematic. Overall, however, NATO unity suffers from serious asymmetry. Collectively, the Alliance has a huge military budget and the largest economy in the world. But many of its members cannot manage greater allocations to defence and at the same time sustain their domestic spending. As well, some feel more threatened by Russia than others.

Russia may feel that it could just wait the EU and NATO out, letting war fatigue undermine their support for Ukraine. Moreover, as 2024 winds down, American domestic politics will keep NATO members and Ukraine holding their breaths.

Even before Stoltenburg's proposition and the huge expropriation made by the US Congress in April 2024, foreign financial aid to Ukraine was vast, providing fuel for Russia's narrative to the effect that it was fighting a proxy war (see table 10.2).

The Kremlin's actions abroad since 2014 have helped ensure that China now leads the East and the United States still leads the West, apparently leaving Russia stuck as a regional power in Eurasia with less clout to wield over

Table 10.2. Foreign Aid to Ukraine, February 2022 to February 2024 in Billions of Euros

United States	66.61
The EU	35.49
Germany	13.71
The UK	8.59
Japan	5.78
Canada	5.53
Denmark	4.87
Poland	4.30
Netherlands	4.09
Sweden	2.54
Norway	2.10
France	1.84
Finland	1.84
Czech Republic	1.32
Italy	1.30
Spain	0.93
Austria	0.75
Lithuania	0.73
Slovakia	0.80

Source: Compiled by the author from data in *Ukraine Support Tracker*, ifw-kiel.de/topics/war-against-ukraine/ukraine-support-tracker/ accessed 23 April 2024.

former clients in the South Caucasus and Central Asia. Moscow and Beijing may not share common interests, values or enemies for long. For instance, whereas China and the United States certainly do not trust each other, they are linked closely economically and both are key players in the global financial system. Russia isn't.

CHANGING FACE OF RUSSIA'S DIASPORA

Russia traditionally has had a smaller diaspora than most other countries. The break-up of the USSR, however, created a new dispersion made up of large ethnic Russian populations residing in newly independent states. Putin remarked on this as early as 2005. Addressing the Federal Assembly, he noted that 'for the Russian nation it [dissolution of the USSR] was a genuine drama. Tens of millions of our co-citizens and compatriots found themselves outside the Russian territory'.[26] Calling this a 'major geopolitical disaster', he was concerned mostly about the displacement of Russians and was not advocating the resurrection of the Soviet Union as so many pundits claimed he was.

The dispersion is nonetheless problematic. To cite but one example, almost one-quarter of Latvia's population of three million are ethnic Russians. They have lived in Latvia all their lives, as did their parents and their grandparents before them when it was the Latvian SSR. Yet, at the beginning of Putin's invasion of Ukraine, the parliament in Riga banned the teaching of Russian in schools, even as a second language. Russian-language websites are banned, as are all TV channels that originate in Russia. Open support for Russia during the war in Ukraine is deemed a crime. Even though 80 per cent of the Russians in Latvia speak Latvian and the younger generation, for the most part, is fluent in it, and they regard themselves as citizens of Latvia with no sense of loyalty to Russia, Latvian nationalists will continue to see them as second-class citizens, or even as potential traitors.

Russians in Estonia (24 per cent) and Lithuanian (5 per cent), and maybe eventually Kazakhstan (16 per cent), face similar problems. In Ukraine, the ethnic Russian population (18 per cent before the war) will be regarded with suspicion and dislike by many, perhaps most, of their ethnic Ukrainian compatriots and their language will be treated harshly by officialdom. Any Ukrainian citizen perceived to harbour pro-Russian sympathies will be in personal jeopardy when the war winds down – as they are now. Given Putin's obsession with the *Russkiy mir*, this situation has become a more dangerous one.

The post-Soviet Russian diaspora has grown since 2022, but the most recent additions are very different in make-up than their predecessors. Many members of the new diaspora are in a state of forced or self-imposed exile and hope to return to their homeland. At least one source claimed that about 700,000 people left Russia in the two months after mobilization was announced. While this number is probably too high, the size of the emigration was nonetheless large. Unable to get into Western Europe easily, they flocked to Turkey, Serbia, Kazakhstan, Armenia, Georgia and Uzbekistan. Known opponents of Putin were able to enter and stay in the Baltic states; others, who were already abroad as students or employees, remained in place. They tend to be well-educated urban dwellers and liberal-democratic in their thinking.[27] Thus, they represent a debilitating brain drain now and, when they go home, will serve as a festering thorn in the side of Putin's Russia.[28]

The above-mentioned brain drain is serious.[29] Graduates of Moscow's Higher School of Economics lead the outflow, with graduates in economics and mathematics following close behind IT specialists. Joining them is an accelerating migration of activist media personnel, other academics, professional people, artists, athletes, environmentalists and students. Germany, Lithuania, Israel and the United States are favoured destinations for anti-Putin, anti-war activists.[30]

A report issued in February 2023 by Russian legal aid group Net Freedom (Setevye Svobody), said that about 1,000 journalists left Russia in 2022. Entire editorial teams and individual bloggers escaped to Europe and the South Caucasus, forming what the report called a second Runet (Russian-language Internet) that uses YouTube and Telegram to carry their political messages to audiences in Russia.[31] It is not clear how much of their message gets through, for Russian journalism has reverted to the sordid days of Glavlit, the abbreviation used in reference to the USSR's Main Directorate for the Protection of State Secrets. Control over the distribution of information, once an invaluable monopoly of the CPSU, is now firmly in the grip of the Putinists.

Journalists and other emigrants took their skills, knowledge and resources with them. The exodus left the workforce depleted and skewed.[32] It is not known how long such tags as 'foreign agents' or 'undesirable' will remain in place after the war. Hundreds of individuals and entities so labelled may never come back and, as in Soviet days, the gaps they left will be filled with sycophants and initiative-free drones. While the old diaspora depends on Russia for cultural and political support, the new diaspora will use the Internet and social media to flail at Russia much more effectively than their Soviet dissident predecessors.

Bear in mind that, although the process starts with Putin, the work of silencing critics is undertaken, often initiated, by tens of thousands of complicit minions: officials with the Ministry of Justice, Ministry of the Interior, the Procurator General's Office, Roskomnadzor, federal and local judges and panels, State Duma and local elected deputies, law enforcement and so on.

They may not only act on the basis of law but also sometimes with the help of snitchers, sometime on personal whim, and sometimes on the basis of a law newly crafted precisely for the action at hand. They will still be in place when the dissidents return.

Diaspora Postscript

It is worth noting here that, as a result of the historic agreement between Russia, the United States and five European countries, 26 prisoners were exchanged on 1 August 2024. Seven anti-war dissidents left Russia's prisons to join the country's activist diaspora. These included Vladimir Kara-Murza and Alsu Kurmasheva, both dual citizens, and Russians Ilya Yashin, Oleg Orlov, Lilia Chanysheva, Ksenia Fadeeva, Sasha Skochilenko, Andrei Pivovarev and Vadim Ostanin.

Russification of Occupied Territories

With the exception of Crimea, which was Russified long before its formal annexation, the forced Russification of occupied territories of Ukraine is well underway. Including Crimea, this comes to about 17.5 per cent of pre-2014 Ukraine.

Institutional integration came first. The process includes martial law, replacing Ukrainian officials in senior oblast and municipal offices with pro-Russia personnel, and removing opponents, sometimes by means of arbitrary detention or enforced disappearances. Rigged referenda, pensions from Moscow, easy access to Russian citizenship and participation in Russian national elections were more for show than representations of reality and could not fill in for the large number of Ukrainians who fled the regions as internal refugees. Bureaucrats are aligning the legal, banking, tax, education and media systems in the annexed areas with Russia's.

The occupiers have seized Ukrainian businesses and handed them over to local supporters of Russia or to Russian business consortia. According to some reports, Ukrainian monuments are taken down, Ukrainian books are removed from libraries and stores, and Russian names replace Ukrainian ones on libraries, theatres and other public venues.[33] The government in Moscow has poured billions into reconstruction and has made certain that contracts for the work has gone to projects managed by Russians. These regions are still subject to lethal attack from Ukrainian armed forces, and the legitimacy of their annexation is rejected by much of the world.

A report on Russia's devastation of Mariupol, published by Human Rights Watch in February 2024, provided clues to the process of Russification: 'Occupying forces are also stripping away markers of Ukrainian identity, including by enforcing a Russian school curriculum and renaming streets. They are requiring residents to obtain Russian passports to apply for certain jobs and benefits'.[34] The report noted as well that new high-rise apartment construction favoured pro-Russian applicants. Over time, as Russians from Russia and other parts of Ukraine move in and Ukrainian residents move out, the process of Russification will be difficult to reverse.

If there are no major changes in the course of the war, the transitional period is set to be complete, tentatively, by January 2026.[35]

QUALITY OF LIFE

In a bid to counter growing public discontent with the quality of life, the Minister of Finance said in October 2022 that about 40 per cent of budget expenditures in 2023 would be on social support measures for people below or near the poverty line. Currently, he said, the financial needy are assigned funds in four categories: single cash payments to families with children from 3 to 17 years old, pregnant women and single parents with children from 8 to 17 years old. A fourth type of support will be a universal allowance based on means criteria.[36] Funds go to families earning less than the minimum wage and, where needed, to those with a family member conscripted into military service.[37]

That said, in late October 2022 the CB predicted that by the end of that year the inflation rate would stand at 11–13 per cent, slightly lower than previously forecast, but still high.[38] As that year ended, Putin announced that the poverty rate had dropped, reaching 10.5 per cent at the end of the third quarter and that the incomes of Russia's poorest people rose by 27.8 per cent. He credited the social support payments noted above for this apparent success. Adding that inflation was under control, he several times mentioned that Russia was doing a lot better than the predictions of doom commonly projected by analysts in the West.[39] He failed to mention that the purchasing power of Russia's higher wages had dropped substantially.

Although the unemployment rate had fallen to less than four per cent, that number did not reflect the fact that many of the new jobs were temporary, without benefits and low-salaried. To offset the rising cost of living the ministry indexed pensions by 4.8 per cent and wages by 6.3 per cent. On 28 December 2022, Putin signed a law increasing pensions for non-working pensioners. The Pension Fund and Social Insurance Fund were merged into a single fund in July 2022 and, in December, the government announced an allocation to it of 1.5 trillion roubles. It was hoped that these actions would ease the economic costs of the war for Russian citizens.[40] They didn't.

Not surprisingly, a large number of new employments were in the defence sector. Putin mentioned this with somewhat misguided pride in February 2024 when he boasted at an 'Everything for Victory!' forum in Tula that Russia had created 520,000 new defence jobs.[41] No one dared point out that these workers had to be removed from other sectors of the economy.

Looking to the future, Putin put grandiose promises forward in his February 2023 address to the Federal Assembly. A decree in early April established a fund 'aimed at guaranteeing a decent life' for soldiers participating in the SVO. Titled 'Defenders of the Fatherland' and connected to the annual holiday of that name, the fund will provide financial assistance to combat veterans of the war in Ukraine, combatants with the armed forces of the DPR and LPR since 2014, and families of soldiers killed 'while performing combat missions' in these areas.[42] The project will cover medical and psychological aid, employment assistance, entrepreneurial development, advanced skill training, long-term home care and other necessary social support. Each veteran is to be assigned a personal social worker. All servicemen will be granted 14 days leave every six months.

For the returning soldiers, the State Duma created a support centre in Moscow to help veterans of the war in Ukraine get re-training, legal and psychological assistance, find employment, register for social benefits and re-integrate into society. The first of these opened in February 2023, but it wasn't clear when, or if, similar centres would be spread around the country.[43] There were even special churches constructed both to honour the dead and wounded and to provide special sanctuaries for veterans. One of these, a large 'Temple of Combat Veterans' under construction in Moscow, sparked protest rallies of local citizens who preferred to save the park and other space for community use.[44]

It is improbable that such a wide range of new social service promises can be fulfilled in the foreseeable future.

Various subsidies could not take into account the deterioration of infrastructure caused by the inability of government to pay the huge costs of war and also sustain everyday quality of life. One example of this dilemma was the breakdown of central heating systems across the country during a very cold spell in January 2024. Heating mains burst, leaving tens of thousands of residents without warmth or hot water. Some of the steel pipes were installed as long ago as the 1960s, and over 40 per cent of utility infrastructure in Russia have long since passed their 'best by' date.[45] Heating and electricity outages regularly force towns, cities and entire regions to declare states of emergency and open warm-up centres.

The war did not eliminate Russia's age-old struggle with corruption, an especially aggravating factor in infrastructure management. Municipal and other officials have been arrested for money laundering related to heating bills, or bribery leading to false inspections of infrastructure (boilers, water pipes, ice and snow clearance). Reports in 2022 that up to 70 per cent of Russia's communal infrastructure was in a state of decay had little effect on the various levels of bureaucracy. Finally acknowledging the crisis, Peskov admitted that it could take up to 15 years to modernize the communal service systems.[46]

He was being optimistic. Russia's roads, public transport, power supplies, water supplies and building maintenance are all in various stages of decay, with few funds available for their repair as the war endures. In the case of infrastructure disrepair, there also was no foreseeable end in sight.

Healthcare

The financial and physical costs of war placed an enormous strain on Russia's healthcare system. The country suffered a serious shortage of doctors even before the war in Ukraine, when Russia was ravaged by COVID-19. Quick-fix legislation improved the number of medical workers and wage subsidies kept workers in the system, but matters worsened again as the war evolved. The MoD began conscripting medical personnel for the front lines, where working conditions for medical employees deteriorated after October 2022 when they were forbidden to take vacations.[47]

Although COVID has not gone away, Russians seem no longer worried about the disease. The health ministry stopped ordering new supplies of Sputnik V in late 2022, claiming that it had some 20 million doses in stock. Supplies of other vaccines, such as epivacorona, were also said to be sufficient.[48] There was much debate and little action about expiry dates on these drugs, even as the Omicron and FLiRT variants spread. Meanwhile, cases of influenza, SARS and RSV were increasing exponentially that year and Putin began urging citizens take flu shots.[49]

They weren't listening. A report released by UNICEF in April 2023 showed that an unusually low percentage of Russians perceived vaccines as important for children. Already a country with one of the lowest levels of faith in child vaccinations before the COVID pandemic, the number of Russians with confidence in childhood vaccinations had fallen from 75 to 54 per cent.[50]

Anxieties related to the war may be the cause of rising levels of cigarette smoking, particularly among the age group of 40–50 years, the results of which are exacerbated by the deterioration of air quality in Russia's industrial cities. Chronic respiratory and other such diseases are spreading. There are signs that alcohol abuse is rising again. These phenomena also contribute to population decline.[51]

A survey conducted by the Levada Centre in February 2023 revealed that 70 per cent of Russian adults would not let themselves be vaccinated against the coronavirus infection, or even against influenza ('gripp').[52] This reluctance may be tested again, for incidents of measles have accelerated as well. According to Anna Popova, head of the Rospotrebnadzor, measles were detected in half of the Russia's regions in April. The hardest hit areas were the North Caucasus, which is also the most non-vaccinated region, and the Volga and Ural federal districts. Looking for scapegoats, the Ministry of Health blamed the outbreaks on migrant workers and immigrants, even those from the Donbas where vaccines have not been available for some time.[53] Doubtless, the potential for another health-care crisis in Russia was growing as war soaked up government revenues.

The Ministry of Health seems to have done nothing about a recent report from Russia's own consumer monitor, Rospotrebnadzor, that there were 60,000 new cases of HIV/AIDS in 2021, more than double that of the previous year, and about ten times the rate of infections in EU countries.[54]

Shortages in imported drugs and medical equipment, especially for diabetics, are another by-product of the war. Although medical equipment and medicinal drugs are not generally subject to sanctions, financial payment restrictions complicate their import, as does the fact that several relevant international pharmaceutical companies left Russia. Some medical equipment previously imported from Europe, such as glucose-monitoring devices for diabetics, now must come from China.[55]

Whatever the significance of the above-mentioned epidemics, the greatest current strain on the Russian healthcare system originates with the huge numbers of wartime casualties. Crude battlefield medical ministrations add to the problem. Doctors, nurses, technicians and medical supplies used on the front line were all taken out of the everyday medical community available to Russian civilians, and wounded veterans filled hospital beds normally used to treat the sick at home.

Hoping to ease some of the problems facing the healthcare sector, Mishustin announced in November 2023 that some 850 million additional roubles were allocated to 14 regions, including Luhansk and Donetsk.[56] These funds will not be enough.

Climate Change and the Environment

Although Russia's agricultural sector is flourishing now, without funding to protect it from the ravages of climate change, vast stretches of Russia's arable terrain will continue to be subjected to extreme heat, drought, floods and wildfires.

Blindly indifferent to environmental issues, the state whittled away at Russia's most important individual and organizational ecological watchdogs. Having stripped its best-known climate activist, Makichyan, of his citizenship, and declaring Russia's internationally linked environment protection agencies, such as the Sakhalin Environmental Watch and Movement 42, 'foreign agents', the Kremlin appears to be fiddling while its lands are burning, drowning or drying.[57]

Typical was Russia's delegation to the UN's COP27, which met in Sharm El-Sheikh for two weeks in November 2022. Without mentioning the war in Ukraine, it lobbied for nuclear power as an alternative to using fossil fuels and called on Western countries to lift sanctions so that Russia could help counter the consequences of climate change. According to Makichyan, these were cynical ploys to ensure a Russia monopoly of the NPP market, and get sanctions out of the way.[58] A year later, Russia's delegation to the UN's COP28 conference in Dubai joined other oil-producing countries opposing language in the final communiqué that called for a quick phase out of coal, oil and gas. The Kremlin needed to peddle fossil fuels to pay for a war.[59]

As resources needed for conservation were transferred to the war effort in 2023, forest fires swept across western Siberia. Mainstream Russian media gave the impression that the Emergency Measures ministry had everything under control. Local residents and firefighters were not so confident.[60] The fires started earlier the next year, dozens of wildfires were reported in Russia's Far East and northern regions as early as mid-March 2024. Prospects for enough preventative assistance from Moscow were slim.[61]

Where there were no fires, there were floods. In August 2023, the Governor of Primorye region, Oleg Kozhemyako, declared a state of emergency because of flooding. Local residents lost their homes after a tropical storm caused a dam to burst. Other towns in the region suffered their worst floods in decades, retail prices soared and government compensation was so frugal that people expressed their anger with demonstrations against local mayors and town councillors. Heavy deluges at the end of the month caused water levels in the region's rivers to far exceed norms, cut off roadways and force evacuations.[62]

No lessons were learned. Eight months later, torrential rains caused another dam to rupture in the southern Orenburg region, forcing tens of thousands to evacuate the cities of Orsk and Orenburg. Dozens of cities and towns close to the Ural River, Europe's third longest, were swamped. In the case of the broken dam at Orsk, authorities opened a criminal case for 'negligence and violation of construction safety rules'.[63] Then parts of a third dam collapsed, this one in southwestern Siberia on the Tom River, causing severe flooding in the city of Tomsk. Before April was even half over, nearly 200 Russian cities, towns and villages were partially submerged across 33 of the country's regions.[64] Demonstrations blaming the government and calling for assistance again spread through the Orenburg, Kurgan and Tyumen regions, areas previously beset by fires.

In terms of wildlife, the Kremlin made matters worse by declaring international associations, such as Greenpeace, the WWF and even the Wild Salmon Centre, 'undesirables', leaving Russian environmentalists and conservationists with no access to international support or independent information on the extent of degradations facing their country. Nor do they have any recourse against corrupt, or indifferent, practices by bureaucrats who ignore such practices as illegal logging, poaching or under-funded fire prevention organizations.[65] There were even accounts of some environmentalists confined to psychiatric hospitals and treated as if they were insane, in the old Soviet style. For the meaning of this, one should have a look at Elena Kostyuchenko's *I Love Russia: Reporting from a Lost Country*, where the process is depicted from the harrowing inside of a psycho-neurological *Internat* facility. Such treatment is an ominous sign of things to come in the environmental protection sector.[66] She also describes life and living in wide-ranging parts of Russia, for which the book won the 2024 Pushkin House Book Prize.

As data showed that 2023 was the world's warmest year on record, and Moscow set a high temperature record on 2 April 2024, Russians awaited 2024's spring and summer of more floods and wildfires with trepidation.[67]

THE POLITICAL HOME FRONT

After dragging Russia out of the economic, political and social quagmire of the 1990s to the extent that Russians enjoyed a much better quality of life, lived longer, earned more, travelled freely and spoke their minds much more openly than they had in Soviet days, Putin switched gears into reverse. His early years in office rekindled expectations among Russians of prosperity and stability at home, and their country's status as a major player abroad restored. Events of February 2014 and 2022 may have rendered these outlooks unattainable.

According to surveys conducted by the Levada Centre after the war in Ukraine started, Russian society gradually consolidated around the 'special military operation', at least for its first two years.[68] The strongest support for the war came from the older generation, many of whom were disengaged from public affairs; that is, they were sheltered, or sheltered themselves, from bad news. The economically optimistic proponents of war were swayed by government intervention to keep inflation under control, raise pensions, offer higher salaries to state employees, and provide payments to participants in the

SVO and their families – and by endless government propaganda. But these ameliorating factors may have a short shelf life.

There were signs that war fatigue was beginning to set in by 2024. Lanes widened in the Russian political world. Youth now had clearly defined opinions that separated them from their elders, urban dwellers drew away from rural people, stay-at-homes grew suspicious of dissidents or IT techies who left the country. Citizens who receive their information from state media, TV or print, and those who rely on social media have much different perspectives on both the past and the future.[69] Putin and his team are still firmly in charge, but seeds of unrest may be germinating.

Special interest advocates in Russia are muffled, but not completely silenced. Feminist organizations (e.g. FAR), the LGBT community and banned religious sects ranging from pacifist Jehovah's Witnesses to militant Islamic extremists have by no means disappeared. Protagonists on behalf of human rights and environmental protection remain observant and poised to recover, given the chance.

While Putin remains in office, they won't get that chance. In the case of the LGBT community, it can only get worse. As OVD-Info put it, 'gay hunting is a common practice in Russia'.[70] Moreover, political activism has been left headless. Navalny is dead, Navalnaia and team (e.g. Leonid Volkov, Kira Yarmysh) are abroad; the old-time oppositionists Mikhail Khodorkovsky and Gari Kasparov are also abroad and can help only with financing; Nadezhdin and Duntsova have been defused; IlyaYashin and Kara-Murza are in prison; and dissident politicians and parties (e.g. Yabloko) are muzzled. YouTube still provides forums for some, such as Lyubov Sobol, but their numbers are few and their profiles are fading.

As Evan Gershkovich passed his first year in detention without a trial, Western journalists remain hesitant about visiting Russia to report first hand, and Russian authorities continue to round up domestic journalists who do not conform. For example, police arrested photojournalist Antonina Favorskaia (Moscow) and RusNews reporter Olga Komleva (Bashkortostan) in late March 2024 on charges of 'extremism' in support of Navalny.[71] Even Telegram is now threatened because investigators allege that it was used to recruit terrorists responsible for the Crocus City attack.[72]

If, as Tatyana Stanovaia has written, the general Russian population is inherently opposed to what they see as Western 'liberal' ideas, believing them corrupt and blasphemous, how can Navalnaia be expected to 'carry on' Navalny's work in Russia? What if there is no audience?[73]

This cannot be explained entirely by political oppression. Domestic propaganda has been very effective, beginning with the label 'special military operation', a term that allowed Russians to distance themselves from the war by not thinking of it as a war. Shifting the descriptive to a 'war' against

Nazism and the collective West was and is also effective because these alleged enemies ring the bells of Russian historical consciousness. Making it difficult for Russians to learn of civilian deaths and the level of destruction in Ukraine kept critical noises at bay as well, as did the obvious futility of resistance. The natural tendency to rally around the flag when the country's young men are sent off to be killed is a factor too, at least for a while – one need only recall the American war in Vietnam to see how that tide could turn. Anti-war sentiment is still there in Russia, but we don't know how deeply instilled, or how widespread it is. Public protest has only one inevitable result for now, but subtle acts of defiance (e.g. graffiti, flowers) continue to surface. 'No to War!' still shows up in a variety of ways. Time will test its resilience and effectiveness. [74]

The state apparatus that controls the common destiny has changed dramatically. Authoritarian and paternalistic practices predominated prior to 2014, but with plenty of ways and means for opponents of the government to express their displeasure in public. That flexibility has ended, and governance reached a level of totalitarianism unseen in Russia since pre-Gorbachev days. The new dictatorship will be anchored in law, ensuring that dystopias portrayed in Zamyatin's *We*, Huxley's *Brave New World* and Orwell's *1984* now resemble the reality of Putin's home front.[75]

CAN ANYONE 'WIN' THIS WAR?

As the dust settled after the presidential election, the most worrisome unknowns related to the war were still: (1) whether NATO countries would put troops on the ground in Ukraine and (2) if Russia would deploy tactical nuclear weapons against Ukraine. Optimism that neither of these unthinkable options would occur was fading. Yet Putin's massive electoral success persuaded him to come out swinging. Recall that his first post-election address was to the FSB.

The lack of trust, current and historical, on all sides ensure that there will be no real winner of this war. On the one hand, Ukraine will have won the moral high ground and earned international admiration for its resilience, but it will emerge from its gallant defence badly wounded in terms of lives and infrastructure, its economy and probably its geography. On the other hand, whatever Russia gains, its image will be tainted, perhaps forever, its international standing greatly diminished, its economy skewed and its people will be restive. Moscow may end up in thrall to Beijing and its own hegemony in Eurasia is already fraying at the edges.

In the long-term, Russia and its people will be the overall losers of Putin's version of *War and Peace*.

NOTES

1. On this generally, see forthcoming book by Michael Kimmage, *Collisions: The Origins of the War in Ukraine and the New Global Instability*. Oxford: Oxford UP, 2024. See also Margaret MacMillan, 'How wars don't end', *Foreign Affairs*, 12 June 2023.

2. Olga Ivshina, 'Russia's meat grinder soldiers – 50,000 confirmed dead', *BBC Russian Service*, 16 April 2024; 'Russia suffers 75,000 military deaths in Ukraine war by end of 2023: Investigation by Mediazona and Meduza', *Mediazona*, 24 February 2024, en.zona.media/article/2024/02/24/75k.

3. Government of Canada, 'Canada starts first process to seize and pursue the forfeiture of assets of sanctioned Russian oligarch', *News Release*. Global Affairs Canada, 19 December 2022; Steven Chase, Robert Fife, 'Ottawa to seize oligarch's funds, will donate money to Ukraine', *Globe and Mail*, 20 December 2022.

4. On this, see Agathe Demarais, 'The unintended consequences of seizing Russian assets', *FP (Foreign Policy)*, 27 November 2023.

5. Huileng Tan, 'The rich are fleeing Russia, and more than 15,000 millionaires – 15% of the country's ultrarich population – are expected to leave this year', *Business Insider*, 14 June 2022.

6. Anastasia Manuylova, 'Naselenie RF sokratilos' na polmilliona chelovek', *Kommersant*, 2 February 2023; 'The labor market: "Shift and shock"', *Economy Times*, 21 November 2022, economytimes.ru/kurs-rulya/rynok-truda-sdvig-i-shok.

7. 'Rosstat: rozhdaemost' v Rossii v aprele snizilas' na 3,6%, smertnost' – na 7,3%', *Kommersant*, 9 June 2023.

8. On this, see Andrei Kolesnikov, 'Russia's second, silent war against its human capital', *The Moscow Times*, 3 March 2023.

9. 'Chislo pribyvshikh v RF bezhentsev s territorii Ukrainy i Donbassa prevysilo 5,4 mln chelovek', *TASS*, 13 March 2023; Civic Assistance Committee, 'How many refugees from Ukraine are in Russia?' 10 March 2023, refugee.ru/dokladyi/how-many-refugees/; Anastasia Tenisheva, 'After 1.5 years of war, Ukrainian refugees in Russia grapple with assimilation question', *The Moscow Times*, 1 August 2023.

10. European Parliament, 'Forcible transfer and deportation of Ukrainian children: Responses and accountability measures', *Work Shop*, 6 December 2023, europarl.europa.eu/RegData/etudes/STUD/2024/754442/EXPO_STU(2024)754442_EN.pdf.

11. See Natalia Antonova, 'Scientists want out of Russia', *FP (Foreign Policy)*, 14 October 2021; 'Russian aerospace engineer sentenced to 12 years for treason – Report', *The Moscow Times*, 26 June 2023; Vladimir Pokrovsky, 'Stung by 'foreign agents' law, Russian scientists regroup', *Science*, 16 November 2015.

12. Ob'edinennaia press-sluzhba sudov Sankt-Peter... 'Maslov priznan vinovnym v gosudarstvennoi izmene (ct.2756 UK RF)', *Telegram*, 21 May 2024, t.me/SPbGS/17645; '3 Russian hypersonic missile scientists jailed for treason, colleagues say', *The Moscow Times*, 17 May 2023.

13. Alexandra Borissova, 'How 2022 wiped out a decade of progress in Russian science', *The Moscow Times*, 8 February 2023; 'High leakage', *Novaia Gazeta Evropa*, 18 January 2024.

14. See Alla Hurska, 'Generation Z: Russia's militarization of children', *Eurasia Daily Monitor*, 18 August 2023.

15. Dina Smeltz, Lama el Baz, Denis Volkov, Stepan Goncharov, 'Generation Putin: Proud Russians but disengaged', *The Chicago Council on Global Affairs*, 18 March 2024.

16. 'Investitsionnyi forum "Rossiia zovet!"', *Kremlin.ru*, 7 December 2023, kremlin.ru/events/president/news/72926.

17. For details, see Florian Zandt, 'The world's most-sanctioned countries', *Statista*, 22 February 2023.

18. 'Infographic – Impact of sanctions on the Russian economy', Consilium. European Council, consilium.europa.eu/en/infographics/impact-sanctions-russian-economy/, accessed 18 January 2023; Agathe Demarais, 'Sanction on Russia are working: Here's why', *FP (Foreign Policy)*, 1 December 2022. For commentary by a former Russian deputy minister of energy, see Vladimir Milov, 'The sanctions on Russia are working', *Foreign Affairs*, 18 January 2023.

19. 'TsB obiazal banki s oktiabria ispol'zovat' rossiiskie servisy pri perevodakh vnutri RF', *Vedomosti*, 20 March 2024; Luke Rodeheffer, 'Russia builds alternative to SWIFT as part of digital sovereignty push', *Eurasia Daily Monitor*, 1 May 2024.

20. 'Reitingi ianvaria 2024 goda', *Levada-tsentr*, 2 February 2024, levada.ru/2024/02/01/rejtjngi-yanvarya-2024-goda-otsenka-polozheniya-del-v-strane-odobrenie-institutov-doverie-politikam-i-rejtjngi-partij/; 'Russia GDP growth reaches 3.6% in 2023 – statistics', *TASS*, 7 February 2024; IMF Executive Board Calendar, 'Russian Federation', imf.org/en/Countries/RUS, accessed 3 March 2024.

21. Dmitrii Medvedev, 'Pochemu nashe delo pravoe', *Telegram*, 4 November 2022, t.me/medvedev_telegram/206; on Medvedev's presidency, see J. L. Black, *The Russian Presidency of Dmitry Medvedev, 2008–12*. Abingdon, UK: Routledge, 2015.

22. On this, see Thomas Graham, *Getting Russia Right*. London: Polity, 2023.

23. See, e.g. Dr. Hasim Turker, 'NATO's Vilnius summit: Hints of a new cold war', *Geopolitical Monitor*, 14 July 2023; Justin Winokur, 'The cold war trap', *Foreign Affairs*, 13 July 2023; Hal Brands, John Lewis Gaddis, 'The new cold war', *Foreign Affairs*, 19 October 2021.

24. On this, see Dr. Andrew G. Ross, 'Will BRICS expansion finally end Western economic and geopolitical dominance?' *Geopolitical Monitor*, 26 January 2024.

25. Bartosz Brzezinski, 'Russia is winning the global grain war', *Politico*, 19 March 2024.

26. Putin, 'Poslanie Federal'nomu Sobraniiu Rossiiskoi Federatsii', *Rossiiskaia Gazeta*, 26 April 2005. For a full English-translation, J. L. Black, ed. *Russia & Eurasia Documents Annual, 2005. The Russian Federation*, Vol. 1. Gulf Breeze, FL: Academic International Press, 2006, pp. 9–19.

27. Filip De Mott, 'Russia's massive brain drain is ravaging the economy – these stunning figures show why it will soon be smaller than Indonesia's', *Business Insider*,

3 September 2023; 'Russians have emigrated in huge numbers since the war in Ukraine', *The Economist*, 23 August 2023.

28. On this, see Andrei Soldatov, Irina Borogan, 'Escape from Moscow', *Foreign Affairs*, 13 May 2022; Georgi Kantchev, Evan Gershkovich, 'Fleeing Putin, thousands of educated Russians are moving abroad', *The Wall Street Journal*, 10 April 2022; Elena Tofanyuk, Julia Sapronova, 'About 700,000 citizens left Russia after September 21', *Forbes*, 4 October 2022.

29. Daria Zakharova, 'Russian state-run media coverage of war-related brain drain', *Russian Analytical Digest*, No. 288, 21 November 2022, pp. 4–7; 'Moscow says 100K IT specialists have left Russia this year', *The Moscow Times*, 20 December 2022.

30. See essays in 'Brain drain from Russia after February 24th 2022', special issue of the *Russian Analytical Digest*, No. 288, 21 November 2022; Daniel Freeman, 'Let's brain-drain Russia', *Institute of Economic Affairs* (UK), 29 September 2022; Yvonne Lau, '"We realized that there's no way we can return": Russia's best and brightest are leaving the country in record numbers. 6 young Russians explain why they left', *Fortune*, 20 August 2022.

31. Setevye Svobody, '2022: Dva Runeta', drive.google.com/file/d/1RiYPt8dkQAOYW6Yz4cO9LP9oChbVeqSd/view'; '1K journalists have fled Russia since Ukraine invasion – Report', *The Moscow Times*, 3 February 2023.

32. Filip De Mott, 'Russia's economy is facing a record worker shortage amid losses in Ukraine', *Markets Insider*, 27 April 2023; 'Russia lost 1.3M young workers in 2022 – Research', *The Moscow Times*, 11 April 2023; Jason Ma, 'Russia's economy faces a "massive brain drain" as over 1 million young workers exit labour force, says former central bank official', *Business Insider*, 5 June 2023.

33. See, e.g. Lidiia Karpenko, 'The world must lift the curtain of Russian culture', *Globe and Mail*, 13 April 2024.

34. Human Rights Watch, 'Ukraine: New findings on Russia's devastation of Mariupol', 8 February 2024, hrw.org/news/2024/02/08/ukraine-new-findings-russias-devastation-mariupol. See also essays in 'Russian occupation in Ukraine', *Russian Analytical Digest*, No. 306, 14 December 2023.

35. On this, see David Lewis, *Occupation: Russian Rule in South-Eastern Ukraine*. London: Hurst, 2024.

36. Anastasia Boyko, 'Maloimushche poluchat 40% vsekh sotsvyplat v 2023', *Vedomosti*, 8 October 2022.

37. Government of Russia, 'Pravitel'stvo vydelilo pochti 363 mlrd rublei dlia novykh vyplat na detei ot 8 do 17 let', 15 April 2022, government.ru/news/45167/; Pravitel'stvo vydelilo eshche 27,5 mlrd rublei dlia vyplat na detei ot 8 do 17 let', *Rossiiskaia Gazeta*, 10 November 2022.

38. 'Real'nye zaplatu rossiian v mae snizilis' na 6,1% v godovom vyrazhenii', *Kommersant*, 27 July 2022; 'Bednost' nedoschitalas' rossiian', *Kommersant*, 8 September 2022; 'Tsentrobank prognoziruet infliatsiiu na urovne 12–13% k kontsu 2022 goda', *Kommersant*, 28 October 2022.

39. 'Zasedanie Soveta po strategicheskomu razvitiiu i natsional'nym proektam', *Kremlin.ru*, 15 December 2022, kremlin.ru/events/president/news/70086.

40. Lusine Balasyan, 'Mintrud proindeksiroval pensii na 4,8%', *Kommersant*, 1 January 2023; Leonid Uvarchev, 'Delovaia aktivnost' v sfere uslyg v RF snizhaetsia tretii mesiats podriad', *Kommersant*, 30 December 2022.

41. 'Vstrecha s aktivom uchastnikov foruma "Vse dlia pobedy!"', *Kremlin.ru*, 2 February 2024, kremlin.ru/events/president/news/73368.

42. Ukaz Prezidenta RF ot 03.04.2023, No. 232, 'O sozdanii Gosudarstvennogo fonda podderzhkii uchastnikov spetsial'noi voennoi operatsii "Zashchitniki Otechestva"', 3 April 2023, publication.pravo.gov.ru/Document/View/0001202304030001; Anastasia Morozova, Evgeniia Dubrovina, 'Putin podpisal ukaz o sozdanii fonda poddershki uchastnikov spetsoperatsii', *Vedomosti*, 3 April 2023.

43. 'V Moskve otkrylsia tsentr podderzhki uchastnikov SVO i ikh semei', *RAPSI*, 28 February 2023.

44. 'A new church for war veterans has Muscovites struggling to save their park', *The Moscow Times*, 2 February 2024; Edinaia Rossiia, 'Stroitel'stvo "Khrama veteranov boevykh deistvii" nachnetsia do kontsa noiabria', 15 November 2023.

45. Mikhail Sergeev, 'Iznos kommunal'noi infrastryktury uvelichivaet riski no novykh avarii', *Nezavisimaia*, 8 January 2024; 'Kremlin steps in as local heating systems collapse', *The Bell,* 16 January 2024.

46. Dmitrii Alekseev, 'Raspravits seti: na modernizatsiiu ZhKKh vydeliat 750 mlrd rublei', *Izvestiia*, 26 August 2022; 'Peskov ob'iasnil otkliucheniia otopleniia morozami i iznosom ZhKKh', *Kommersant*, 9 January 2024; '"Total disgrace": Anger, frustration as mass heating failures across Russia leave thousands in the cold', *The Moscow Times*, 11 January 2024.

47. 'Vrachei ne seiut i ne zhnut', *Kommersant*, 13 October 2022; 'Vrachebnym vyplatam 5 meniaiut protseduru', *Kommersant*, 23 October 2020.

48. 'Russia drops remaining Covid-19 restrictions', *The Moscow Times*, 1 July 2022.

49. For details, Egor Gubernatorov, 'Chto proiskhodilo s virusom COVID-19 v 2022 godu. I pochemu "ytroinaia epidemiia" vozmozhna, no ne strashna', *Vedomosti*, 31 December 2022. On FLiRT, see 'What to know about COVID FLiRT variants', Johns Hopkins, Bloomberg School of Public Health, @ publichealth.jhu.edu/2024/what-to-know-about-covid-flirt-variants.

50. UNICEF, 'New data indicates declining confidence in childhood vaccine of up to 44 percentage points in some countries during the COVID-19 pandemic', 20 April 2023, unicef.org/rosa/press-releases/new-data-indicates-declining-confidence-childhood-vaccines-44-percentage-points-some.

51. 'Nado snova men'she pit', *Kommersant*, 15 January 2024; 'Is it still possible to somehow find out how many Russians died in the war? . . . Discussing with demographer Igor Efremov', *Meduza*, 13 December 2022.

52. 'Koronovirus, gripp i vaksinatsiia', *Levada-tsentr*, 15 February 2023.

53. Anna Kiselova, 'V Rossii rastet zabolevaemost' kor'iu', *Vedomosti*, 10 April 2023; Anna Kisleva, 'Nado li povtorno vaktsinirovat'sia ot kori iz-za oslozheniia situatsii s zabolevaemost'iu', *Vedomosti*, 22 April 2023.

54. 'Rospotrebnadzor: uroven' zabolevaemosti VICh v Rossii v desiat' raz vyshe, chem v stranakh ES', *Novaia Gazeta*, 29 September 2021; Felix Richter, '10 Countries account for almost half of new HIV infections', *Statista*, 1 December 2022.

55. 'Minzdrav: kazhdyi 15-i rossiianin stradaet diabetom', *Kommersant*, 3 September 2022; 'Diabet podlechat den'gami', *Kommersant*, 16 May 2022; Yanina Sorokna, 'Diabetics in Russia suffer wartime supply disruption, price rises', *The Moscow Times*, 17 October 2022.

56. 'The cabinet of ministers will allocate more than 850 million rubles to modernize healthcare in the regions', *RAPSI*, 29 November 2023.

57. On this, see 'Sakhalin environmental watch organization will close after being named a "foreign agent"', *Meduza*, 17 December 2022; Dvizhenie 42, 'My zakryvaemsia', *Telegram*, 10 January 2023, t.me/shiesnews/370; Tony Wood, 'How green is Russia?' *London Review of Books*, Vol. 44, No, 19 (6 October 2022), a review essay on Thane Gustafson, *Klimat: Russia in the Age of Climate Change*. Cambridge, MA: Harvard UP, 2021.

58. Arshak Makichyan, 'Russia's cynical approach to COP27 only confirms its global pariah status', *The Moscow Times*, 21 November 2022.

59. On this, see Laura A. Henry, Lisa McIntosh Sundstrom, 'Climate policy constraints: Yet another negative reverberation of Russia's war in Ukraine?' *Russian Analytical Digest*, No. 297 (24 July 2023), pp. 2–6.

60. MChS Rossii [Emergency Measures]. 'Zaiavlenie glavy MChS Rossii i gubernatora Kurganskoi oblasti po itogam raboty v regione', *Telegram*, 8 May 2023, t.me/mchs_official/8734; 'O lesopozharnoi obstanovke v Rossii na 00:00 msk 08.05.2023', *FBY "Avialesookhrana"*, 8 May 2023, aviales.ru/popup.aspx?news=7943; 'V Kurganskoi oblasti lokalizovali bol'shinstvo prirodnykh pozharov', *Vedomosti*, 8 May 2023; Svetlana Dobrynina, Irina Nikitina, Valentina Pichurina, 'Sil'neishie pozhary bushuiut po vsei territorii Ural'skogo federal'nogo okruga', *Rossiiskaia Gazeta*, 8 May 2023.

61. 'Russia unprepared for "alarming" 2024 wildfire season, experts warn', *The Moscow Times*, 19 March 2024. See also essays in 'Russian environmentalism during the war', *Russian Analytical Digest*, No. 311, 11 March 2024.

62. Kozhemiako /ofitsial'no. 'ChS regional'nogo masshtaba vvoditsia v Primor'e! . . .', *Telegram*, 14 August 2023, t.me/kozhemiakoofficial/1265; 'Flood-hit region in Russia's far East declares emergency to expand disaster relief', *The Moscow Times*, 15 August 2023. 'V Primor'e ob'iavili ChS iz-za sil'nogo zatopleniia', *Vedomosti*, 31 August 2023. For photos, 'Intense rainfall brings floods to Russia's far East Primorye region', *The Moscow Times,* 31 August 2023.

63. Sofia Veksler, 'V Orske pogibli chetyrew cheloveka', *Vedomosti*, 8 April 2024; 'Polovod'e mozhet podtopit' riad sel i raionov Kurganskoi oblasti', *Vedomosti*, 8 April 20–24; 'Russia flood situation "critical" in orsk after burst dam', *The Moscow Times*, 8 April 2024.

64. 'V Rossii kolichestvo podtoplennykh pavodko zhilykh domov prevysilo 15,6 tys.', *TASS*, 15 April 2024; 'Partial dam collapse in Siberia's Tomsk region as river swells', *The Moscow Times*, 15 April 2024.

65. Irina Kravtsova, 'Any way the wind blows' (on wildfires), *Novaia Gazeta Europa*, 8 May 2023; 'Russia's war on environmental NGOs robs country of conservation resources', *The Moscow Times*, 21 July 2023.

66. 'Prinuditel'naia psikhiatriia', *Ekologo-krizisnaia gruppa* (EKG), 21 July 2023, help-eco.info/forced-psy/; '"Urban Madmen": Russia's environmental activists targeted with soviet-style punitive psychiatry', *The Moscow Times*, 8 December 2023; Elena Kostyuchenko, *I Love Russia: Reporting from a Lost Country*. Toronto: Random House, 2023. Translated by Bela Shayevich & Ilona Yazhbin Chavasse.

67. National Oceanic and Atmospheric Administration. US Department of Commerce, '2023 was the world's warmest year on record by far', 12 January 2024.

68. 'Reitingi ianvaria 2024 goda', *Levada-tsentr*, 2 February 2024, levada.ru/2024/02/01/rejtingi-yanvarya-2024-goda-otsenka-polozheniya-del-v-strane-odobrenie-institutov-doverie-politikam-i-rejtingi-partij/

69. 'Osnovnye istochniki informatsii Rossiian', *Levada-tsentr*, 3 November 2022, levada.ru/2022/11/03/osnovnye-istochniki-informatsii-rossiyan/.

70. The Dissident, 'Pride month: A brief history of oppression', *OVD-Info Newsletter*, 6 June 2024, mail.yahoo.com/d/folders/1/messages/70939?.intl=ca&.lang=en-CA.

71. Sudy obshchei iurisdiksii goroda Moskvy, 'Sud Moskvy izbral meru presecheniia zhurnalistu', *Telegram*, 29 March 2024, t.me/moscowcourts/2823, with photos; '2 Russian journalists detained in Navalny "extremism" case', *The Moscow Times*, 28 March 2024; Nataliia Savoskina, 'Svoboda favorskoi', *Novaia Gazeta*, 30 March 2024.

72. 'Russian officials target Telegram over Moscow concert hall attack', *The Bell*, 2 April 2024.

73. Stanovaya Tyaga, 'Iuliya Naval'naya ob'iavila, chto budet prodolzhat; delo Alekseya . . .', *Telegram*, 19 February 2024, t.me/stanovaya/1757. For Stanovaya's remarks about Russians, see Eva Hartog, Sergei Goryashko, 'Who is Yulia Navalnaya, Putin's new enemy?' *Politico*, 19 February 2024; Ilya Yashin, 'I have no doubt that Putin killed Navalny', *The Moscow Times*, 20 February 2024.

74. These questions are discussed by Alexander Archagov in, 'Why haven't Russians rebelled against the war? Psychology has answers', *The Moscow Times*, 11 March 2024.

75. On this, see Nigel Gould-Davies, 'How the war has changed Russia', *International Institute for Strategic Studie*s (IISS), 24 February 2023; Svetlana Stephenson, 'Decivilizing Russia', *Novaia Gazeta Europa*, 16 March 2023.

Appendix
Further Reading

With few exceptions, these 'Further Reading' and bibliographic lists include only books published during the period of writing and those referenced in the main text. Similar extensive lists exist in each volume in this series.

Baidaus, Eduard, *An Unsettled Nation: Moldova in the Geopolitics of Russia, Romania, and Ukraine*. Stuttgart: Ibidem, 2023.
Bartel, Fritz, *The Triumph of Broken Promises: The End of the Cold War and the Rise of Neoliberalism*. Cambridge, MA: Harvard UP, 2022.
Braithwaite, Rodric, *Russia: Myths and Realities*. Cambridge, UK: Pegasus, 2022.
Buchanan, Elizabeth, *Red Arctic: Russian Strategy Under Putin*. Lanham, MD: Rowman & Littlefield, 2023.
Figes, Orlando, *The Story of Russia*. New York: Metropolitan Books, 2022.
Galeotti, Mark, *Putin's Wars: From Chechnya to Ukraine*. Oxford, UK: Osprey, 2022.
Giles, Keir, *Russia's War on Everybody: And What it Means for You*. London: Bloomsbury, 2023.
Gorbachev, Mikhail, *The New Russia*. Cambridge: Polity, 2023. Translated by Arch Tait.
Hess, Maximilian, *Economic War: Ukraine and the Global Conflict between Russia and the West*. London: Hurst & Co., 2023.
Khan, Samra Sarfraz, *Sino-Russian Policies in the Center and Periphery: A Comparative Analysis*. Lanham, MD: Lexington Books, 2022.
Khodorkovsky, Mikhail, *How to Slay a Dragon: Building a New Russia after Putin*. Cambridge, UK: Polity, 2023.
Khodorkovsky, Mikhail, *The Russia Conundrum: How the West Fell for Putin's Power Gambit — and How To Fix It*. New York: St. Martin's, 2022. Written with Martin Sixsmith.
Kimmage, Michael, *Collisions: The Origins of the War in Ukraine and the New Global Instability*. Oxford: Oxford UP, 2024.

Kolodko, Grzegorz W., *Global Consequences of Russia's Invasion of Ukraine: The Economics and Politics of the Second Cold War*. Cham: Springer, 2023. E-book.

Popova, Maria, Oxana Shevel, *Russia and Ukraine: Entangled Histories, Diverging States*. New York: Wiley, 2024.

Radchenko, Sergey, *To Run the World: The Kremlin's Cold War Bid for Global Power*. Cambridge: Cambridge UP, 2024.

Radvanyi, Jean, Marlene Laruelle, *Russia: Great Power, Weakened State*. 2nd edition. Lanham, MD: Rowman & Littlefield, 2023.

Slider, Darrell, Stephen K. Wegren, eds. *Putin's Russia*. 8th edition. Lanham, MD: Rowman & Littlefield, 2022.

Smith, Christopher M., *Ukraine's Revolt, Russia's Revenge*. Lanham, MD: Rowman & Littlefield, 2022.

Takach, George S., *Cold War 2.0: Artificial Intelligence in the New Battle Between China, Russia, and America*. New York: Pegasus Books, 2024.

Tsygankov, Andrei P., *Russia's Foreign Policy*. 6th edition. Lanham, MD: Rowman & Littlefield, 2022.

Uehling, Greta Lynn, *Everyday War: The Conflict Over Donbas, Ukraine*. Ithaca, NY: Cornell UP, 2023.

Van Herpen, Marcel H., *Putin's Wars: The Rise of Russia's New Imperialism*. 3rd edition. Lanham, MD: Rowman & Littlefield, 2024.

Zygar, Mikhail, *War and Punishment: Putin, Zelensky, and the Path to Russia's Invasion of Ukraine*. New York: Scribner, 2023.

Bibliography

This bibliography includes books cited in the present volume. It does not include the many references to Russian- and English-language items from scholarly journals, popular periodicals, newspaper and government agencies found in endnotes to each chapter.

Abely, Christine, *The Russia Sanctions: The Economic Response to Russia's Invasion of Ukraine*. Cambridge: Cambridge UP, 2023.
Arel, Dominique, Jesse Driscoll, *Ukraine's Unnamed War: Before the Russian Invasion of 2022*. Cambridge: Cambridge UP, 2023.
Arutunyan, Anna, *Hybrid Warriors: Proxies, Freelancers and Moscow's Struggle for Ukraine*. London: Hurst, 2022.
Black, J.L., *Eternal Putin?: Confronting Navalny, the Pandemic, Sanctions, and the War with Ukraine*. Lanham, MD: Lexington Books, 2023.
Black, J.L., *Putin's Third Term as Russia's President, 2012–18*. Abingdon, UK: Routledge, 2019.
Black, J.L., *Russia After 2020: Looking Ahead After Two Decades of Putin*. Abingdon, UK: Routledge, 2022.
Dowler, Wayne, *A History of Education in Modern Russia: Aims, Ways, Outcomes*. New York: Bloomsbury Academic, 2021.
Graham, Thomas, *Getting Russia Right*. Cambridge, UK: Polity, 2023.
Harding, Luke, *Invasion: The Inside Story of Russia's Bloody War and Ukraine's Fight for Survival*. London: Vintage, 2022.
Herszenhorn, David, *The Dissident: Alexey Navalny: Profile of a Political Prisoner*. New York: Twelve, 2023. Kindle edition.
Karp, Masha, *George Orwell and Russia*. London: Bloomsbury Academic, 2023. Kindle edition.
Kostyuchenko, Elena, *I Love Russia: Reporting from a Lost Country*. Toronto: Random House, 2023. Translated by Bela Shayevich & Ilona Yazhbin Chavasse.

Lewis, David, *Occupation: Russian Rule in South-Eastern Ukraine*. London: Hurst, 2024.

Matthews, Owen, *Overreach: The Inside Story of Putin's War Against Ukraine*. Glasgow: Mudlark, 2023.

McGlynn, Jade, *Memory Makers: The Politics of the Past in Putin's Russia*. London: Bloomsbury, 2023.

Medvedev, Sergei, *A War Made in Russia*. Cambridge, UK: Polity, 2023. Translated from the Russian by Stephen Dalziel.

Mendel, Iuliia, *The Fight for Our Lives: My Time with Zelenskyy, Ukraine's Battle for Democracy, and What It Means for the World*. New York: Atria/One Signal Publishers, 2022.

Monaghan, Andrew, *The New Politics of Russia*. 2nd Edition. Manchester, UK: Manchester UP, 2024.

Moshes, Aerkady, Ryhor Nizhnikau, eds. *Russian Policy Toward Belarus After 2020: At a Turning Point?* Lanham, MD: Lexington, 2023.

Nhemachena, Artwell, Aaron Rwodzi, Munyaradzi Mawere, eds. *The Russia-Ukraine War from an African Perspective*. Lanham, MD: Lexington, 2023.

Onuch, Olga, Henry E. Hale, *The Zelensky Effect*. London: Hurst, 2022.

Petersson, Bo, *The Putin Predicament: Problems of Legitimacy and Succession in Russia*. Stuttgart: Ibidem-Verlag, 2021.

Petro, Nicolai N., *The Tragedy of Ukraine: What Classical Greek Tragedy Can Teach Us About Conflict*. Boston and Berlin: De Gruyter, 2022.

Pirchner, Herman Jr., *Post Putin: Succession, Stability and Russia's Future*. Lanham, MD: Rowman & Littlefield, 2019.

Plokhy, Serhii, *The Russo-Ukrainian War: The Return of History*. New York: W.W. Norton, 2023.

Ramani, Samuel, *Putin's War on Ukraine: Russia's Campaign for Global Counter-Revolution*. London: Hurst, 2023.

Romandash, Anna, *Women of Ukraine: Reportages from the War and Beyond*. New York: Columbia UP, 2023.

Sakwa, Richard, *Frontline Ukraine: Crisis in the Borderlands*. London: I.B. Taurus, 2015.

Sakwa, Richard, *The Lost Peace: How the West Failed to Prevent a Second Cold War*. New Haven, CT: Yale UP, 2023.

Short, Philip, *Putin*. New York: Henry Holt & Co., 2022.

Shuster, Simon, *The Fight Is Here: Volodymyr Zelensky and the War in Ukraine*. New York: HarperCollins, 2024.

Stoeckl, Kristina, Dmitry Uzlaner, *The Moralist International: Russia in the Global Cultural Wars*. New York: Fordham UP, 2022.

Suyslov, Mikhail, *Putinism: Post-Soviet Russian Regime Ideology*. Abingdon, UK: Routledge, 2024.

Sweeney, John, *Killer in the Kremlin*. London: Transworld, 2023.

Trofimov, Yaroslav *Our Enemies Will Vanish: The Russian Invasion and Ukraine's War of Independence*. Toronto: Random House (Penguin), 2024.

Wood, Mary, *Everything Is Possible: Words of Heroism from Europe's Bravest Leader, Ukrainian President Volodymir Zelensky*. New York: Skyhorse, 2022.

Name Index

Abramovich, Roman, 279
Akar, Hulusi, 20
Akunin, Boris, 162, 197, 255
Amorim, Celso, 204
Antonova, Anatolia, 298
Arakhamia, David, 203
Austin, Lloyd, 20, 70

Babchenko, Arkady, 161
Bach, Thomas, 201
Bachmin, Vyacheslav, 156
Baerbock, Annalena, 204
Balitsky, Yevgeny, 90
Bandera, Stepan, 237, 254, 268–69
Bastrykin, Aleksandr, 16, 129
Bauer, Adm. Robert, 73
Bekbulatova, Taisiya, 162
Belousov, Andrei, 278
Bely, Ruslan, 161
Bennett, Naftali, 11, 203
Berdimuhamedow, Serdar, 99
Berdnikov, Lt. Gen. Roman, 15
Berkovich, Yevgeniia (Zhenya), 131, 132
Biden, Joseph, 1, 10, 17, 21, 23, 27, 33, 38, 40, 46, 74, 75, 96, 142, 143, 189, 199, 226, 254, 255, 262
Blinken, Antony J., 66, 101, 190, 195, 263

Bogner, Matilda, 173, 258
Bondarev, Boris, 183–84
Bonner, Yelena, 156
Borrell, Josep, 73, 239
Bosov, Katerina, 158
Budanov, Kyrylo, 93
Byalyatski, Ales, 156
Bykov, Dmitry, 255

Capote, Truman, 165
Carlson, Tucker, 107, 208, 269
Chanysheva, Lilia, 141
Chekalov, Valery, 103
Chernov, Mstyslav, 76
Chernysheva, Anastasia, 126
Chikov, Pavel, 160
Chubais, Anatoly, 122
Colonna, Catherine, 37
Croo, Alexander De, 74

da Silva, Lula, 204
Davankov, Vladislav, 109
Davis, Diana, 202
Djokovic, Novak, 201
Dolgov, Konstantin, 59
Duda, Andrzej, 46
Dugin, Aleksandr, 16
Dugina, Darya, 16, 134
Duntsova, Yekaterina, 108–9, 143, 296

Erdogan, Recep Tayyip, 11, 75, 187, 189, 191, 195, 196

Fadeeva, Ksenia, 289
Favorskaia, Antonina, 296
Felgenhauer, Tatyana, 158
Filiponenko, Mikhail, 65
Filonova, Natalia, 126

Gabbasov, Ruslan, 158
Gabuev, Aleksandr, 159
Gafurova, Dilya, 165
Galkin, Maksim, 158
Gatilov, Gennady, 67
Gerasimov, Valery, 39, 58, 59, 268
Gershkovich, Evan, 131, 132, 296
Girkin, Igor (Strelkov), 104, 134
Gladkov, Vyacheslav, 59
Goralik, Yulia, 161
Gorbachev, M.S., 256, 297
Grebenshchikov, Boris, 162
Gref, German, 226
Gudkov, Dmitry, 186
Gudkov, Gennady, 159
Guriev, Sergei, 159
Gurulyov, Andrei, 252
Guterres, Antonio, 193, 195

Hartog, Eva, 132
Heger, Eduard, 46
Hitler, Adolf, 254
Huxley, Aldous, 297

Ivanov, Dmitry, 125
Ivanov, Roman, 131

Jaishankar, Subrahmanyam, 221
Japarov, Sadyr, 99
Johnson, Boris, 11

Kadyrov, Ramzan, 15, 21, 39, 128
Kalinin, Aleksandr, 162
Kanygin, Pavel, 161
Kapustin, Denis, 45
Karaganov, Sergei, 209

Karakulov, Gleb, 97, 100
Kara-Murza, Vladimir, 125, 135, 157, 289, 296
Kasparov, Garri, 186, 254, 296
Kasyanov, Mikhail, 135
Kazantseva, Asya, 163
Khananashvili, Nodari, 162
Kharitonov, Nikolai, 109
Khodorkovsky, Mikhail, 186, 254, 296
Kholodny, Daniel, 141
Khusnullin, Marat, 97
Kirby, John, 72
Kirill, Patriarch, 89, 170, 206, 256
Kiriyenko, Sergei, 93, 267
Kiriyenko, Vladimir, 93
Klimenko, Ihor, 11
Kochkin, Semyon, 158
Kolokoltsev, Vladimir, 160
Komleva, Olga, 296
Kondakova, Sargylana, 162
Kostyuchenko, Elena, 165, 295
Kozak, Dmitry, 11
Kozhemyako, Oleg, 294
Krasnov, Ivan, 161
Kravtsov, Sergei, 266, 268–69
Krivtsova, Olesya, 127
Kudrin, Aleksei, 89
Kuleba, Dmytro, 33, 41, 75, 188
Kurilla, Ivan, 162
Kurmasheva, Alsu, 289
Kuyayev, Oleg, 158
Kuzmenkov, Col. Gen. Aleksei, 49
Kyva, Illia, 66

Lapin, Col. Gen. Aleksandr, 39
Lauréns, Anna-Lena, 132
Lavrov, Sergei, 17, 20, 33, 40, 63, 73, 99, 101, 105, 107, 183, 184, 186, 192–93, 203, 204, 207–9, 256
Lecornu, Sebastien, 20
Levinson, Aleksei, 105
Leyen, Ursula von der, 37, 74, 204, 206, 225, 239
Li Hui, 204
Lobanov, Mikhail, 162

Lobanovskaya, Ira, 128
Lugovskikh, Elizaveta, 202
Lukashenka, Alyaksandr, 38, 63, 94, 99, 172, 192
Lvova-Belova, Maria A., 172, 173

Macron, Emmanuel, 20, 37, 42, 44, 74, 204
Makichyan, Arshak, 161, 294
Malinkovich, Sergei, 137
Marshenkulova, Zalina, 169
Maslov, Anatoly, 281
Matviyenko, Valentina, 108, 134, 269
Medvedchuk, Viktor, 66
Medvedev, Danil, 201
Medvedev, Dmitry, 12, 16, 33, 34, 37, 38, 40, 48, 66, 67, 72, 77, 89, 90, 106, 144, 169, 206, 208, 260, 284
Melikov, Sergei, 102
Melkonyants, Grigoriy, 160
Meloni, Giorgia, 74
Milei, Javier, 194
Milner, Yuri, 121
Mironov, Sergei, 96
Mirziyoyev, Shavkat, 99
Mishustin, Mikhail, 91, 99, 101, 107, 136, 206, 219, 226, 227, 235
Mizintsev, Col. Gen. Mikhail, 49, 59
Modi, Narendra, 190, 191
Molochnikov, Aleksandr, 263
Monaghan, Andrew, 1
Monetochka, 158
Mongait, Anna, 159
Morozov, Pavel, 127
Mosin, Aleksei, 125
Moskaleva, Masha, 126
Moskalev, Aleksei, 126–27
Moskalkova, Tatiana, 140, 171
Muntyan, Pavel, 158
Murashko, Mikhail, 167
Muratov, Dmitry, 123, 129, 161

Nabiullina, Elvira, 234
Nadezhdin, Boris, 109, 143, 144, 296
Naryshkin, Sergei, 207

Navalnaia, Yulia, 110, 134, 140, 143–44, 296
Navalny, Aleksei, 101–3, 108, 109, 122, 124, 139–44, 157–58, 240, 253, 267, 296
Nebenzia, Vassily, 172, 185
Nechaev, Aleksei, 96, 109
Novak, Aleksandr, 226–27
Nuland, Victoria, 6

Oleshchuk, Mykola, 76
Oreshkin, Maksim, 229, 266
Orlov, Oleg, 125
Orwell, George (E.A. Blair), 125, 270, 297
Ostanin, Vadim, 141, 289
Ovchinnikov, Vladimir, 130
Ovsyannikova, Marina, 123

Pamfilova, Ella, 107, 110–11, 137, 144
Pandor, Naledi, 186
Parshkova, Anna, 123
Pasechnik, Leonid, 90
Patrushev, Dmitry, 241
Patrushev, Nikolai, 14
Pavel, Metropolitan, 170
Peskov, Dmitry, 10, 41, 44, 49, 65, 73, 77, 98, 103, 104, 130, 140, 142, 144, 195, 196, 205, 260, 261, 292
Petriychuk, Svetlana, 131–32
Pivovarev, Andrei, 289
Plyushchev, Aleksandr, 158
Podolyak, Mykhailo, 47, 206, 222
Ponomarenko, Maria, 125
Ponomarev, Ilya, 132, 134, 162
Ponsonby, Sir Arthur, 252
Popov, Oleg, 66
Popova, Anna, 293
Poroshenko, Petro, 260
Pozdyankov, Vladislav, 258
Prigozhin, Yevgeny, 2, 13, 46, 47, 58–59, 62–64, 107, 134–35, 199, 257, 263, 278
Prilepin, Zakhar, 134
Primakov, Yevgeny, 8

Pugacheva, Alla, 158
Pushilin, Denis, 90, 103
Putin, Vladimir, 32, 87–111, 136, 166–67, 290; and 'collective West', 14, 19, 45, 48, 61, 73, 126, 203, 254, 255, 259, 262; and the economy, 217–50; and education, 264–69; elections, 107, 111, 139, 144; and family values, 155–82; and foreign policy, 183–216; and history, 100, 101, 194, 254, 267, 269, 277; as Hitler, 255–56; and martial law, 19; and mobilization/recruiting, 11, 13, 64, 66, 127–28; motives for war, 1, 2, 12, 90–91, 260–61; New Year's Addresses, 41, 107; and nuclear weapons, 2, 9, 10, 17, 19, 23, 33, 39, 43, 48, 59, 67–68, 74, 110, 190; and patriotism, 96–98, 100, 134; and Russian civilization, 9, 41, 89–91, 96, 184; and snitching, 126–27; succession, 124. *See also* Nazism

Qin Gang, 192

Rahmon, Emomali, 99
Ramaphosa, Cyril, 60, 105, 194, 204–5
Reshetnikov, Maksim, 227
Reznik, Maksim, 129
Reznikov, Oleksiy, 43
Roberts, Geoffrey, 2
Rodnyansky, Aleksandr, 158
Roizman, Yevgeny, 125, 159
Rumyantsev, Vladimir, 124
Rybakov, Nikolai, 135

Sabalenka, Aryna, 201
Sachkov, Ilya, 162
Sakwa, Richard, 1
Saldo, Vladimir, 90
Sanchez, Pedro, 204
Scholz, Olaf, 23, 74, 142, 204
Schröder, Gerhard, 11, 203
Serenko, Daria, 169
Shevchenko, Taras, 129
Shishkov, Aleksandr, 129
Shmyhal, Denys, 37, 188
Shoigu, Sergei, 12, 14, 20–21, 33, 38–39, 46, 58, 59, 64, 99, 101, 107, 192, 207, 219, 278
Shtein (Stein), Lyudmila, 262
Shumanov, Ilya, 158
Simonyan, Margarita, 21, 100, 252, 257
Skochilenko, Sasha, 123–24, 289
Slepakov, Semyon, 161
Slutsky, Leonid, 96, 109, 135, 138
Smolkin, Gleb, 202
Sobchak, Anatoly, 124
Sobchak, Ksenia, 124
Sobol, Lyubov, 296
Sobyanin, Sergei, 89, 138–39, 219
Sokolov, Sergei, 129
Solovyov, Vladimir, 100, 252
Stalin, Josef, 135, 157
Stanovaia, Tatyana, 296
Stent, Angela, 209
Stoltenberg, Jens, 43–44, 46, 67, 74, 142, 188, 189
Støre, Jonas Gahr, 197
Stronsky, Nik, 122
Sukhanov, Kirill, 124
Sunak, Rishi, 34, 72, 142
Sun Tzu, 1
Suraykin, Maksim, 137
Surovikin, Gen. Sergei, 15, 19, 21, 39, 59, 64
Suslov, Mikhail, 95

Tatarsky, Vladlen, 134
Tokaev, Kassym-Jomart, 99, 190–91
Tolstoy, Leo, 270
Trepova, Daria, 134
Trofimova, Sardana, 202
Trudeau, Justin, 74
Trump, Donald J., 60, 104
Tsukanova, Olga, 92
Tsvetkova, Yulia, 166
Türk, Volker, 258
Turlov, Timur, 121

Ukrainka, Lesya, 129
Ulitskaya, Lyudmila, 163
Ushakov, Yuri, 206
Utkin, Dmitry, 103

Vasiliev, Vladimir, 96, 136
Vedel, Semiel, 125–26
Virolainen, Daria, 202
Vishnevsky, Boris, 129
Volkov, Leonid, 108, 139, 144, 296
Volodin, Vyacheslav, 57, 67, 68, 122, 132, 142, 165, 254
Volozh, Arkady, 122

Wallace, Ben, 20, 22
Woolf, Virginia, 165

Xi Jinping, 38, 44, 48, 189–91, 214, 285

Yakovenko, Igor, 161
Yakunin, Andrei, 197
Yakunin, Vladimir, 197
Yanukovych, Viktor, 5–6, 260
Yarmysh, Kira, 296
Yarosh, Dmytro, 254

Yashin, Ilya, 124, 135, 157–58, 296
Yathothu, Pani, 237
Yatsenyuk, Arseniy, 6
Yavlinsky, Grigory, 108
Yeltsin, Boris, 16, 122, 141, 156, 256
Yermak, Andriy, 208

Zakharova, Maria, 23, 77, 134, 197, 207, 260, 270
Zamyatin, Yevgeny, 270, 297
Zanko, Olga, 90
Zelenska, Olena, 37
Zelensky, Volodymyr, 7, 9, 11, 15, 37–38, 43, 68, 93, 111, 142, 157, 170, 237, 253, 255; meets world leaders, 42, 44, 60, 67, 74, 188, 189, 204–5; and peace talks, 20–22, 70, 75, 190, 204, 207–8
Zhemkova, Yelena, 157
Zhirinovsky, Vladimir, 99, 135
Zhuravlev, Col. Gen. Aleksandr, 15
Zolotov, Viktor, 199
Zuppi, Cardinal Matteo Maria, 206
Zygar, Mikhail, 158
Zyuganov, Gennady, 96, 109

Subject Index

Only countries or cities with a major stake in the war will be indexed here. References to the United States (US) and the United Kingdom (UK) are too plentiful to be indexed usefully.

abortion, 167–68, 280
Afghanistan, 91, 192
Africa, 13, 35, 60–61, 186–87, 190, 193, 195, 203–6, 209, 221, 231, 235, 237, 268, 278, 284
Africa Union, 190
Agora, 160. *See also* human rights
agriculture, 195–97, 239–41. *See also* grain corridor/exports
aid to Ukraine, Western, 8, 10, 17–18, 21, 34, 38, 41–43, 45, 58, 70, 74, 76–77, 283. *See also* Ukraine at war
All-Russia Centre for Research on Public Opinion (VTsIOM), 88, 94, 99, 105, 138
All-Russia People's Front (ONF), 36, 92, 133, 155
annexations, 7, 15, 31, 35–38, 90, 105, 132, 170, 185, 220, 289. *See also* occupied zones
anti-Government movements. *See* opposition, domestic political
anti-Semitism, 6, 208, 237
Armenia, 99, 122, 128, 183–84, 187, 190–92, 194, 232, 238, 284, 288

arming Ukraine. *See* Ukraine at war
arms control, 33–34; CTBT, 67–68; New START, 33, 43, 67, 96, 190
arms sales, 226
Association of Southeast Asian countries (ASEAN), 189–90, 203, 206, 238
atrocities. *See* war crimes
Australia, 17, 201, 205, 217, 228, 230–31, 240, 282
Azerbaijan, 128, 183, 191, 192, 194, 225, 284
Azov Battalion, 10, 254, 265

Bakhmut, 39, 46–47, 58–59, 62, 258
Baltic States, 63, 73, 128, 174, 188, 194, 200, 225, 228, 288
Batkivshchyna, 6
Belarus, 38, 48, 59, 63, 73, 95, 172, 186, 189, 191–92, 194, 200, 224, 231–33, 236
Belgorod, 19, 59, 69, 71, 72, 75, 76
Belt and Road Initiative (China), 183, 191, 203, 230, 233

315

Black Sea, 7, 9, 71, 76, 170, 176–77, 205, 212, 230, 286
Black Sea Fleet, 47, 65, 195
bloggers, pro war, 39, 103–4, 133–35, 169
Brazil, 35, 91, 185, 187, 204–6, 208, 221, 231, 233, 240
BRICS, 105, 186–87, 190, 192–94, 203, 204, 206; New Development Bank, 192
Bulgaria, 23, 155, 196, 197, 199, 225

Canada, 12, 18, 34, 40, 45, 74, 143, 173, 200, 201, 217, 220, 228, 232–35, 240, 279, 286
censorship, 131, 165, 253
Central Election Commission (CEC), 107–10, 137
Chechnya, 92, 128. *See also* Kadyrov, Ramzan
children: Russian, 106–7, 133, 135, 156, 164, 167–68, 171, 264, 272–77, 280, 290, 292; Ukrainian, 17, 97, 123, 171, 173, 181, 206, 257, 261, 280. *See also* Russian Children's Centre; youth
China, 37, 38, 42–44, 48, 60, 68, 71, 91, 173, 183, 184, 186, 187, 190–93, 203–6, 208, 217, 219, 221, 224–27, 229, 278, 281–87
citizenship, 170–71, 268, 289; renounced/lifted, 122, 161, 163, 202
Civic Initiative Party, 109
civilizations, 96; wars between, 94, 183, 256, 259, 268
climate change, 161, 185, 187, 205, 227, 293–95. *See also* environmentalism/ists
Club of Angry Patriots, 104, 134
Collective Security Treaty Organization (CSTO), 105, 187, 190–91, 203, 207
Committee for the Protection of National Interests, 133
Commonwealth of Independent States (CIS), 194
Communist Party of the Russian Federation (CPRF), 96, 109, 135, 137–39, 162, 255

Communist Party of Ukraine, 6
Communists of Russia, 137
conscription, 12–13, 39, 47–48, 64, 92, 127–29, 163, 165, 167, 171; 'Go by the Forest', 169
corruption: Russian, 13, 38, 66, 111, 137, 160, 256, 291; Ukrainian, 188. *See also* Foundation for the Fight Against Corruption (FBK)
Council of Wives and Mothers, 92–93. *See also* women
COVID-19, 292–93
Crimea, 6–8, 11, 16, 22, 32, 48, 66, 73, 76, 87, 89, 97, 110, 134, 138, 171, 204, 254, 266, 289
Crimean Tatars, 134
Cuba, 232
cybersecurity, 46, 162, 174, 185
cyber space, 185
Czech Republic, 128, 143, 200, 286

denunciations. *See* snitching
diaspora, Russian, 89, 166, 237–38, 262, 287–89
Donetsk People's Republic (DPR), 7, 23, 34, 35, 90, 94, 103, 173. *See also* referendums
DOXA, 161
Dozhd, 143, 159, 261, 262

Eaglets of Russia, 266
Eastern Economic Forum, 104, 237–38
economics, 155–82, 277, *passim*; companies leaving Russia, 221–25; 'frozen' Russian assets, 219, 240, 279, 282; 'pivot to the East', 184, 191, 236, 282–84; SPIEF, 59, 233, 237. *See also* energy; pipelines; sanctions; St. Petersburg International Economic Forum (SPIEF)
education, 47, 98, 100, 110, 126, 128, 162, 264–69, 278, 281, 289; *vospitanie*, 264
Egypt, 35, 60, 91, 190–92, 194, 196, 204, 207, 231

elections, 76–77, 261, 289; municipal, 12, 34, 88, 91, 122; national, 100, 137–39; presidential, 99–101, 104, 107–11, 297
emigration, 128, 233, 280, 288; brain drain, 281, 288
energy, 7, 140, 186, 194, 217, 219–21, 226, 227, 230, 231, 237, 245, 263, 285; gas, 230; LNG, 225, 226, 232, 239; NPPs, 231–32; oil, 193, 194, 206, 217, 219–22, 225, 230–31, 236, 237, 260; price cap (oil), 230–31. *See also* Nord Stream; pipelines
energy sites, Ukrainian targets, 17, 19, 21, 23, 32, 76
environmentalism/ists, 136, 159, 174, 206, 241, 278, 293, 295–96. *See also* climate change; *Kedr*
espionage, 94, 197–99
Eurasian Economic Union (EEU), 203, 232–33
Eurasianism, 16, 282
European Parliament (PACE), 172
European Union (EU), 6, 14, 38, 45, 60, 70, 73, 74, 76, 128, 143, 173, 183–85, 188, 194, 204, 217, 218, 222–23, 229, 235, 254, 284

fascism, 125, 261. *See also* Nazism
feminism, 123–24, 167–69
Feminist Anti-War Resistance (FAR). *See* opposition organizations
Finland, 31, 39, 44, 64, 128, 187, 188, 198, 202, 206, 220–21, 224, 286
Fond obschestvennoe mnenie (FOM), 94, 105
food, 91, 102, 240, 278. *See also* agriculture
food security, 61, 190, 206, 207
'foreign agents' label, 24, 125, 133, 156, 158–66, 168, 169, 253, 261, 281, 284–85, 288, 294. *See also* 'undesirables'
Foreign Policy Concept, 203
For Truth, 134

Foundation for the Fight Against Corruption (FBK), 108, 139, 159, 267
France, 5, 7, 34, 35, 37, 40, 44, 72, 74, 143, 188, 200, 226, 229, 283
Freedom of Russia Legion. *See* military
FSB. *See* law enforcement

G-7. *See* summits
G-20. *See* summits
gas. *See* energy
gays. *See* LGBT
Gazprom, 93, 165, 219, 222, 225, 230, 231, 235, 237
Georgia, 128, 183, 225, 288
Georgian Legion, 14
Germany, 5, 7, 34, 35, 40, 46, 48, 58, 60, 72, 74, 91, 143, 188, 198, 204, 221, 225, 227, 229, 230, 237, 252
global majority. *See* Global South
Global South, 187, 193, 207–9, 283
Golos, 138, 139, 144, 159, 160
governance, Russia, 91–92, 133
Government Coordination Council, 91, 219
graffiti protest art, 130, 297
grain corridor/exports, 21–22, 32, 44, 58, 75, 190, 192, 195–97, 205, 209, 229, 240–41
GrayZone, 103, 133
Great Patriotic War, 255, 265. *See also* World War II (Great Patriotic War)
Greece, 225, 231

healthcare, 292–93. *See also* COVID-19; HIV/AIDS
Helsinki Group, Moscow, 155–56. *See also* human rights
HIV/AIDS, 293
Holland. *See* Netherlands
human rights, 155–82
Human Rights Monitoring Mission in Ukraine (UN), 32, 258
Human Rights Watch, 173, 182, 271, 280
Hungary, 44, 71, 187, 196, 220, 225, 229, 230, 269

imports. *See* trade, Russian foreign
India, 37, 43, 91, 102, 184–87, 190–93, 201, 203, 206, 208, 217, 221, 224, 226, 231–32, 237, 238, 282, 283
inflation. *See* quality of life
International Criminal Court (ICC), 48, 97, 98, 172–73, 186–87, 194, 206
International Legion of Territorial Defence, 14
International Monetary Fund (IMF), 74, 187, 193, 236, 238, 283
Iran, 91, 186, 190–94, 233, 240, 242, 282, 284
Islam, 131; radical Islam, 76, 77, 111, 131, 278, 296. See *also* religion
Israel, 11, 68, 76, 105, 106, 121, 122, 124, 169, 190, 284, 288
Israeli-Hamas war, 68, 76, 105–6, 190, 208
'I Want to Live' project, 61, 169

Japan, 193, 217, 223, 224, 226, 228, 240, 286
Jehovah's Witnesses, 169, 296
A Just Russia, 96, 127, 134

Kazakhstan, 91, 128, 183, 190–92, 194, 231–33, 287, 288
Kedr, 159
Kerch Strait Bridge, 16–17, 32, 65, 88
Kharkiv, 9, 10, 18, 19, 22, 31–32, 39, 73, 88, 171, 252
Kherson, 9, 12, 15, 21–23, 31–32, 98
Kholod, 162, 255
Korea, North, 186
Korea, South, 205, 238
Kyrgyzstan, 99, 183, 191, 192, 194, 232

Latin America, 186, 203, 209, 221, 235, 268, 278
law enforcement, 124; FSB, 13, 63, 101, 111, 124, 130, 131, 162, 163, 198, 253, 297; Investigative Committee, 16, 129
Levada Centre, 57, 61, 69, 75, 94, 99, 101, 104, 105, 107, 136, 184, 205, 260, 283, 295

LGBT, 123, 130, 159, 161, 163–66, 255, 296; 'LGBT propaganda', 163–65
Liberal Democratic Party of Russia (LDPR), 96, 109, 135, 138, 251
LNG. *See* energy
Luhansk (Lugansk) People's Republic (LPR), 7, 34, 35, 65, 66, 90, 94, 98, 279, 293. *See also* referendums

Maidan (Euromaidans), 5, 6, 251, 254, 260
Male State, 258
Mariupol, 9–10, 32, 39, 48, 97–98, 289
media: foreign, 9, 94, 130, 133, 160, 172, 208, 257–58, 285; Russian, 10, 18, 19, 21, 32, 34, 35, 57, 62, 88, 98, 101, 109, 111, 131, 140, 163, 166, 171, 252, 253, 255, 288, 294; social, 16, 48, 59, 61, 69, 93, 102, 121, 129, 184, 269; Ukrainian, 66
Mediazona, 70, 131, 259, 261
Meduza, 160–61, 164, 259, 261, 279
Memorial, 128, 129, 156–57
mercenaries. *See* volunteer battalions
Middle East, 76, 106, 134, 203, 220, 225, 231, 283
military, Russian, *passim*; volunteer organizations, 14, 45, 58–59, 70, 74–75, 132. *See also* conscription; recruiting
Military Industrial Commission, 89
Minsk Protocols, 7
mobilization. *See* conscription
Moldova, 22, 183, 184, 199, 225, 232
Munich Security Conferences, 43–44

National Guard, 64, 199
nationalism. *See* patriotism
National Republican Army, 132, 134
National Resistance Centre (NRC) (Ukraine), 65, 81
NATO, 7, 9, 10, 12, 14, 15, 19, 23–29, 31, 43–44, 48, 59, 91, 97, 183, 198, 259, 263, 265, 285–86; arming Ukraine, 17, 18, 33, 37, 39, 43, 45, 46, 97; expansion, 8, 107, 198, 206, 208, 256,

262, 286; Ukraine membership, 11, 15, 22, 31, 60, 188. *See also* summits; 'war against the West'
NATO-Ukraine Council, 72, 188, 189
Navalny (film), 140
Nazism, 135, 265; accusations of, 12, 41, 59, 63, 98, 111, 141, 157, 206–10, 260, 262–63; 'de-Nazify', 8, 40, 71, 237. *See also* fascism; *Praviy sektor*
Netherlands, 35, 48, 59, 221, 223, 226, 286
New People party, 96, 109
Nobel prizes, 123, 156, 163, 174
Nord Stream, 6, 45, 203, 254, 262, 265, 269. *See also* pipelines
Norway, 59, 197, 198, 220
Novaia Gazeta, 122–23, 127, 129
Novaia Gazeta Evropa, 108, 123, 128, 161, 261, 262, 281
nuclear weapons. *See* weapons

occupied zones, 16, 34–37, 90, 105, 289–90; martial law in, 92; referendums, 6, 22, 31–35, 90, 220, 262. *See also* annexations
Oculus, 130
Odesa, 9, 22, 32, 71, 110, 195, 196
Odesa Massacre, 260
oil industry. *See* energy
oligarchs, 66, 88, 89, 100, 102, 121, 124, 221, 226, 238, 279
opposition, domestic political, 121–53
opposition-in-exile, 261–63
opposition organizations, 124–26; Eighth Resistance Group Feminist Project 'Labyrinth', 124, 168; Feminist Anti-War Resistance (FAR), 123, 167–68; Protesting MGU, 125; Soft Power, 124, 168; SotsFem Alternative, 124, 168; *Vesna*, 127, 155, 164, 167, 168
opposition publications. *See Dozhd*; *Kholod*; *Meduza*; *Novaia Gazeta Evropa*; *Perviy otdel*

Organization for Security and Cooperation in Europe (OSCE), 7, 8, 206, 280
Organization of Oil Exporting Countries (OPEC), 226, 231, 233, 285
Orthodox Church, Russian, 89, 126, 164, 167–70, 280
Orthodox Church, Ukrainian, 170

Pakistan, 186, 191, 192, 231, 240, 284
pandemic. *See* COVID-19
Parliamentary Assembly of Europe (PACE), 157
PARNAS, 135
Party of Regions (Ukraine), 6
patriotism, Russian, 48, 61, 64, 96–98, 100, 122, 125, 135, 251, 255–56, 264–68; Club of Angry Patriots, 104, 134
peace plans, 11, 17, 20–22, 36, 38, 40–42, 60, 65, 70, 75, 187, 203–7, 277; African, 60–61; Brazilian, 204; Chinese, 44–45, 49, 204; Indonesian, 60; Russian, 190; Russian public opinion on, 57, 61, 75, 87, 94, 100–101, 108–9; South African, 204–5; Ukrainian, 21–22, 204, 206–8; Vatican, 206
Perviy otdel, 162
pipelines: *Druzhba*, 47, 230; Nord Stream, 219, 222, 223; Power of Siberia, 225, 232, 235; Tikhoretsk-Baku, 194; TurkStream, 17. *See also* energy
Poland, 6, 34, 39, 46, 59, 63, 64, 70, 71, 74, 174, 188, 194, 196, 198, 200, 204, 208, 216, 222, 225, 228–30, 240, 269, 286
politics, Russian, 121–53, 295–97, *passim*
population, Russian, 168, 280
Praviy sektor, 6, 254, 260
presidency, Russian, 87–119, *passim*; elections for, 99, 105–11; succession to, 89–90. *See also Golos*; Putinism

Prigozhin mutiny, 2, 64, 101–4, 134, 199, 263. *See also* Prigozhin, Yevgeny; Wagner Group
prisoner exchanges (RF-Ukraine), 21, 32, 72, 185, 206, 257
propaganda, 10, 20, 36–37, 39, 41, 43, 60, 69, 71, 92, 130, 132, 134, 172, 174, 183–84, 208, 209, 229, 251–52, 256, 260, 267–68, 281, 296
protests, 121–53, 155–82
Public Chamber, 97, 137, 268
public opinion polls, Russian, 42, 47–48. *See* Levada Centre
Pussy Riot, 131, 144, 160, 261
Put' domoi, 106, 168; Kovcheg, 168–69
Putinism, 95, 167, 278. *See also* Putin, Vladimir

quality of life, 110, 278, 290–92, 295; inflation, 104, 218, 228, 234, 238, 278, 290, 295; pensions, 228, 238, 289, 290, 295; taxes (personal), 138, 221, 289; wages/salaries, 16, 48, 64, 66, 96, 106, 167, 228, 234, 238, 278, 290, 292, 295. *See also* unemployment

recruiting, 13, 16, 47, 64, 66, 92, 139. *See also* conscription
referendums. *See* occupied zones
refugees, Ukrainian, 36, 163, 173, 280
religion, 169–70. *See also* Islam; Jehovah's Witnesses; Orthodox Church, Russian; Orthodox Church, Ukrainian
Reporters Without Borders, 253
Romania, 22, 174, 184, 197, 199, 225, 269
Rosfinmonitoring, 106, 127, 166
Roskomnadzor, 122, 127, 130–31, 158, 162, 165, 229, 288
Rosneft, 222
Rostourism, 224
Russia-China Business Forum, 226, 230
Russian Children's Centre, 266
Russian Imperial Legion, 45
Russian World. *See Russkiy mir*

Russia Today (RT), 100, 252, 257. *See also* Simonyan, Margarita
Russkiy mir, 1, 89, 92, 95, 98, 164, 256, 287
Russophobia, 9, 88, 203, 206, 208
Rybar, 133–35

sabotage, in Russia, 16, 45, 65, 70–71, 102, 104–5, 162, 172, 198
Sakharov Centre, 156
Sakharov Prize, 156, 157, 253
sanctions: combatted by Russia, 74, 98, 107, 110, 131, 186, 187, 191, 204, 217, 228–30, 237, 266, 294; impact of, 121, 226; *vs*. Russia by West, 7, 9, 23, 41, 42, 44, 49, 66, 74, 100, 195, 205, 218–21, 227, 228, 238–41, 282, 283; by Ukraine, 170
Saudi Arabia, 106, 186, 187, 190, 205, 206, 208, 225, 226, 231, 233, 240
schools. *See* education
Sea of Azov, 9
Serbia, 36, 201, 288
Shanghai Cooperation Organization (SCO), 102, 185, 191–92, 233. *See also* summits
Siberia, 68, 241
Siberian Legion, 14
siloviki, 88, 89
snitching, 11, 124, 126–27, 162, 166, 198, 258–59, 289
Social Revolutionaries, 127
Soldiers Widows, 133
Solidaires du people ukrainien, 37
South Africa, 60, 105, 186, 190, 193–94, 206, 230, 233. *See also* Ramaphosa, Cyril
SOVA, 156
Soviet Union, 36, 184, 265, 266, 287
space, outer, 185, 187, 285
Special Military Operation (SVO), *passim*
spies. *See* espionage
sport: domestic, 159, 202, 214; international, 199–203

Stalingrad, 99–100
St. Petersburg Economic Forum. *See* St. Petersburg International Economic Forum (SPIEF)
St. Petersburg International Economic Forum (SPIEF), 59, 233, 237
summits: Arab League, 205; BRICS, 193–210; CIS, 163, 192, 194; EU, 42, 223, 244; G-7, 205–6; G-20, 17, 29, 105, 189–90; NATO, 188–89; peace, 20, 65, 84; RF-China, 65, 75; RF-Ukraine, 192; SCO, 102, 191, 233
Svoboda, 6, 254
Sweden, 32, 39, 44, 64, 72–73, 187, 189, 198, 206, 222, 229, 286
SWIFT, 219, 222, 282, 283

Tajikistan, 183, 191, 192, 194
Taliban, 192
Telegram, 45, 46, 69, 72, 106, 123, 125, 127–31, 141, 143, 163, 167, 169, 257, 258, 284
terrorism, Islamic, 76–77; Crocus City, 76; Hamas, 68, 76, 105–6, 190, 208; Hezbollah, 76; IS-Khorosan, 76–77
trade, Russian foreign, 225–27, 235. *See also* economics
Turkey, 11, 20, 23, 75, 102, 128, 185, 188–89, 191, 195, 197, 207, 220, 224, 230, 235, 239, 240, 282, 285, 286. *See also* Erdogan, Recep Tayyip; pipelines

UDAR, 6
Ukraine at war, 5–29, 31–55, 57–85; civil war, 7; foreign support, financial, 10, 17, 21, 23, 37, 38, 60, 66, 71, 73, 285–86; foreign support, weapons, 22–23, 34, 38–40, 45–46, 58, 67, 68, 70, 72–74. *See also* Zelensky, Volodymyr
Ukrainian World Congress, 38–39, 51
'undesirables', 42, 159–61, 171, 288, 295. *See also* 'foreign agents' label
unemployment, 66, 234, 236, 290

United Arab Emirates (UAE), 72, 106, 186, 190, 193, 194, 231, 232, 235, 236, 239
United Nation Office for Human Rights, 32
United Nations: UNGA, 9, 22, 75, 155, 183, 185, 186, 209; UNICEF, 186, 292; UNSC, 185, 192–93, 222, 284
United Russia (UR), 12, 88, 99, 106, 108, 136, 139
United States. *See* Biden, Joseph; Blinken, Anthony J.
Uzbekistan, 91, 128, 191–92, 194, 201, 231, 232, 288

'V', 133, 137
Valdai Discussion Club, 91, 184
Vatican, 60, 206
Venezuela, 193
Vepr, 131
Victory Day, 57, 98
Vietnam, 205, 221, 226, 238, 297
VKontakte, 92–93, 127, 131, 136
volunteer battalions, 14. *See also* Azov Battalion; military; Wagner Group
vospitanie. *See* education

wages. *See* quality of life
Wagner Group, 13–15, 23, 39, 45–47, 58–59, 62–64, 102, 103, 199, 257
'war against NATO', 40, 59, 73, 101, 110, 188, 297
'war against the West', 32, 64–66, 73–74
war crimes, 10–11, 171–74, 257–59; Bucha, 10, 25, 257
war dead, 12–13, 49, 69, 259, 279
weapons: cluster bombs, 17, 189; general, 17–18, 32–34, 39; long-range, 18, 21, 33, 43, 72, 254; nuclear, 12, 20, 252, 297. *See also* arming Ukraine; Medvedev, Dmitry; Putin, Vladimir
White Armbands, 133
women, 167–69. *See also* Feminist Anti-War Resistance (FAR)

World Bank, 60
World Economic Forum (Davos), 72, 93, 208
World Trade Organization (WTO), 217
World War II (Great Patriotic War), 99, 268
World Wildlife Foundation, 159

Yabloko, 95, 108, 121, 129, 135, 162, 296
Yeltsin Centre, 156
youth, 251–76; Yunarmiya, 266. *See also* education

'Z', 97
Zaporizhzhia NP, 9, 76

About the Author

Joseph Laurence (Larry) Black grew up in a small village in the province of New Brunswick, Canada. He has degrees from three universities, culminating in a doctorate awarded by McGill University, Montréal. He has been a secondary school teacher; rugby, football and basketball player and coach; and for many years served as a professor of history and international affairs at Laurentian University (9 years) and Carleton University (30 years), both in Ontario. At Laurentian University, in Sudbury, he chaired the History Department and sat on the academic senate. At Carleton, in Ottawa, he was a member of the History Department, director of the Institute of Soviet and East European Studies for a decade, founding director of the Centre for Research on Canadian-Russian Relations and was the first faculty member to be elected directly to the university's board of governors. He is now professor emeritus and was re-designated distinguished research professor by Carleton in 2023.

Black has been a researcher for NATO, instructor for recruits to Canadian Security and Intelligence Service and consultant with Canada's Immigration and Refugee Board. He is the author, co-author or editor of over 50 books on Imperial Russia, the USSR and present-day Russia – and three on local Canadian history.